P9-EGM-041

FREE COPY NOT FOR RESALE FREE COPY NOT FOR RESALE FREE COPY

Children's Literature

FREE COPY NOT FOR RESALE FREE COPY NOT FOR RESALE FREE COPY

FREE COPY NOT FOR RESALE FREE COPY NOT FOR RESALE FREE COPY

FREE COPY NOT FOR RESALE FREE COPY NOT FOR RESALE FREE COPY

FREE COPY NOT FOR RESALE FREE COPY NOT FOR RESALE FREE COPY

FREE COPY NOT FOR RESALE FREE COPY NOT FOR RESALE FREE COPY

FREE COPY NOT FOR RESALE FREE COPY NOT FOR RESALE FREE COPY

Children's Literature

An Invitation to the World

Diana Mitchell

Co-Director, National Writing Project, Michigan State University
Consultant to Public Schools

with

Pamela Waterbury, *Aquinas College*
Rose Casement, *University of Michigan, Flint*

Boston | New York | San Francisco
Mexico City | Montreal | Toronto | London | Madrid | Munich | Paris
Hong Kong | Singapore | Tokyo | Cape Town | Sydney

FREE COPY NOT FOR RESALE FREE COPY NOT FOR RESALE FREE COPY

FREE COPY NOT FOR RESALE FREE COPY NOT FOR RESALE FREE COPY

Series Editor: Aurora Martínez Ramos
Developmental Editor: Alicia Reilly
Editorial Assistant: Beth Slater
Senior Marketing Manager: Elizabeth Fogarty
Editorial-Production Administrator: Annette Joseph
Editorial-Production Service: Lifland et al., Bookmakers
Text Designer: Deborah Schneck/Carol Somberg
Electronic Composition: Monotype Composition
Composition and Prepress Buyer: Linda Cox
Manufacturing Buyer: Megan Cochran
Cover Administrator: Linda Knowles
Cover Designer: Studio Nine

For related titles and support materials, visit our online catalog at *www.ablongman.com.*

Copyright © 2003 Pearson Education, Inc.

All rights reserved. No part of the material protected by this copyright notice may be reproduced or utilized in any form or by any means, electronic or mechanical, including photocopying, recording, or by any information storage and retrieval system, without written permission from the copyright owner.

To obtain permission(s) to use material from this work, please submit a written request to Allyn and Bacon, Permissions Department, 75 Arlington Street, Suite 300, Boston, MA 02116 or fax your request to 617-848-7320.

Between the time website information is gathered and then published, it is not unusual for some sites to have closed. Also, the transcription of URLs can result in unintended typographical errors. The publisher would appreciate notification where these errors do occur so that they may be corrected in subsequent editions.

Library of Congress Cataloging-in-Publication Data

Mitchell, Diana.
    Children's literature : an invitation to the world/Diana Mitchell with Pamela
Waterbury, Rose Casement.
        p. cm.
    Includes bibliographical references and index.
    ISBN 0-321-04915-2
    1. Children's literature—History and criticism. I. Waterbury, Pamela. II. Casement,
Rose. III. Title.

PN1009.A1 .M54 2002
809´.89282--dc21   2002067584

Printed in the United States of America

10 9 8 7 6 5 4 3 2 1   VHP   07 06 05 04 03 02

Chapter-opener art by Ted Lewin

Text credits: *Credits appear on page 402, which constitutes a continuation of the copyright page.*

FREE COPY NOT FOR RESALE FREE COPY NOT FOR RESALE FREE COPY

FREE COPY NOT FOR RESALE FREE COPY NOT FOR RESALE FREE COPY

To my mother, Mary Dawson, who read to me

To Leah Graham and Joan Tresize, who reawakened my love for children's literature

To Virginia Blanford, who helped me shape my vision and believed in me

To my husband, Robert, who is my constant support

FREE COPY NOT FOR RESALE FREE COPY NOT FOR RESALE FREE COPY

FREE COPY NOT FOR RESALE FREE COPY NOT FOR RESALE FREE COPY

FREE COPY NOT FOR RESALE FREE COPY NOT FOR RESALE FREE COPY

FREE COPY NOT FOR RESALE FREE COPY NOT FOR RESALE FREE COPY

FREE COPY NOT FOR RESALE FREE COPY NOT FOR RESALE FREE COPY

FREE COPY NOT FOR RESALE FREE COPY NOT FOR RESALE FREE COPY

$\mathscr{B}$RIEF $\mathscr{C}$ONTENTS

FREE COPY NOT FOR RESALE FREE COPY NOT FOR RESALE FREE COPY

FREE COPY NOT FOR RESALE FREE COPY NOT FOR RESALE FREE COPY

FREE COPY NOT FOR RESALE FREE COPY NOT FOR RESALE FREE COPY

FREE COPY NOT FOR RESALE FREE COPY NOT FOR RESALE FREE COPY

FREE COPY NOT FOR RESALE FREE COPY NOT FOR RESALE FREE COPY

FREE COPY NOT FOR RESALE FREE COPY NOT FOR RESALE FREE COPY

CONTENTS

CHAPTER 1

An Introduction to Children's Literature

2

CHAPTER 2

Evaluating and Selecting Children's Literature

28

FREE COPY NOT FOR RESALE FREE COPY NOT FOR RESALE FREE COPY

FREE COPY NOT FOR RESALE FREE COPY NOT FOR RESALE FREE COPY NOT FOR RESALE FREE COPY NOT FOR RESALE FREE COPY

CHAPTER 3
The World of Picture Books 70

CHAPTER 4
Responding to Books Through Talk, Art, Writing, Drama, Movement, and Music 108

FREE COPY NOT FOR RESALE FREE COPY NOT FOR RESALE FREE COPY

FREE COPY NOT FOR RESALE FREE COPY NOT FOR RESALE FREE COPY NOT FOR RESALE FREE COPY NOT FOR RESALE FREE COPY

C H A P T E R 5
The Delights of Poetry

140

FREE COPY NOT FOR RESALE FREE COPY NOT FOR RESALE FREE COPY

C H A P T E R 6

The Context of Children's Literature

170

C H A P T E R 7

Multicultural and International Literature

198

FREE COPY NOT FOR RESALE FREE COPY NOT FOR RESALE FREE COPY

FREE COPY NOT FOR RESALE FREE COPY NOT FOR RESALE FREE COPY

CHAPTER 8

Traditional or Folk Literature

226

CHAPTER 9

Realistic and Historical Fiction

258

Contents **xiii**

CHAPTER 10
Modern Fantasy and Science Fiction

300

CHAPTER 11
Nonfiction Books

324

FREE COPY NOT FOR RESALE FREE COPY NOT FOR RESALE FREE COPY

CHAPTER 12

Biography and Autobiography

356

FREE COPY NOT FOR RESALE FREE COPY NOT FOR RESALE FREE COPY

FREE COPY NOT FOR RESALE FREE COPY NOT FOR RESALE FREE COPY

FREE COPY NOT FOR RESALE FREE COPY NOT FOR RESALE FREE COPY

FREE COPY NOT FOR RESALE FREE COPY NOT FOR RESALE FREE COPY

FREE COPY NOT FOR RESALE FREE COPY NOT FOR RESALE FREE COPY

EATURES

Favorite Authors and Illustrators...

Criteria for...

Applying the Criteria...

Taking a Look at the Research

Children's Voices...

Response to First Reading of a Book

CHAPTER 1

An Introduction to
Children's Literature

Chapter Outline
What Is Children's
Literature? 4
What Can You Expect
to Find in the Field of
Children's Literature? 4
Looking at Controversy in
Children's Literature 5
Exploring Genre 5
The Connection Between
Children's Literature and
Reading 6
The Reading Autobiography 7
Different Readers, Different Readings 7
Getting Started as a Reader of Children's
Literature 9
Child Development and the Selection of
Children's Literature 11
Piaget's Stages of Development 11
Piaget's Three Processes: Assimilation,
Accommodation, and Equilibration 12
What Makes a Book Accessible? 12
Accessibility in Early Reader Books 14
Accessibility in Chapter Books 18
Reasons for Reading 19
What's Changed About Children's
Literature Since You Were in Elementary
School? 21
The Influence of Sociopolitical and Cultural
Factors 21
The Influence of Trends in Marketing and
Technology 23

Children's Literature: An Invitation to the World is designed to help readers appreciate the beauty and depth of children's literature. Unlike any other text, this text asks readers to take a *world view* of literature—discussing what it is, how to recognize one's own, and how to recognize an author's—and encourages readers to see children's literature through a lens that includes people not like themselves. The text tackles tough issues such as gender and racial bias and how they can be insidiously promoted in literature. No other text on the market engages readers to such an extent in its material. By working with and exploring the literature, readers will become confident in their ability to evaluate and select literature for children. Above all, this text's purpose is to encourage readers to delight in children's literature and to discover works that resonate deep within.

This book grew out of my love for children's literature and my desire to invite readers into the literature, instead of simply telling them about it. Rather than just presenting topics, the text asks, "What can we learn from them?" Thus, although this textbook covers all aspects of children's literature, it is accessible and informal in style. In addition, it contains visual aids for readers to facilitate comprehension, such as use of boldface italics within the text to denote titles of recommended books. Attending to the "affective" aspects of literature rather than focusing strictly on a cognitive interpretation of literature, the text asks, "What about the affective?" This question is directly and indirectly answered; along with the information presented is an explanation of why it's important. This thread is woven throughout, as readers are asked to examine as evaluative

PREFACE

criteria the *emotional* and *imaginative* impact of books in each genre. For example, instead of simply telling about poetry, Chapter 5 shows readers what it does for children. And instead of just explaining art terminology, Chapter 2 shows readers how that terminology can help them understand their reactions to the visual in children's literature.

This text is organized in such a way as to encourage immediate immersion in the literature. Although most of the chapters deal with specific genres, several unique chapters are organized around issues:

- Chapter 1 focuses on the close connection between reading and children's literature.

- Chapter 4 presents an expanded view of responses to literature, including talk, art, writing, drama, movement, and music.

- Chapter 6 explores the context of children's literature, taking a critical look at authors' world views, the implicit values contained in literature, and the presence of sexism, racism, and classism.

- Chapter 7, Multicultural and International Literature, offers in-depth coverage of multicultural topics not always found in other texts, as well as an international focus that is truly unique in the marketplace.

Instructors may choose to use the material in any order that they find suitable for their classes.

This book has the following distinctive features.

1. **Favorite Authors and Illustrators.** An annotated list in every genre chapter gives readers the information they need to seek out and select books written by respected authors and illustrated by talented artists.

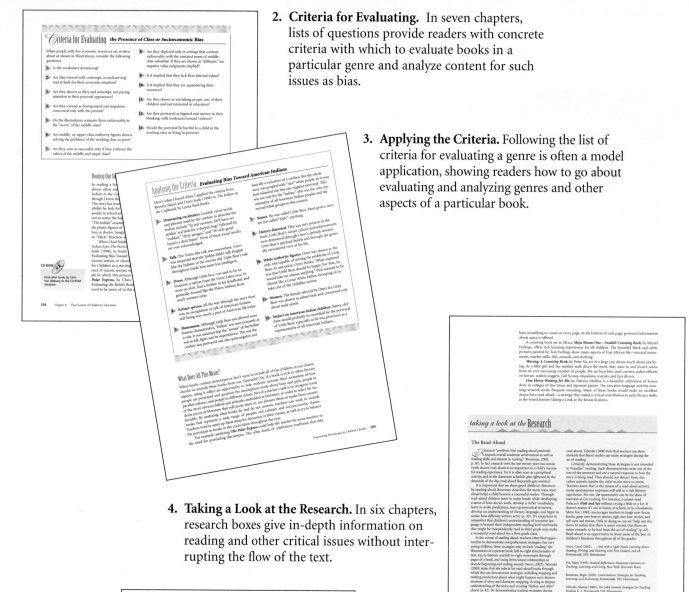

2. Criteria for Evaluating. In seven chapters, lists of questions provide readers with concrete criteria with which to evaluate books in a particular genre and analyze content for such issues as bias.

3. Applying the Criteria. Following the list of criteria for evaluating a genre is often a model application, showing readers how to go about evaluating and analyzing genres and other aspects of a particular book.

4. Taking a Look at the Research. In six chapters, research boxes give in-depth information on reading and other critical issues without interrupting the flow of the text.

5. Children's Voices. In every chapter, quotations from children talking about real books bring children's perspectives to the text, allowing readers to hear what children have to say about the genre and book selection.

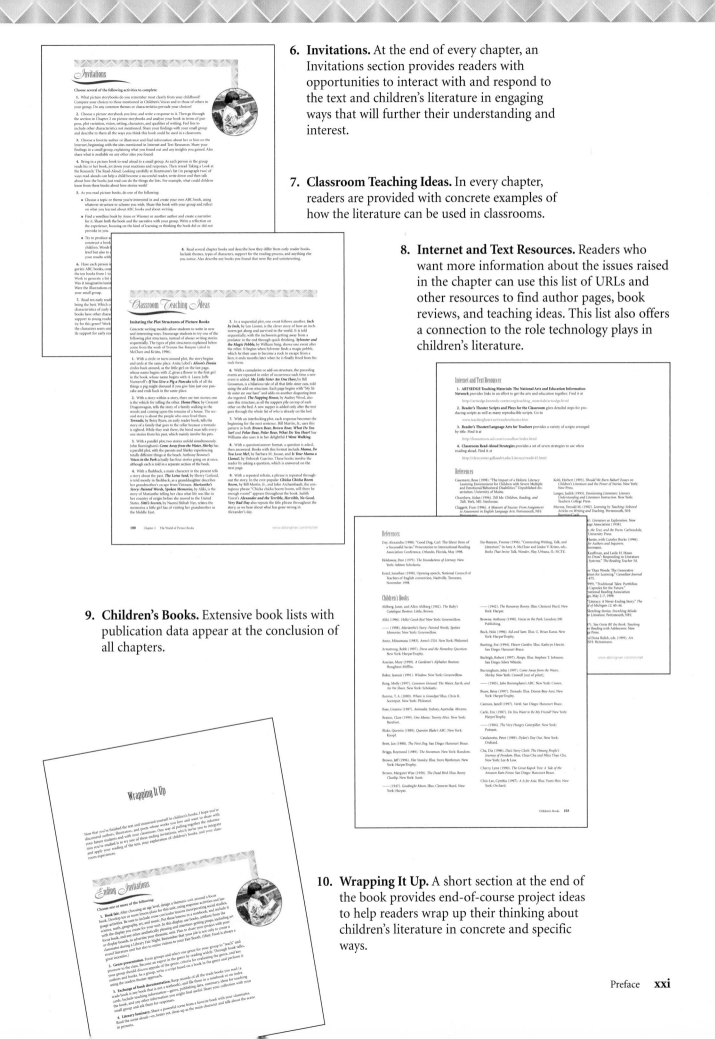

6. Invitations. At the end of every chapter, an Invitations section provides readers with opportunities to interact with and respond to the text and children's literature in engaging ways that will further their understanding and interest.

7. Classroom Teaching Ideas. In every chapter, readers are provided with concrete examples of how the literature can be used in classrooms.

8. Internet and Text Resources. Readers who want more information about the issues raised in the chapter can use this list of URLs and other resources to find author pages, book reviews, and teaching ideas. This list also offers a connection to the role technology plays in children's literature.

9. Children's Books. Extensive book lists with publication data appear at the conclusion of all chapters.

10. Wrapping It Up. A short section at the end of the book provides end-of-course project ideas to help readers wrap up their thinking about children's literature in concrete and specific ways.

Children's Literature

An Introduction to Children's Literature

tepping into a library or bookstore filled with children's books is like stepping into a magical world, filled with adventure, amazing people, intriguing places, and beautiful language. Books call out to readers: *Touch me—my glossy pages will entice you. Look at me—my illustrations will transport you. Hear me—my beautiful sounds will delight you and my voices will mesmerize you. Read me—my story will enfold you.* When we open books, touching their smooth pages and sinking into their colors, we become enveloped in the worlds they create as we listen to and learn from their characters.

Books entrance children, too. A toddler will spontaneously dig through a toy collection to drag out a book for a parent to read. The eyes of school-age children light up when they enter a new classroom and discover an array of books, ready for them to explore. Older children will bury themselves for hours with a book in a favorite reading corner. Literature can touch children's lives, as well as teach and entertain them.

What Is Children's Literature?

Although many people define children's literature as any book children read, not all of these books are considered to be literature. Several important characteristics distinguish "kids' books" from children's literature. These include the author's passion, interest, and intention; authenticity; literary merit; the high quality of the illustrations and the effectiveness with which they interact with the text; and the richness of the themes. Obviously, these criteria are subjective, but their consideration nonetheless is important. Excellent children's literature is marked by appealing content and clear writing; the characters are often children, people familiar to children, or animals. The settings generally are places well known to children or places children would love to go. The themes speak to children and their concerns.

Children's literature embraces every genre, including picture books, poetry, realistic fiction, fantasy, historical fiction, biography, informational books, and traditional stories such as myths, fables, and fairy tales. It includes multicultural and international literature across the genres. Much of what children read, however, is not written with children in mind. Christopher Paul Curtis, who won the Newbery Award and the Coretta Scott King Award, never intended to write for children (Curtis, 1997). He wrote the story he had to tell in the voice that seemed best for it. In his first version of the book *The Watsons Go to Birmingham—1963,* he started the story from the point of view of Byron, the older brother. The story didn't work well from that point of view, and so he changed to that of the younger brother, Kenny. Similarly, Newbery Award winner Madeleine L'Engle did not have children in mind when she wrote her award-winning story *A Wrinkle in Time,* which was rejected by more than ten publishers before one saw possibilities in it. According to a television interview, even J. K. Rowling had trouble selling her first book, *Harry Potter and the Sorcerer's Stone,* because publishers said it was too long to be a children's book.

Often, marketing considerations define whether a book is considered a children's book or an adult book. In a children's book, publishers look for young characters, not too many pages, frequent use of dialogue, minimal description, and wide appeal to children. Today, even many picture books, which are traditionally thought of as children's books, are not written strictly with children as their audience. For instance, *The Secret Knowledge of Grown-Ups,* by David Wisniewski, is a satire that older students and adults will enjoy. Some older children read books intended for adults, such as the work of Stephen King. Since the line between children's and adults' literature is sometimes hard to draw, this text will focus on books that have been categorized either by publishers' marketing departments or by libraries as books for children.

What Can You Expect to Find in the Field of Children's Literature?

CD-ROM

The CD-ROM offers descriptions of the writing of many authors listed in the Favorite Authors section. For more examples of authors known for their rich language use, go to Favorite Authors and do a word search for *language.*

The first thing you'll notice about children's literature is the sheer abundance of it. It comes in a variety of shapes, sizes, formats, and genres. Visit any bookstore or children's section of a library and you'll be stunned by the rich selection of books, which offer unlimited possibilities for reading, responding, and teaching. You'll find classics, award winners, and just plain good books, as well as mediocre, poorly written, and poorly conceived books.

Some of the first books you are drawn to may be books you remember from your childhood, many of them classics. *Classics* are defined as books that have withstood the test of time and are favorites of children from generation to generation. Their enduring qualities include universal themes that speak across time and generations, memorable

Although *Charlotte's Web* was originally published 50 years ago, the appeal of Charlotte, the spider, and Wilbur, the pig, is still strong for children today.

(Cover art from *Charlotte's Web* by E. B. White, illustrated by Garth Williams. Used by permission of HarperCollins Publishers.)

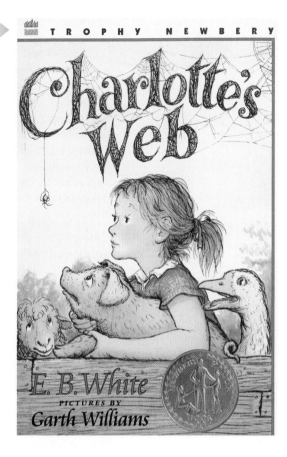

characters that live on in readers' minds, elements that create a strong emotional pull, rich language, and even a memorable rhythm. Such books include **The Wind in the Willows** (1908), by Kenneth Grahame; **The Raggedy Ann Stories** (1920), by Johnny Gruelle; **The Complete Tales and Poems of Winnie-the-Pooh** (1926), by A. A. Milne; **Millions of Cats** (1928), by Wanda Gag; **The Little Engine That Could** (1929), by Watty Piper; **Mike Mulligan and His Steam Shovel** (1939), by Virginia Lee Burton; **Make Way for Ducklings** (1941), by Robert McCloskey; **The Poky Little Puppy** (1942), by Janette Sebring Lowrey; **Goodnight Moon** (1947), by Margaret Wise Brown; **Charlotte's Web** (1952), by E. B. White; **Green Eggs and Ham** (1960), by Dr. Seuss; and **Where the Wild Things Are** (1965), by Maurice Sendak. Books such as these are reprinted because of their constant readership. As years pass, many books are added to the list of those that children turn to again and again. At the same time, some books considered classics by previous generations may lose favor with the current generation of children and slip off the list.

Some especially notable books have a sticker on the cover, signifying receipt of an honor such as the Caldecott, Newbery, or Coretta Scott King award. But because only a small percentage of the more than 5,000 children's books published yearly receive awards, many non-award-winning books are still so engaging that children will embrace them and as adults will share them with future generations. Working with the criteria in Chapter 2 will assist you in determining the literary merit of these books.

Looking at Controversy in Children's Literature

Selecting books for children often includes an element of controversy, as adults' views about what is appropriate for children may clash. Some adults think that children need protection from the harsh realities of life; others believe that letting children explore such topics as loss and death will alleviate their fear of the unknown. The vital questions of who decides what books to produce for children, who makes the decisions about what books to buy for libraries, and how books are selected for use in the classroom are typically ignored. These issues will be addressed in Chapters 2 and 9.

Other issues that arise out of the study of children's literature will be discussed throughout this book. There is controversy about whether people outside a culture should write books about that culture (Chapter 7). Another issue is whether books are simply their words and pictures or whether they contain cultural values and messages (Chapter 6). Although much children's literature takes you away to other times and places, looking beneath the words of the text will often bring you in contact with unexpected issues. Should beautiful award-winning books be eliminated from reading lists because of sexism or racism? Are multicultural and international books important only for the community they describe or for all children in the larger society (Chapter 7)?

Exploring Genre

Although the definitions of genres are not absolute or exclusive of one another, they do provide a framework for categorizing children's literature. *Genre* is a term used to designate the types, or categories, into which literary works are grouped, usually by style, form, or content.

This kind of classification implies that works of the same type have some common characteristics, regardless of time or place of composition, author, or subject matter. Poetry, for instance, is a genre that has a range of specific elements such as the use of rhythm and stanzas, but the subject matter may be almost anything. Dividing literature into genres is simply a way to grapple with a large body of writing and organize our thinking. The term *form* or *format* is sometimes used interchangeably with *genre,* but form is usually the pattern, structure, or organization used to give expression to the content. Although some would categorize picture books as a form of fiction, in this text picture books will be treated as a genre. Picture books are distinguished by specific elements, such as the close connection of the words and the illustrations, and they comprise too large a body of work to be discussed without their own category. You will find common threads as you read through the chapters on the various genres, but there are distinctive characteristics that identify the seven categories.

1. As you begin reading picture books, you'll notice their variety, beauty, and depth. Chapter 2 is intended to help you figure out ways to identify differences in literary and artistic quality by looking at both the text and the art. Chapter 3 focuses on the range of picture books and the characteristics of ABC, counting, and concept books; wordless books; books for the earliest reader; and transitional or chapter books. A thorough look at the purposes for which picture books have been written will alert you to the many reasons children respond so positively to them.

2. Poetry books for children may surprise you, particularly if you haven't been a fan of poetry. In Chapter 5, you will find that not only are the text and pictures closely wed, but themes range from friendship, family, and feelings to historical events and the natural world. By immersing yourself in poetry books and allowing yourself to experience them, you will find poems that speak to you.

3. Traditional literature, which includes folk tales, fairy tales, tall tales, myths, and fables (Chapter 8), is amazing in its variety. You could lose yourself in this genre, in which many excellent books on or from a multitude of cultures have recently been published. The stories contain much cultural information, so the books can be used in many ways with students in the classroom.

4. Realistic fiction and historical fiction are packed with themes to which children can relate. These genres have widespread appeal to children partially because the children can live vicariously through the characters' experiences. Looking at the narrative structures used in realistic fiction and historical fiction will give you a way to organize your thinking about these genres. Evaluative criteria described in Chapter 9 will help you delineate the qualities of excellent books in these areas.

5. Modern fantasy and science fiction, ever popular with the younger set, are now becoming popular with older children, as evidenced by the success of J. K. Rowling's **Harry Potter** series. The appeal of these genres is looked at closely in Chapter 10 and their significance in developing imagination is explored.

6. Nonfiction and informational books (Chapter 11) have benefited from the explosion in the graphic capability of computers. Now, beautiful photographs are found in many of these books. The photos and design add to the accessibility of the information to the reader. Notable contemporary informational books are carefully researched.

7. Biography, often seen as a genre to be read only for reports, also offers much variety in the way stories are written and the kinds of people written about.

CD-ROM

Use the CD-ROM, under Favorite Authors, to find authors who specialize in writing *biographies.*

The Connection Between Children's Literature and Reading

It's important to get children involved in a story so that they can experience what readers do—participate, comment, question, predict, and savor—in short, personally interact with the text and construct meaning from it. If children remain outside a story, they may focus only on decoding without becoming fully engaged readers.

Good books delight children, make them laugh, excite them, intrigue them, mystify them, encourage them to think of themselves as inside the story. Thus, good literature is essential to entice children into the world of reading.

Once children are willing to read, we have to understand what keeps them reading, what pulls them further into books, what pulls them back to books, and what pushes them away from books. Some children come to school or the library eager to read because they have been read to at home and associate being read to with being nurtured and engaging in conversations. What we ask students to do in response to a book can help or hinder their growth as readers.

The relationship between reading and children's literature is reciprocal. Children learn to read by reading, and good literature encourages children to read. Through this reading, they develop an understanding of the process of reading (described in Chapter 4) and in turn become more eager to read good literature.

W

To get help locating good literature for children, go to **Booktalks—Quick and Simple** at http://nancykeane.com/booktalks/.

The Reading Autobiography

All of your past experiences, both at home and at school, contributed to the kind of reader you are today. What kinds of books call out the deepest responses in you? Which books do you remember the most vividly? What do you remember about being taught to read? What experiences encouraged or discouraged your reading? What were you asked to do with the books you read in school? Did anyone ever give you guidance in your reading?

Everything that happens to you shapes the way you feel about reading. Writing your own *reading autobiography* can give you insight into the way you view the activity of reading. Discussing what drew you to reading and what pushed you away from it can give you insight into how you can best involve your students in reading. Looking at what you read over your years in school can help you be patient when students seem to get stuck in "series" books such as *Goosebumps,* since you may have read series such as *Nancy Drew* or *The Babysitters Club.* One person's reading autobiography might reveal that the writer associates being read to with warmth and nurturing and caring, while another might associate reading with being made to feel stupid by being placed in a low reading group. Still another might associate reading with having to answer hated questions at the end of the piece that asked for the "main idea" of the story.

Reading is much more than decoding words on a page. A willingness to read is vital, and it seems to come about when children are nurtured and helped, not labeled and treated differently.

Different Readers, Different Readings

When we share our views on a book that we love or hate, we are often jolted to find out that others responded in entirely different ways. One person may despise a character we love; another may be bored by a book that we were engrossed in. The uniqueness of each reader's response to a piece of literature is explained by theorist Kathleen McCormick (1994), who says that our perspectives are influenced by our sociocultural background, the roles we play, and our unique viewpoints, formed by our past experiences. Each of us brings all our experiences and memories with us when we read.

As readers, we all have personal histories that include our attitudes about gender, race, religion, values, regional biases, politics, lifestyle, love, education, and so on. Becoming more aware of the facets of our histories that influence the way we read helps us to become critically literate, active readers, alert to the ways our own "repertoires" are embedded within our larger culture.

Being able to talk about how we are situated in our own histories and how they influence the way we "read" a text allows us to support our own reading and see many ways to approach a book. We can think about which part of our social history affects us the most in a particular reading. McCormick's work can help us realize that we are all reading from a certain context and a certain point of view and that we are reading in our own present historical time. These elements will affect and influence our reading. It also can help us to learn why others read differently. By sharing literature reactions with others, we climb into someone else's reading perspective.

Students, too, should understand the perspectives they are reading from so that they can support their right to that reading. For instance, a black South African man who read *The Story of Babar, the Little Elephant,* by Jean De Brunhoff, told Herbert Kohl (1995) that students in his community would not find this an endearing story about an orphaned elephant taken in by a nice, rich, white lady. Students would focus on the fact that a man wearing the clothing of a colonial oppressor (pith helmet and rifle) had needlessly killed an elephant and had never been brought to justice. Because of the experiences in South Africa with dominant colonials who were white supremacists, they also would see the move to clothe the naked elephants as overtly racist and insulting (p. 18). The fact that children from other cultures may react strongly to other elements of the story, such as how sad the death of Babar's mother was, does not invalidate the reading of the South African. Because every reader doesn't see the oppression in the text doesn't mean it's not there.

McCormick's work empowers readers of literature by helping them articulate the importance of context in literature and what contributes to that context for them. With an understanding of the ideas of McCormick, you will be better prepared to listen to what your students see in the books they read, validate the histories they bring to their readings, and help them become engaged readers and lovers of books. Students need a comfortable and supportive learning environment so that they can fully explore their responses and share them with others as they work toward building meaning.

Creating a Community of Readers Through Talk

Most of us need to feel connected to a community; it makes us feel accepted and worthwhile. When we attend a new school, we want to know where to find the bookstore, the advising office, the bathrooms, and the snack bar or coffee shop. More importantly, we want to establish a sense of our identity in the new school. We want comfortable relationships with others—our classmates, our professors. If we feel connected to the community, we no longer have to prove our worthiness every day—our attractiveness, our intelligence, our wittiness. Comfortable relationships make us feel safe and more willing to take risks, ask questions, test our opinions. This sense of ease lets us focus on the more important issue—our learning.

The same is true in a classroom. If we feel we are part of a community, working toward the goal of learning, we feel connected to others and we learn to listen to and value others' opinions. In turn, we feel we can speak freely and not be ridiculed because we have become overly enthusiastic about a book under study. We also want to learn from others. Can they show us another way to look at a character or theme? Creating a community in the classroom is as important in kindergarten as it is at the college level. In such classrooms, students feel they have something to contribute to the class, have the freedom to work with others, and are part of something larger than the individual. The boxed feature Taking a Look at the Research: Creating Classroom Communities provides additional information about the importance of community in the classroom. Here you will also find resources to guide you in developing a classroom community.

Building this sense of community takes time and usually begins with the instructor. The teacher must work to connect with the class and show that student talk is valued. Students then need time to work in small groups, talking with others about responses to books, sharing reading autobiographies, and responding to other group members' ideas. When students see that others value reading and enjoy books enthusiastically, they will feel more ready to participate wholeheartedly.

Creating a community of readers has an even bigger payoff for students than for teachers. They get the opportunity to see how others react to books, thus broadening and enriching their personal views. Talking with others after reading and responding to a book often has surprising effects. After they listened to the views of their classmates, students in classes I have taught have been willing to take a new look at characters they disliked immensely. Talk about books is essential to stretching our own understandings and to the continued pursuit of making meaning. Students will come to see responses to the books they read as "works in progress," not immutable renderings of the meaning of a book. Often, students will mull these works over in their minds and compare characters to other characters they have read about, think about how

Creating Classroom Communities

Creating a community within the classroom begins the moment students arrive on the first day of school. The community is shaped throughout the year, as students grow in their relationships with one another, the teacher, and themselves. Its cohesiveness develops through listening and talking, shared problem solving, and risk taking. In order to create a caring community, individuals must know that within the community there is a commitment that each student will be valued "as a human being, as one who has much to give, much to demonstrate, much to teach others" (Avery, 2002, p. 58). Only within this atmosphere can one expect that children will feel safe to share their responses to the learning they are engaged in. Routman (2000) suggests that a teacher examine the tone of the classroom community by asking, "What would it be like to be a student in this classroom?" (p. 543).

At all grade levels, working to create a caring and respectful community requires establishing predictable routines and clear expectations for community members' behaviors. In order to be effective, these routines and expectations should be developed through discussions within the group itself, in which members define what they want in their classroom community. "It is only when students negotiate acceptable behaviors and routines with the teacher and assume responsibility for putting them into practice that we can effectively teach" (Routman, 2000, p. 539).

Time and space are required for community building. Some teachers set aside an area of their classroom as a meeting space. Taberski (2000) describes this space as the hub of her classroom. Her students gather there at the beginning and end of reading and writing workshop, as well as for a variety of literacy activities including read aloud, shared reading and writing, discussions of text, and mini lessons that demonstrate strategies children might want to employ in their reading and writing. Setting aside time and space for classroom meetings that allow students to share with peers, collaborate, and dialogue—and involve students in establishing the organization and expectations for such meetings—validates the importance of community in the classroom.

Avery, Carol (2002). *. . . And with a Light Touch: Learning About Reading, Writing, and Teaching with First Graders,* 2nd ed. Portsmouth, NH: Heinemann.

Routman, Regie (2000). *Conversations: Strategies for Teaching, Learning, and Evaluating.* Portsmouth, NH: Heinemann.

Taberski, S. (2000). *On Solid Ground: Strategies for Teaching Reading K–3.* Portsmouth, NH: Heinemann.

books are similar thematically, or marvel over an author's use of craft to create a compelling story. In classes where community has been created, books are talked about over and over again and pulled out of the files of students' minds whenever the stories or characters have something to add to a book they are currently reading. Once students have experienced a literary community, they feel cheated when books aren't shared through discussion. The proliferation of adult book clubs reveals how central sharing is to our experience of reading.

Getting Started as a Reader of Children's Literature

The best way to learn about children's literature is to be a reader of children's literature. Read the books, talk about the books, respond to the books, even analyze the books. Read everything you can get your hands on. Share books in class. Haunt the local public library, sampling the various sections of the children's area. Go to the children's section of your local bookstore, sit down, and sample books from the shelves.

Although at first you may want to read those glorious picture books without annotating them, it will stand you in good stead later if you respond to each one, keeping good records of what you read. As a future teacher or librarian, you'll want information about books for your students at your fingertips. At the time you read the book, it may seem you'll never forget it, but after you read hundreds of books, memories of them tend to run together.

Eventually, you'll probably want to develop your own way of keeping track of what you've read, but one way to keep good records is to use the chart in the boxed feature

(W)

*To see examples of children's book reviews, go to **The Bulletin of the Center for Children's Books** at www.lis.uiuc.edu/ puboff/bccb/.*

Responding to and Analyzing Children's Books

Author:

Title of Book:

Genre (circle one):
picture storybook, poetry, traditional literature, realistic fiction, historical fiction, science fiction, fantasy, informational book, biography, and autobiography

Subject or theme:

Brief summary of plot or format:

How I responded or reacted to the book:

What I want to remember about the book:

Characters:

	Name	M/F	Age	Race	Socioeconomic Class	Actions
Main character						
Main character						
Secondary character						
Secondary character						

Setting (circle one):
rural, urban, suburban, home, school, outside, in a country outside the U.S., other (explain below)

Additional features (circle one):
multicultural, international, strong female character, good role model, written from more than one point of view, literary qualities (such as figurative language, good beginning, good use of dialogue, excellent description), other (explain below)

Possible classroom connection, or how you could foresee using this book in a classroom or library:

Responding to and Analyzing Children's Books. A consistent method for recording what you read along with information about the book allows you to easily retrieve your thoughts and evaluations of books. Some of the suggested categories (gender, age, race, socioeconomic class, and actions of the characters) nudge you to become aware of the values embedded in the books (see Chapter 6 for a fuller discussion of the values in children's literature).

Child Development and the Selection of Children's Literature

Views of child development and how it affects the literature children are drawn to have been greatly influenced by the work of Jean Piaget. Based on his observations of children, Piaget identified four stages of child development. These four stages, according to Piaget, are experienced by children at approximately the same age, and each must be completed before the child can enter the next one.

Applying Piaget's theory of cognitive development to the world of children's literature can help us provide children with books that will enhance their cognitive, emotional, and social development. It must be remembered, however, that children move through the different stages in their own time and that social, motivational, and experiential factors will influence their development.

Piaget's Stages of Development

Piaget's stages of development are sensorimotor (birth to approximately two years), preoperational (approximately two years to seven years), concrete operational (approximately seven years to eleven years), and formal operational (approximately eleven years and older) (Siegler, 1991).

Sensorimotor Stage

In the sensorimotor stage, infants to two-year-olds actively engage with their environment, employing all of their senses to make discoveries of the world. During this stage, the child moves from simple reflexes to more sophisticated intentional actions. Books that interest children in this stage include books that are colorful, that make sounds, and that describe movements the reader and child can do together, as well as books with rhymes, poetry, and songs. For this group, who like to chew what they read and have not yet learned the fine art of turning pages carefully, board books, cloth books, and vinyl books offer an opportunity to hold and manipulate books.

Preoperational Stage

The preoperational stage is characterized by self-orientation, or viewing the world only from one's own perspective. It is in this stage that children develop understandings about the real world, increase their understandings first of themselves and then of those around them, and begin to develop logical reasoning skills (Elliot, Kratochwill, Littlefield, and Travers, 2000). In this stage, in which children develop language rapidly and gradually move away from their egocentricity, they need to continue to manipulate with hands-on experiences. In many ways, it is during this stage that children gather the tools, skills, understandings, and strategies that will allow them to "operate" in the next stage. Books that are appropriate for this stage include everyday stories with characters children can identify with; stories in which relationships with others build family, friendship, and community understandings; stories that use a rich, natural, and authentic language; stories that provide children with opportunities to make predictions; and stories that allow for a variety of active responses such as drama, drawing, conversation, and writing.

quatrain, provided the subject is within the realm of their experience. Another way predictability is enhanced is by establishing the main characters, setting, and problem in the first few pages. Then children can see the main elements in the story and work to understand how all the elements will be played out. After children have been read to for a while, they begin to develop an understanding that stories follow a regular sequence. They can see that problems need resolution, so they begin to think about and guess what might happen.

Young readers also like repetition of actions, phrases, and sentence structure. These predictable structures make stories easier for children to listen to and comprehend. Again, repetition allows children to participate—to be readers, not outsiders to the reading process. Predictable structures also allow authors to introduce surprising or unusual elements successfully within a carefully constructed familiar context, which usually delights children since they love surprises.

Conceptual Information

Young readers have to have conceptual information about the topic in order for a book to be accessible to them. If they have never heard about Arctic winters or how people live in the Arctic, a book that assumes knowledge of the Arctic might not make much sense to them or might make them work too hard to understand. Though based on known conceptual information, the book also needs to contain new information that interests the reader. Students respond positively when a book refers to experiences that they know about. Having some background information gives students a place to put the new information in their minds. If they have never heard of or seen a train station or airport, then vocabulary like *ticket counter, luggage return, conductor, stewardess,* and *boarding passes* will not make much sense to them, and they will need more experiences for it to become part of their language system.

Thus, all readers—even proficient ones but most particularly insecure readers—can benefit from thematic studies that provide background information and connectedness through conceptually related materials and ideas. Classrooms that encourage discussion, questions, and student research offer the curricular support learners need to make sense of texts that might otherwise be too difficult for them.

Room to Make Inferences

Young readers find books more accessible if there is room to make inferences (draw conclusions from facts) and have these inferences confirmed or rejected within the story. For example, a reader might infer that one character will be a good friend based on what he says to another character. Readers draw inferences from the intersections of their lives and the text. They try to figure out how a character will act based on what they know of people or what might happen within the constraints of the setting. Proficient readers go beyond the author's explicit information; they tap into the vast store of knowledge gained from their lives, including experiences with literature. When books make room for inferences, children are drawn into them and work to use what they know to make sense of the text.

Language

Young readers find books accessible if the language is natural for the text and for them. Calling an elephant an elephant, even though the word is a three-syllable one, will not confuse children if the story is indeed about an elephant. Whereas adults may think that children can handle only short, simple words, often it's easier for them to learn the longer, more difficult word as long as it makes sense in the context of the story. Think how frustrated children must feel when they are unable to enter into a story because the language is not language that resonates with them; not being the language of childhood, it is not something familiar that prepares them to read. Students respond to familiar language. If the words chosen by the author seem to speak to the true spirit of childhood, even beginning readers will be able to get involved in the story.

Literary Quality

If the story is well written, the theme is one children can relate to, and the pace keeps the reader turning the pages, the book probably has the literary quality needed to be accessible to children. Something in the plot line must move the story along or add to the overall mood of the book. If the story is poorly organized, if the theme isn't meaningful, if the characters aren't multidimensional, or if the language doesn't ring true, children will have trouble motivating themselves to read further.

Relevance of Illustrations

Drawings that work well to extend and support the text are necessary to make a picture book accessible. The earliest readers can read books somewhat independently if illustrations enable them to do some accurate guessing. When they are not overwhelmed by detail, illustrations support the earliest readers' efforts to focus on the central aspects of the pictures, which contribute to understanding the meaning of the words in the book.

Authentic Social/Cultural Significance

Books are more accessible to children if they can easily identify with the story and discuss similar situations of their own. A book doesn't have to deal with the weighty issues of the world to be authentic; but the issues it discusses must be real to the lives of the children. Children like to hear about others who lose a tooth, who get a new sibling, who worry about doing the wrong thing. While these might not be important issues in adult lives, such situations loom large in the life of a child.

As Ken Goodman, noted reading theorist, reminds us in much of his writing, readers must be looking at authentic texts and must be invited to bring to the texts their thoughts, languages, and lives. Reading is a complex activity. The boxed feature Taking a Look at the Research: Literature-Based Reading Programs reflects on the strategies that children use

CD-ROM

To find resources on the many aspects of *reading,* go to the References database on the CD-ROM.

taking a look at the Research

Literature-Based Reading Programs

Literature is the centerpiece of some teachers' reading and writing instruction. They believe that, by reading quality children's literature, not only do children learn to read—they also learn to love reading. The goals of a literature-based reading program are that children will learn to read, that they will understand what they read, and that they will choose to read for pleasure and information (Routman, 2000).

Belief in a literature-based reading program is supported by research on how children read. Researchers have learned about how children read by studying the miscues, or unexpected responses, they make as they read. Studies conducted by Ken and Yetta Goodman in the 1960s indicate that readers use three cueing systems, which work simultaneously to help them read.

The graphophonic cueing system is based on the physical characteristics of individual words. Children look at a word and identify its letters and their sound associations. The syntactic cueing system relies on children's informal understanding of the structure or grammar of language, which they have learned from their experiences as listeners and speakers. Children use familiar sentence structure to make predictions about how the sentence will read. The semantic, or meaning-making, cueing system is invoked as children reflect on their reading, asking, "Does this make

sense?" or "What would make sense here?" in order to self-correct before going forward. They read through the lens of their understanding of their world, with each young reader constructing his or her own meaning while transacting with the text (Goodman, 1996).

When basal readers are written with a controlled vocabulary on the assumption that children will learn to read best if they are introduced to words selectively, slowly, and in isolation, they may not have a familiar syntax. Without a familiar syntax, it is more difficult to make predictions, which are important for reading fluency. Also, the stories often lack the real literary elements that create a rich story and meaning. Goodman (1996) explains that a simplistic view of reading as just a set of words not only produces vacuous text but actually confuses the reader by taking away significant cues for comprehending text. "Authentic texts, on the other hand, not only control their own vocabulary but also have predictable, authentic grammar and thus provide natural grammatical cues to readers" (p. 77).

Goodman, Ken (1996). *On Reading: A Common-Sense Look at the Nature of Language and the Science of Reading.* Portsmouth, NH: Heinemann.

Routman, Regie (2000). *Conversations: Strategies for Teaching, Learning, and Evaluating.* Portsmouth, NH: Heinemann.

when they read. It traces the early investigation of meaning-based reading, which supports the literature-based reading programs used in the classroom today.

Accessibility in Chapter Books

Chapter books get their name from the simple fact that, unlike books for early readers, they are divided into chapters. Children are thrilled to make the move to chapter books because it signals that they are becoming independent readers. The problem with this designation, however, is that it's not clear where it ends, since almost all books read by adults also contain chapters. Some chapter books are transitional and provide continued support through illustrations (these are discussed in Chapter 3). The kinds of chapter books discussed here are the books children read independently from the time they move from transitional books up through the time they are ready for what has been categorized as young adult literature. The following elements contribute to how accessible a chapter book is to students.

Appeal of Topic

Interest is probably the main factor in accessibility of chapter books to students. If students are dying to know more about basketball, they will approach a book on Michael Jordan with zest. If students want to know how other children deal with stepparents in their life, they will approach a book on that subject with interest. Humor also draws students into books. Books with topics that appeal to children include *Because of Winn-Dixie*, by Kate DiCamillo, which begins with a ten-year-old girl's finding and getting to keep a dog; *Stuart Little*, by E. B. White, which tells of a mouse being adopted into a human family; *The ~~Worst~~ Best School Year Ever*, by Barbara Robinson, about misadventures at school; and *Bunnicula: A Rabbit-Tale of Mystery*, by Deborah Howe and James Howe, about the adventures of a talking dog.

Book Appearance and Format

A visually appealing book cover will draw children to a book and entice them to at least consider whether they want to read it. What is written on the back cover is also important, since that is often the thing children read before selecting a book. Thick books with dense type, narrow margins, long paragraphs, and long chapters do not appeal to younger people. These features alone signal that a book may be too hard for them. Chapter books may have a larger format than traditional paperback books and generally run from about 85 pages to 150 pages. The chapters are short, running from a few pages to about 15 pages. Paragraphs are usually no more than five sentences long. Type size is larger than in traditional paperback books, and there is more space between the lines, with fewer lines on a page. All of these features give younger readers breathing space and the feeling that the book is approachable.

Predictability in Structure

Can the reader count on the structure of the story to be predictable, with a beginning, middle, and ending? Younger

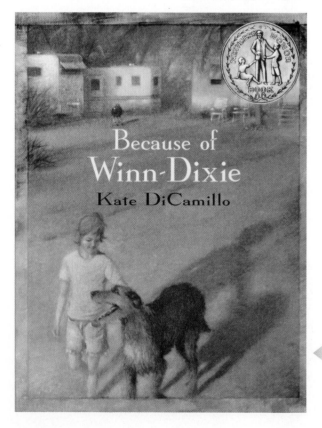

Children are drawn to this book because of the humor and the solid relationship between the little girl and her dog.
(BECAUSE OF WINN-DIXIE. Copyright © 2000 Kate DiCamillo. Cover illustration © 2000 Chris Sheban. Reproduced by permission of the publisher Candlewick Press, Inc., Cambridge, MA.)

readers often are not ready for story structures that break the conventions of how a story is normally told. They need to be able to count on the structure that a story of the kind they are reading provides. Mysteries, for instance, usually begin with a problem or a crime. They move to a look at several characters who might be suspects and end with a solution. As readers get more experienced and gain confidence and skill in their reading abilities, they become ready to tackle books that aren't written in a conventional manner.

Room to Make Inferences

None of us wants to have conclusions drawn for us or someone in the book tell us what we should be learning. We stay away from heavy-handed didactic books, preferring to infer the message from the book. Children also prefer and are drawn to books that don't insult their intelligence and that allow them to blend their own thinking into the story. Readers don't want everything spelled out for them; if it is, reading the book is no longer an adventure since someone has already done the reader's work. Readers want to draw their own conclusions based on information and actions and dialogue from the book. This allows the reader to be an active part of the reading process.

Language

Natural-sounding language in familiar sentence patterns, with familiar vocabulary or new vocabulary embedded in an easily understood context, makes books accessible. Younger readers especially are put off by archaic language and elaborate sentence structures with which they have had no experience. Younger readers often lack the patience to overcome the hurdle of antiquated language in order to get to the ideas. Introducing a book like *Great Expectations,* by Charles Dickens, with its rich but long descriptions, antiquated vocabulary, lengthy sentences, and complicated and unfamiliar sentence structures might work against inviting younger children into the literature.

Use of First-Person Narrator

By using the first-person narrative voice, authors control how much of the story the reader hears at a time. First person is the least complicated point of view, because all information comes from one character. There is no jumping around from character to character, and readers know that what they are hearing is coming from one person's point of view. As readers get more experienced, they can easily move to third-person narration and even omniscient narration, where the author has access to the thinking of several characters. The majority of novels for children are written with a first-person narrator.

Literary Qualities

When literature is well written, it is much more accessible to children. If the writing is well organized and easy to follow, if the settings are familiar and vivid, if the themes touch on the lives and interests of students, if the plot is fluid enough that readers want to keep going to see what happens, and if the language is natural sounding, with clear, direct sentences, the book will be one that children will be interested in reading.

Reasons for Reading

Although our experiences with reading are vastly different—some good, others painful—the reasons we choose to read are universal. We read to escape and disappear into books. We read for the sheer pleasure of it. We read to find out new and exciting information. We read to make sense of our lives, to experience new realities, to find answers to the big questions that haunt us. We read because we are enamored with the beauty of literature and how that beauty echoes in our own lives when we read. As parents or older siblings, we watch the children in our families read for the same reasons during their preschool and ele-

Other essays can be found at **Online Journals and Adolescent Literature** *at* http://eric.indiana.edu/www/ #JOUR.

mentary years. As teachers, we watch our students read for similar reasons. Try to identify the reasons you read as a child and while growing up. Why do you read now?

Work by G. Robert Carlsen, professor of English education and scholar in adolescent literature, may help to shed light on some of the stages you went through and continue to live out as a reader. In his essay "Literature IS . . . ," Carlsen (1974) identifies five roles literature plays in readers' lives and cites key grades in which readers seek each role from literature. The stages of literary appreciation are merely approximations; clearly, the roles overlap and continue to have an impact throughout our lives once we become readers.

Unconscious Delight

We read for unconscious delight, for the sheer pleasure and joy of entering an imaginary world. Many of us remember being so mesmerized by a book that we hated to have it end, but this unconscious delight is especially evident in young children, for whom reading or being read to is almost magical. Young children and beginning readers have no difficulty entering the world of make believe. A world of talking animals, elves, fairies, dragons, gremlins, and monsters hiding in closets is as real as their everyday world. Although preschool children who are read to obviously enter with ease into this make-believe world, Carlsen identifies this stage as being at its peak in grades three to seven.

Vicarious Experience

Avid readers delight in learning about places, times, and people about which they know little. We long to experience another's reality through books. Historical fiction may give us a glimpse into what our lives would have been like if we had lived during World War II. Books with themes of survival and adventure address our need to experience life vicariously through literature. We can discover what it means to live in a city or on a farm by reading books. Reading permits us to experience emotions of fear or terror that we might not want to experience in real life. Children in grades seven to nine are most often in this stage.

Seeing Oneself

We read to encounter our own realities. We want to see people like us so that we can better understand ourselves and know why we behave as we do. Seeing people who are like us struggle with problems similar to our own helps us to universalize our own experiences. Students in grades nine to eleven identify with this stage.

Philosophical Speculations

We read to make sense of our world and our role in it. Through reading, we encounter "the mystery of the human experience" and struggle with those issues, dilemmas, and questions that have troubled humans from the beginning of existence. We read to make sense of death, love, the loss of love, evil, authority and its abuses, and what it means to be human and act with integrity and courage. Students in grades eleven through fourteen are usually in this stage.

Aesthetic Appreciation

We read for the pleasure we gain from the beauty and craftsmanship in literature. We delight in the richness of its themes and the skill with which they are woven through the work and developed through characters, plot, setting, and language. We admire the unity of a work and in that unity find reassurance that our lives have the same inner harmony. People in grade fourteen and up often experience this stage.

Although these stages overlap, there are clear implications for us as teachers and librarians in the scaffolding that Carlsen has identified. Children do not pick up books primarily for the aesthetic experience of the literature. They do not read to trace foreshadowing, examine metaphor, and identify where the climax of the story occurs. Nor do they read to do story mapping or an analysis of the characters through Venn diagrams. They read primarily for the sheer pleasure of reading; they want to be swept away into the literature.

They also read for all the other reasons we read literature as adults—seeing oneself, philosophical speculation, and aesthetic appreciation.

Not only do children read to gain information, to seek answers, to see themselves and others, and to find hope and meaning in an often confusing modern world; they also read to gain the approval of adults in their lives who value reading. It's important to provide literature and literature experiences that feed children's reading needs at a developmentally appropriate level—both a developmentally appropriate reading level and a developmentally appropriate appreciation level. We should not try to turn them into readers at a more adult stage than is appropriate. If we let them read literature at the level appropriate for their experiences and interests, they will move into the next stage naturally.

What's Changed About Children's Literature Since You Were in Elementary School?

If you haven't read children's literature in the last five to ten years, you may be surprised by the multitude of changes that are now in evidence mainly because of sociopolitical and cultural shifts in our society and because of trends in marketing and technology. Attention to sociopolitical and cultural factors is embedded throughout the text and specifically addressed in Chapter 6.

The Influence of Sociopolitical and Cultural Factors

Children's literature reflects our changing views of children, of the world, and of what literature is and should look like. In fiction, there is a broader view of characterization. Girls are shown in more active roles (*Amazing Grace,* by Mary Hoffman; *Mountain Valor,* by Gloria Houston; and *Sammy Keyes and the Hotel Thief,* by Wendelin Van Draanen). Boys are depicted expressing emotions and nurturing others (*Crazy Lady!,* by Jane Leslie Conly; *Belle Prater's Boy,* by Ruth White; and *Follow the Moon,* by Sarah Weeks). Minority characters are portrayed in a broader range of roles with less stereotyping (*I Hadn't Meant to Tell You This,* by Jacqueline Woodson; *Second Daughter: The Story of a Slave Girl,* by Mildred Pitts Walter; and *Francie,* by Karen English).

Topics continue to broaden but still reflect the hesitancies of our society. For instance, our tangled views of the Arab world often preclude the publishing of fiction about this part of the world (Naomi Shihab Nye's books that focus on Arab families, *Habibi* and *Sitti's Secrets,* are two of the few fictional books published about the Arab world). Our "hands-off" attitude toward books with religious themes is softening (*Armageddon Summer,* by Jane Yolen and Bruce Coville; *The Tent,* by Gary Paulsen; and *I Believe in Water: Twelve Brushes with Religion,* a book of short stories edited by Marilyn Singer). Gradually books with homosexual characters are being published (*Good Moon Rising,* by Nancy Garden; *From the Notebooks of Melanin Sun,* by Jacqueline Woodson; and *Am I Blue? Coming Out from the Silence,* edited by Marion Dane Bauer).

Fiction is still the most prominent genre published, as evidenced by the awarding of the Caldecott and Newbery medals primarily to fiction. The 2001 Newbery winner (*A Year Down Yonder,* by Richard Peck) and all three honor books were fiction. The 2000 Caldecott did go to a nonfiction book (*So You Want to Be President?,* written by Judith St. George and illustrated by David Small), but all the honor books were fiction.

Picture books continue to hold a secure place in the publishing world. As our ideas on what books are appropriate for whom broaden, many more picture books written for older readers are being published. Books for older readers are discussed in Chapter 3.

Many picture books are breaking established conventions to present a "more complex visual image in terms of line, color use and composition, increased use of multiple perspectives, disintegration of the page surface, an altered conceptualization of

W

To find picture books with positive, powerful women characters, go to Only the Best for My Child at www.oz.net/ ~walterh/biblio.html.

the actual page of the book, and a loss of narrative and visual linearity" (Goldstone, 1999, p. 335). Examples of this trend can be found in books illustrated by Jannell Cannon, Peter Catalanotto, David Macauley, Peggy Rathmann, Lane Smith, and David Wisniewski.

The popularity of series books in fiction continues, with themes reflecting the changing, as well as the typical, tastes of children. Visit any bookstore or library and you'll see rows of R. L. Stine's *Goosebumps,* the *American Girl* historical fiction series, and the action-packed *Animorphs* books. Children still like the predictability that series books offer.

High-quality early reader books are being published that allow developing readers to read on their own. Easy-to-read books and series that provide light or humorous reading reflect a trend in school practices away from exclusive reliance on basals, which emphasize controlled or limited vocabulary, to inclusion of trade books (Harris, 1996). Excellent authors of early readers include Betsy Byars and Patricia Reilly Giff.

A new stress on authenticity and research in biography and nonfiction (Fisher, 1997) has made this genre more vigorous and exciting [Kathleen Krull's ***Lives of the Artists: Masterpieces, Messes (and What the Neighbors Thought),*** and Sneed B. Collard III's ***1,000 Years Ago on Planet Earth***]. Instead of being "sanitized," history discusses human frailties. The idea of "heroes" has expanded to include more than just well-known people (***Honoring Our Ancestors: Stories and Pictures by Fourteen Artists,*** edited by Harriet Rohmer). In keeping with the current view that it is natural to learn through mistakes, richer, more accurate information is now included about the history of this country (***Amistad: A Long Road to Freedom,*** by Walter Dean Myers). The advent of literature-based teaching and cross-curricular approaches has increased the demand for well-written nonfiction, which can be used with fiction.

Historical fiction has become more interesting as authors have done increased research on the past in order to portray a particular time as accurately as possible. This increase in accuracy reflects the view that children should be given a full picture of this country's past, blemishes and all (***Dragon's Gate,*** by Laurence Yep; ***Bat 6,*** by Virginia Euwer Wolff; and ***So Far from the Sea,*** by Eve Bunting).

More and better multicultural literature is now available, although it still represents only a small portion of what is published. ***My Heroes, My People: African Americans and Native Americans in the West,*** by Morgan Monceaux and Ruth Katcher, showcases two cultures, describing African Americans and American Indians who played prominent roles in the West. Of the multicultural books published, the largest number focus on African Americans, although there has been a slow increase in books representing American Indians and Asian Americans (Michael Dorris's ***Morning Girl,*** Huynh Quang Nhuong's ***Water Buffalo Days: Growing Up in Vietnam,*** Minfong Ho's ***The Clay Marble,*** and Dia Cha's ***Dia's Story Cloth: The Hmong People's Journey of Freedom***). Part of this increase is due to the strides that have been made in introducing books by authors and artists from diverse cultures into the ranks of publishing (Elleman, 1995).

There has been a burst in the poetry market for children, with many more Latino, Asian American, and African American voices in evidence. Francisco X. Alarcon, Eloise

The bold use of color in the illustrations and the inclusion of subjects of many ethnicities lets readers know that this book will offer a fresh look at the impact ancestors have made.

(Image from *Honoring Our Ancestors: Stories and Pictures by Fourteen Artists.* Reprinted with the permission of the publisher, Children's Book Press, San Francisco, CA. Book project copyright © 1999 by Harriet Rohmer. Individual images copyright © 1999 by Nancy Hom; copyright © 1999 by Maya Christina Gonzalez; copyright © 1999 by Helen Zughaib; copyright © 1999 Stephen Von Mason.)

Greenfield, Nikki Grimes, Juan Felipe Herrera, Pat Mora, Gary Soto, Joyce Carol Thomas, and Janet Wong are among those who have made a significant contribution to widening the repertoire heard in children's poetry (Hade, 2000).

Boundaries between the kinds of literature are being pushed more and more. A blurring of distinctions between genres is becoming apparent with the publication of such books as *The Magic School Bus* series, by Joanna Cole, whose subject matter is science, threaded with fantastical elements.

CD-ROM

Search the CD-ROM References for additional resources on *multiculturalism*.

The Influence of Trends in Marketing and Technology

Advanced technology has led to improvements in many picture books in the area of illustrations (Yolen, 1997). This same technology has allowed for a new emphasis on photos and graphics in nonfiction, making for stunning presentations (Elleman, 1995). However, graphics technology may be overshadowing other considerations that are equally important. Some critics believe that we have let design and appearance factors overpower the content of the books while "going beyond the artistic knowledge of young readers" (Fisher, 1997).

Interactive approaches to books have been developed in reaction to the CD-ROMs and other media being released. Publishers want to give readers something to be involved with, to change, to manipulate. *The Magic Eye* books, which require readers to locate pictures within frames of colored dots, have intrigued both adults and children and have become international best sellers (Elleman, 1995). The rise of audio books has given teachers and parents another way to involve children in literature.

More tie-in artifacts, such as lunch boxes and dolls, are being manufactured to accompany books. As the number of publishing houses shrinks, manufacturing of these artifacts rises.

Pop-up, scratch-and-sniff, and paper-engineering products for young children are proliferating. Some fear that these are less literary and more commercial than traditional books (Yolen, 1997).

Production of board books (books printed on cardboard for sturdiness), which toddlers love so much, is increasing. Today's board books offer much more than simple concepts such as colors and objects. Some board books contain images of children of color.

Mass marketing of books in supermarkets, mall bookstores, and drugstores, along with the rise of book clubs in schools, has changed the way books are selected. Before, a teacher or librarian led children to books after explaining their merits. Now, often the appeal of the cover alone sells the book. Some fear that the diversity of published material may decline as distribution lines narrow (Taxel and Ward, 2000).

Because of a tax on warehoused goods, books go out of print quickly if sales aren't high. This often makes it difficult to find a book you loved as a child—or even a book you read about in a review written two years ago (Taxel, 2000).

With the consolidation of publishing houses into a few megacompanies, unknown authors are having a harder time finding a publisher. The tradition of a family-owned publishing house, nurturing and leading along authors and illustrators, has all but disappeared.

Invitations

Choose several of the following activities to complete:

1. Write about your history as a reader. Include in your reading autobiography answers to some of the following questions:

- What are your earliest memories of reading at home and at school?
- Did you share reading with friends and family?
- What books/authors/subjects did you tend to focus on?
- Which adults most encouraged you as a reader? Why? Discouraged you as a reader?
- In upper elementary school, how did your reading patterns change? Why?
- Do you consider yourself a good reader? Why or why not? What characteristics do good readers have that you would like to develop?
- What roles does reading play in your life now—beyond required reading for classes? Who are some of your favorite authors, and what are some of your favorite books?

2. After sharing parts of your reading autobiographies in a group, create a list of the things that drew you to reading and those that pushed you away. What generalizations can you draw about what contributes to making "readers"? What experiences discouraged people in your group from reading? Did anything surprise you as you shared?

3. Write down in your notebook all the repertoires from which you read (aspects of your personal history or perspective). Share these with your group, and add to your list any mentioned by other group members that you think apply to you. Continue adding to this list as you go through the course so that you get a better understanding of all the parts of your history that affect your reading.

CD-ROM

To get a preview of how often group work is offered in the Invitations section, do a word search for *group* under Invitations.

4. What books that you read as a child do you consider to be children's classics? Jot down the titles of books you believe are classics and why you think their appeal is lasting. Share your list with others in your group. What discoveries did you make? Did you agree on what makes a book a classic?

5. Get comfortable in the library with a stack of picture books next to you. Read through ten books, noting what you think makes them accessible to children. Do the pages seem to turn in the right places? Does the text flow naturally when you read it aloud? How does it sound? Do you notice elements of patterned language? Are there sentence or plot structures that make the story predictable? Do the illustrations work with the text and add to the meaning of the story? As you read children's books, use your favorites to formulate statements about what you believe the purpose of children's literature is.

6. One way to build community is to share books you love. Share a favorite story you remember from childhood. Discuss the various repertoires from which you and other members of your group read the book.

7. The boxed feature Taking a Look at the Research: Creating Classroom Communities describes various aspects of creating a classroom community. Think back over your own schooling. In which classes or grades do you remember feeling part of a classroom community? In which classes or grades did you not feel part of a community? Explain to a small group what contributed to these feelings. As a group, come up with a list of dos and don'ts for creating a community in the classroom.

8. Select one website that your group will explore and report back to the class on. If possible, access the site together and then decide which person will familiarize himself or herself with each part of the site. As a group, prepare a written report for the class, explaining what they can find on your site.

Classroom Teaching Ideas

The best teaching ideas will come from your own interests and needs and the experiences you and your children are having within your unique setting. Many ideas will be spontaneous and teach to the moment. The ones shared here and at the conclusion of each future chapter may be useful, may serve as a springboard for other ideas more perfectly suited to you, or may not be helpful at all. In any case, read, enjoy, and have fun!

1. Have students write or record their own reading autobiographies, in which they share what they remember best about books from their earlier years.

2. Work together with your students to determine what kind of community you want your classroom to be. Talk through and write down rules that will help shape a caring and respectful environment. Remember to keep the rules to a minimum and adhere to them consistently.

3. Share yourself with your students. Perhaps even before school begins, write to your prospective students to introduce yourself. Talk about what interests you, your friends, your pets, your wonderings, and the things you like to do. Include photocopies of photos. Ask your students to bring items about themselves to share during the first days of school. These could include, among other things, photos or favorite toys.

4. Many students make text-to-text connections through their familiarity with authors and illustrators. Select an author or illustrator to study. Have students find as many of the person's works as they can, research biographical material, make a bulletin board display, or bring in foods mentioned or shown in the person's work. Consider having a birthday party on the person's birthday.

Internet and Text Resources

Following are some of the largest websites devoted to children's literature. Several of these will be cited again in the specific chapters to which they pertain. Please note that if a web address is no longer operational, you can often locate the new address by going to a search engine and typing in the name of the site.

1. American Library Association provides lists of Best Books for Young Adults, Quick Picks (books for reluctant readers), and information about award-winning books. Find it at

www.ala.org/parents

2. Booktalks—Quick and Simple has over 400 booktalks arranged alphabetically by author and book. Go to

http://nancykeane.com/booktalks/

3. The Bulletin of the Center for Children's Books contains book reviews, recommended books, in-depth discussions of featured books, and so on. Go to

http://lis.uiuc.edu/puboff/bccb/

4. Carol Hurst's Children's Literature Site recommends books, some teaching guides, and activities. Find it at

www.carolhurst.com

5. The Children's Literature Web Guide is a great site, packed with information on children's and young adults' books, authors, awards, and many links, even though it hasn't been updated recently. Find it at

www.ucalgary.ca/~dkbrown/

6. Northwest Regional Educational Library is another excellent resource, with links to a number of teacher resources. Go to

www. nwrel.org/sky/index.asp?ID=3

7. ERIC REC Web Resources provides links to various children's and adolescents' literature resources online. Find it at

http://eric.indiana.edu/www/indexwr.html

8. Once Upon a Time: A Children's Literature Website offers readers a myriad of resources. Go to

nova.bsuvc.bsu.edu/~OOmevancamp/clrw.html

9. Subject Guide to Children's Literature is an Australian site that allows the searcher to find books, journal articles, Internet sites, and background information. Go to

www.deakin.edu.au/library/srchgdes/SearchChildLit.html

10. Online Journals on Children's and Adolescents' Literature also lists special library collections. Find it at

http://eric.indiana.edu/www/#JOUR

References

Carlsen, G. Robert (1974). "Literature IS . . . ." *English Journal 63,* 23–27.

Curtis, Christopher Paul (1997). Keynote address. National Conference of Teachers of English Annual Convention, Detroit, Nov. 20–24, 1997.

Elleman, Barbara (1995). "Toward the 21st Century—Where Are Children's Books Going?" *The New Advocate 8,* 151–165.

Elliot, Stephen N., Thomas R. Kratochwill, Joan Littlefield, and John F. Travers (2000). *Educational Psychology: Effective Teaching, Effective Learning.* New York: McGraw-Hill.

Fisher, Leonard Everett (1997). "From Xenophon to Gutenberg." *The New Advocate 10,* 203–209.

Goldstone, Bette (1999). "Brave New Worlds: The Changing Image of the Picture Book." *The New Advocate 12,* 331–343.

Goodman, Ken (1996). *On Reading: A Common-Sense Look at the Nature of Language and the Science of Reading.* Portsmouth, NH: Heinemann.

Hade, Daniel D., and Lisa Murphy (2000). "Voice and Image: A Look at Recent Poetry."*Language Arts 77,* 344–352.

Harris, Violet (1996). "Continuing Dilemmas, Debates, and Delights in Multicultural Literature." *The New Advocate 9,* 107–122.

Kohl, Herbert (1995). *Should We Burn Babar? Essays on Children's Literature and the Power of Stories.* New York: The New Press.

McCormick, Kathleen (1994). *The Culture of Reading and the Teaching of English.* New York: Manchester University Press.

Siegler, Robert S. (1991). *Children's Thinking* (2nd ed.). Englewood Cliffs, NJ: Prentice Hall.

Taxel, Joel, and Holly M. Ward (2000). "Publishing Children's Literature at the Dawn of the 21st Century." *The New Advocate 13,* 51–59.

Yolen, Jane (1997). "Taking Time: Or How Things Have Changed in the Last Thirty-Five Years of Children's Publishing." *The New Advocate 10,* 285–291.

Children's Books

Bauer, Marion Dane, ed. (1994). *Am I Blue? Coming Out from the Silence.* New York: HarperCollins.

Brown, Margaret Wise (1947). *Goodnight Moon.* Illus. Clement Hurd. New York: Harper & Row.

Bunting, Eve (1998). *So Far from the Sea.* Illus. Chris K. Soentpiet. New York: Clarion.

Burton, Virginia Lee (1939). *Mike Mulligan and His Steam Shovel.* New York: Houghton Mifflin.

Cha, Dia (1996). *Dia's Story Cloth: The Hmong People's Journey of Freedom.* Stitched by Chue and Nhia Thao Cha. New York: Lee & Low.

Collard, Sneed B., III (1999). *1,000 Years Ago on Planet Earth.* Illus. Jonathan Hunt. Boston: Houghton Mifflin.

Conly, Jane Leslie (1993). *Crazy Lady!* New York: HarperTrophy.

Curtis, Christopher Paul (1999). *Bud, Not Buddy.* New York: Delacorte.

—— (1995). *The Watsons Go to Birmingham—1963.* New York: Delacorte.

De Brunhoff, Jean (1966). *The Story of Babar, the Little Elephant.* New York: Random [1931].

DiCamillo, Kate (2000). *Because of Winn-Dixie.* Cambridge, MA: Candlewick.

Dickens, Charles (1861). *Great Expectations.* Philadelphia: Peterson.

Dorris, Michael (1992). *Morning Girl.* New York: Hyperion.

English, Karen (1999). *Francie.* New York: Farrar, Straus & Giroux.

Gag, Wanda (1928). *Millions of Cats.* New York: Coward-McCann.

Garden, Nancy (1996). *Good Moon Rising.* New York: Farrar, Straus & Giroux.

Grahame, Kenneth (1983). *The Wind in the Willows.* Illus. Ernest H. Shepard. New York: Scribners [1908].

Gruelle, Johnny (1920). *The Raggedy Ann Stories.* Chicago: Volland.

Ho, Minfong (1991). *The Clay Marble.* New York: Farrar, Straus & Giroux.

Hoffman, Mary (1991). *Amazing Grace.* Illus. Caroline Binch. New York: Dial.

Houston, Gloria (1994). *Mountain Valor.* New York: Philomel.

Howe, Deborah, and James Howe (1979). *Bunnicula: A Rabbit-Tale of Mystery.* Illus. Alan Daniel. New York: Avon.

Krull, Kathleen (1995). *Lives of the Artists: Masterpieces, Messes (and What the Neighbors Thought).* Illus. Kathryn Hewitt. San Diego: Harcourt Brace.

L'Engle, Madeleine (1980). *A Wrinkle in Time.* New York: Farrar, Straus & Giroux [1962, Ariel; 1973, Yearling].

Lowrey, Janette Sebring (1942). *The Poky Little Puppy.* Illus. Gustaf Tenggren. New York: Simon & Schuster.

McCloskey, Robert (1941). *Make Way for Ducklings.* New York: Viking.

Milne, A. A. (1988). *The Complete Tales & Poems of Winnie-the-Pooh.* Illus. Ernest H. Shepard. New York: Dutton [1926].

Monceaux, Morgan, and Ruth Katcher (1999). *My Heroes, My People: African Americans and Native Americans in the West.* New York: Farrar, Straus & Giroux.

Myers, Walter Dean (1998). *Amistad: A Long Road to Freedom.* New York: Dutton.

Nhuong, Huynh Quang (1997). *Water Buffalo Days: Growing Up in Vietnam.* Illus. Jean and Mou-Sien Tseng. New York: HarperCollins.

Nye, Naomi Shihab (1997). *Habibi.* New York: Simon & Schuster.

—— (1997). *Sitti's Secrets.* Illus. Nancy Carpenter. New York: Simon & Schuster.

Paulsen, Gary (1995). *The Tent.* San Diego: Harcourt Brace.

Peck, Richard (2000). *A Year Down Yonder.* New York: Dial.

Piper, Watty (1929). *The Little Engine That Could.* Illus. George and Doris Hauman. New York: Putnam [reissued in 1990].

Robinson, Barbara (1994). *The Worst Best School Year Ever.* New York: HarperTrophy.

Rohmer, Harriet, ed. (1999). *Honoring Our Ancestors: Stories and Pictures by Fourteen Artists.* San Francisco: Children's Book Press.

Rowling, J. K. (1997). *Harry Potter and the Sorcerer's Stone.* New York: Scholastic.

Rylant, Cynthia (1995). *Henry and Mudge and the Best Day of All.* Illus. Suçie Stevenson. New York: Aladdin.

Sendak, Maurice (1965). *Where the Wild Things Are.* New York: Harper.

Seuss, Dr. (1960). *Green Eggs and Ham.* New York: Random.

Singer, Marilyn, ed. (2000). *I Believe in Water: Twelve Brushes with Religion.* New York: HarperCollins.

St. George, Judith (2000). *So You Want to Be President?* Illus. David Small. New York: Philomel.

Van Draanen, Wendelin (1998). *Sammy Keyes and the Hotel Thief.* New York: Knopf.

Walter, Mildred Pitts (1996). *Second Daughter: The Story of a Slave Girl.* New York: Scholastic.

Weeks, Sarah (1995). *Follow the Moon.* Illus. Suzanne Duranceau. New York: HarperCollins.

White, E. B. (1952). *Charlotte's Web.* Illus. Garth Williams. New York: Harper & Row.

—— (1945). *Stuart Little.* Illus. Garth Williams. New York: Harper & Row.

White, Ruth (1996). *Belle Prater's Boy.* New York: Yearling.

Wisniewski, David (1998). *The Secret Knowledge of Grown-Ups.* New York: Lothrop, Lee & Shepard.

Wolff, Virginia Euwer (1998). *Bat 6.* New York: Scholastic.

Woodson, Jacqueline (1995). *From the Notebooks of Melanin Sun.* New York: Scholastic.

—— (1994). *I Hadn't Meant to Tell You This.* New York: Bantam Doubleday Dell.

Yep, Laurence (1993). *Dragon's Gate.* New York: Scholastic.

Yolen, Jane, and Bruce Coville (1998). *Armageddon Summer.* New York: Harcourt Brace.

Evaluating and Selecting Children's Literature

Although evaluating and selecting children's books can at first seem like an intimidating and overwhelming task, deciding what to read is important not only for you but also for your students. No one wants to waste time reading mediocre books, especially when one lifetime is hardly enough time to read all the wonderful children's books that have been published. One of the goals of this text is to help you discover what books are worth your and your students' time. Learning why you feel the way you do about particular books will give you more confidence in the choices you make for your students.

Your reactions to the books you choose for your personal reading are based on your own needs, values, experiences, and preferences with respect to style; the same is true of  your reactions to children's books. But when, as a teacher or librarian, you are also making choices for students, you want to make sure that you stretch your range of possibilities so that you select books based on the very best criteria possible. If you know little about a subject, your choices are limited. You need to immerse yourself in the world of children's literature. There are, however, ways to fairly quickly come to understand which books are worth your and your students' time. This chapter will help you clarify possible criteria you might use to evaluate books. The boxed feature Children's Voices gives a glimpse of what some middle-grade students like in books.

THE POLAR EXPRESS

A train, its light dimmed by the quietly falling snow, pulls up in front of a house to transport one boy into the experience of a lifetime.

(Cover, from THE POLAR EXPRESS. Copyright © 1985 by Chris Van Allsburg. Reprinted by permission of Houghton Mifflin Company. All rights reserved.)

In a similar way, the language in *The Whales' Song* enchants and lulls: "Lilly's grandmother told her a story. 'Once upon a time,' she said, 'the ocean was filled with whales. They were as big as the hills. They were as peaceful as the moon. They were the most wondrous creatures you could ever imagine.'" The ending kindles a quiet joy and a belief that all life is connected: "Lilly thought she must have been dreaming. She stood up and turned toward home. Then from far, far away, on the breath of the wind, she heard 'Lilly! Lilly!' The whales were calling her name."

In both of these books, I am entranced by the story line and wonder where it will take me. I want Lilly to hear the whales sing, as her grandmother has, though Frederick's strong presence and attitudes make me question whether Lilly will be able to defend her beliefs. In *The Polar Express,* once the boy is at the North Pole and receives his gift, I wonder what will happen next. The plot lines provide tension that makes me read each book to the end.

I am also enamored of *Roll of Thunder, Hear My Cry,* by Mildred D. Taylor, because I feel very connected to the characters—smart, no-nonsense Mama; kindly but strict Papa; sometimes-sassy Cassie. Although surrounded by prejudice and hate, the family members do not let it warp their spirits. The parents teach their children that the people who hate them are ignorant, so the children don't turn their hurt inward, wondering what they have done wrong. Strong families with strong beliefs about themselves and the world I find compelling. I am always trying to figure out how black people survived discrimination and why whites acted as if it were acceptable. Sometimes human beings' behavior stuns me. The tension in the book is constant, beginning with Cassie's confrontation with the teacher over the inferior books given to the children and ending with TJ's being brought to trial. The action never stops.

Cassie gazes straight out at us from Jerry Pinkney's soft watercolor illustration, giving us a hint of her very direct nature.
("25TH ANNIVERSARY COVER" from ROLL OF THUNDER, HEAR MY CRY by Mildred D. Taylor, illustration by Jerry Pinkney. Copyright 1976 by Mildred Taylor, text. Copyright 2001 by Jerry Pinkney, illustration. Used by permission of Dial Books for Young Readers, an imprint of Penguin Putman Books for Young Readers, a division of Penguin Putnam Inc.)

Generalizing the Process

What do my reactions to these books have in common? On what basis do I evaluate books? Emotional impact seems important, as does as the vision the author has of the world. For example, the mood of **The Whales' Song** reverberates; the playfulness of the whales and the timelessness of the water move me, making me want to celebrate the mysteries of the universe. Well-drawn characters are also vital, as are themes that make me think about the books long after I have read them. Themes that involve the resiliency of the human spirit keep me interested. Beautiful language enchants me.

I tend to pay attention to other qualities of writing after I have finished a book. Although I do not specifically think about the setting, I must feel a part of the story's world and "see" the setting, or else engagement with the book is difficult. Envisioning the setting allows me to move around in the world of the characters, seeing the ocean or the North Pole or rural Mississippi. I'm absorbed into books with richly drawn worlds.

The Place of Elements of Literature in Evaluation

Looking at literary elements can help us to see a piece of literature from multiple perspectives and thus experience it more deeply. Probably the first thing we do as readers, before using any other evaluative screen, is decide whether we like a book. Once we have initially connected with a book, we are ready to look at particular literary elements to see whether the book has a universal richness. These elements help us appreciate the craft of the writing.

Although it is important for teachers to know and use the elements of literature in order to select books that will hold up under the scrutiny of children, we all tend to respond holistically on a first read. Then we turn to the elements of literature to see how they can be used to extend our thinking about and evaluation of the book. As you read the following discussion of the elements of literature, think about whether and how each is important to you when you evaluate the merit of a book.

Plot

The plot answers the questions "What is happening in the story?" and "What is the sequence of events?" Some stories have simple and straightforward plots. Others have complex plots that make the reader think and ask questions: Who solves problems? What allows the tension to be dissolved? Herbert Kohl (1995) says, "Studying how tension and dissonance are dealt with in a plot is another way of discovering the role of power relations in a story" (p. 24). For instance, in **The Whales' Song,** although Frederick is ornery and outspoken, he is not able to change the mythic and magical views that Lilly and her grandmother have of the whales. The pace at which the plot unfolds is also important. Stories that flow well keep the reader involved and interested. For some readers, unraveling or solving one plot line doesn't offer enough complexity—they prefer a book to be multidimensional.

Characters

Characterization addresses the questions "Who are these people?" and "Are they believable?" Characters need to be authentic for the reader to connect with them. Readers are looking for multidimensional characters so well developed that they seem to be real people. When characters are flat, given life through stereotyping and predictable actions, readers are not likely to become sufficiently involved with their lives to want to finish the book. Readers seek characters whose humanity touches theirs. Both the grandmother and Lilly in *The Whales' Song* are easy to relate to and believe in, partly because of their sensitivity. It's easy to empathize with the boy in *The Polar Express* and imagine what it would be like going to the North Pole and meeting Santa Claus. In *Roll of Thunder, Hear My Cry,* the characters of Cassie, her mother, and her father are so well developed that it's possible to imagine having whole conversations with them. Characters come to life for us through what they say, their actions, and what others say about them.

Setting

Setting informs the reader of where the story is taking place. It answers the questions "Where am I?" and "What will I see if I walk around here?" Occasionally, the setting is so prominent—for example, when it includes a hurricane, a tidal wave, or a storm—that it almost becomes another character. More frequently, the setting falls into the background, and the reader is not particularly aware of it. Readers know immediately, however, when the setting is not well drawn, because they can't get a sense of where they are. In *The Polar Express,* the language and illustrations evoke a fairy-tale world. In *The Whales' Song,* conversations about the whales and the immediacy of the illustrations of the ocean surround the reader.

Theme

Theme answers the question "What is this story telling me?" Readers want to come away from a story with ideas that they can turn over and over in their mind. The reader may well ask: Have I taken away something of substance by reading the book? Is this something that will help me think about issues within myself? What did I learn about people and society or myself? What kinds of connections to people and society did this book give me? Did this book show me possibilities and make me excited about thinking further about issues? Is the content worth exploring? The theme and the worth of the content are closely intertwined.

Style

Style defines the *qualities of writing,* answering the question "How has this book been written to engage the reader?" Readers often are not aware of the qualities of good writing while they read, but they almost always are jolted by poor or inadequate writing. Hearing the author's voice, the reader realizes that there is someone behind the words. If point of view is not presented effectively, which character is thinking what becomes unclear. Authors who can move smoothly from one point of view to another keep their readers involved. Well-chosen words, rich language, and the skillful use of literary devices make an impact on the reader. Sometimes a beautiful metaphor will take the breath away or cause the reader to linger over the words, savoring the image. Sometimes the richness of the language will stun or simply delight the reader. So, when looking at the qualities of writing, don't simply identify them, but recognize the impact each has on you and how it contributes to the effectiveness of the overall story.

Other Considerations

In addition to the elements of literature, books can also be evaluated on emotional impact, imaginative impact, and vision.

Emotional Impact

Did this book connect you to your own humanity and that of others? Did this piece of literature make an impact on you? The purpose of literature is to make an impact, so if you felt nothing or said "So what?" the book doesn't meet key criteria. If you were moved by the beauty of the language, by the glimpses into the characters' personalities, by the ideas and issues dealt with, or by the actions of the characters, then the book has merit. In ***Roll of Thunder, Hear My Cry,*** Cassie's rage at the injustice she faces from Lillian Jean and the white world becomes our rage.

Imaginative Impact

Books can spark imagination, show possibilities, stretch thinking, pique curiosity, and make the reader think in different ways. Herbert Kohl (1995) identifies the value of this element: "Children's imaginations are lively and are fed by the stories they are told and the images provided them by their culture" (p. 62). Kohl maintains, "Books can be vehicles for sparking utopian and hopeful imaginings" (p. 63). If we don't provide stories that allow young people to "fundamentally question the world as it is and dream it as it might be, resignation, defiance, or the quest for personal success become the only imaginable options . . . " (p. 65).

One of the central characteristics of the imagination is that it crosses borders and categories. The only way we can jump over the boundaries of our own thinking is through imagination, so we need stories that spark it. ***The Polar Express*** makes a strong impact because it not only puts the reader in the center of the little boy's experience, but also makes the reader feel the wonder and beauty of believing in something beyond the self.

Sometimes, this sparking of the imagination can be attributed to plot, character, or theme. But it's much more than any one of these parts—it's the overall quality of the story that makes us wonder or feel awe or think of a million questions we want answered. Since, as Carlsen (1974) pointed out (see Chapter 1), early childhood is a key age for unconscious delight, it's important to offer books that feed the imagination of young students.

Vision

Vision is the view authors have of the world and the people in it, and their attitudes toward both. How are people shown? Are they good or evil? Are they inherently competitive or cooperative? Are some people viewed as less worthy because they are not beautiful or rich, or are all characters portrayed as equal in worth? Does this book connect what happens in the story to "who has the power and how the power is distributed among the characters" (p. 5)? Kohl asks us to look at the way power is represented in the story, "since power relationships in literature reveal the politics of both the story and, frequently, the author. Power relationships also provide examples and models for children of social and moral behavior" (p. 4). In other words, by seeing who makes the decisions, who gives the orders, and who obeys, readers make discoveries about power.

In ***The Whales' Song,*** Frederick, although he is gruff and forceful in his speech, doesn't get the last word. Lilly listens to her gentle grandmother and follows her heart. She doesn't let someone who views the world in utilitarian ways steal her hope and longing for beauty. Thus, power here is somewhat equitably distributed; the overbearing adult doesn't win out. The author's vision of the world encourages children to recognize the importance of their own feelings and not to feel inadequate because someone has a totally different view. Likewise, in ***Roll of Thunder, Hear My Cry,*** the author's vision is of an equitable world where all people can live in peace and not be denied opportunities. The issue of power is, of course, at the forefront, since the story takes place in the 1930s in the South. Although the white people have the upper hand, with the law supporting them, the rightness of this view is challenged throughout the book. An author's vision can have a powerful impact on the reader.

The Visual

Color leaping off the page. Lines wiggling, waving, or standing straight. Shapes smoothly rounded or abruptly angular. Art includes all of these elements but is much, much more. Art makes an impact on us as we view it, representing one piece of the artist's

W

To locate books that appeal to children of different age groups, go to **Database of Award-Winning Children's Literature** at www2.wcoil.com/~ellerbee/childlit.html.

world view and giving us another way to look at the world. Yet, for those of us who are not visual artists ourselves, the idea of evaluating illustrations in books can be intimidating. To evaluate children's literature, we do not need to become art critics; we merely need to learn to trust our own instincts and responses. It is not necessary to know how to name techniques and styles in order to evaluate art. Our descriptions of how the art moves us can provide the beginnings of ways to talk about the art.

Once I asked an artist friend what I was supposed to do when I looked at a picture and what I had to know in order to appreciate art. She told me to start with what moved me and what I noticed about the picture. I now have two beautiful pieces in my living room that I bought for the shapes and the colors. Whenever I look at the abstract shapes in one of the pieces, something pleases me. I can't even name the technique the artist used. All I know is that those colors and shapes put me in touch with deep, deep parts of myself and keep me in touch with my humanness. Now I never buy a painting unless it moves me, adds warmth and beauty to my house, shows me something new every time I look at it, and enriches my life. So, although I am not an artist, I know what I love; I know what moves me and involves me.

As a reader, you too respond to illustrations in books. So we will begin our investigation of art in children's literature with our own responses, considering such issues as whether the pictures please us and make us want to look harder.

Responding to the Visual

First I will tell you what I notice when I look at pictures that attract me or interest me. After responding to a few particular illustrations, I'll make some generalizations about my responses. Then I'll suggest some other ways of responding to art and some ways of understanding what might have elicited a particular response.

I have read many, many Brian Wildsmith books to my children over the years. We all fell in love with his drawings. At first, I couldn't identify why they captivated me, until I described what I saw. His illustrations in *Fishes,* in which the brushstrokes are very obvious, draw me into the pictures. In the picture of "a hover of trout," he uses many shades of blues and purples in the water. Because it's not just a solid blue mass, I feel as if I could find a way to enter into the water. Shadows and openings seem to be created for me. The golds, yellows, and oranges look luminous, as if the fish were lit up by something inside of them. The fish nearer the top seems brighter and has more intense colors, as it is closer to the sun. Their contrasting dark black eyes draw me into their depths, making the fish come alive and giving me an empathy for them as fish. The composition of the fish is balanced, but the fish are moving forward, off the page, and my eye follows them in that direction. The bodies of the fish are covered with red, aqua, and black dots that seem to draw the fish toward me, almost out of the illustration itself. Wildsmith's lines are delicately drawn, adding to the floating quality of the pictures. His pictures are certainly not what would be called realistic or representational because of the blurring of parts of the fish, the obvious strokes, and the way the color seems to be laid on.

In *Mama, Do You Love Me?,* written by Barbara M. Joosse and illustrated by Barbara Lavallee, I immediately notice the shapes and the colors. In the picture of the mother leaning over to receive a hug from her child, the half-elliptical shape makes the mother and daughter seem like one person. Although the art is stylistic, with the faces divided and shaded and the eyes represented by curved lines, this illustration beams with love and affection. The oranges and reds of the mother's dress, which is covered with a cheery flower design and has borders around the neck, sleeves, and bottom ruffle, radiate acceptance and warmth. Even the browns and reddish oranges of the faces are warm and seem to glow. The little girl's positioning—her arms around her mother's neck, her head flung back to receive her mother's kiss, straining on her tiptoes to be as close to her mother as possible—exudes love and trust, suggesting that this child feels completely secure with her mother. This feeling of warmth and the way the artist has positioned the two figures are the most important features of the picture. The doll is a nice touch because it snuggles, with arms flung open, in the little girl's arm and reinforces the feeling of openness to love and affection. The mother,

CD-ROM

To find other books by Brian Wildsmith, go to the CD-ROM database.

Fishes by Brian Wildsmith

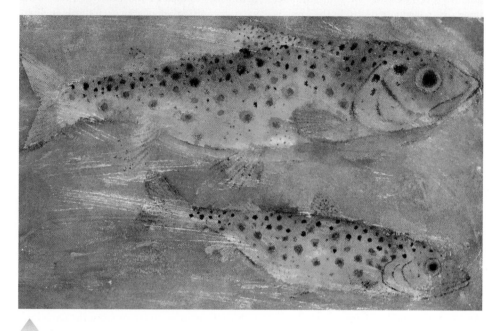

Brian Wildsmith creates a floating, almost ethereal feeling with his use of color, shadows, and brushstrokes.

(Cover illustration from **Fishes** by Brian Wildsmith, by permission of Oxford University Press.)

the child, and the doll all wear similar shoes and leg coverings. These repeated elements serve to show how much the three have in common. The beautiful curving shape of the mother as she bends over the child speaks of softness and yielding. The curve is repeated in the mother's head and arm, the child's head, the doll's head, and even the shoes. There are no sharp, straight lines in the picture to detract from the soothing smoothness. Because the embracing mother and child are right in the middle of the page, nothing takes our eyes away from this display of affection and love. The design of the little girl's dress, with hearts everywhere, reinforces the presence of love. Both mother and daughter are standing on a bluish, shaded area, which holds them together and centered.

In both Wildsmith's and Lavallee's pictures, color adds to the illustrations, as does composition (where objects are placed in a picture). The reader's eye is drawn by the lines and shapes, which also contribute to the impact. The brushstrokes and repeated elements are particularly striking in these two pictures. You may find, however, that you frequently are at a

How much?

Barbara Lavallee's stunning composition and use of line and color create an image bursting with love.

(From *Mama, Do You Love Me?* by Barbara M. Joosse, illustrated by Barbara Lavallee © 1991. Reprinted by permission of Chronicle Books, San Francisco.)

loss for words to describe your reaction to art. The purpose of the following sections is to give you the language to express what you are responding to in the art. By learning the basic vocabulary of art, you also will indirectly acquire another tool for looking at the world. The goal isn't to have you—or your students—memorize a bunch of vocabulary terms, but to open up an evaluative lens. In the same way we use a particular vocabulary to evaluate literature, we can use one for art.

Looking at the Art

When you set out to look at the art in a book, you can learn much by paging through the book quickly, just to get a feel for it. In a quick look through the illustrations, pay attention to colors, lines, shapes, texture, and composition.

Colors

Are the colors bright or dark? How are the pictures shaded? What's in the shadows? Are the colors warm or cool? Do they make the pictures seem joyous or solemn? In **The Painter's Eye,** Jan Greenberg and Sandra Jordan (1991) say, "Paintings filled with intense red, orange or yellow can be exciting or even violent. The duller the color, the softer it seems, as in the blue-grey of dusk or the pale blue of a misty day. Artists use intensity of color to convey mood" (p. 32).

Lines

Are the lines straight, jagged, curved, vertical, thick, thin, long, short, or smooth? Each kind can convey a mood. Horizontal lines may be interpreted as peaceful, depressed, or serene. Vertical lines may be seen as strong, rigid, formal, or even religious. Jagged lines may indicate excitement, anger, or energy, whereas curved lines often are sensuous, organic, or rhythmic, according to Greenberg and Jordan. Brushstrokes also contribute to the overall feel. They can be big and bold or delicate and whispery.

The soft, almost furry quality of this image in *Toby, Where Are You?* emphasizes the gentle, loving nature of the family.
(© 1997 by Teryl Euvremer. Used by permission of HarperCollins Publishers.)

Shapes

Artists use shapes and forms as well as lines to control the direction of our eye movements within an illustration. Curved shapes often represent objects in nature, whereas angular shapes tend to represent man-made objects. According to Greenberg and Jordan (1991), whereas triangles, circles, and rectangles are geometric shapes we're used to seeing in our daily lives, "organic shapes are freer and less defined. These shapes often remind us of animal, human, or natural forms such as a shell or a cloud" (p. 24). Some shapes look strong or dense; others appear soft or floating. Shapes contribute to the overall impression we get from a picture, moving us with their power or inviting us in with their gentleness or softness.

Texture

Do the surfaces of the shapes have a rough, smooth, or soft appearance? When actual material is attached to a canvas, it gives a picture a three-dimensional look. Greenberg and Jordan (1991) say, "Sensing whether the surface is rough or smooth, grainy or gossamer contributes to our feelings about the painting" (p. 30). Because texture appeals to our tactile sense, it can give a strong sensual feeling to artwork. The soft texture of Teryl Euvremer's pictures in *Toby, Where Are You?,* by William Steig, seems to emanate love; we feel almost caressed by the pictures. The smooth texture of Richard Egielski's work in *Buz* adds to the pictures' unreality because nothing can stick to the glossy, impenetrable images. The high gloss doesn't invite us to look deeply *into* the picture—we have to stay on the surface. When a work has a rough texture, we may get a sense of depth. Clearly, texture can have a definite impact on our responses to illustrations.

Composition

Does the placement of objects make them seem to be in harmony with one another? Do they seem unified, or do they stand in contrast or opposition to one another? The sizes of the objects in relation to one another and the perspective from which the picture is drawn are also part of its composition.

In Debra Frasier's *Out of the Ocean,* the balanced, layered composition of the illustrations gives us a feeling of harmony, oneness, and serenity. In *To Market, To Market,* written by Anne Miranda and illustrated by Janet Stevens, the composition of the picture on the eighth page

Uh-oh!

The goose was let out.

Janet Stevens's composition captures the chaos and disorder of the situation, since even the goose can't stay on the page.
(Illustration from TO MARKET, TO MARKET by Anne Miranda, illustrations copyright © 1997 by Janet Stevens, reprinted by permission of Harcourt, Inc.)

clearly shows chaos and disharmony. The lady is almost reaching outside the frame of the picture to catch the goose; the pig is partly outside the frame. Nothing appears orderly. As you can see, composition creates distinct impressions in the viewer.

Artists' Media and Materials

After the first quick look-through, you may want to linger over certain pictures that really strike you. Sometimes, knowing the terms for the media and materials the artist used in creating the picture will help you to describe the impression you got from the picture.

Drawing

Artists may draw with pen and ink, pencil or graphite, pastels, or a sharp instrument on scratchboard. The characteristics of each medium affect the impressions it makes.

Pen and ink creates a very defined effect. The strong lines make the objects seem very sure of themselves. Chris Van Allsburg's ***Ben's Dream*** is drawn in pen and ink, and the lack of color makes the viewer focus more closely on the objects. This medium seems a little more aggressive than other media, as everything has to have an outline and muted areas are rare. However, some artists—like James Stevenson in ***"Could Be Worse!"***—use pen and ink and then color the images with watercolors. This creates a softer effect, but the emphasis is still on the outlined shapes. This medium also makes the illustrations look purposeful, as if every single thing in the picture had a definite and important place.

James Stevenson uses the definite lines created by pen and ink to ensure that readers don't miss one thing in this humorous story, which is told largely through the illustrations.
(Cover art from *"Could Be Worse!"* by James Stevenson. Used by permission of HarperCollins Publishers.)

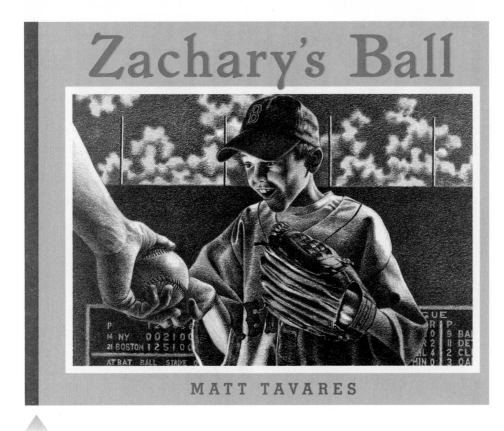

Matt Tavares's use of pencil, with its emphasis on lights and darks, focuses the reader's attention on the emotions the boy is experiencing.

(ZACHARY'S BALL copyright © 2000 Matt Tavares. Reproduced by permission of the publisher Candlewick Press, Inc., Cambridge, MA.)

Pencil or graphite allows for a full range of lights and darks, creating different moods and a sense of depth with shadow. Chris Van Allsburg's **The Garden of Abdul Gasazi** and **Jumanji** offer excellent examples of the sense of depth that can be created. Matt Tavares's use of pencil in **Zachary's Ball** highlights the contrast between light and dark, causing readers to focus on the luminescent expression on the face of the young boy.

Pastels are powdered colors mixed to the desired shade with white chalk and held together with liquids. Because pastels are used in a form that resembles chalk, they have a soft quality and often a muted appearance. Pastels are wonderful for creating moods, as they can so easily be used to suggest subtleties. In **Hoops,** written by Robert Burleigh and illustrated by Stephen T. Johnson, there is a dreamlike quality to the pictures which works well with the text, because readers can imagine themselves in the pictures shooting baskets. Caldecott-winning artist Ed Young often draws in pastels. His drawings in **Lon Po Po: A Red-Riding Hood Story from China** create a mood of danger and foreboding through the muted colors and the floating quality of the soft edges of the illustrations. No harsh, straight lines detract from this illusion. Howard Fine's use of pastels in Margie Palatini's **Piggie Pie!** to achieve a bright effect shows their versatility.

Scratchboard is a technique in which the artist uses a sharp instrument to scratch a picture into a two-layered (usually black-and-white) board. Brian Pinkney does almost all of his work in scratchboard. As he did in **Duke Ellington,** written by Andrea Davis Pinkney, Brian Pinkney often overpaints his illustrations with oil to add color to the sharp black-and-white contrasts. This technique gives the illustrations a rough appearance and implies that everything is not smooth beneath the surface. The deepness of the scratches suggests that they are purposeful and deliberate. The fact that everything is outlined and has a definite shape contributes to a serious mood or tone.

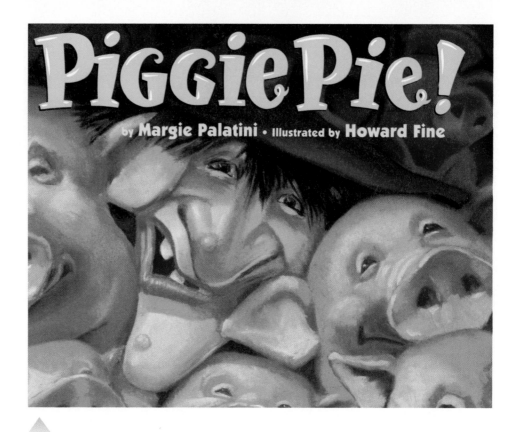

In *Piggie Pie!*, a story of deception, the soft, often blurry look created by the pastels helps mute or hide the truth.

(Cover of PIGGIE PIE! by Margie Palatini, illustrated by Howard Fine. Reprinted by permission of Clarion Books/Houghton Mifflin Co. All rights reserved.)

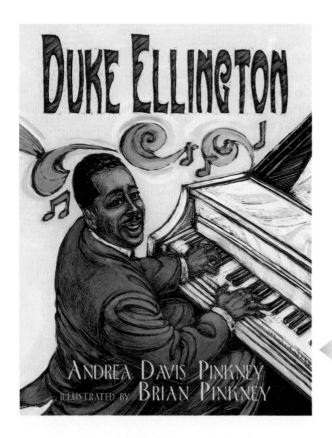

Painting

Painting emphasizes the use of color and tone to convey meaning and emotions. There are many kinds of paints. As Kathleen Horning (1997) explains in *Cover to Cover: Evaluating and Reviewing Children's Books,* each type of paint "begins as a finely ground pigment that is mixed with a different type of binder to adhere to a surface, and as such has its own distinctive properties" (p. 113). Most people will not be able to identify the type of paint used simply by looking at the illustrations, although watercolor seems the most easily distinguishable to me. The reason I am including descriptions of different types of paint is so that when you read in a review that the illustrator used *gouache* or *tempera,* you will be familiar with the term as well as the effects that type of paint can have on a picture.

Gouache (pronounced "gwash") is a type of water-based paint that is used when an "opaque," or solid, even color is

Pinkney's use of scratchboard with its deep, distinct markings helps convey the strength and deliberateness of Duke Ellington's character.

(Illustration reprinted with the permission of Little, Brown and Company from *Duke Ellington* by Andrea Davis Pinkney. Illustrations copyright © 1998 by Brian Pinkney.)

Helen Oxenbury's use of gouache, with the even colors and lack of blurriness, lets viewers directly experience the openness and affection given and received.
(Illustration © 1994 Helen Oxenbury. SO MUCH by Trish Cooke. Reproduced by permission of the publisher Candlewick Press, Inc., Cambridge, MA, on behalf of Walker Books Ltd., of London.)

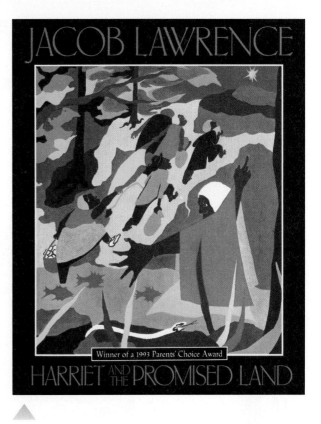

Jacob Lawrence's use of poster paint in bold primary colors gives a distinct, no-nonsense feel to this painting, leaving no doubt that people are hurrying toward the North Star and away from slavery.
(Reprinted with the permission of Simon & Schuster Books for Young Readers, an imprint of Simon & Schuster Children's Publishing Division from HARRIET AND THE PROMISED LAND by Jacob Lawrence. Copyright © 1968, 1993 Jacob Lawrence.)

wanted. It is powdered color mixed with an opaque white. In **So Much,** written by Trish Cooke and illustrated by Helen Oxenbury, the entire surface of the paper is covered with paint, the lines are distinct, the colors are even, and there are no blurry or muted areas. These qualities give the illustrations a straightforward feel—nothing is hidden; everything is as it is shown. The even, solid quality of the paint gives the illustrations substance, as if you couldn't look through them to find something else. No mystery is implied, consistent with pictures about daily life. Like **More More More Said the Baby,** most of Vera B. Williams's books are done in gouache, with the vivid colors expressing the zest for living of her characters.

Poster paint is a coarser version of gouache in which the color pigment is not as finely ground. I find it difficult to distinguish among gouache, tempera, and poster paint. Jacob Lawrence's **Harriet and the Promised Land,** which is done in poster paint, looks very much like his **The Great Migration: An American Story,** described in the next paragraph.

Tempera is a quick-drying paint that can yield bright, solid colors or can be mixed with water for softer effects. Jacob Lawrence's **The Great Migration: An American Story,** done in tempera, features fully covered surfaces and clearly defined lines, which create a feeling of substance. The often-evident brushstrokes give an impression of scarcity of paint or carelessness in the painting, since everything is not covered evenly. By using this medium, the artist extends the subject of the painting, suggesting the scarcity in the lives of the people migrating North and the carelessness in the way others treated them.

Watercolor is a type of paint that is mixed with water, which decreases its opacity and allows it to appear transparent. Paintings done in watercolors often have a delicate, dreamlike quality. The color may be very uneven; some watercolor paintings even have water spots. It's

CD-ROM

To find illustrators known for their use of watercolor, search for the term *watercolor* in Favorite Authors.

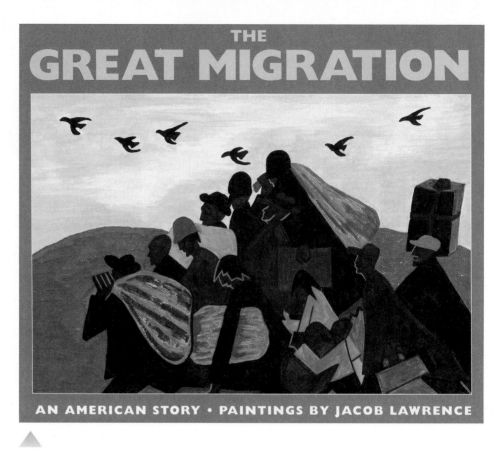

THE
GREAT MIGRATION

AN AMERICAN STORY • PAINTINGS BY JACOB LAWRENCE

The tempera used in Jacob Lawrence's painting helps convey the contrast between the burdened people, portrayed in solid dark colors, and the birds, flying free in a sparsely colored light blue sky. (*The Great Migration* by Jacob Lawrence. Used by permission of HarperCollins Publishers.)

The delicate effect created by E. B. Lewis's watercolor suggests the fragility of the blossoming relationship between the two young girls.
("Illustrations," copyright © 1998 by E. B. Lewis, illustrations, from THE OTHER SIDE by Jacqueline Woodson, illustrated by E. B. Lewis. Used by permission of G. P. Putnam's Sons, an imprint of Penguin Putnam Books for Young Readers, a division of Penguin Putnam Inc.)

James Ransome's use of oil paint gives a feeling of substance to the relationship between the young girl and her uncle, suggesting that this affection is not shortlived.

(Reprinted with the permission of Simon & Schuster Books for Young Readers, an imprint of Simon & Schuster Children's Publishing Division from UNCLE JED'S BARBERSHOP by Margaree King Mitchell, illustrated by James Ransome. Illustrations copyright © 1993 James Ransome.)

easy to show many shades, either by adding layers of paint or by adding water to the paint after it has been applied to the paper. Watercolor is the most popular medium for picture books because it can so easily express moods and capture the emotions of the characters. Because the shapes need not have definite lines and one color can bleed into the next, watercolor suggests that there is more beneath the surface. The absence of sharp, straight lines conveys a sense of fluidity, the possibility of blending or melding. The blurring suggests permeability—that we, too, can find ways to enter into the picture. The colors are usually muted and gentle, inviting us into the picture. In Jacqueline Woodson's **The Other Side,** E. B. Lewis uses soft, blurred colors and somewhat indistinct images in the distance, suggesting that there is more to the picture, that it goes on and on. Nothing is sharply delineated, so we can go beyond what is on the page to imagine what might be beyond the fence.

Carole Byard's use of acrylic, with its thick, textured surface and evident brushstrokes, suggests that the child picking cotton has a rough, multilayered life that can't be seen at first glance.

(Cover illustration from WORKING COTTON by Sherley Anne Williams. Illustration copyright © 1992 by Carole Byard, reprinted by permission of Harcourt, Inc.)

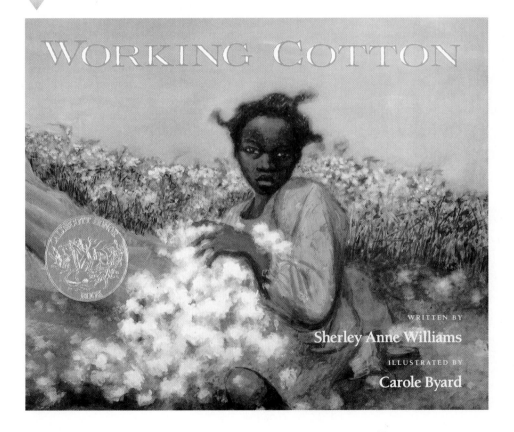

Oil paint is powdered color mixed with linseed oil. Its heavy look is used to create texture, which gives a sense of depth and substance. Oil paint doesn't seem ethereal; it's not going to disappear, and you can't walk through it. ***Uncle Jed's Barbershop,*** written by Margaree King Mitchell and illustrated by James Ransome, provides a beautiful example of how oil can be used. Highlights on the people's faces, as well as the lines and colors, express a wide range of emotions. The rich jewel-like tones suggest the richness and depth of the lives of the people. The often-evident brushstrokes imply roughness and toughness—the fact that nothing has been smooth or easy.

Acrylic paint is powdered color mixed with water-based plastic. Like oil paint, acrylic paint can be applied thickly to create a textured surface. It is difficult for me to tell the difference between oil and acrylic. In the books I looked at, I did notice that some illustrations done in acrylic, such as Carole Byard's work in ***Working Cotton,*** by Sherley Anne Williams, are blurred or indistinct. Because acrylic has been put on thickly, the cotton in the background of the cover picture almost seems to rise up off the plants. The brushstrokes in the pictures suggest the roughness of the life the characters lead. In ***Something Is Growing,*** by Walter Lyon Krudop, the paint covers the page fully; the people are less distinct, and although the lines are apparent, the tree edges are a bit blurred. These pictures have a flat appearance because the paint does not appear to have been put on thickly.

Printmaking

Printmaking is a time-consuming process that is used only occasionally today because of advances in printing technology. The artist creates a backward image on a surface such as wood, linoleum, metal, or cardboard. This surface is then inked and pressed against paper so that the image is transferred to the paper. Most of the earliest children's books were illustrated with wood prints, but the process is used by only a few artists today. By using wood prints to illustrate *A Gardener's Alphabet,* Mary Azarian created substantial images with definite lines. This medium yields a direct look and a very sharp effect.

Collage

Collages are made by attaching bits of paper, cloth, or other materials to a flat surface such as paper. Cut-paper collage often produces crisp pictures with clean lines. Colors are usually solid and uniform, giving illustrations a straightforward look devoid of subtleties. Although the technique sounds simple on the surface, it can be very complex, as Debra Frasier, author and illustrator of ***Out of the Ocean,*** explains in the Illustration Notes at the end of the book. She says, "The illustrations include photocopies of these photographs [of life along the beach], still-life photographs, and two kinds of cut paper—Canson paper for the flat color and hand-embellished pastepaper for the waves." Producing the images incorporating shells, sea glass, and other actual objects took several steps. "Each page of objects was first arranged in a tray of sand and photographed, carefully leaving space for the later addition of other elements. These still-life images were then combined with photographic images of the paper cutouts. Finally, the framed illustrations of the silhouetted figures were added, along with the text."

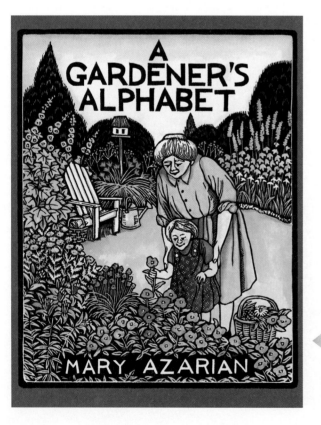

Through distinct lines, which outline every aspect of the image, the woodcuts created by Mary Azarian convey a very definite impression.

(Cover, from A GARDENER'S ALPHABET by Mary Azarian. Jacket Art © 2000 by Mary Azarian. Reprinted by permission of Houghton Mifflin Company. All rights reserved.)

The back and front covers of Frasier's *Out of the Ocean,* done in mixed media collage, include the ocean and cut-paper flowers and waves, all photographed against a box of sand to create a sense of the variety and beauty of the ocean.

(Cover illustration from OUT OF THE OCEAN, copyright © 1998 by Debra Frasier, reprinted by permission of Harcourt, Inc.)

Photography

Most frequently used in nonfiction books, photography has recently found its way into more children's fiction. Photography can give the viewer a feeling of intense realism; sometimes the subjects seem to be looking out at us. ***Stranger in the Woods,*** by Carl R. Sams II and Jean Stoick, is a photographic fantasy in which wildlife often stares directly out of the page. Capturing these shots obviously took great patience, for the animals are shown coming close to and then nibbling on the vegetable parts of a snowman. In this delightful book, the concept of creating a fictional piece around photographs of wildlife works well.

Mixed Media

Whenever two or more of the above media are employed, the artist is said to be using mixed media. Artists are always exploring the endless possibilities for combining media to create visual effects. Janet Stevens, illustrator of ***To Market, To Market,*** by Anne Miranda, uses acrylic, oil, pastel, and colored pencil along with photographic and fabric collage elements to create the bright but chaotic effects throughout the book. In ***Verdi,*** Janell Cannon uses acrylic and colored pencil to help us see the lushness of the jungle habitat. Dom Lee applies encaustic beeswax to paper, then scratches out images, and finally adds oil paint and colored pencil to create the stark but poignant images in ***Passage to Freedom: The Sugihara Story,*** by Ken Mochizuki. In ***Black Cat,*** Christopher Myers combines photography with collage, ink, and gouache to create stunning, unusual effects that make the reader want to look closer. Myers began with photographs that he took in Harlem and in his Brooklyn neighborhood. The very textured look created by the mixing of media and the unusual composition of the pictures makes the viewer realize the complexity and depth of the city. It makes us aware that simply by looking at the surface we cannot see the city in all the ways the black cat does.

This information about different media and their effects will become more important to you, and thus be easier to remember, if you have the chance to try some of them for yourself

A PHOTOGRAPHIC FANTASY

Stranger in the Woods

Carl R. Sams II & Jean Stoick

This photograph of deer examining a snowman is so intense that you feel as if you were right there. (Photography © 2000 Carl Sams from *Stranger in the Woods*. Reproduced by permission of Carl Sams.)

Combining photography of the city with ink and gouache paintings allows Christopher Myers to render a complicated, textured view of the city.
(From BLACK CAT by Christopher Myers. Copyright © 1999 by Christopher Myers. Reprinted by permission of Scholastic Inc.)

and see what effects they can produce. Understanding the possibilities of various media can help us as teachers to see how art and words work together to make an impact on readers.

Styles of Artists

Style refers to particular manners of artistic expression that have developed over time and can be defined by broad characteristics. It also refers to the features in an artist's work that make it recognizable and distinctive. Identifying styles is a way to categorize types of art so that we can talk about them more easily.

Artists don't start out thinking about style; they start out thinking about the subject and the impact they want to make. When they set out to illustrate a book, they look for the emotional nuances. Javaka Steptoe (1999) explains that, before he created the illustrations for ***In Daddy's Arms I AM TALL: African Americans Celebrating Fathers,*** he read each poem over and over again. Then he worked to capture the feeling through his art. David Diaz (1998) talks about looking closely at the art of William Steig and realizing that Steig's technique was subsumed by meaning: "I drew a parallel between what he did and where I was with my background in the super-realist movement. I thought, what's really important here is the essence of what's there, not just the technique" (p. 4).

Understanding the terminology used to describe artists' styles is not essential for appreciating and responding to illustrations in picture books. But this terminology does give us a shorthand with which to discuss the visual in books. If we were struggling to explain why the art in Faith Ringgold's ***Tar Beach*** was so striking and what was so different about it, we could start by explaining that it was done in the naive style. This label would tell the listener that the pictures were drawn one-dimensionally and simply, often appearing as if they could have been drawn by a child. Knowing the names of styles can help us to explain what we are responding to so that our listeners can picture what we are talking about. The following categories encompass the styles most commonly used in children's picture books.

Realism

Realistic, or representational, style is usually the easiest to recognize, since the artist is working to show things the way they really look. Oftentimes illustrations done in this style have an almost photographic quality. The shapes are recognizable, and the objects are in the proper perspective and proportion. Mike Wimmer's illustrations in ***All the Places to Love,*** by Patricia MacLachlan, are representative of this style. His artwork is precisely rendered, with great attention to detail. Other artists known for painting realistically are Jerry Pinkney, Floyd Cooper, and Allen Say.

Expressionism

In the expressionistic style, artists represent their emotional, subjective responses to the subject. Abstractions are often used to highlight what artists see as the essence of their reality. This style is widely used in picture books. Excellent examples include the artwork in Sharon Dennis Wyeth's ***Always My Dad*** (illustrated by Raúl Colón), Vera B. Williams's ***A Chair for My Mother,*** and Sherry Garland's ***The Lotus Seed*** (illustrated by Tatsuro Kiuchi).

Impressionism

The impressionistic style was developed by French painters of the nineteenth century who used dabs of color to re-create the sense of constant changes in light and color. Because they were concerned with changing effects, they worked to capture the subjective, sensory impression of a scene or object rather than a sharp, detailed description of it. In impressionistic work, figures might seem blurred or marginal, colors might be placed next to each other to suggest a mingling or mixing of colors. It is as if the contours of reality were softened. E. B. Lewis (whose drawing appears on page 44), Ed Young, and Peter Catalanotto often paint in this style.

This crisp, photo-like painting from *All the Places to Love* is so realistic that viewers have a sense of witnessing this scene filled with obvious warmth and caring.

(COPYRIGHT © 1994 BY MIKE WIMMER. Used by permission of HarperCollins Publishers.)

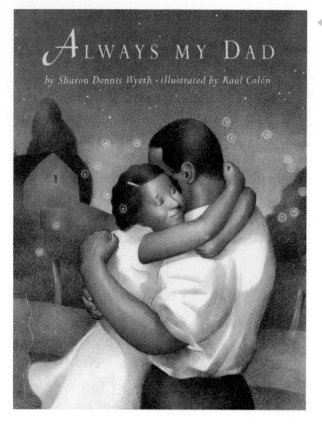

Intense love leaps from this image, done in the expressionistic style.

("Cover illustration" by Raúl Colón, copyright © 1994 by Raúl Colón, from ALWAYS MY DAD by Sharon Dennis Wyeth. Used by permission of Alfred A. Knopf Children's Books, a division of Random House, Inc.)

Surrealism

In the surrealistic style, realistic images are given an unreal or almost dreamlike quality, often through unnatural or unexpected juxtapositions of objects and people. Sometimes the image is photographically represented with very precise details, but what you see couldn't happen. For instance, in Anthony Browne's *Voices in the Park,* the trees and shrubs reflect the characters' outlook and mood. One character sees trees with little foliage, while another sees the same trees bursting with blooms. In David Wiesner's *Tuesday,* we see very realistic frogs on lily pads, except they are flying! So, although the pictures look very real, they are actually surreal because they simply could not happen in the natural world.

Naive Art and Folk Art

Naive and folk art styles are similar in that they are both pre-perspective—that is, all people and objects appear flat and one-dimensional. Naive art simplifies what is seen and experienced. Tomie dePaola's work is largely done in naive style, as is Faith Ringgold's. David Diaz often paints in the naive style, as he does in Eve Bunting's *Smoky Night.* There is much variation in folk art style, since it reflects the aesthetic values of the culture from which it comes. The use of color, stylized patterns, and simple shapes seem to permeate the folk art style.

CD-ROM

To locate illustrators whose style is *surrealistic,* search for the term in Favorite Authors.

Anthony Browne paints surrealistic images in which the objects surrounding a character represent how the character views the world. In this case, the little girl viewing a mother and son on a park bench sees the world in positive, fruitful ways.

(Reprinted from *Voices in the Park,* copyright © 1998 Anthony Browne. Permission granted by Dorling Kindersley, Inc.)

The naive style used in this image by David Diaz, with its flat, one-dimensional people, simplifies what is seen and thus focuses viewers' attention on the emotional content of the picture.
(Cover illustration of *Smoky Night* by Eve Bunting, copyright © 1994 by David Diaz, reproduced by permission of Harcourt, Inc.)

Cartoon Art

Cartoon art is easily recognizable by the use of lines to create exaggerated characters. Cartoon art is used in humorous books and also to lighten a heavy subject. James Stevenson, William Steig, and James Marshall, all masters of this style, use cartoon art to express an amazing range of emotions.

This information on style was provided to help you develop a vocabulary that gives quick ways to talk about illustrations. You have probably already noticed, as you have looked at picture book illustrations, that there is a great deal of overlap in these styles and many illustrations cannot be neatly placed into a category. If this terminology is helpful in describing illustrations, use it. If you find that it interferes with your ability to describe or even respond to a book, don't use it. Sometimes I find myself working very hard to figure out what style a book is drawn in, and I have to admit that this takes me away from the book and isn't productive. So, remember that the point of this information is not to categorize all the picture books you read by style. Artists rarely talk about their style in terms of these categories, which they believe are simply labels overlaid onto their work when it is finished. Using the vocabulary of style is important only if it helps you to describe to yourself and others what you are seeing.

Here are some questions you can ask about illustrations to get at style: Do they have an almost photographic quality? Do the images seem blurry and indistinct, or are they sharp and crisp? Is there a lack of perspective in the pictures, making everything seem flat? Are they cartoonish?

Evaluating the Art

When I evaluate and respond to art in picture books, I first look to see if it invites me in and delights me and makes me want to look closer. Then I look to see how it extends and works with the story. Answering the following four questions is a good place to begin in evaluating the artwork in a picture book.

1. Does it delight and involve you? Babette Cole's books, which she both writes and illustrates, are absolutely delightful. Her whimsical cartoons reflect her rather irreverent attitudes. For instance, in **The Trouble with Mom,** we first see mom wearing a tall, pointy black hat that has a mouse looking off of it and a snake wound around it. Mom also has skull-and-bones earrings, a tattered dress, and unruly hair. On the second full-page spread, we can clearly see that the trouble with mom is that she is a witch, since she takes her child to school on a broomstick!

Richard Egielski's **Buz** is another delightful book. His unusual perspectives, his bright colors, and his clean and uncluttered composing style are very appealing. The pictures on the first pages draw the reader right in. A very large hand holds a spoon that contains not only cereal, but also a bug. The spoon is being put into a very large mouth, and we can see the tonsils as well as the teeth. We wonder right away what will happen to the bug.

Likewise, **To Market, To Market,** written by Anne Miranda and illustrated by Janet Stevens, delights and intrigues the reader immediately. A woman with a large pig in her grocery basket is just something you don't expect to see. The artist surprises us with the look on the pig's face as well as the frazzled actions of the woman shopper. The backgrounds of both the market and the home are done in black and white so that the woman and her pig take center stage.

Wonderful examples of art in children's literature from 1870 to 1920 can be found at **Children's Literature— The Art Gallery** at www.arts.uwaterloo.ca/ENGL/ courses/engl208c/gallery.htm.

David Small's ability to enhance and extend the story through his art is demonstrated in this double-page spread. Occurring after the story told through the text is over, it is a tangible representation of Uncle Jim's love for Lydia.

(Excerpt from THE GARDENER by Sarah Stewart, illustrated by David Small. Pictures copyright © 1997 by David Small. Reprinted by permission of Farrar, Straus and Giroux, LLC.)

level as the picture, and still other times we seem to be looking up into the picture. It amazes me that the artist can keep us so interested in the story and the illustrations when the scene is a rather common one.

What does an artist do to create variety? An artist might create a frame around some pictures but leave other pictures unframed; use borders; mix media from page to page; change where shapes are placed in relation to each other; change where the text is placed in relation to the illustration; change the sizes of the objects from page to page; change the shading or the tones of the colors; or change the size of the illustration itself from quarter page to half page to full page to double-page spread.

Book Awards

A tool often used in selecting books is book awards. Although awards are helpful, it is important to know that selection committees are made up of individuals whose distinct values color their choices of best books. Awards such as the Newbery and the Caldecott carry great weight. They create excitement about a book and help distinguish it from the

Suzanne Duranceau keeps readers interested in this little turtle through her ability to show a range of perspectives, including this closeup of his head with his eye directed at us.
(ART COPYRIGHT ©1995 BY SUZANNE DURANCEAU. Used by permission of HarperCollins Publishers.)

thousands of other books published each year. Because awards put books in the public eye, award-winning books sell better. Almost every bookstore has a section called "Award-Winning Books," which alerts parents and other buyers of books that a committee has put its stamp of excellence on these particular works. This status inspires confidence in teachers, librarians, and other buyers, and thus these books are more often used in the classroom. Two questions come up about classroom use: "What makes these books good?" and "What do these awards mean in terms of what children learn about the world?" Both questions will be addressed in the following discussion.

The Award Selection Process

Just as you and I weigh different factors in our evaluation of books, so too do committees that are selecting an award-winning book. The Caldecott and Newbery awards, the best-known awards for children's books, each have a committee made up of fifteen people who must agree on the selection of a single winner as most outstanding book. Similarly, the Hans Christian Andersen Award committee is made up of fifteen people, representing many countries. Every two years, they give an award internationally for the body of work by a single author.

In reflecting on her four terms as chair of the Andersen Award committee (from 1987 to 1994), Eva Glistrup (1994) explained that each juror comes to the task from a unique perspective, which depends on his or her cultural and professional background, personal taste, view of children and childhood, view of children's literature, and sense of humor or lack of it. Even though aesthetic standards and value structures differ significantly across the different nations and cultural heritages, the group still is able to select a winner.

Juror Maria Antonieta Cunha from Brazil wanted books not only to appeal to children but also to attract and hold her attention. She wanted the aesthetic qualities of the work to take precedence over any moralizing intentions of the author. Originality—surprise, newness, paths never taken before—was important to her. She also believed that characters had to be credible, not stereotyped, and capable of capturing and sustaining the interest of the reader.

Further, the story must not contain prejudices which might lead to a lack of comprehension or respect toward what is different.

Another juror on the same committee, Ruth Mehl of Argentina, sought books that affirmed human values such as peace, understanding, justice, freedom, and the inherent value and richness of differences between races and cultures. The need for love, friendship, and honesty was present in the books she believed were excellent. She wanted to see these values interwoven in a text that brought joy and aesthetic pleasure, that promoted the exercise of critical thinking. Through the promotion of these values, she wanted children to find themselves represented, to have a voice that spoke for them. She wanted stories or poems that made sense, told something truly unforgettable, captured our emotions, and stimulated our reflection. She looked for authors who created characters that became lovable or despicable and went on living with the readers; she wanted these characters to take on some little piece of childhood's predicament so that the reader would gain through vicarious experience. She concluded her discussion by saying: "Finally I would demand from an Andersen Award winner some kind of emotion and magic. I do not know beforehand how this is going to come into play or where it will be appropriate, but I am sure I will recognize the occasion when it comes" (p. 60).

A third juror, Jeff Garrett from the United States, ended his list of criteria by saying: "We need to keep in mind that by giving this award to an individual writer or illustrator we are sending messages to the world about what we see as great writing and illustrative art for children, and only secondarily for ourselves. . . . Finally I think the 'politics' we must be aware of have to do with our perceptions of the social conscience of the author and depth of social and political responsibility this writer imparts to young readers, not the politics represented by a writer's government" (pp. 60–61).

It's easy to see, just from examining the criteria a few members of one committee share, that the impact a book has, the values embedded in it, and the significance of the topic are central. It's also evident that there is no such thing as total objectivity in evaluating books.

Looking at Award-Winning Books

As you can see from the statements made by just three jurors of the Andersen Award committee, each person brings to the committee his or her own experiences and tastes. Thus, committees vary year to year in how they define excellence. Because award winners are held up as models of excellence, they should be able to withstand close scrutiny. One way to judge their merits is to look at them in terms of literary considerations, educational considerations, and sociopolitical considerations.

We can be fairly sure that these award winners have exemplary literary qualities, since that is the major concern of the selection committee. However, as we can see from just a glimpse at the standards that three members of the Hans Christian Andersen Award committee brought with them, educational and sociopolitical qualities are also important. Studies have been done over the years of both Newbery and Caldecott winners, and both have on occasion been found to be lacking in educational and sociopolitical qualities, sometimes even promoting stereotypes.

Peggy Albers (1996) has expressed concern about whether award-winning books attend to the pluralism and democracy that schools strive for. She looked closely at Caldecott literature to see which groups wield power and which ethnic groups are represented and how. She believes that award-winning picture books "need to be examined in light of whose knowledge is considered the best and whose lives are being represented in these books" (p. 269). She looks past the issue of how many times groups are represented and instead examines the representations created. Albers found that the "roles and representations tend to be quite traditional. . . . The roles dominated by white males continue to be more positive and exciting, while many of the roles of females and people of color are traditional, stereotyped, and/or negative" (p. 278).

Although we can count on the literary quality of award-winning books, Albers's research suggests that we have to look carefully at what these books teach about people and whom they show as important. The boxed feature Criteria for Evaluating Award-Winning

*Take a look at how Newbery Award winners have been ranked across the years at **Newbery Books Ranked** at www.acpl.lib.in.us/Childrens_Services/newberyranking.html.*

Books is intended to provide you with the tools you need to evaluate award-winning books, as well as other books.

Kinds of Awards

Book awards are created to draw attention to books. The best-known awards are the Newbery Award, given to the best-written children's book, and the Caldecott Award, given to the artist of the most distinguished picture book. Both the Newbery and the Caldecott have a long history of favoring the genre of fiction; nonfiction and poetry rarely win. Poetry awards and nonfiction awards have evolved to recognize outstanding books in these genres. Likewise, groups that were not often included as winners and admirers of genres not usually represented have sought to draw attention to the excellent books in their areas by instituting awards.

The Newbery Award is presented by the American Library Association to the author of the book chosen as the most distinguished contribution to American literature for children published the previous year in the United States. The author must be a citizen or resident of the United States. After the winner is chosen, the committee decides whether to name honor books and, if so, how many.

CD-ROM

Award-winning authors cited in Favorite Authors on the CD-ROM can be found by searching for the word *award-winning.*

Criteria for Evaluating Award-Winning Books

Literary Considerations:

1. **Plot.** What drives the plot and keeps the reader interested? How do conflicts unfold? Is the plot rich and multilayered? Is the story unforgettable?

2. **Character.** What makes the characters memorable? Will these characters go on living with you? Did you live through a vicarious experience with a character? Is there an absence of stereotyping?

3. **Setting.** Can you enter the setting easily? Is it woven into the story?

4. **Theme.** Are the themes significant ones? Were they worked into the plot, or does the author moralize?

5. **Style—qualities of writing.** Is a strong voice apparent? Does the writing make an impact through careful choice of words, descriptions, dialogue, and figurative language?

6. **Aesthetic qualities.** What is original about this book? What makes it pleasing? Is there some kind of emotion or magic in the book?

Educational Considerations:

1. What do readers learn about people and about the world?

2. What traits of people are emphasized?

3. Whose knowledge is considered best?

4. Does this book introduce your students to groups of people they may not be familiar with?

5. Is the theme one that would involve or interest your students?

6. What could your students gain from reading this book? What do you consider to be extremely strong about the book?

7. What questions do you have about this book as an award winner? Do you believe it merits the award it won?

Sociopolitical Considerations:

1. Which groups are represented in the book? Which are left out?

2. Is a range of characters represented? What kinds of roles do they have?

3. Is a range of socioeconomic levels represented? How is each group represented?

4. Who is shown to have power? What is the power based on?

*For links to the major children's book awards, look at **Children's Book Awards and Other Literary Prizes** at http://falcon.jmu.edul~ ramseyil/awards.htm.*

The Caldecott Award is given by the American Library Association to the artist of the book deemed the most distinguished contribution to American literature for children published the previous year in the United States. The artist must be a citizen or resident of this country. Once the winner is chosen, the committee decides whether to name any honor books and, if so, how many.

The Aesop Prize is awarded by the American Folklore Society to the most outstanding book or books incorporating folklore and published in English for children or young adults. The Aesop Prize committee compiles a useful Aesop Accolade List, an annual roster of exceptional books among Aesop Prize nominees.

The Jane Addams Children's Book Award is given by the Women's International League of Peace and Freedom to recognize the children's book from the preceding year that most effectively promotes the cause of peace, social justice, and world community. Books geared to children of any age, preschool to high school, are eligible, including translations and titles published in English in other countries.

The Américas Award for Children's and Young Adult Literature is sponsored by the National Consortium of Latin American Studies Programs. It is given in recognition of U.S. works of fiction, poetry, folklore, or selected nonfiction (from picture books to works for young adults) published in the previous year in English or Spanish that authentically and engagingly portray Latin America, the Caribbean, or Latinos in the United States. Winners are selected for their distinctive literary quality; cultural contextualization; exceptional integration of text, illustration, and design; and potential for classroom use.

The Mildred L. Batchelder Award was established by the American Library Association to recognize American publishers for issuing quality children's books in translation. The award is given not to the author, illustrator, or translator, but to the publisher. The book must be an outstanding work of literature, it must have a good overall design, the original illustrations must have been retained, and the text must reflect the flavor of the original work and not be unduly "Americanized."

The Pura Belpré Award, established in 1996, is given biennially to a Latino/Latina author and illustrator who best portray, affirm, and celebrate the Latino cultural experience through their outstanding books for children.

The Boston Globe–Horn Book Award is presented jointly by the *Boston Globe* newspaper and the *Horn Book* magazine to recognize excellence in literature for children and young adults. Awards are given to a picture book, a work of fiction, and a work of nonfiction. Like the Newbery and the Caldecott, the award can be given only to a book published in the United States, but unlike the Newbery and Caldecott, it may be given to a book written by a citizen of any country.

The Coretta Scott King Awards, established in 1970, are presented to authors and illustrators of African descent whose distinguished books promote an understanding and appreciation of the "American Dream." Since 1980, this award has been affiliated with the American Library Association.

The NCTE Poetry Award for Excellence was established in 1977 by the National Council of Teachers of English to honor a living American poet for his or her aggregate work. Originally awarded annually, since 1982 it has been awarded only once every three years. The NCTE website has a description of what the group is looking for in the winner: "In short, we're looking for a poet who can write clean, spare lines; use language and form in fresh ways; surprise the reader by using syntax artistically; excite the reader's imagination with keen perspectives and sharp images; touch the reader's emotions. A maker of word events is what we're looking for."

The Scott O'Dell Historical Fiction Award is presented by the American Library Association annually to a work of historical fiction published by a U.S. publisher and set in the New World. This award is named after the highly respected author of children's historical fiction. A list of O'Dell Award winners may be particularly helpful to teachers who want to use children's literature to enhance the social studies curriculum.

The Orbis Pictus Award for Outstanding Nonfiction for Children is given by the National Council of Teachers of English to a nonfiction or informational book that meets their criteria of being outstanding in accuracy, organization, design, and writing. In addition, the book should be useful in the classroom, encourage thinking and more reading, model exemplary expository writing and research skills, share interesting and timely subject matter, and appeal to a wide range of students.

The Edgar Allan Poe Award, instituted in 1945 by the Mystery Writers of America, is given to distinguished works in various categories of the genre. The two categories for children's books are the Best Juvenile and the Best Young Adult mystery.

The Michael L. Printz Award, instituted in 2000 by the American Library Association, celebrates outstanding literature for young adults and honors the late Michael L. Printz, a Topeka, Kansas, school librarian. The winning book, which can be fiction, nonfiction, poetry, or an anthology, must exemplify literary excellence.

The Kate Greenaway Medal, instituted in 1956, is awarded by The [British] Library Association annually for the most distinguished work in the illustration of children's books published in the United Kingdom.

The Carnegie Medal is awarded annually by The [British] Library Association for an outstanding book for children and young people. It was first won in 1936 by Arthur Ransome and has since been won by many of the great names in children's literature, including C. S. Lewis.

The Appendix contains a list of the winners of these awards from 1980 to 2002.

Selecting Books

Selecting books to use with children is a joyous task if you have the time to savor the reading of many books. If you love the literature you use, your passion and excitement will come across to the children, who like to see adults get excited about things! This is one way they have to measure how important things are to you. If you seem blasé about a book, children will get the message that literature isn't important or that it's not worth immersing themselves in. Use books that you love, and your students will love them too.

Katherine Paterson (2001), a Newbery Award–winning author, gives this advice:

- In general, look for plots that grip and satisfy, characters to deeply care about, a world you can believe in, a book worth all the trees that will sacrifice their lives to make it.

- Select a book for the joy of it, not for how you can "use" it. That's just a by-product. The first thing children should learn is the joy of books and what they can do for you.

- Never take anyone else's recommendation about a book you're going to use with students, because you know your kids better than anybody.

- You shouldn't be using a book you don't like or aren't comfortable discussing.

- There's a good reason to choose "hard books" because they give adults and children a place to talk, but only if the adult has carefully read them too. Never stop children from reading difficult books, but always be around when they finish.

In selecting books across the year for classroom use, I ask myself these questions: Do I love or value it? What is my purpose for using it—what is it I want students to know or appreciate? Are my students, with their backgrounds, interests, and age level, the right audience? Am I creating a balance as far as kinds of books selected and kinds of people portrayed? It is important to remember that, through the books we bring into the classroom, we teach students what is important to think about, talk about, write about, and draw.

Value

Every book you share with a child reflects what you value. I want children to be aware of beauty in the world and in their natural surroundings. I want children to be stimu-

4. Herbert Kohl (1995) said, "There has never been a period in my lifetime when it has been so urgent for children to know that there is more than one way to organize society, and understand that caring and cooperation are not secondary values or signs of weakness so much as affirmations of hope and life" (p. 93). What are Kohl's underlying values? Can you find books in your reading that you think would meet these goals? Create your own list of criteria for selecting books for your classroom. What are the overriding themes you're looking for?

5. Do a study of an artist. Glean information about the artist's style and the media the artist uses by reading several books illustrated by your artist. Evaluate the art, using the criteria in this chapter or other criteria you find more appropriate. Find biographical information on your artist by looking in Pat Cummings's three volume *Talking with Artists* or any other source you can locate. Do a presentation to your whole class, focusing on the major accomplishments or strengths of the artist.

6. Select Caldecott winners from a period of about ten years. Read the books and analyze them in terms of the trends they reflect.

7. Select a book from Harste's list of books that invite critical conversations (p. 63). Discuss it in your group in such a way that critical issues are raised. Record your reaction to the discussion in your notebook. What did this experience make you aware of as far as raising critical issues in a classroom?

8. After reading the research box Vygotsky and Literature for Children, share a memory of a time in your learning when, given assistance by other students or the teacher, you accomplished something you couldn't do before. Can you explain your own ZPD in terms of something you're currently trying to learn?

CD-ROM

To see further examples in Invitations and Classroom Teaching Ideas of how ranking can be used in the classroom, begin your search with the word *ranking.*

Classroom Teaching Ideas

1. To help your students understand that illustrations can convey feelings, have them take out their crayons and draw lines or shapes that would show that they were angry, that they were shy, that they were tired, and that they were happy. Then have them look at the strokes and colors used. Were the strokes thin and delicate or bold and broad? Were the colors soft or loud? Talk about their discoveries and how they can relate this information to the picture books they read.

2. To help students become aware of what influences them when selecting a book, use butcher paper to make a chart (which students could later turn into a graph) with three categories: picture, topic, author. When children select books from the library, ask each one whether they selected the book because of the pictures, because of the topic, or because it was written by an author they knew and liked. Have students add their name to the column corresponding to the factor that influenced them most.

3. After reading a picture book aloud with students, go back through the book with them and do some "picture reading." Ask students to look closely at the pictures to see what kinds of information they can get just from the pictures. Students enjoy commenting on details while they do this.

4. After students have written their own "book" or story, have them illustrate it in the style of an illustrator they admire. Give them time to go through your bookshelves or those in the library, looking for a book illustrated in a style that they would like to use for their own story. This provides students with a real reason to think about many elements of composition, such as whether they want their pictures to have a background, whether they want to put boxes or frames or borders around their pictures (as Jan Brett does) or just have the pictures come to the edge of the page, whether they want to use bright colors (as Eric Carle does) or dark colors, whether they want to use cut paper (as Lois Ehlert does) or paint, whether they want to use watercolor or poster paint. After the illustrations are complete, have the students talk about the choices they made.

5. Bring in a collection of works by different illustrators, and have the children identify the illustrator by the style or medium used. Eric Carle, Jerry Pinkney, Tomie dePaola, Brian Pinkney, Patricia Polacco, and Barbara Cooney are illustrators whose work is well suited for this activity. For added effect, you may wish to bring in Cooney's first book, which illustrates Chaucer's tale **Chanticleer and the Fox.** It has a very different style from her later works and will show students that artists can change their style or choice of medium.

Internet and Text Resources

1. Basic Reference Tools for Children's Literature includes lists of books about selecting books in all genres, as well as about using literature in classrooms. Find it at

www.library.arizona.edu/users/kwilliam/kiddy.html

2. David Brown's Website on Children's Literature has a part called Children's Book Awards, which provides links to sites containing the award winners in children's literature. Find it at

www.ucalgary.ca/~dkbrown/ala97.html

3. Children's Book Awards and Other Literary Prizes links not only to the major children's book awards but also to award-winning audiovisual materials, multicultural books, nonfiction, and poetry. Go to

http://falcon.jmu.edu/~ramseyil/awards.htm

4. The Art Gallery allows access to some wonderful art in children's literature from the 1870s to the 1920s. Find it at

www.arts.uwaterloo.ca/ENGL/courses/engl208c/gallery.htm

5. Database of Award-Winning Children's Literature allows users to search for books by ethnicity, genre, age, setting, and so on. It also has links to the award sites. Go to

www2.wcoil.com/~ellerbee/childlit.html

6. Newbery Books Ranked looks at the winners across the years and ranks them from top to bottom. This site could provoke great discussions. Go to

www.acpl.lib.in.us/Childrens_Services/newberyranking.html

7. Smith, Henrietta M. (1999). *The Coretta Scott King Award Book 1970–1999*. Chicago: American Library Association.

8. Association for Library Service to Children (1999). *The Newbery and Caldecott Awards: A Guide to the Medal and Honor Books*. Chicago: American Library Association.

References

Albers, Peggy (1996). "Issues of Representation: Caldecott Gold Medal Winners 1984–1995." *The New Advocate 9,* 267–285.

Carlson, G. Robert (1974). "Literature IS . . . ." *English Journal 63,* 23–27.

Cummings, Pat, ed. (1992). *Talking with Artists: Volume One.* New York: Bradbury.

—— (1995). *Talking with Artists: Volume Two.* New York: Simon & Schuster.

—— (1999). *Talking with Artists: Volume Three.* New York: Clarion.

Diaz, David (1998). "It's All About Process: Talking with David and Cecelia Diaz." *The New Advocate 12,* 1–9.

Glistrup, Eva (1994). "Comparing the Incomparable: The Work of the Hans Christian Andersen Jury, 1987–94." *Bookbird 32,* 55–63.

Greenberg, Jan, and Sandra Jordan (1991). *The Painter's Eye.* New York: Delacorte.

Harste, Jerome (1998). "Supporting Critical Conversations in Classrooms." Lansing, MI: Michigan Council of Teachers of English, Oct. 9, 1998.

Harwayne, Shelley (1996). "Weaving Literature into the School Community." *The New Advocate 9,* 61–74.

Horning, Kathleen (1997). *Cover to Cover: Evaluating and Reviewing Children's Books.* New York: HarperCollins.

CHAPTER 3

The World of Picture Books

The name *picture books* evokes images of brightly colored, beautifully illustrated books that beg to be read. No matter what our age, most of us still enjoy reading them because of their vibrant pictures, rich and evocative language, and poignant and meaningful themes. Picture books speak to us in the same way photographs do. They touch our emotions, delight our senses, appeal to our whimsy, and bring back memories of our childhood. Picture books invite us to curl up and read them.

The plethora of picture books is both a gift and a bane. It's easy to feel overwhelmed by their sheer number. As you come to know the genre and develop criteria for evaluating books, you will feel more secure about selecting

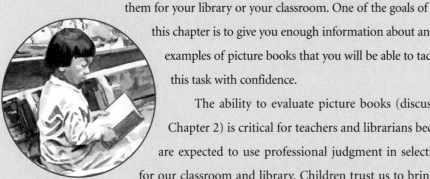

them for your library or your classroom. One of the goals of this chapter is to give you enough information about and examples of picture books that you will be able to tackle this task with confidence.

The ability to evaluate picture books (discussed in Chapter 2) is critical for teachers and librarians because we are expected to use professional judgment in selecting books for our classroom and library. Children trust us to bring in picture books relevant to them and to their lives. Whether as a parent, a friend, a teacher, or a librarian, we can do for one or several children what Kozel (1998) wishes for every child: "I wish that teachers would insist that every little child in our country—rich or poor; black, brown, or white; whatever origin or background—would have the chance to read books not for any other reason than the fact that books bring joy into our lives, not because they'll be useful for a state examination, not because they'll improve SAT scores, but solely because of the intense pleasure that we get from books. If [adults are] not willing to defend the right of every child to enjoy the treasures of the earth, who will?"

Many, many kinds of picture books are produced today. In an effort to give you some meaningful ways to sort them out and think about them, the following categories will be examined: ABC books, counting books, concept books, wordless books, books for the earliest readers, transitional or chapter books, and picture storybooks for older readers. Other categories of picture books exist, such as toy books, participation books, and board books, but the categories included here are the ones most widely used in schools.

Purposes of ABC Books

The phrase *ABC books* sounds so ordinary and straightforward that it's hard to imagine the richness and variety that can be found in these books. Although some are written only to teach the alphabet, many others are written to play with language, present information on a topic, tell a story, or accent the visual.

Teaching the Alphabet

There is no better book than **Brian Wildsmith's ABC** for beginning to teach letter names and the sounds they make as initial letters. The words he has selected to represent the letters and corresponding letter sounds are ones small children would probably know, such as *apple, butterfly, cat, dog,* and *elephant.* But it's his art that will hold the children's attention. The paintings have both depth and luminosity, inviting children to return to the book frequently.

Flora McDonnell's ABC is an exuberant introduction to the alphabet for children. The beautiful color pictures show one very large object or animal along with a small object or animal on each page. The *Dd* page shows dinosaurs and a duck and the *Ll* page a lemon and a ladybug. Humor and wit abound in the juxtaposition of these objects and in the way she portrays them. The dinosaurs appear to be watching the lone duck.

Helen Oxenbury's **ABC of Things** has whimsical drawings that make the reader feel warm and nurtured. Love and caring are embedded in the pages. For instance, on the *Cc* page, a huge *cow* sits on a *couch,* with one leg *crossed* over the other, next to a *cat;* they both look happily at the *crow* bringing in a *cake* with *candles.* The expressions in the eyes of the people and animals bring them to life. Each page has objects familiar to children.

John Burningham's ABC is filled with humorous colored-pencil drawings that invite children to look at them repeatedly. An adorable little boy is in all the pictures, doing unusual things that would appeal to children: riding an *Ostrich;* with a *Parrot* sitting on his head; sticking out his tongue at a *Snake,* which has its tongue out too. Each page has only a single word—the name of the animal—but each picture tells a story.

The illustrators of the best ABC books tap into children's deep needs and wants, as well as into what delights children. They know that a book must be visually interesting to keep children coming back over and over again. When you select ABC books to teach the alphabet and initial sounds to children, be sure that the objects used to illustrate the letters are familiar to children so that they are not trying to absorb too much new information at once.

CD-ROM

For other books by Helen Oxenbury, search the CD-ROM database.

The bright colors and familiarity with the objects and their contrasting sizes make this alphabet book appealing to children. (*Flora McDonnell's ABC* copyright © 1997 Flora McDonnell. Reproduced by permission of the publisher Candlewick Press, Inc., Cambridge, MA, on behalf of Walker Books Ltd., of London.)

Playing with Language

When the sounds of words delight children, they are motivated to want to learn about language and to use language. Language that delights, through the use of such devices as alliteration and rhyming, makes children laugh and feel joyful, eliminating anxiety and self-consciousness about learning. These are prime moments for learning because the filters or blocks are down and new information can be enjoyed and absorbed. Through language play, children gain a heightened sensitivity to the sounds and rhythms of language and become aware of the function and power of words. Books that play with language comprise the largest single category of alphabet books. They can be used to stimulate writing, as well as vocabulary growth and an interest in language.

One of my favorites is Anita Lobel's **Alison's Zinnia,** which is filled with large, gorgeous paintings of flowers. Beneath the painting of the flower, in a long rectangular box, is a girl who will give the flower to another girl, who will do something to or with it. For instance, "Leslie left a Lady's slipper for Maryssa; Maryssa misted a Magnolia for Nancy; and Nancy noticed a Narcissus for Olga." In her author's note, Lobel says, "It took a bit of weeding before I found a way to connect flowers to girls' names. Once I found the verbs, it seemed wickedly simple. Girl—verb—flower. I wrote it A to Z on the plane ride back to New York." The paintings, which took Lobel more than a year, stimulate a desire to know more about flowers and to look closely at those delicate, detailed drawings. Children could use this word pattern as a model for making up their own books on any number of other topics.

Steven Kellogg's **Aster Aardvark's Alphabet Adventure** is a collection of alliterative stories—one for each letter. His skill in both drawing the illustrations and creating the clever and amusing stories invites children to return to the book again and again. A sampling of less than a quarter of this alliterative story reflects how much fun it would be to imitate: "Hermione, a hefty hyperactive hippo, hurt her hip hurling herself into the Hawaiian Hula Hoop Happening."

Other alphabet books focus on rhyme. **Quentin Blake's ABC** rhymes across two pages with such entries as "K is for Kittens, all scratching the chair. L is for Legs that we wave in the air." These rhymes are accompanied by wild, crazy, messy cartoon-like figures. In the *L* picture, the whole family is down on the floor, lying on their backs as they wave their legs in the air. Underwear shows and hairy legs are exposed, as Blake exhibits his sense of the ridiculous!

Books based on alliteration include Graeme Base's **Animalia,** an alphabet book that you can use for a whole year without tiring of it. Each page is resplendent with lush, detailed paintings containing a myriad of things beginning with a particular letter, accompanied by an alliterative sentence for that letter.

ANTICS, by Cathi Hepworth, is a captivating book in which words beginning with every letter of the alphabet have *ant* in them somewhere. *Lieutenant* represents *L,* and the picture shows an ant with a scarf around his neck flying an old World War I plane. *M* is represented by *Mutant,* and a very large ant hovers over an anteater. The zany illustrations alone keep you turning the pages.

Presenting Information Using the Alphabet Scheme

Many alphabet books are packed with fascinating information organized around the letters of the alphabet. Jerry Pallotta is a master at writing alphabet books that easily could be used to introduce students to science concepts or units. In *The Ocean Alphabet Book,* as in all his other books, he writes clear, interesting prose with intriguing information that speaks directly to children. "B is for Bluefish. Everyone loves to catch Bluefish because they love to fight. Their teeth are very, very sharp so don't ever put your fingers in their mouth. C is for Cod. Some grow to be as big as a ten-year-old boy or girl." He keeps his tone upbeat and light, making his books very appealing.

Roger Tory Peterson's ABC of Birds, by Linda Westervelt, shows bright birds from around the globe photographed or painted by this century's foremost birder, who has written many bird field guides. The beautiful language in the text illuminates our knowledge about birds.

Among the alphabet books that could be used in a social studies curriculum is *A Is for Africa,* by Ifeoma Onyefulu, which captures what the people of Africa have in common. One entry is "O is for Ornaments to adorn our bodies. African people love to dress up and look beautiful. In some tribes people wear beaded strands around their waists or across their chests. Body markings are another kind of ornament." Children learn new information in manageable ways.

A Is for Asia, by Cynthia Chin-Lee, gives us glimpses into this area of the globe—which, as the author points out, is one-third of the entire world. We learn that *B* is the letter for *batik, L* is for *lotus,* and *M* is for *monsoon.* Each entry is followed by a few sentences explaining it more fully.

A Gardener's Alphabet, by Mary Azarian, portrays the difficulty and delight of gardening through dazzling, detailed wood prints with strong, clear images related to the theme. Each is accompanied by only a single word for each letter of the alphabet.

A book that teaches children American Sign Language is Laura Rankin's *The Handmade Alphabet.* The hand sign for each letter of the alphabet is paired with a hand holding or pointing to something that begins with that letter. So *A* shows the hand in the "A" position holding asparagus, the "V" signing hand is holding a valentine, and so on. Children will delight in seeing and perhaps learning the whole sign alphabet.

Tomorrow's Alphabet, by George Shannon, is a decidedly different kind of alphabet book. It teaches thinking skills as it pushes readers to figure out why *C* is for *milk* or *E* is for *campfire.* Of course, the answer is that the milk is tomorrow's cheese and the campfire is tomorrow's embers. Readers have to think about how things begin or start. To compile such an alphabet, children would have to think about what things are made of and what they produce.

Telling a Story Using the Alphabet Scheme for Structure

A Long Trip to Z, by Fulvio Testa, has the story embedded in the alphabet structure. In this story, an airplane climbs out of a book and goes on an adventure out of the house and across the world. Each page features a different letter of the alphabet as the plane makes its way.

The ABC Bunny, written by Wanda Gag and illustrated by Howard Gag, is a timeless story, with a rhyming alphabet scheme centered around the activities of a bunny. The pictures of the bunny's adventures convey much of the meaning. "C is for crash, D is for dash, E is for elsewhere in a flash. F is for frog—he's fat and funny. 'Looks like rain,' says he to Bunny."

Doug Cushman's *The ABC Mystery* is a fast-paced chase after an art thief. It begins, "A is the Art that was stolen at night. B is the Butler who sneaks out of sight. C is the Clue that's left in the room. D is Detective Inspector McGroom." The illustrations add depth to the story because they contain clues not mentioned in the text.

Accenting the Visual to Foster Learning

The Graphic Alphabet, a Caldecott Honor book by David Pelletier, is an unusual book in which the illustration of the letter form retains the natural shape of the letter, as well as representing the meaning of the word pictured. For instance, the letter *K* is represented by the word *knot* and the *K* has a knot in its middle. The *M* makes a snow-topped *mountain*. The author is mainly interested in the relationship between the image and the meaning.

Alphabet City, by Stephen T. Johnson, encourages viewers to find the shapes of letters in their surroundings. Johnson wants his paintings to inspire children and adults to look at their surroundings in a fresh and playful way. In the author's note, he says that in doing so "they will discover for themselves juxtaposition of scale, harmonies of shadows, colorful patterns in surface textures, and joy in the most somber aspects of a city, by transcending the mundane and unearthing its hidden beauty." *E* is the side view of a traffic light, *G* is formed from the elaborate ironwork in a street light, and *M* is the two arches of a bridge.

Alphabet books are a source of delight and learning about the alphabet as well as many other things. As you read them, look for other patterns and other purposes.

Purposes of Counting Books

Just as many alphabet books do much more than teach the alphabet, many counting books do much more than teach numbers. Some present information on a topic; others tell a story.

Teaching Numbers

Denise Fleming's **Count!** presents the numbers via the antics of animals—four kangaroos bounce, five giraffes stretch, seven worms wiggle. Each page has the number clearly shown on the left side along with blocks of color so that children can count the blocks of color as well as the animals.

Stephen Kellogg's **Frog Jumps: A Counting Book** is an action-packed, continuous-counting book. Each phrase is repeated before the new number is added. For example, the fifth page says "One frog jumps, two ducks dive, three elephants trumpet, four rabbits run, and five bats bat." The pages get very crowded by the end of the book. Although the pictures are terrific, the pages may be too overloaded to truly teach counting. This would, however, be a wonderful book for students to read along with a teacher to reinforce their counting skills.

The M&M's Counting Book, by Barbara Barbieri McGrath, teaches numbers, six colors, and three shapes through the use of M&M's. It also teaches sets by asking children to arrange the M&M's. This fun, interactive book functions best if the child has M&M's to work with.

Bert Kitchen's **Animal Numbers,** which shows exotic and familiar animals with the specified number of infants, asks the reader to figure out how many babies are in each mother's brood. Beautiful illustrations depict swans, squirrels, lizards, and opossums frequently in unusual positions in relation to the number. The goldfish swim inside the number 8, and salamanders crawl around the number 9.

One Moose, Twenty Mice, by Clare Beaton, uses another device to keep children involved. In each of the photos of the stitched pictures, which also use felt, beads, and buttons, a cat is hiding. Each page asks readers to locate the cat. This book is so playful that children will want to keep reading.

The Crayon Counting Book, by Pam Muñoz Ryan and Jerry Pallotta, has children counting by twos, as well as considering the concepts of odd and even, as they learn about color.

Presenting Information Using the Counting Scheme

Authors use the counting scheme as a way to organize and present information so that it will involve the reader. **Blast Off! A Space Counting Book,** written by Norma Cole and illustrated by Marshall Peck, III, teaches about space travel. Rhymed couplets are accompanied by pictures of child astronauts inside a spaceship. The numbers appear at the sides of the pages, along with dots, arrows, or some other kind of representation so that children

Raymond Briggs's **The Snowman** shows us a little boy who has the fantastic experience of interacting with a snowman who has come to life. This snowman takes him flying to show him another view of the world. Although the book was published more than 20 years ago, it is still popular because it taps into human longings.

Will's Mammoth, written by Rafe Martin and illustrated by Stephen Gammell, offers another favorite childhood fantasy. In spite of his parents' assurance that mammoths have been gone for over 10,000 years, when Will goes out to play in the deep hills of snow, he finds a mammoth and rides him. Together, they spend the day traveling past many prehistoric sights. When they return, the mammoth reaches through the snow and gives Will a flower, which he sleeps with that night. The lovely paintings, the sympathetic mammoth, and the little boy who enjoys every minute of his adventure make this an unforgettable story.

Ben's Dream, by Chris Van Allsburg, takes the commonplace experience of dozing off while studying (in this case, studying geography) and turns it into a dream. In his dream, Ben finds himself in his house, floating past many of the great monuments of the world. When he is awakened by his friend, he realizes that his friend had the same dream, and he remembers waving to her as her house bobbed past the Great Sphinx in Egypt!

Eric Rohmann engages us in more imaginative wanderings in his Caldecott Honor–winning book **Time Flies,** in which a bird enters a dinosaur museum and then thinks about how he would feel if he were their prey. His wonderings put flesh on the dinosaurs and thrust them all back to prehistoric times, where he narrowly escapes being dinosaur lunch. The rich colors, the unusual perspectives, and the detailed illustrations make reading this book a stimulating experience.

Characteristics of Wordless Books

Outstanding wordless books seem to have several characteristics in common.

1. They almost always have rich pictures, full of details that make readers look carefully on every reading. Readers drink in the illustrations with their eyes, finding just one more thing they hadn't noticed on the first or second or third reading.

2. They use action to develop the characters. The plot shown through the pictures is the driving force that keeps readers turning the pages.

3. They deal with intriguing or interesting themes.

4. The setting is often a big part of the story line. The illustrations must have enough detail to make the place recognizable. Readers have to have enough knowledge to enter and feel comfortable in the story world. This explains why so many fantasies start in a known place, like a child's bedroom or some other part of the house. From there, readers can make leaps into the story world.

5. They demonstrate an expansive vision of the world, in which wanting adventure and using imagination is a normal part of living. When they view the world as an exciting, unfolding place in which we can see and perceive in many different ways, illustrators add to the fascination of the world.

6. They often make a strong emotional impact on the reader, leaving the reader wondering and thinking. Many of these books show people in caring, affirming situations, so readers come away feeling nurtured.

7. Of course, many of these books have a very distinct imaginative impact on us, since they are created for just that reason. But even when wordless books are created mainly to ask us to participate in the story, they require us to use our imaginations in order to enter into the story.

This mouse father with his mismatched pajamas enjoys entertaining his children with stories.
(COPYRIGHT © 1972 by ARNOLD LOBEL. Used by permission of HarperCollins Publishers.)

Characteristics of Books for the Earliest Readers

Although books for the earliest readers do not have the gloriously lush illustrations of many picture books, there is still much to entice the young reader. Series such as *I-Can-Read*, *Step into Reading*, and *Dell Picture Yearlings* were created to support the child who is starting to read without adult help. Early reader books, probably the first books children will read entirely on their own, share many characteristics.

Uncomplicated Pictures

The pictures, usually done in cartoon style, provide clues to the text. Because the pictures are designed to support the children's reading by providing illustrations of words they may not be familiar with, detail is often minimal. Since the illustrator wants the child to see in the pictures what will be helpful in the reading, extraneous objects and unnecessary backgrounds are not included. The illustrations are still delightful; *Frog and Toad Are Friends,* an early reader by Arnold Lobel, has won a Caldecott Honor award. The cartoon style is perfect for these kinds of books, because the strong lines used to create characters and objects make them easy to identify.

Humorous or Delightful Touches

Often the illustrations will delight children by showing them something unexpected, as in Arnold Lobel's *Mouse Tales,* where the father mouse is shown with a moustache and mismatched pajama top and bottom. Unexpected things happen, too, such as the wishing well yelling "ouch" every time a coin is thrown into it. Lobel usually draws miniature pictures, which young children adore.

The *Little Bear* books, by Else Holmelund Minarik, have whimsical illustrations by Maurice Sendak that endear the characters to the reader. But it isn't just the illustrations that are delightful and humorous; much humor is used in the text itself.

In *Henry and Mudge in Puddle Trouble,* by Cynthia Rylant, Henry's father at first is unhappy that Henry and Mudge are rolling around in a puddle of water. But after Mudge shakes himself off all over the father, the father smiles and jumps in the puddle himself, telling Henry, "Next time, ask me along!"

Solid Themes of Interest to Children

Among the themes repeated in many early reader books are the longing for and importance of friendship; adults and children making mistakes and still being accepted; celebration of special events, birthday parties, or Valentine's Day parties; the joy of having a pet; reluctance to go to bed; being afraid or having fears; children being adventurous or creative or doing something unexpected; the need to be nurtured and taken care of; the difficulty of being considered "little"; children having problems with other children; and children's

CD-ROM

To locate authors who are known for humor in their writing, do a word search for *humor* under Favorite Authors.

Booklists of Children's Literature offers lists of books by theme. Go to www.monroe.lib.in.us/ childrens/children_booklists.html.

A little girl asks her neighbors and shopkeepers what they have that is beautiful.
(From SOMETHING BEAUTIFUL, by Sharon Dennis Wyeth and illus. by Chris K. Soentpiet, copyright © 1998 by Sharon Dennis Wyeth. Illustrations copyright © 1998 by Chris K. Soentpiet. Used by permission of Random House Children's Books, a division of Random House, Inc.)

grow up and change into a less lively green snake. Over the course of the story, he learns to accept himself and not judge others by how they look. *Leo the Late Bloomer,* by Robert Kraus, depicts a young lion who isn't developing skills as fast as others his age. Luckily, he has a patient, understanding mother to help him through the experience. In *Emma's Rug,* by Allen Say, a very talented young artist learns that the creativity she displays in her paintings comes from within her, not from the rug she has had since she was a baby. And in *Where the Wild Things Are,* by Maurice Sendak, Max learns that he can have emotional outbursts, be "bad," and still be loved.

Children want to know that what they experience and feel is not strange or unusual. Books that assure them that others have fears are *Goodnight Moon,* by Margaret Wise Brown, which shows a child frightened of going to bed, and *Ira Sleeps Over,* by Bernard Waber, which depicts a little boy too embarrassed to bring his teddy bear to a sleepover with his good friend, who also sleeps with a teddy bear. In the very popular *Lilly's Purple Plastic Purse,* by Kevin Henkes, Lilly, who loves school, writes mean things to her teacher when he takes away her purple plastic purse for the day because she is distracting the class with it. The story shows how her parents help her deal with her dilemma and apologize to her teacher.

Learning About the World

CD-ROM

Find historical picture books by *theme* by searching the CD-ROM database.

Picture storybooks dealing with the historical, geographical, and natural world can help children to understand their experiences. Historical picture storybooks abound today. Ann Turner's stunning *Drummer Boy: Marching to the Civil War* gives children a close-up view of one very young boy's experiences in the Civil War. Patricia Polacco's *Pink and Say* relates two boys' experiences in the same time period.

In *The Rock,* by Peter Parnall, respect for nature underscores all that is said as we see the interconnectedness of humans, animals, and the land. *Old Turtle,* by Douglas Wood, is a beautiful story about environmental interdependence and Old Turtle's wisdom in reminding others about the beauty of the fragile earth. *Follow the Moon,* by Sarah Weeks, shows a little boy caring for a small turtle and helping him find his way to his home. Many, many books are written today about caring for the natural world and appreciating its beauty.

Margaret Wise Brown's *The Dead Bird* shows three children burying a bird and creating a ceremony for its burial. This little book introduces children to death in nature and shows how some respond to such a death. On a lighter note, *Livingstone Mouse,* by Pamela Duncan Edwards, is about a mouse who needs to find a home after his mother tells him it's time for him to live on his own. He wants a special place and has heard that China is nice, so he searches in his field for China. After many false starts, he finally finds the home he desires in a china pot, letting children know that while "home" is important, it can be many things. A different aspect of living in the world is shown in Sharon Dennis Wyeth's *Something Beautiful,* in which a little girl who lives in the projects with a graffiti-scarred door asks everyone she knows what they think is beautiful. This book affirms that people can find beauty anywhere around them, especially within other people. Many books in this category can be used in social studies and science

A Sampling of Picture Storybooks That Can Be Used Across the Curricula

Social Studies

Grandfather's Trolley, by Bruce McMillan, takes us back to the trolley days of the early 1900s and would be a good starting point for awareness of transportation at this time in our country's history.

To get a glimpse of Hmong history and how the Hmong immigrated to the United States following their alliance with the Americans in the Vietnam War, read **Dia's Story Cloth: The Hmong People's Journey of Freedom,** by Dia Cha. The story is told through a story cloth of hand-embroidered pictures and symbols. The end of the book has two full pages about the history of the Hmongs, and reading the story will make students very interested in hearing it.

Sitti's Secrets, by Naomi Shihab Nye, offers a good beginning to a study of the Middle East. This book introduces Jerusalem and the everyday customs of the Arab people who live there through the life of a little girl's grandmother, or *sitti.* This story gives a very human face to the area so that students can see the similarities among peoples as well as cultural differences.

Note: Many books cited in Chapter 9 on historical fiction can also be used in social studies classes.

Science

Out of the Ocean, by Debra Frasier, could be part of a study of the ocean and what comes to shore. At the end of the book, Frasier includes an "ocean journal," in which she talks about such things as shells, turtle tracks, driftwood, and sea urchins. Frasier's **On the Day You Were Born** introduces the natural world of animals, the sun and the moon, gravity, the sea, and much more.

Common Ground: The Water, Earth, and Air We Share, by Molly Bang, directly confronts the question of how we use the earth's resources and where it will get us.

Jeannie Baker's wordless **Window** visually shows us the effects of our actions on the environment.

Lynn Cherry's **The Great Kapok Tree: A Tale of the Amazon Rain Forest** works well as an introduction to the rain forest and what it supplies to its creatures and plants.

curricula, as demonstrated in the boxed feature A Sampling of Picture Storybooks That Can Be Used Across the Curricula.

Learning About People, Relationships, and Feelings

Two books that feature older people are **My Great-Aunt Arizona,** by Gloria Houston, and **Grandpa's Town,** by Takaaki Nomura. In the first book, we see the exuberant Great-Aunt Arizona explaining how she got an education on her own and fashioned her life around a teaching career that inspired many students to travel and fulfill their life dreams. **Grandpa's Town** shows a little boy visiting his grandfather because he is worried that, since his grandmother died, his grandfather will have nothing meaningful in his life. His notions are dispelled when he sees the full, rich life grandfather experiences in his town with his friends. Children can broaden their views of what older people are like through contact with books such as these.

Children can expand their views of the roles of men and women by reading such books as **Mama Is a Miner,** by George Ella Lyon, in which a child talks lovingly about her mother and her demanding job. **Bently and egg,** by William Joyce, shows a male—in this case, a frog—caring for the egg of his duck friend who is called away on family business. Although Bently is at first unhappy with this job, he eventually becomes very involved in caring for the egg and thus very attached to the duckling when he emerges from his shell. In **Tea with Milk,** by Allen Say, a young Japanese woman, raised in California until she was seventeen, goes back to Japan with her parents and cannot adjust to the different view of women held by that culture. When her parents try to arrange a marriage for her, she leaves, goes to the city to work, and eventually meets the man she will marry. This story of Say's mother (and father) gives us a picture of an independent, capable woman in the earlier part of the 20th century.

Many stories show children how people solve problems and get along with other people. In **That Toad is Mine!,** by Barbara Shook Hazen, two boys fight over a toad, lose him, and then resume their friendship. They work through their conflict themselves. In **The Sweetest Fig,** by Chris Van Allsburg, a selfish, mean-spirited man gets his comeuppence when his dog eats the last magic fig and turns the tables on him. In **Chester's Way,** by Kevin Henkes, children see how to be a friend as they watch Chester play with his friends.

Picture storybooks give children a peek into others' family lives, as they see what others do together within the family. An extended family that looks out for each other through hard times is pictured in **Uncle Jed's Barbershop,** by Margaree King Mitchell. When his niece needs an operation, Uncle Jed uses the money he was saving for a barbershop. This beautiful book also shows many other aspects of human behavior, including the importance of "holding fast to dreams." **Daddy Calls Me Man,** by Angela Johnson, gives us a glimpse of what it's like growing up in a family of artists. **Ma Dear's Aprons,** by Patricia C. McKissack, depicts the life of one hard-working single mother from the point of view of her young son. In T. A. Barron's **Where is Grandpa?,** a father explains to his children where his own father is since he died. All of these books show children not only the wide variety of families today, but also how these families handle life, conflicts, and death.

Having Fun

Read-Aloud Books Too Good to Miss, 2000–2001 provides lists of books children will want to hear at www.ilfonline.org/ Programs/Read%20Aloud/ readaloud.htm.

Picture storybooks can help children to learn that the world can be a humorous place and that having fun is a part of living. Some books seem to be written just for the joy and fun they bring to others. One such book written in rhyme, **Mrs. McNosh Hangs Up the Wash,** by Sarah Weeks, shows a woman hanging up just about everything in her house, including herself! **Grandpa's Teeth,** by Rod Clement, plays on the absurd. Grandpa's lost dentures are placed on the Wanted list, and detectives in the city try to locate them. This funny book has zany illustrations, as well as a marvelous surprise ending. In the playful **If You Give a Pig a Pancake,** by Laura Joffe Numeroff, we are shown a series of hilarious things that will happen if you give a pig one pancake. Audrey and Don Wood's **The Napping House,** a rhyming story, is a playful, funny account of what happens when the household all wants to take a nap. The illustrations burst with life and humor. In Anne Miranda's **To Market, To Market,** an old woman goes to market to buy a fat pig, but when she gets him home, he begins to wreck her house. With every additional animal she brings home, it gets worse! This funny rhyming book holds many surprises for the reader. Books in this category often make readers laugh out loud and discover the fun and joy that are part of life.

Stimulating the Imagination

Picture storybooks can help awaken children to the power and pleasure of the imagination. Many books portray the dreams and wishes of children by taking readers off to new places full of wonder. They stimulate imagination, pique curiosity, and fuel the desire to learn and know more. Some books show us new worlds created in the minds of the characters. The lushly illustrated **A Summertime Song,** by Irene Haas, takes us on a journey with Lucy to a birthday party for an owl. Lucy becomes the size of the little animals and can talk to them. She becomes part of their world before finding her grandmother's long-lost doll and returning home, where she regains her human size.

◀ In this circular, outrageous plot, one thing leads to another just because a little girl gives a pig a pancake.
(Cover art from *If You Give a Pig a Pancake* by Laura Joffe Numeroff, illustrated by Felicia Bond. Used by permission of HarperCollins Publishers.)

Lucy takes a magical journey when she's invited by a frog to attend a birthday party.
(Reprinted with the permission of Margaret K. McElderry Books, an imprint of Simon & Schuster Children's Publishing Division from A SUMMERTIME SONG by Irene Haas. Copyright © 1997 Irene Haas.)

Several books feature dreams about this world. *The Wreck of the Zephyr,* by Chris Van Allsburg, tells the story of why a sailboat is marooned on top of a mountain. Tapping into our desire to experience freedom by soaring on the wind like birds, this book makes us aware of our capabilities and limitations. *A Dragon in a Wagon,* by Lynley Dodd, is a delightful rhyming book in which a little girl imagines that her dog has turned into all sorts of wonderful, scary things. Another beautiful fantasy is William Joyce's *The Leaf Men,* in which an ill old woman who cannot water her dying garden is helped by the beetles. In their quest to save the garden, they hear the old tale that to call on the help of the leaf men they must go to the top of a tree and call to them. In spite of great perils, the beetles accomplish this task, the leaf men come, and a doll who has lain lost in the garden comes to life to complete the mission of helping the old woman get well.

Two books that give us examples of the imagination in action are *Cherries and Cherry Pits,* by Vera B. Williams, and *Art Dog,* by Thacker Hurd. In *Cherries and Cherry Pits,* a little girl's world is transformed through her imagination and creativity, which are ignited when she draws. In *Art Dog,* a security guard in an art museum is not recognized as the artist who expresses his joy and love of life by painting the city. The artists in both these books are shown expressing their personal power as they engage in a pursuit that brings them great pleasure.

Appreciating Beauty

Picture storybooks can help children to experience the wonder and awe of beauty in language and in the visual. Many, many picture books help children to experience the wonder of language. Jane Yolen's *Nocturne,* a poetic lullaby illustrated by Anne Hunter, is beautiful to read because she has such a feel for language and such a sense of playfulness. Her love of language, as well as her ability to hear the sounds of language and to pull in or create just the right word, is apparent throughout the book. Hunter's ethereal paintings take us into the night, where we are enfolded by the sounds of Yolen's words.

Book, by George Ella Lyon, ties the beauty of language with the beauty of the visual. Peter Catalanotto's rich-toned watercolors help us feel that we too are inside the book, taking a journey just like the little girl. The words and pictures are wedded perfectly and transport us to the world of imagination that we experience every time we open a wonderful

Ⓦ

*Get information on some of these authors and illustrators at the website of **Fairrosa Cyber Library of Children's Literature—Authors and Illustrators.** Find it at www.fairrosa.info/ cl.authors.html.*

book. Children remember having such experiences with picture books, as the comments in the boxed feature Children's Voices indicate.

Characteristics of Picture Storybooks for Older Readers

Picture storybooks for older readers are those that can be used from fourth grade up through middle school and beyond. Just because a book is designed for older readers doesn't mean that it can't be used by younger readers. With the help of an enthusiastic teacher or parent or librarian, younger children can appreciate these books. Some of the books mentioned in this section are commonly used by younger children. Picture storybooks for older readers are usually distinguished by a more sophisticated theme, more reflective text, or more academically oriented topic.

Sophisticated Themes or Subject Matter

The Caldecott winner *Snowflake Bentley,* by Jacqueline Briggs Martin, is a biography of a man who spent most of his life photographing snowflakes and revealing their beauty to the world. *Hoops,* by Robert Burleigh, is a poetic description of basketball. *Harlem,* by Walter Dean Myers, is a picture book poem about Harlem. All of these are books whose themes appeal to older readers. Allen Say's *The Sign Painter* is the story of a teenage artist who lands a job as an artist and then realizes that he is not willing to do the kind of commercial art the job requires. He strikes out on his own to live his dream of creating art that is important to him.

Longer and More Reflective Text

Toyomi Igus has written two relatively long and quite reflective picture storybooks, with pictures by Michele Wood. *Going Back Home: An Artist Returns to the South* is about Michele Wood's journey back to the South to capture the history of her African American family in her paintings. This visually stunning book tells the story of each picture both in terms of what it represents in her family and in terms of the symbols used in the paintings. *i see the rhythm* is a visual and poetic introduction to the history of African American music. Not only do the rich tones, lines, and shapes draw us into each era, but Igus's poems capture perfectly the essence of each kind of music. In addition, there is a one- or two-line summary describing each type of music, such as ragtime, swing, or gospel, as well as a brief summary of the events in history that shaped this music. This beautiful book is packed with tantalizing glimpses into African American musical history. *What's the Most Beautiful Thing You Know About Horses?,* by Richard Van Camp, gently prods us into thinking reflectively about these lovely animals, as the narrator asks his friends and family the question in the title. The answers he gets from his family—who, as part of the Dogrib nation, know little about horses because they have always used dogs—are both delightful and profound. George Littlechild's bright, vivid paintings, done in the folk tradition, add an element of playfulness to the book. Because this book pushes readers to think in fresh, positive ways, children find it provocative.

Topics That Relate to Other School Studies

*Find books on specific topics or concepts at **Children's Picture Book Database** at Miami University at www.lib.muohio.edu/pictbks/.*

At the top of the list of academically oriented books that can inspire students to think, research, or write are books that can enrich social studies courses. *Drummer Boy: Marching to the Civil War,* by Ann Turner, and *Pink and Say,* by Patricia Polacco, both show the Civil War from young boys' points of view. The Caldecott winner *Golem,* by David Wisniewski, tells of the year 1580 in Prague, when Jews were being set upon and accused of using the blood of Christian children to make matzoh, the Passover bread. To protect them from angry mobs storming the walls of their ghetto, a Golem, or shapeless man, was created by the chief rabbi. This fascinating legend might encourage students to do research in order to learn more about the persecution of the Jews and the nature of the

Children's Voices

On memories of picture books . . .

It's about a dog and little girl and a teacher and a mom but it doesn't have any words in it. I like it because it has a lot of pictures.
—Jessica, 2nd grade

*My favorite picture book is **Outside My Window—Good Day Spider** because this kid liked the duck, the spider, and the dog. The spider said "hello" to the duck and the spider looked sad.* —Ashley, 2nd grade

I can't think of the name of it. It's got a cat in it and the house burns down. I like it because it's got a cat in it. —Sarah, 2nd grade

*The best one I've ever heard of is **Goldilocks**. It has good pictures.* —Elizabeth, 2nd grade

*I like **Hey Al!** because the pictures are colorful and bright.* —Andy, 3rd grade

***Search for Santa's Helpers** because you get to search for elves.* —Amber, 3rd grade

I love Mercer Mayer's books because they have good pictures. —Casey, 3rd grade

***Werewolf of Fever Swamp** because it's scary.* —Nathan, 3rd grade

***There's a Wocket in My Pocket** because it's a tongue twister sort of.* —Amanda, 3rd grade

***Arthur** books make my mind say, "I think this author did a neat job!"* —Jenna, 3rd grade

I liked Eric Carle when I was younger because he did his own artwork. —Jake, 4th grade

*The one picture book that stands out in my memory is **The Little Engine That Could**. It's my favorite book because it reminds me every time I read it about how I need to keep trying. Lots of children's books we read as children we still remember today. They actually help us go through life.* —Jacob, 6th grade

*I loved **Brown Bear, Brown Bear** not because of the words but because of the pictures.* —Joshua, 6th grade

I can't say I remember any picture books but I can remember I liked them when I was little. —Scott, 6th grade

*The book that was called **I Think I Can.** I like it 'cause it tells me not to give up.* —Leon, 6th grade

***Chicka, Chicka, Boom Boom** because when I was in the second grade that was my favorite book.* —Monique, 6th grade

*I remember **Where the Wild Things Are.** I always liked art and the pictures to me were so cool.* —Bridget, 7th grade

I remember Dr. Seuss books when I began reading. What I think I enjoyed the most is how he could use his imagination and how everything rhymed. —Marie, 7th grade

***Rose Blanche** sticks in my mind. I like the unfinished wording and the way the pictures are watercolors and sort of blurry.* —Jeff, 7th grade

***Berenstain Bears** are great. They are colorful and they have a moral. They were great especially when I was young because they helped me understand what not to do.* —Jessica, 7th grade

*My favorite picture book of all time is **If You Give a Mouse a Cookie.** I like this book because it is animals talking and I think it would be cool to meet a talking mouse that wanted a cookie and milk.* —Drew, 7th grade

*I like **Green Eggs and Ham** because I remember how stubborn Sam I Am was.* —Ben, 7th grade

Older readers are drawn to this picture book because of the topic and the illustrations, which pique their interest.

(Reprinted with permission of the publisher, Children's Book Press, San Francisco, CA. *I See the Rhythm* paintings © 1998 by Michele Wood and text copyright © 1998 by Toyomi Igus.)

allegations made against them. Paul Goble's **Death of the Iron Horse** shows an American Indian point of view on the coming of the railroad and what it meant to the native people's way of life. It would be interesting to use this book as a way to talk about point of view and how every instance in history of taking lands can be seen from at least two points of view. Perhaps students studying this time period in history could write about other events from the point of view of the American Indians. Sherry Garland's **The Voices of the Alamo** is the story of the many people who lived on the land surrounding the Alamo or had a hand in fighting there. It is told through poems from the points of view of Indians who first lived there, farmers, Texians (Mexicans who lived in Texas), the military, and many others. Students could work to generate multiple points of view on other historical events or sites.

Students who are learning about Harriet Tubman and her heroic work to save thousands of people from slavery will enjoy two very different accounts of Tubman's accomplishments in Faith Ringgold's **Aunt Harriet's Underground Railroad in the Sky** and Jacob Lawrence's **Harriet and the Promised Land.** In Ringgold's version, a young girl in the present day finds Harriet's railroad in the sky and experiences what escaping slaves did, traveling from safe house to safe house. Ringgold's paintings make the story leap to life. Lawrence's version is written in rhymed verse, accompanied by his rich-hued, stylized illustrations. These two stories cry out to be compared, and students could get involved in looking at which events the artists depicted, which ones they left out, and the impact of each book. These books together show students in very vivid ways how writing about historical events still involves selection and choice on the part of the author; there is no such thing as "just the facts," since the facts to be presented must be selected.

Ringgold's **Dinner at Aunt Connie's House** is another book older readers find interesting. Two children go upstairs at Aunt Connie's house, where the subjects of her paintings of outstanding African American women talk to the children about who they are and what they've done. This marvelous book introduces new information in an interesting way. It provides a good starting point for learning more about the twelve women in the paintings.

An abundance of books are available to introduce or reinforce concepts in science. *Window,* by Jeannie Baker (discussed in the wordless book section), is a book older readers respond to, since they can see so clearly the negative effects of humans' actions on the environment. A book students could use as a starting point for research on how early man lived is Jan Brett's **The First Dog,** set in an Ice Age landscape. **Buddy,** by William Joyce, the true story of a gorilla raised in the New York mansion of Gertrude Lintz, could be used to kick off a unit on animal rights. What happens to Buddy raises many provocative questions students would be eager to explore.

Many picture storybooks can be used to stimulate writing by students. **Tea with Milk,** by Allen Say, could inspire students to unearth the story of how their parents or grandparents met. **Aunt Flossie's Hat (and Crab Cakes Later),** by Elizabeth Fitzgerald Howard, which describes Aunt Flossie's memories of what she experienced as she wore each of her different hats, could lead students to write about memories revolving around an object or memories of aunts and uncles.

The books of Chris Van Allsburg, Jon Scieszka, and Babette Cole are sure to be a hit with older students. Van Allsburg's **The Garden of Abdul Gasazi, Jumanji,** and **The Mysteries of Harris Burdick** all cry out to be viewed closely and repeatedly and talked and written about. These books are nothing short of intriguing. Scieszka's books— **The Stinky Cheese Man and Other Fairly Stupid Tales; Squids will be Squids: Fresh Morals, Beastly Fables; The True Story of the Three Little Pigs by A. Wolf;** and **The Frog Prince Continued**—are riotously funny. They require repeated readings to catch all of the subtleties and humor; they also seem to ask us to create our own tales, just as he does. In combination with his outrageous sense of humor, his breaking of literary conventions

This illustration of two chimpanzees and a surprised girl cries out for an explanation.
(Cover, from JUMANJI. Copyright © 1981 by Chris Van Allsburg. Reprinted by permission of Houghton Mifflin Company. All rights reserved.)

results in highly unusual and entertaining tales. Babette Cole writes and illustrates unconventional, hysterically funny books. *The Trouble with Mom, Winni Allfours,* and *Drop Dead* are all books older students would giggle at. It turns out that mom is a witch, Winnie prefers to be a horse, and Grandad and Gran had very interesting, unconventional lives. These story lines could easily be imitated in students' own tales.

The books mentioned here are only a small sampling of those that could be used with older readers. The best way to find books to use with the older age groups is simply to go to the children's section in the library and sample books.

Favorite Authors and Illustrators of Picture Books

Thousands of picture books are published each year. To help you navigate through the sea of choices until you become familiar with the authors and illustrators and find some you love, I offer the list in the boxed feature Favorite Authors and Illustrators of Picture Books.

Favorite Authors and Illustrators of Picture Books

Aliki creates endearing drawings filled with multiethnic characters in the books she writes, which often deal with the affective.

Graeme Base, author and illustrator, creates books filled with lush, colorful, detailed drawings that beckon readers back to look for what they might have missed the first time through.

Quentin Blake is known for doing humorous, often outrageous drawings in cartoon style, in both his own books and those of others.

Margaret Wise Brown authored some endearing stories, dealing with fears and doubts, that continue to be read to very young children today.

Anthony Browne writes delightful books filled with his exquisitely detailed images, often done in a surrealistic style.

Ashley Bryan, poet and illustrator, creates paintings in the naive style, using bright, bold colors that exude happiness.

Eve Bunting, a very prolific author, writes stories that often touch on the harder "real life" issues such as homelessness, urban riots, and memories of war losses.

John Burningham, author and illustrator, creates delightful picture books that often border on the outrageous.

Janell Cannon, author and illustrator, uses bright colors and clear images to involve the reader in the thoughtful stories she creates.

Eric Carle, author and illustrator, is a master of the cut-paper collage. His books use bright, cheerful colors and sharply delineated illustrations.

Peter Catalanotto, author and illustrator, is a watercolorist whose often-surrealistic illustrations have a dreamlike quality.

R. Gregory Christie is an illustrator known for drama, an effect he achieves through angular representations, outsized heads and hands, and striking perspectives.

Rod Clement's humorous illustrations enhance the reader's enjoyment of the story, whether he is illustrating his own work or a book authored by another.

Babette Cole, author and illustrator, creates zany books with cartoonlike figures. One cannot help but smile at her whimsical characters.

Bryan Collier, author and illustrator, dazzles with his stunning, bold, watercolor and cut-paper-collage compositions. His stylized drawings capture the essence of his subjects.

Barbara Cooney, a Caldecott Award–winning illustrator, also writes lovely books. Simple forms, soft colors, and a sometimes-somber mood characterize her illustrations.

Floyd Cooper, author and illustrator, creates oil-wash illustrations. Some have glowing color, while others are soft and muted. His choices capture the mood of whatever story he is illustrating.

David Diaz, illustrator, is known for the vibrant colors he uses, a collage-like effect, and a naive style.

Leo and Diane Dillon are a husband-and-wife team. They have worked together to create brilliant illustrations for a wide variety of texts authored by some of children's literature's best authors.

Richard Egielski is an author and illustrator. His award-winning illustrations reveal not only a wonderful imagination, but a versatile artistry as well.

Lois Ehlert, author and illustrator, creates cut-paper collage, often embedded with fascinating designs and bright colors.

Mem Fox writes stories for young readers in which the text often has magical repetition, making it predictable and very "readable." The sense that she purposefully chooses concise words with a poetic feel permeates Fox's work.

Wanda Gag created the classic story of a little kitten that emerged out of hundreds, thousands, millions, and billions of prospective pets to become part of an elderly couple's home. Her artwork holds up well in today's competitive field of illustrations.

Stephen Gammell is an illustrator and author whose work has a whimsical quality. He can record a fun family get-together but can also convey the mood of a story with a scary or sad theme.

Kevin Henkes, author and illustrator, creates endearing mice in cartoon style and writes about issues near and dear to the hearts of children.

Ronald Himler is an illustrator who works in watercolors. The stories that he illustrates or creates often deal with sensitive issues, and his watercolors capture the dignity of the characters and themes in the text.

Shirley Hughes is an author and illustrator whose books for preschoolers and young readers are well written and entertaining. Her colorful, soft illustrations capture the expressions of the story's characters.

William Joyce is an author and illustrator who, along with illustrating other authors' work, writes creative, fun stories that capture a child's imagination with their bright, colorful, stylized illustrations.

Ted Lewin is a Caldecott Honor–winning illustrator who has worked with many wonderful authors. His beautiful watercolors illustrate this textbook.

E. B. Lewis is an outstanding illustrator whose watercolors are rich in detail and highly luminescent, complementing the texts of leading children's authors.

Leo Lionni is a popular author and illustrator whose work continues to be reprinted. His illustrations are easily recognizable with their cut paper and soft hues.

Arnold Lobel is a prolific illustrator who became an author as well. His stories, characterizing the many aspects of friendship between a frog and a toad, are wonderful texts for early readers.

Thomas Locker, author and illustrator, has won numerous awards for his work. His magnificent realistic paintings are breathtaking, and they capture the essence of the text.

George Ella Lyon, author, is best known for her loving use of language and her willingness to approach subjects in unusual ways.

James Marshall, author and illustrator, illustrates his engaging, humorous stories with delightful cartoon characters.

Robert McCloskey has authored and illustrated some classic children's stories, often set on the East Coast. His subjects range from the life of a family of ducks in a large city to life in a quiet coastal setting.

Barry Moser, book designer and illustrator, creates amazingly beautiful illustrations that reach to the heart of the book.

Helen Oxenbury, author and illustrator, creates whimsical, delightful, cartoonlike characters, using bright, bold colors that capture the essence of the characters.

Margie Palatini is an author whose books delight the young reader. Using dialogue that has been described as riotous, she tickles the funny bone of her readers.

Peter Parnell often illustrates the books of Byrd Baylor, depicting the Southwest in beautiful yellows and oranges against a white background, with finely woven features created with black lines. Illustrating his own New England story led him to use a very different color scheme.

Patricia Polacco illustrates her own stories and poems, which have an extraordinary immediacy. She is known for the breadth of her work across different genres, as well as her inclusiveness of multiracial and ethnic characters in her stories.

Brian Pinkney's work is almost always quickly recognizable. His use of scratchboard is outstanding and captures the feel of the text.

Jerry Pinkney is an amazing watercolorist whose attention to detail, use of soft-hued colors, and authenticity contribute to any book he illustrates.

Chris Raschka, author and Caldecott Honor–winning illustrator, reaches for the never-been-tried-before in his unusual books.

Faith Ringgold, both an author and an illustrator, is known for her naive style and richly colored, detailed pictures, often used in stories that deal with the human desire to be free.

Cynthia Rylant is an author whose themes nudge the boundaries of children's literature. Whether she is writing in prose or in poetry, for

(continued)

older readers or for the very young, her writing finds a way to the heart.

Allen Say, illustrator and author, creates illustrations that have a crisp, photographic quality. His lovely stories are steeped in emotion and human experience.

Jon Scieszka is a zany author whose humorous story lines break literary conventions and make readers pay attention.

Maurice Sendak has authored numerous children's books and illustrated even more. He is best remembered for a story he authored and illustrated about a little boy who imagines a wild adventure after being sent to his room for misbehaving.

Dr. Seuss, often cited as a favorite author/illustrator, made a permanent place for himself in children's literature with his mischievous cat and odd-colored eggs. His books range from simple rhymes creating silly images to books with messages about conservation and life choices.

David Shannon, illustrator and author, often uses bright, splashy colors and cartoonlike characters whose actions children can relate to. When he illustrates for other writers, he demonstrates his range and depth.

David Small, illustrator and author, has a quiet style. His illustrations, usually with soft colors and great attention to detail, wonderfully extend the story.

Chris K. Soentpiet, illustrator for many popular authors, creates stunning images with exciting use of light in his photolike pictures.

William Steig, both author and illustrator, uses a cartoon style and animals with whimsical expressions to make his characters leap to life.

James Stevenson, both author and illustrator, is known for his softly colored cartoons, his gentle characters, and his wit and humor, which make his stories memorable.

Sarah Stewart is a writer who creates gentle, quiet stories, which are often evocative of earlier times.

Ann Turner is an author whose beautiful artistry with words lets her say volumes in just a few words, whether she writes in prose or in poetry.

Chris Van Allsburg is an author and illustrator who uses light masterfully. His surrealistic pictures often startle readers into looking closely at the details.

Rosemary Wells is a versatile author/illustrator who has created many of her own books for young children. Her huggable animal characters, painted in bright colors, live out many stories that young children can relate to.

David Wiesner is an illustrator and author of wordless books that tickle the imagination and create countless texts in the reader's mind. Because of his use of the surreal, interest in his

books extends to the middle school student.

Vera B. Williams, author and illustrator, uses vibrant, rich colors to illustrate her lovely stories, often featuring working-class people.

Mike Wimmer is an illustrator noted for his stunning use of light in pictures that touch the heart of the story.

Jacqueline Woodson is an author relatively new to children's literature. Both her picture books and her young adult realistic fiction tackle difficult issues, opening the way to meaningful discussion with even the youngest readers.

Jane Yolen is a prolific author who writes in a multitude of genres. Her language is always lovely, and she has the ability to wrap the reader in the essence of her stories.

Ed Young, both an author and an illustrator, is known for his soft-hued watercolors and the dreamlike quality of many of his illustrations.

Paul O. Zelinski's strikingly beautiful illustrations have ensured him a place among notable children's literature artists. By retelling and illustrating folk tales, he has brought new beauty and interest to these familiar tales.

Invitations

Choose several of the following activities to complete:

1. What picture storybooks do you remember most clearly from your childhood? Compare your choices to those mentioned in Children's Voices and to those of others in your group. Do any common themes or characteristics pervade your choices?

2. Choose a picture storybook you love, and write a response to it. Then go through the section in Chapter 2 on picture storybooks and analyze your book in terms of purpose, plot variation, vision, setting, characters, and qualities of writing. Feel free to include other characteristics not mentioned. Share your findings with your small group and describe to them all the ways you think this book could be used in a classroom.

3. Choose a favorite author or illustrator and find information about her or him on the Internet, beginning with the sites mentioned in Internet and Text Resources. Share your findings in a small group, explaining what you found out and any insights you gained. Also share what is available on any other sites you found.

4. Bring in a picture book to read aloud to a small group. As each person in the group reads his or her book, jot down your reactions and responses. Then reread Taking a Look at the Research: The Read-Aloud. Looking carefully at Routmann's list (in paragraph two) of ways read-alouds can help a child become a successful reader, write down and then talk about how the books just read can do the things she lists. For example, what could children learn from these books about how stories work?

5. As you read picture books, do one of the following:

- Choose a topic or theme you're interested in and create your own ABC book, using whatever structure or scheme you wish. Share this book with your group and reflect on what you learned about ABC books and about writing.

- Find a wordless book by Anno or Wiesner or another author and create a narrative for it. Share both the book and the narrative with your group. Write a reflection on the experience, focusing on the kind of learning or thinking the book did or did not provoke in you.

- Try to produce an early reader yourself so that you can see how much skill it takes to construct a book with 120–1,000 words that still has a sense of story and engages children. Words have to be selected carefully not only to take into account reading level but also to delight and interest children so as to engage them in the text. Share your results with your group.

6. Have each person in your group select and read ten books in one of the following categories: ABC books, counting books, concept books, or picture books for older readers. Rank the ten books from 1 to 10, with 1 being the best, and explain the reasons for your decisions. Work to generate a list of the characteristics that caused you to rank each book as you did. Was it imaginative/unimaginative pictures? Did the language delight/fail to delight you? Were the illustrations engrossing or too obscure to involve you? Share your findings with your small group.

7. Read ten early reader books in the library. Rank the ten books from 1 to 10, with 1 being the best. Which ones did you personally find most interesting to read? Do any of the characteristics of early reader books apply to or describe the books you read? Did your books have other characteristics that weren't mentioned? What qualities in these books give support to young readers? Did you find books that you did not consider to be of high quality for this genre? Work to name the qualities that put you off. Did you find stereotypes? Did the characters seem uninteresting? Were the illustrations mediocre? Did there seem to be little support for early readers? Share your findings with your group.

Miranda, Anne (1997). *To Market, To Market*. Illus. Janet Stevens. San Diego: Harcourt Brace.

Mitchell, Margaree King (1993). *Uncle Jed's Barbershop*. Illus. James Ransome. New York: Aladdin.

Mochizuki, Ken (1995). *Heroes*. Illus. Dom Lee. New York: Lee & Low.

Mullins, Patricia (1998). *One Horse Waiting for Me*. New York: Simon & Schuster.

Myers, Walter Dean (1997). *Harlem*. Illus. Christopher Myers. New York: Scholastic.

Neitzel, Shirley (1989). *The Jacket I Wear in the Snow*. Illus. Nancy Winslow Parker. New York: Greenwillow.

Nomura, Takaaki (1995). *Grandpa's Town*. Trans. Amanda Mayer Stinchecum. New York: Kane/Miller.

Nye, Naomi Shihab (1994). *Sitti's Secrets*. Illus. Nancy Carpenter. New York: Simon & Schuster.

Numeroff, Laura Joffe (1985). *If You Give a Mouse a Cookie*. Illus. Felicia Bond. New York: HarperCollins.

—— (1998). *If You Give a Pig a Pancake*. Illus. Felicia Bond. New York: HarperCollins.

Onyefulu, Ifeoma (1993). *A Is for Africa*. New York: Cobblehill.

Oxenbury, Helen (1971). *Helen Oxenbury's ABC of Things*. New York: Franklin Watts.

Pallotta, Jerry (1986). *The Ocean Alphabet Book*. Illus. Frank Mazzola, Jr. Watertown, MA: Charlesbridge.

Parnell, Peter (1991). *The Rock*. New York: Macmillan.

Pelletier, David (1996). *The Graphic Alphabet*. New York: Orchard.

Polacco, Patricia (1994). *Pink and Say*. New York: Philomel.

Rankin, Laura (1991). *The Handmade Alphabet*. New York: Dial.

Ringgold, Faith (1992). *Aunt Harriet's Underground Railroad in the Sky*. New York: Crown.

—— (1993). *Dinner at Aunt Connie's House*. New York: Hyperion.

Rohmann, Eric (1994). *Time Flies*. New York: Crown.

Ryan, Pam Muñoz, and Jerry Pallotta (1996). *The Crayon Counting Book*. Illus. Frank Mazzola, Jr. Watertown, MA: Charlesbridge.

Rylant, Cynthia (1996). *Henry and Mudge in Puddle Trouble*. Illus. Suçie Stevenson. New York: Aladdin.

Say, Allen (1996). *Emma's Rug*. Boston: Houghton Mifflin.

—— (1993). *Grandfather's Journey*. Boston: Houghton Mifflin.

—— (2000). *The Sign Painter*. Boston: Houghton Mifflin.

—— (1999). *Tea with Milk*. Boston: Houghton Mifflin.

Scieszka, Jon (1991). *The Frog Prince Continued*. Illus. Steve Johnson. New York: Puffin.

—— (1998). *Squids will be Squids: Fresh Morals, Beastly Fables*. Illus. Lane Smith. New York: Viking.

—— (1992). *The Stinky Cheese Man and Other Fairly Stupid Tales*. Illus. Lane Smith. New York: Viking.

—— (1989). *The True Story of the Three Little Pigs by A. Wolf*. Illus. Lane Smith. New York: Puffin.

Sendak, Maurice (1962). *Chicken Soup with Rice: A Book of Months*. New York: Harper & Row.

—— (1963). *Where the Wild Things Are*. New York: Harper & Row.

Serfozo, Mary (1988). *Who Said Red?* Illus. Keiko Narahashi. New York: McElderry.

Seuss, Dr. (1968). *The Foot Book*. New York: Random.

—— (1970). *Mr. Brown Can Moo, Can You?* New York: Random.

Shannon, George (1995). *Tomorrow's Alphabet*. Illus. Donald Crews. New York: Greenwillow.

Sierra, Judy (1996). *Wiley and the Hairy Man*. Illus. Brian Pinkney. New York: Lodestar.

Sis, Peter (1988). *Waving: A Counting Book*. New York: Greenwillow.

Smith, Janice Lee (1995). *Wizard and Wart at Sea*. Illus. Paul Meisel. New York: HarperCollins.

Spinner, Stephanie, and Ellen Weiss (1997). *Born to Be Wild: The Weebie Zone #3*. New York: HarperCollins.

Steig, William (1969). *Sylvester and the Magic Pebble*. New York: Windmill.

—— (1997). *Toby, Where Are You?* Illus. Teryl Euvremer. New York: HarperCollins.

Stevenson, James (1996). *Yard Sale*. New York: Greenwillow.

Tafuri, Nancy (1989). *The Ball Bounced.* New York: Greenwillow.

Testa, Fulvio (1992). *A Long Trip to Z.* San Diego: Harcourt Brace.

Turner, Ann (1998). *Drummer Boy: Marching to the Civil War.* Illus. Mark Hess. New York: HarperCollins.

Van Allsburg, Chris (1982). *Ben's Dream.* Boston: Houghton Mifflin.

—— (1979). *The Garden of Abdul Gasazi.* Boston: Houghton Mifflin.

—— (1981). *Jumanji.* Boston: Houghton Mifflin.

—— (1984). *The Mysteries of Harris Burdick.* Boston: Houghton Mifflin.

—— (1993). *The Sweetest Fig.* Boston: Houghton Mifflin.

—— (1983). *The Wreck of the Zephyr.* Boston: Houghton Mifflin.

Van Camp, Richard (1998). *What's the Most Beautiful Thing You Know About Horses?* Illus. George Littlechild. San Francisco: Children's Book Press.

Viorst, Judith (1972). *Alexander and the Terrible, Horrible, No Good, Very Bad Day.* Illus. Ray Cruz. New York: Atheneum.

Waber, Bernard (1972). *Ira Sleeps Over.* Boston: Houghton Mifflin.

Waddell, Martin (1992). *Farmer Duck.* Illus. Helen Oxenbury. Cambridge, MA: Candlewick.

Weeks, Sarah (1995). *Follow the Moon.* Illus. Suzanne Duranceau. New York: HarperCollins.

—— (1998). *Mrs. McNosh Hangs Up Her Wash.* Illus. Nadine Bernard Westcott. New York: HarperCollins.

Westervelt, Linda (1995). *Roger Tory Peterson's ABC of Birds.* Illus. Roger Tory Peterson. New York: Universe.

Wiesner, David (1992). *July 29, 1999.* New York: Clarion.

—— (1991). *Tuesday.* New York: Clarion.

Wildsmith, Brian (1981). *Animal Shapes.* London: Oxford University Press [out of print].

—— (1962). *Brian Wildsmith's ABC.* London: Oxford University Press.

Williams, Sue (1990). *I Went Walking.* Illus. Julie Vivas. San Diego: Harcourt Brace.

Williams, Vera B. (1986). *Cherries and Cherry Pits.* New York: Greenwillow.

—— (1990). *More More More Said the Baby.* New York: Greenwillow.

Wisniewski, David (1996). *Golem.* New York: Clarion.

Wood, Audrey (1996). *The Napping House.* Illus. Don Wood. Duluth, MN: Red Wagon.

Wood, Douglas (1984). *Old Turtle.* Illus. Cheng-Khee Chee. San Diego: Harcourt Brace.

Wyeth, Sharon Dennis (1998). *Something Beautiful.* Illus. Chris K. Soentpiet. New York: Doubleday.

Yolen, Jane (1992). *Nocturne.* Illus. Anne Hunter. San Diego: Harcourt Brace.

—— (1987). *Owl Moon.* Illus. John Schoenherr. New York: Philomel.

On becoming immersed in the story world . . .

I like science fiction and mysteries. They make it easy for my mind to see the scene and what's going on and they help my imagination wander.
—Jimmy, 7th grade

Sometimes without even realizing it at the time, I get so caught up in the book at the suspenseful parts that I start to read really fast. I sometimes put myself in the position of the main character. I then think about what I would do if it were me instead.
—Angela, 7th grade

When I read I try to put myself in the characters' shoes, try to think what they think, I try to be them. So the more interesting the book I read is, the more I like it.
—John, 7th grade

I mostly like to read an action type of book. In these books I get so into it that I don't want to stop. I say to myself "I'll stop next page." I never do. I always keep going.
—Jacob, 7th grade

*I read **Redwall** books, **Mossflower** books, and ghost books because they keep you on the edge of your seat.* —Arnie, 7th grade

I don't care for science fiction and fantasy. I can't feel that I'm part of the story when it sounds so fake. —Ashlynn, 7th grade

I like fiction books mostly including dragons or magic. I like them because they draw me in and keep me reading. —Renee, 7th grade

2. Considering cultural or psychological nuances

3. Filling in the gaps by using clues and evidence in the text to draw conclusions

4. Evaluating how the author's ideas fit with one's prior knowledge or experience

5. Challenging the text

6. Demonstrating an understanding of the work as a whole

7. Paying attention to the structure of the text and how parts work together

8. Showing aesthetic appreciation of such features as language use and depth of theme

9. Alluding to or relating specific passages in order to validate ideas

10. Demonstrating emotional engagement with the text

11. Reflecting on the meaning and universal significance of the text

12. Making connections between the text and one's own ideas and experiences

As good readers we use various strategies to help us comprehend and interact with what we read. Every time we read something that is in a new genre or is particularly difficult, we add to our strategies for meaning-making so that we can better understand what we are reading. Like us, students are continually learning how to read. Helping students recognize the reading strategies they use and teaching them new strategies are both vital activities. We all need ways to get the most out of our reading, while keeping the impact of the literature at the center.

Ellin Oliver Keene and Susan Zimmermann (1997) redefine comprehension as new thinking. They point out that teachers already teach children to use webbing and mapping processes to remember significant actions taken by characters. Many of these comprehension tools are primarily enrichment activities. Although they help teachers find out what children remember from their reading, these activities do little to actually change children's thinking while they read. Keene and Zimmermann identified a need to explicitly teach strategies so that students could not only read better but also get more out of their reading. They found that the difference between just talking about books and talking about the thinking processes a proficient reader uses to understand them is subtle but key. They encourage students as young as kindergartners and first-graders to make text-to-self, text-to-world, and text-to-text connections, a self-reflective process that helps readers think as they read. When readers make text-to-self connections, thinking about their own experiences as they read, they understand the story better. For example, when reading a book about a grandfather, readers can more deeply understand the character and his feelings if they think about their interactions with their own grandfathers. These "connection" experiences may cause the children to question the text, which is something else good readers do.

Text-to-world and text-to-text connections also deepen a reading. Children learn to make text-to-world connections as they become more aware of the events of the world through travel, media, and reading. They start to recognize connections between a story they are reading and actual events. Children begin to make text-to-text connections when they associate texts they have read before with the one they are reading. Perhaps the plot or setting is similar or a character reminds them of someone in another story. They may also begin to recognize the work of particular authors or illustrators. What readers already know will change because of what they read. When students focus on their thinking as they read, they are doing more than simply pointing out strategies; they are discovering that thinking helps them understand and interact with the story. They are learning that reading is about making meaning of stories and of their own lives. As mature readers, we usually go through this process unintentionally, silently making text-to-self, text-to-world, and text-to-text connections as we read. This is part of what makes us good readers. Children need to be explicitly taught to do this so that they, too, can understand what they read at deep levels. Understanding what good readers do helps us create meaningful response activities for our students so that they practice good reading strategies.

Initial Responses

Since we all see different things as we read, it isn't appropriate to expect each reader to notice the same details or even view characters in the same way, especially after just a first reading. To get a closer look at the process of how we read and how we make sense of text, let's look at two very different responses to the same book: *We Had a Picnic This Sunday Past,* written by Jacqueline Woodson and illustrated by Diane Greenseid. The boxed feature Response to First Reading of a Book: A Response Log for a Picture Book contains my responses to the picture book as I read it for the first time, including the things I was conscious of noticing and reacting to as I read (see page 116). Then the boxed feature Response to First Reading of a Book: A College Student's Response gives the response of a college student to the same text (see page 117).

The bright colors and smiling faces seem to invite readers to the picnic, too.

(From WE HAD A PICNIC THIS SUNDAY PAST by Jacqueline Woodson. Text Copyright © 1997 by Jacqueline Woodson. Illustrations Copyright © 1997 Diane Greenseid. Reprinted by permission of Hyperion Books for Children.)

Children's Talk in Book Clubs

One multi-age first- and second-grade class in a rural area has a teacher who understands literacy and literature. Renee Webster (1996) has her students in book club groups, making meaning from the books she reads them. Webster describes how her students write and talk about books through book clubs:

> Book clubs encourage students to organize their response to a text in a personal way, which stimulates their prior experiences, abilities, and ideas. Conversing through book talks provides students with the experience of sharing a text as more than an exercise in decoding, supporting a belief that the role of a reader goes beyond the reciting of words to discover the multiple interpretations of a text. (p. 42)

The boxed feature First- and Second-Graders Discuss *Henry and Beezus* is a transcript of three first-graders and one second-grader discussing Beverly Cleary's story **Henry and Beezus.** The first few minutes of this student-led discussion focus on how Henry actually discovered 49 packages of bubble gum in a vacant lot and the events that led up to the discovery.

Webster points out that we can see from this discussion how the students are moving through the story to construct meaning. In lines 1 through 4, Mary and Ellie work to clarify a description of a vacant lot, which is not a familiar landmark for these rural students. They end up agreeing that it is not exactly an alley but like an alley. In line 6, Mary summarizes her interpretation of Henry's discovery of the gum. Ellie and Ron then begin questioning what actually happens in the story. Their inquiries take the form of restating or describing mental images of what they are trying to learn. These learners take ownership of their learning within a community that demands listening and participation. Webster points out that if a large-group discussion or individual worksheets had been used, these students might never have had the opportunity to scaffold each other's construction of knowledge concerning their understanding of this text.

First- and Second-Graders Discuss *Henry and Beezus*

1. M: He found it in the . . . alley.
2. E: It's not an alley, really.
3. M: It's like one.
4. E: Yeah.
5. M: Henry's dog ran up to chase a cat and . . . he found a package of something and he looked at it and it was gum.
6. E: I don't remember any cat.
7. R: Neither do I.
8. T: I do.
9. M: There was . . .
10. T: A cat.
11. R: I thought that was a dog.
12. E: It was a dog. There was a dog there.
13. R: There was.
14. E: Yeah.
15. T: There was a cat and a dog.
16. M: The dog started chasing the cat and he found the package of something.
17. E: Oh yeah!
18. M: And he opened it and it was gum.
19. T: Neat.
20. E: The dog didn't open it.
21. R: Yeah, the dog didn't open it.
22. T: The dog chased the cat and THEN he found it.
23. R: The dog didn't find it.
24. E: Yes, he did.
25. M: The dog (inaudible)
26. E: The dog found the package.
27. T: Yeah!
28. R: The dog found the cat.
29. E: Yeah, and that was when Henry opened the package and there was gum in there.
30. M: And then he ran to his friend's house and asked for a barrow.
31. R: Ah, no, not a barrow, a . . .
32. ALL: A wagon.

Awareness of the works of Langer (1995) and Claggett (1996) helps us see what these children are doing through their talk. They are in Stance Two (Being In and Moving Through an Envisionment), where they need time to share and build on each other's understandings. They are not yet ready to talk about the story in terms of themselves or to compare it to other stories. We can also see, as Langer points out, that the students each pay attention to different details and don't remember the same things from the story. This kind of book club talk helps them fill in the picture. Their questioning indicates that they are intellectually engaged with the text. They are also filling in gaps by using clues and evidence from the story to draw conclusions. They allude to and relate specific passages to validate their ideas. By deciding that the dog didn't open the package they demonstrate that they are evaluating the story in terms of how the author's ideas fit with their prior knowledge or experience. These children are exhibiting some characteristics of good readers, and they will continue to develop as readers as they are given more occasions to try out behaviors that good readers use.

What Talk Does

Talk is not only a medium for thinking, it is also an important means by which we learn how to think. From a Vygotskian perspective thinking is an internal dialogue, an internalization of dialogues we've had with others. Our ability to think depends upon the many previous dialogues we have taken part in—we learn to think by participating in dialogues. (Dudley-Marling and Searle, 1991, p. 60)

When students have opportunities such as those just described to talk to each other about books, the understanding comes from within. They've had to think about the book, share responses and questions, pull from their memories pieces of the book, and negotiate meaning with others. Because students are actively involved in this talk, the understandings they come away with are authentic. The talk changes and extends their understanding and teaches them to see through other people's eyes. It shows in a very concrete way that even when we all read the same text, we remember or pay attention to very different things. So this kind of talk enriches all our readings, because it gives us a broader understanding of the many meanings in the text, beyond the ones we found. By examining and weighing possible interpretations through talk, students discover new layers of meaning. One common way to begin this kind of talk in the classroom is through the use of reading aloud. The boxed feature Implementing the Read-Aloud in the Classroom explains the hows and whys of reading aloud to a class (see page 124).

Classroom Read-Aloud Strategies provides even more ideas on implementing this process. Find it at http://clerccenter.gallaudet.edu/Literacy/readit45.html.

Art

When we read, we see images in our minds—full-blown pictures or flashes of color and shapes. These mental images are what make reading real to us, what make it retrievable, what help us talk about literature. Images have always been a part of the reading process, even though little attention has been paid to them. By talking about these images or sketching them, we can become more closely linked to our reading. But drawing can do even more than that. For too long, we non-artists have not understood the power or the function of art. Now, especially through the work of Karen Ernst, Ruth Shagoury Hubbard, Phyllis Whitin, Dennie Palmer Wolf, and Dana Balick, we are beginning to understand that drawing is another way to make meaning, to process thought, to represent our worlds, and to better understand what we think and feel. It is a vehicle for learning, a tool for expressing and organizing ideas. We have to learn what Karen Ernst (in Hubbard and Ernst, 1996) says kindergartners know naturally: "A picture is a form of expression, holds meaning, and is a story, a poem, a reflection of thinking" (p. 146). We also have to recapture that freedom kindergartners have to just draw. All of us have the capacity for visual expression, even though many of us are frightened by the idea of drawing or sketching.

When we script, role-play, or act out a piece of literature, we increase our comprehension of the literature because we enter into it as a character. Performing parts of scenes provides a forum for discussing a piece of literature, as we learn to express orally a range of meanings and emotions. We understand characters and therefore people better when we role-play, or "try on," their actions, seeing how it feels to do or say what the character did. When we create our own script from a piece of literature, we learn how to select its essence and how to get the meaning and tone across to others. Creating and performing a script is fun and highly motivational because others will see our performance and respond to it.

Scripting

Scripting usually involves selecting a scene or chapter from a book, eliminating extraneous material from it, and adding a narrator to set the scene and provide transitions or information that the characters do not speak in dialogue. Scripting changes the format of the writing into all speaking parts.

A chapter selected for a reader's theater script should have the following characteristics:

- The characters are interesting and quickly understood through their dialogue.

- The dialogue carries the action, leaving little need for supplementary information.

- The writing is clear and concrete, yet rich in the choice and placement of words.

- The scene will encourage others to want to change parts and seek other interpretations of the material.

- The scenes will stir the imagination and interest of the listeners.

Other characteristics you might look for include the following:

- The depth of emotion or characterization will be better understood through performance.

- The scene will be a good introduction to the rest of the book.

- The scene will give listeners a better understanding of an historical period, a contemporary problem, the people of another culture, or a new genre of literature.

- The scene will introduce listeners to an author or a series, enticing them to do more reading.

When you respond to a book by creating a reader's theater script, your goal is to capture the essence of the book or its conflicts through the chapter you select to script. If the script is read aloud, you will feel the power of performance, of hearing the words spoken with emotion. Short scripted pieces of stories should make us wonder what will happen to characters, how a problem will be resolved, or what will happen next and thus make us want to read the whole story.

Many novels do not lend themselves to easy adaptation without significant rewriting. Oftentimes, to unleash the power of a scene, you will have to leave out great hunks of the writing so as to uncover the essence of the scene for your listeners. If the narrator seems to have a very heavy reading load, you might consider using more than one narrator to keep the pacing lively. The Internet resources at the end of the chapter provide sites where scripts are available.

Role-Playing

Role-playing thrusts us inside a piece of literature, as we work to think and speak like the character we are playing. When a character is puzzling to you, when you would like to figure out why she reacted as she did to another character, find a partner and role-play the parts. In a two-person role-play, each person is forced to think of explanations for the

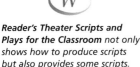

Reader's Theater Scripts and Plays for the Classroom not only shows how to produce scripts but also provides some scripts. Go to *www.teachingheart.net/ readerstheater.htm.*

actions and attitudes of his or her character—to think like the character. Or, if everyone in the class has read the same book, you could take the part of a character and be interviewed by the whole class, answering questions as that character. Interviewers might ask how you feel about taking care of your brother, whether you think your parents were fair, and so on. Another way to role-play is simply to have students enact the story, as the boxed feature The Drama Connection illustrates.

Using drama builds understanding and involvement. Seeing, doing, or touching helps us understand. Drama also provides the opportunity to repeat and review. When you have trouble understanding a characterization, role-play can help you figure out the character's thinking. Through involvement in drama, students cease being observers of a conflict in a text. Instead, they become active agents and participants in a real human dilemma, using language to work toward resolution of that dilemma.

To experience the power of role-play, find a scene in a book that puzzles or troubles you and start role-playing. Books that work well for role-playing or scripting include *The Giver* and *Number the Stars,* both by Lois Lowry; *Red Scarf Girl: A Memoir of the Cultural Revolution,* by Ji Li Jiang; *Ella Enchanted* and *Dave at Night,* both by Gail Carson Levine; *Freak the Mighty,* by Rodman Philbrick; *Bud, Not Buddy* and *The Watsons Go to Birmingham—1963,* both by Christopher Paul Curtis; *Tuck Everlasting,* by Natalie Babbitt; and *Roll of Thunder, Hear My Cry,* by Mildred D. Taylor.

The Drama Connection

It is always amazing when children who have been quoted in their school reports as hating reading fall in love with read-aloud and enthusiastically interact with text. This was the case in Rose Casement's (1998) classroom of children diagnosed with severe behavioral and emotional disabilities. Early years in skill-and-drill literacy programs had convinced them that they could not read. For many of them, *The Frog and Toad* stories by Arnold Lobel were a captivating segue into text. One day, as the teacher and students gathered on the floor for a read-aloud, Julia picked *Frog and Toad Are Friends* (1970) and Casement read the chapter called "The Story." Julia sat where she could see the text; as Casement read, she stopped and Julia filled in the words. This oral-to-print literacy teaching strategy promotes a focus on meaning, or the semantic cueing system. Julia responded enthusiastically.

In the story, Toad goes through several antics, trying to get an idea for a story. Everyone in the class cracked up when Toad stood on his head and later when he poured water on his head. They almost fell out of their seats when he hit his head on the wall. No one wanted to let go of the story.

Julia suddenly remembered that the class the year before had done a dramatization of another *Frog and Toad* story, "Spring." It was her idea to dramatize *Frog and Toad Are Friends,* and Casement suggested that the class focus on the part where Frog tells Toad the story they have created through their own actions.

Julia's four classmates joined in the excitement of the play. The teacher quickly turned to the story for possibilities. After the initial casting of Frog and Toad, the real work began. "OK, who will be the water?" "Who will be the wall?" And then there was the role of the narrator. As the play commenced, the water dutifully splashed, and the wall did its best to just stand flat. The part of the narrator was filled with each child in turn, some of whom could read the entire story and others who required various degrees of support from Casement. Everyone played his or her part and readily switched as they re-performed the story. Not only did everyone have fun; the students also saw the text come alive and realized that they could interact with it in a way that was meaningful for them. As Jeffrey Wilhelm (1997) suggests in *You Gotta BE the Book: Teaching Engaged and Reflective Reading with Adolescents,* using drama with reluctant and less proficient readers "may help such students enormously as we come to more fully understand actual processes of making meaning through reading" (p. 112).

The story plays that these students performed involved community building as part of the production. Each of the parts, even those that might have seemed mundane, had some fun aspect. The wall, after all, wasn't such a bad part when one remembered that Toad, as part of the story, was to pretend to hit his head on it. But the "lead roles" and "secondary roles" and even the role of a flat wall didn't seem to matter. It was being part of the drama that counted.

Interestingly, for the students in Casement's classroom, drama not only enhanced their engagement with text but also improved their interactions with the other students in the class. The activity of story play—and the requirements that came with it of active participation and consideration for others—helped build community.

Internet and Text Resources

1. **ARTSEDGE Teaching Materials: The National Arts and Education Information Network** provides links in an effort to get the arts and education together. Find it at

    http://artsedge.kennedy-center.org/teaching_materials/artsedge.html

2. **Reader's Theater Scripts and Plays for the Classroom** gives detailed steps for producing scripts as well as many reproducible scripts. Go to

    www.teachingheart.net/readerstheater.htm

3. **Reader's Theater/Language Arts for Teachers** provides a variety of scripts arranged by title. Find it at

    http://hometown.aol.com/rcswallow/index.html

4. **Classroom Read-Aloud Strategies** provides a set of seven strategies to use when reading aloud. Find it at

    http://clerccenter.gallaudet.edu/Literacy/readit45.html

References

Casement, Rose (1998). "The Impact of a Holistic Literacy Learning Environment for Children with Severe Multiple and Emotional/Behavioral Disabilities." Unpublished dissertation. University of Maine.

Chambers, Aidan (1996). *Tell Me: Children, Reading, and Talk.* York, ME: Stenhouse.

Claggett, Fran (1996). *A Measure of Success: From Assignment to Assessment in English Language Arts.* Portsmouth, NH: Heinemann.

Cummings, Pat, ed. (1992). *Talking with Artists—Volume 1.* New York: Bradbury.

—— (1995). *Talking with Artists—Volume 2.* New York: Simon & Schuster.

—— (1999). *Talking with Artists—Volume 3.* New York: Clarion.

Dudley-Marling, Curt, and Dennis Searle (1991). *When Students Have Time to Talk.* Portsmouth, NH: Heinemann.

Ernst, Karen (1994). *Picturing Learning.* Portsmouth, NH: Heinemann.

Greene, Maxine (1995). *Releasing the Imagination: Essays on Education, the Arts, and Social Change.* San Francisco: Jossey-Bass.

Griss, Susan (1998). *Minds in Motion: A Kinesthetic Approach to Teaching Elementary Curriculum.* Portsmouth, NH: Heinemann.

Hansen, Jane (1998). *When Learners Evaluate.* Portsmouth, NH: Heinemann.

Harwayne, Shelley (1999). *Lasting Impressions.* Portsmouth, NH: Heinemann.

Hubbard, Ruth Shagoury, and Karen Ernst, eds. (1996). *New Entries: Learning by Writing and Drawing.* Portsmouth, NH: Heinemann.

Keene, Ellin O., and Susan Zimmermann (1997). *Mosaic of Thought: Teaching Comprehension in a Reader's Workshop.* Portsmouth, NH: Heinemann.

Kohl, Herbert (1995). *Should We Burn Babar? Essays on Children's Literature and the Power of Stories.* New York: New Press.

Langer, Judith (1995). *Envisioning Literature: Literary Understanding and Literature Instruction.* New York: Teachers College Press.

Murray, Donald M. (1982). *Learning by Teaching: Selected Articles on Writing and Teaching.* Portsmouth, NH: Boynton/Cook.

Rosenblatt, Louise (1996). *Literature as Exploration.* New York: Modern Language Association [1938].

—— (1978). *The Reader, the Text, and the Poem.* Carbondale, IL: Southern Illinois University Press.

Short, Kathy, and Jerry Harste, with Carolyn Burke (1996). *Creating Classrooms for Authors and Inquirers.* Portsmouth, NH: Heinemann.

Short, Kathy G., Gloria Kauffman, and Leslie H. Hawn (2000). "'I Just Need to Draw': Responding to Literature Across Multiple Sign Systems." *The Reading Teacher 54,* 160–171.

Spiegel, M. (1995). "More Than Words: The Generative Power of Transmediation for Learning." *Canadian Journal of Education 20,* 455–475.

Trussell-Cullen, Alan (1999). "Traditional Tales: Portfolios from the Past—Time Capsules for the Future." Presentation to International Reading Association Conference, San Diego, May 2–7, 1999.

Webster, Renee (1996). "Literacy: A Never-Ending Story." *The Language Arts Journal of Michigan 12,* 40–44.

Whitin, Phyllis (1996). *Sketching Stories, Stretching Minds: Responding Visually to Literature.* Portsmouth, NH: Heinemann.

Wilhelm, Jeffrey D. (1997). *You Gotta BE the Book: Teaching Engaged and Reflective Reading with Adolescents.* New York: Teachers College Press.

Wolf, Dennie Palmer, and Dana Balick, eds. (1999). *Art Works!* Portsmouth, NH: Heinemann.

Children's Books

Allen, Pamela (1990). *Who Sank the Boat?* New York: Coward McCann.

Avi (1990). *The True Confessions of Charlotte Doyle.* New York: Orchard.

Babbitt, Natalie (1975). *Tuck Everlasting.* New York: Farrar, Straus & Giroux.

Björk, Christina (1985). *Linnea in Monet's Garden.* Illus. Lena Anderson. New York: R & S.

Browne, Anthony (1998). *Voices in the Park.* New York: DK Publishing.

Bunting, Eve (1997). *Ducky.* Illus. David Wisniewski. New York: Clarion.

Cleary, Beverly (1983). *Henry and Beezus.* Illus. Louis Darling. New York: Morrow.

Coles, Robert (1995). *The Story of Ruby Bridges.* Illus. George Ford. New York: Scholastic.

Collodi, Carlo (1914). *Pinocchio.* Philadelphia: Lippincott.

Curtis, Christopher Paul (1999). *Bud, Not Buddy.* New York: Delacorte.

—— (1995). *The Watsons Go to Birmingham—1963.* New York: Delacorte.

dePaola, Tomie (1989). *The Art Lesson.* New York: Putnam.

—— (1988). *Now One Foot, Now the Other.* New York: Putnam.

Fox, Mem (1988). *Koala Lou.* Illus. Pamela Lofts. San Diego: Voyager.

Garland, Sherry (1993). *The Lotus Seed.* Illus. Tatsuro Kiuchi. San Diego: Harcourt Brace.

Giff, Patricia Reilly (2000). *Nory Ryan's Song.* New York: Delacorte.

Glass, Andrew (1982). *Jackson Makes His Move.* New York: Frederick Warne.

Henkes, Kevin (1991). *Chrysanthemum.* New York: Greenwillow.

Jiang, Ji Li (1997). *Red Scarf Girl: A Memoir of the Cultural Revolution.* New York: HarperCollins.

Johnston, Tony (1994). *The Tale of Rabbit and Coyote.* Illus. Tomie dePaola. New York: Putnam.

Joosse, Barbara M. (1991). *Mama, Do You Love Me?* Illus. Barbara Lavallee. San Francisco: Chronicle.

Kaldhol, Marit, and Wenche Oyen (1987). *Goodbye Rune.* Trans. Michael Crosby-Jones. New York: Kane/Miller.

Kraus, Robert (1971). *Leo the Late Bloomer.* Illus. Jose Aruego. New York: Windmill.

Krull, Kathleen (1995). *Lives of the Artists: Masterpieces, Messes (and What the Neighbors Thought).* Illus. Kathryn Hewitt. San Diego: Harcourt Brace.

Lester, Helen (1988). *Tacky the Penguin.* Illus. Lynn Munsinger. Boston: Houghton Mifflin.

Levine, Gail Carson (1999). *Dave at Night.* New York: HarperCollins.

—— (1997). *Ella Enchanted.* New York: HarperCollins.

Lionni, Leo (1991). *Matthew's Dream.* New York: Knopf.

—— (1988). *Six Crows.* New York: Knopf [out of print].

—— (1963). *Swimmy.* New York: Knopf.

Lobel, Arnold (1970). *Frog and Toad Are Friends.* New York: HarperCollins.

Lowry, Lois (1993). *The Giver.* Boston: Houghton Mifflin.

—— (1989). *Number the Stars.* Boston: Houghton Mifflin.

Martin, Jacqueline Briggs (1998). *Snowflake Bentley.* Illus. Mary Azarian. Boston: Houghton Mifflin.

Martin, Rafe (1989). *Will's Mammoth.* Illus. Stephen Gammell. New York: Putnam.

McDonald, Megan. (1996). *My House Has Stars.* Illus. Peter Catalanotto. New York: Orchard.

Miller, William (1997). *Richard Wright and the Library Card.* Illus. Gregory Christie. New York: Lee & Low.

Miranda, Anne (1997). *To Market, To Market.* Illus. Janet Stevens. San Diego: Harcourt Brace.

Mochizuki, Ken (1993). *Baseball Saved Us.* Illus. Dom Lee. New York: Lee & Low.

Paterson, Katherine (1977). *Bridge to Terabithia.* New York: Crowell.

—— (1980). *Jacob Have I Loved.* New York: Crowell.

Philbrick, Rodman (1993). *Freak the Mighty.* New York: Scholastic.

Prelutsky, Jack (1976). *Nightmares—Poems to Trouble Your Sleep.* Illus. Arnold Lobel. New York: Greenwillow.

Ringgold, Faith (1991). *Tar Beach.* New York: Crown.

Rylant, Cynthia (1988). *All I See.* Illus. Peter Catalanotto. New York: Orchard.

Samton, Sheila White (1985). *The World from My Window.* New York: Crown.

Scieszka, Jon (1989). *The True Story of the 3 Little Pigs!* Illus. Lane Smith. New York: Penguin.

Sheldon, Dyan (1991). *The Whales' Song.* Illus. Gary Blythe. New York: Dial.

Spinelli, Jerry (1997). *Wringer.* New York: HarperTrophy.

Stewart, Sarah (1997). *The Gardener.* Illus. David Small. New York: Farrar, Straus & Giroux.

Taylor, Mildred D. (1976). *Roll of Thunder, Hear My Cry.* New York: Dial.

Turner, Ann (1998). *Drummer Boy: Marching to the Civil War.* Illus. Mark Hess. New York: HarperCollins.

Venezia, Michael (1988). *Rembrandt.* San Francisco: Children's Book Press.

Walsh, E. S. (1989). *Mouse Paint.* San Diego: Harcourt Brace.

Weiss, George, and Bob Thiele (1995). *What a Wonderful World.* Illus. Ashley Bryan. New York: Atheneum.

White, E. B. (1952). *Charlotte's Web.* Illus. Garth Williams. New York: Harper & Row.

Winter, Jeanette (1992). *Follow the Drinking Gourd.* New York: Knopf.

Woodson, Jacqueline (1997). *We Had a Picnic This Sunday Past.* Illus. Diane Greenseid. New York: Hyperion.

Wyeth, Sharon Dennis (1995). *Always My Dad.* Illus. Raúl Colón. New York: Knopf.

Sensory Details

Poets use details of the senses to help a reader see, hear, smell, touch, and even taste. In *Listen to the Rain,* when Bill Martin, Jr., and John Archambault say, "leaving all outdoors a muddle,/a mishy mushy muddy puddle," we can almost feel that mud squishing through our toes.

Figurative Language

Poets use similes, metaphors, personification, and other nonliteral descriptions to "provide clarification and intensity of thought," according to Mary Oliver (1998) in *Rules for the Dance: A Handbook for Writing and Reading Metrical Verse* (p. 67). Figurative language, which is at the heart of many poems, is present in the form of personification, simile, and metaphor in this Maya Angelou poem:

> ### I Love the Look of Words
>
> Popcorn leaps, popping from the floor
> of a hot black skillet
> and into mouth.
> Black words leap,
> snapping from the white
> page. Rushing into my eyes. Sliding
> into my brain which gobbles them
> the way my tongue and teeth
> chomp the buttered popcorn.
>
> When I have stopped reading,
> ideas from the words stay stuck
> in my mind, like the sweet
> smell of butter perfuming my
> fingers long after the popcorn
> is finished.
>
> I love the book and the look of words
> the weight of ideas that popped into my mind
> I love the tracks
> of new thinking in my mind.

("I Love the Look of Words" by Maya Angelou, copyright ©1993 by Maya Angelou, from SOUL LOOKS BACK IN WONDER by Tom Feelings. Used by permission of Dial Books for Young Readers, an imprint of Penguin Putnam Books for Young Readers, a division of Penguin Putnam Inc.)

Line Breaks and White Space

Another way poets make meaning is through the use of empty space and printed lines. By directing us where to pause and where to rush on, poets use line breaks to emphasize meaning. In Maya Angelou's poem, the way she separates adjectives from their noun and nouns from their prepositional phrase tells us what to pay attention to or give weight to. For instance, when she ends the line with "white," she makes us pause and wonder what will come after it. In the last stanza, when she ends the line with "tracks," the pause before "of new thinking in my mind" makes us experience the impact of reading on her.

Repetition

Poets often use the same phrases or words over and over again for emphasis and rhythmic pleasure. David McCord's "Five Chants, III" reads:

> The pickety fence
> The pickety fence

Give it a lick it's
The pickety fence
Give it a lick it's
A clickety fence
Give it a lick
It's a lickety fence
Give it a lick
Give it a lick
With a rickety stick
Pickety
Pickety
Pickety
Pick

(From ONE AT A TIME by David McCord. Copyright © 1952 by David McCord. By permission of Little, Brown and Company (Inc.).)

Compact Language

Poets distill language so that we get the essence of an experience. Sometimes the words bump into each other to create an impression. Douglas Florian is a master at distilling language. Although the poem "The Beaver" is but four words long, every word is packed with imagery and meaning:

Wood-chopper
Tree-dropper
Tail-flopper
Stream-stopper.

(Reprinted with permission of Harcourt, Inc. from *Mammalabilia: Poems and Paintings,* by Douglas Florian. Copyright © 2000 Douglas Florian.)

 he Many Types of Poetry

Poetry comes in many shapes and sizes. The types most often used with children are narrative poems, lyric poems, poems with special forms (including limericks, haiku, cinquains, and clerihews), free verse, concrete poetry, and nursery rhymes.

Narrative Poems

Narrative poems tell a story. Gary Soto often writes poetry in a narrative form, as he does in "Sarape" from **Canto Familiar.** It begins

It's itchy
Against my skin,
This sarape
In the backseat
Of our Chevy,
Faded Aztec rainbow
That was a hand-me-down
From a friend
Of a friend
That Papi no longer remembers.

(Reprinted with permission of Harcourt, Inc. from *Canto Familiar,* by Gary Soto. Copyright © 1995 Gary Soto.)

Diane Siebert's lovely picture book–length poem **Sierra,** the story of the mountain ranges, is told from the point of view of the mountain. It describes how the mountain was formed millions of years ago, what activities it views, and its worries about its future.

PoetryTeachers.com is packed with information on poems, poetry writing, and poetry teaching. Find it at www.poetryteachers.com.

Encourage students to browse through poetry books and share their favorites in small groups or as a class. Ashley Bryan (1996) reinforces the importance of reciting poetry: "Poetry is an oral art. Hearing a poem is as necessary to the art of poetry as hearing a song is necessary to the art of song. To know song only from sight-singing music is as limited an experience as knowing poetry only from sight-reading the words" (p. 222). Children respond to the oral and love to be part of orchestrated choral readings of poems. Because they can feel and hear the poetry, they make a connection to it. Some of my favorite classroom memories are of children reciting together David McCord's "The Pickety Fence" from *One at a Time* and chanting "What Night Would It Be?" from *You Read to Me, I'll Read to You,* by John Ciardi. They were totally immersed in the experience, moving their bodies to the beat of the words and expressing the exuberance and joy they felt from making music together.

Once children have become captivated by poetry, they are ready to try more sophisticated poetry and will willingly work to make it their own. In the hands of a skillful or enthusiastic teacher, sophisticated poetry is not beyond the reach or appreciation of even young students. Moving students to another level in the kinds of poetry used in the classroom calls for teacher modeling. Taking advantage of Vygotsky's zone of proximal development, teachers can aid children in moving beyond what they can do on their own to what they can accomplish with the help of others.

Give poetry a prominent place in your classroom, letting children hear it frequently. Slip it into the small spaces of the day, and let it work its magic on your students. Children share some of their thoughts on poetry in the boxed feature Children's Voices.

Children's Voices

Children like poetry because . . .

It's funny. —Drew, 2nd grade

It rhymes, is funny and crazy. —Janae, 6th grade

It sounds musical to my ears. —Trent, 6th grade

It comes from the heart. —Brentin, 6th grade

It's sweet and loving when I hear it. —Aloushia, 6th grade

I can make a rap out of it. —Angel, 6th grade

It is very deep. —Jasmin, 6th grade

The rhyme is fun. —Kent, 7th grade

A lot of thought is put into it. I like poems that relate to emotion and feelings.
—Chris, 7th grade

It's just thought. It doesn't have to have a plot or a main character. It's just itself.
—Camille, 7th grade

Poetry is soft and soothing to listen to. —Molly, 7th grade

It tells a story in a couple paragraphs or less. —Brittany, 7th grade

I like how they put feelings and emotions in a different point of view and make you see something so significant that it has a totally new meaning. —Maria, 7th grade

Funny, zany poems that make me laugh. —Jenny, 7th grade

Poems appeal to me when they point out certain things about something.
—Samantha, 8th grade

Children like poetry because . . .

I like poems that go slowly and smoothly. Ones that rhyme. —Matthew, 8th grade

Poetry only appeals to me when I can relate to it or it makes me feel something. —Chris, 8th grade

What appeals to me about poetry is eloquent words that are put together well. I like Robert Frost's poetry. —Erin, 8th grade

Some don't like it . . .

I hate poetry. I think it is pointless. —Billy, 7th grade

I don't like poetry. I had to memorize a poem out of the Outsider. *The poem was by Robert Frost.* —Jennifer, 7th grade

Other thoughts on poetry . . .

Right now I'm really into writing my own poems, not reading others. Because I think mine could be better than somebody that's getting paid. —Adrik-Dominique, 6th grade

I like poetry but don't really read a lot of poetry in school. My grandma always reads them to me. —Elizabeth, 7th grade

Poetry! I love it. I love reading it and writing. It's easy to read because it goes fast. —Sunny, 7th grade

I don't like nontraditional poetry but limericks are fun. —Carlyn, 7th grade

I like to write poems at home myself. —Eden, 7th grade

I like poetry in a way—funny, goofy poems. —Ashlynn, 7th grade

I enjoy poetry, although we don't spend much time with it at school so I don't really have memories of it. —Sara, 8th grade

Poetry can confuse me, but I like some of the funny silly poems by Shel Silverstein and others. —Hannah, 8th grade

How Poetry for Children Reflects a Changing World

Poetry, like other genres, reflects the changing sociocultural landscape of society, as well as its changing views of childhood. Contemporary poetry for children reveals trends in what is considered important to share with children, as well as what subject matter is considered appropriate for them to explore.

1. Poetry is directed more toward children's experience. Many poems have as their topic school, siblings, feelings, childhood experiences, pets, or friends. The world isn't presented to children so that they can see what it is like; it is shown from the child's point of view. This trend is easier to see if you compare a book of poetry written today to poetry written before 1950, such as the well-loved *A Child's Garden of Verse,* by Robert Louis Stevenson.

2. Poetry is written by a broader array of people, including children. More ethnically diverse poets are being published today, although the number still does not reflect the demographics of this country. Poems written in two languages are also being published; these collections are mentioned in Chapter 7. Children's voices are appearing more frequently, often in collections dealing with the hard social issues that are part of their lives.

CD-ROM

To find poets from diverse backgrounds, go to Favorite Authors and key in *poem.*

Paul Fleischman. Both books are written for two people to read aloud and so are perfect for performance. *It's Show Time: Poetry from the Page to the Stage,* by Allan Wolf, is filled with scripted poems and hints on enhancing student performance. Poems written from the point of view of children are also marvelous ones to perform. One such collection is Brod Bagert's *Let Me Be . . . The Boss: Poems for Kids to Perform.* Of course, any poems that are rhythmic or have a definite rhyme scheme work well too.

Sports

If sports-loving children need an enticement to read poetry, these books will do the trick. *Extra Innings: Baseball Poems,* selected by Lee Bennett Hopkins, is filled with energetic poems, illustrated with brilliant paintings by Scott Medlock. Arnold Adoff's *The Basket Counts* is packed with his exuberant poems about young people playing basketball. *Hoops,* by Robert Burleigh, is a picture book–length poem about playing a game of basketball. *For the Love of the Game: Michael Jordan and Me,* by Eloise Greenfield, is a lovely poem comparing Michael Jordan's love of the game of basketball to love of the game of life.

Science connections

Since both scientists and poets are close observers of nature, poetry makes a natural complement to science.

Natural world

Lee Bennett Hopkins's *Spectacular Science: A Book of Poems* contains poems about science and the questions it suggests. *Once Upon Ice: And Other Frozen Poems,* poems selected by Jane Yolen, shows students the power and beauty of ice in its many different configurations. Myra Cohn Livingston's *Sky Songs,* illustrated by Leonard Everett Fisher, is a stimulating and beautiful collection of poems that challenge our minds and enrich our visions of the universe. The poems Jane Yolen has selected for *Mother Earth, Father Sky: Poems of Our Planet* pay tribute to our fragile world. Frank Asch's *Cactus Poems* is about the desert, while his *Sawgrass Poems: A View of the Everglades* puts us in the heart of the Everglades in Florida. Kristine O'Connell George's *Old Elm Speaks: Tree Poems* engages us to view trees in original ways through poems laced with humor and imagination.

Animal world

Douglas Florian's *In the Swim: Poems and Paintings* and *On the Wing: Bird Poems and Paintings* will delight youngsters who are learning about fish or birds. *Weird Pet Poems,* compiled by Dilys Evans, and *Words with Wrinkled Knees: Animal Poems,* by Barbara Juster Esbensen, playfully involve students in new ways to think about animals. Alice Shertle's *How Now, Brown Cow?* is a collection of poems exclusively about cows. Some show us the cow's point of view, some remind us of the many aspects of a cow's life, and some simply make us laugh out loud. *The Originals: Animals That Time Forgot,* by Jane Yolen, is a book of story poems that intrigue and inform as we learn about animals that have hardly changed over centuries.

Social studies connections

Celebrating life/people/diversity

Joseph Bruchac's *The Circle of Thanks: Native American Poems and Songs of Thanksgiving* will help students understand that for American Indians, every day is a day to give thanks. *The Tree Is Older Than You Are: A Bilingual Gathering of Poems and Stories from Mexico,* edited by Naomi Shihab Nye, gives readers a taste of the everyday aspects of this culture. The poems in *All the Colors of the Race,* by Arnold Adoff, are written from the point of view of a child who has a white father and a black mother. *Bein' with You This Way,* by W. Nikola-Lisa, celebrates the diversity among people. *Canto Familiar,* by Gary Soto, focuses on the pleasures and woes that Mexican American children experience growing up.

Historical events

Ann Turner's *Grass Songs* reveals the intensity of the pioneer experience for the women who journeyed west. Many of the poems are in the voice of real women whose writings Turner read. Exposure to poems such as these gives children a more balanced view of what actually happened during the westward movement. *I Have Heard of a Land,* by Joyce Carol Thomas, is a book-length poem inspired by Thomas's family's westward journey to Oklahoma. This lovely poem is the story of black settlers surviving and thriving, a story not often told in history books. *The Ballad of the Pirate Queens,* by Jane Yolen, is based on two women who were arrested and tried in England in 1720 on charges of being pirates.

Selecting Poetry for the Classroom

As you select books of poetry to bring into the classroom, take into consideration what you know about your children and what you want to accomplish. You might want to answer the questions in the boxed feature Criteria for Evaluating Poetry.

In bringing poetry into the classroom, variety is essential. You don't want children to think that there is only one kind of poem, or only one subject written about in poetry, or

Criteria for Evaluating *Poetry*

1. **Appeal and impact.** Will the poem interest children? Can you see them becoming involved in the poetry? Do you think it will have an impact on them because of the power of the words, the topic or theme, or the presentation?

2. **Purpose.** Does the poem meet the purpose for which you want to use it? Does it infect children with a joy for language? Does it make them want to perform it? Does it enhance a topic? Will it make them want to know more?

3. **Complexity.** How understandable is the poetry? Will it be accessible to your students in terms of content, language, and structure?

4. **Uses of poetic elements.** Does the poem offer surprises? Is the language fresh or used in unusual and satisfying ways? Does the rhyme or rhythm give the poem an infectious quality? Does the figurative language provide clear ways to view the topic?

5. **Visual images.** Do the pictures complement and extend the words? Do the illustrations make the tone of the poetry collection obvious? In other words, if the poems are scary, can you tell from the illustrations? Are the illustrations ones children will want to look at more than once?

---

only one characteristic that marks all poems. So when selecting poems, keep in mind the categories in the boxed feature Ensuring Variety in the Poetry Selected for the Classroom.

It is often difficult to know where to begin to select poetry for your classroom. The boxed feature Favorite Authors and Anthologists of Children's Poetry provides a bit of information on some people you can count on to provide high-quality writing and strong appeal to children.

Ensuring Variety in the Poetry Selected for the Classroom

1. Mood and tone. Bring in funny poems, serious poems, sad poems, happy poems, poems that will soothe, and poems that will elicit hand-clapping.

2. Form. Bring in narrative poems, lyric poems, concrete poems, and poems written in specific formats. Bring in long poems and short poems.

3. Content. Bring in poetry about friendship, family, the moon, ice, animals, and counting. Use poetry with math, with science, with social studies, in conjunction with books read, and just for fun.

4. Poetic characteristics. Bring in poems with rhyme, without rhyme, with rhythm, in free verse, with strong images, with repetition, with onomatopoeia, with figurative language, and with sound devices.

5. Purpose. Bring in poetry that calls forth stories and experiences, poetry that opens students' eyes to new ways of seeing, poetry that validates what they are experiencing, poetry that creates a mood, poetry that shows them the wonder and beauty in a subject, poetry written in response to literature, and poetry that uses language in unusual ways.

6. Visual images. Bring in poetry illustrated in a variety of ways so that children can enjoy a range of images and artistic styles and media. Beautiful art can call out an even deeper response to the poetry and add to the children's delight.

7. Range of difficulty. Bring in poetry that is fun and easy to experience, as well as poetry that may at first seem just beyond the children's reach. *Talking to the Sun: An Illustrated Anthology of Poems for Young People,* edited by Kenneth Koch and Kate Farrell, is filled with every kind of poem and would be a good choice to broaden the range of sophistication in the poems read to a class. Another collection that can be used for the same purpose is Nancy Willard's *Step Lightly: Poems for the Journey.* When children read "Child on Top of a Greenhouse," by Theodore Roethke, they will fall in love with his work and want to hear more.

words in their poems and underline them. Are there other words they might want to use instead to better convey what they intended? As with other writing, the decision is theirs.

6. Ask students to find a poem (from the library or your bookshelves) that in some way relates to a book read in science, social studies, or math.

Internet and Text Resources

1. **A Pocketful of Rhymes** is full of poems for kids. Find it at

   www.hometown.aol.com/Bvsangl/pocket.html

2. **PoetryTeachers.com** is packed with information on poetry, poetry writing, and poetry teaching. Go to

   www.poetryteachers.com

3. **Bob's Byway: Glossary of Poetic Terms** does just what its name implies. Find it at

   www.poeticbyway.com/glossary.html

4. **ISLMC Poetry for Children** provides elementary and middle school teachers with resources that can be used across the curriculum. Find it at

   http://falcon.jmu.edu/%7eramseyil/poechild.htm

5. **Kristine O'Connell George's website** is inviting and kid-friendly. Go to

   www.kristinegeorge.com/

6. **Poetry Month: The Academy of American Poets** is a site where you can look up a particular poem or poet, as well as ideas on celebrating National Poetry Month. Find it at

   www.poets.org/npm

7. **The Academy of American Poets: Teaching Tips** provides creative suggestions for making poetry a more important part of school life. Go to

   www.poets.org/npm/teachtip.cfm

8. Heard, Georgia. *Awakening the Heart: Exploring Poetry in Elementary and Middle School.* Portsmouth, NH: Heinemann, 1999. Tools, examples, and stories useful for implanting poetry in the classroom and the hearts of children.

9. Hopkins, Lee Bennett. *Pass the Poetry, Please!* 3rd ed. New York: HarperCollins, 1998. Indispensable help in selecting poetry, involving children in poetry, and integrating poetry into the classroom.

10. Koch, Kenneth. *Rose, Where Did You Get That Red?* New York: Random, 1973. Wonderful ideas for introducing classic poems to children.

11. Koch, Kenneth. *Wishes, Lies, and Dreams: Teaching Children to Write Poetry.* New York: Vintage, 1971.

12. Larrick, Nancy. *Let's Do a Poem: Introducing Poetry to Children.* New York: Delacorte, 1991. A handbook full of lively ideas on how to bring children and poetry together in imaginative and interactive ways.

References

Bryan, Ashley (1996). "The Sound of the Voice in the Printed Word." In Amy A. McClure and Janice V. Kristo, eds., *Books That Invite Talk, Wonder, and Play.* Urbana, IL: NCTE.

—— (2001). Speech at the National Council of Teachers of English Spring Conference, Birmingham, Alabama, March 29–31, 2001.

Grimes, Nikki (2000). "The Power of Poetry." *Booklinks, 9,* 32–35.

Harrison, Barbara, and Gregory Maguire, eds. (1987). *Innocence & Experience: Essays and Conversations on Children's Literature.* New York: Lothrop, Lee & Shepard.

Hodgins, Francis, and Kenneth Silverman, eds. (1985). *Adventures in American Literature.* San Diego: Harcourt Brace.

Kennedy, X. J., and Barbara Kennedy (1982). *Knock at a Star: A Child's Introduction to Poetry.* Illus. Karen Ann Weinhaus. Boston: Little, Brown.

Oliver, Mary (1998). *Rules for the Dance: A Handbook for Writing and Reading Metrical Verse.* Boston: Houghton Mifflin.

Perfect, Kathy (1999). "From Rhyme and Reason: Poetry for the Heart and the Head." *The Reading Teacher 52,* 728–737.

Sloan, Glenna (1998). "Poetry and Linguistic Power." *Teaching and Learning Literature 8,* 69–79.

Children's Books

Abeel, Samantha (1994). *Reach for the Moon.* Illus. Charles R. Murphy. Duluth, MN: Pfeifer-Hamilton.

Adedjouma, Davida, ed. (1996). *The Palm of My Heart: Poetry by African American Children.* Illus. R. Gregory Christie. New York: Lee & Low.

Adoff, Arnold (1982). *All the Colors of the Race.* Illus. John Steptoe. New York: Beech Tree [out of print].

—— (2000). *The Basket Counts.* Illus. Michael Weaver. New York: Simon & Schuster.

—— (1997). *Love Letters.* Illus. Lisa Desimini. New York: Scholastic.

—— (1995). *Street Music: City Poems.* Illus. Karen Barbour. New York: HarperCollins.

—— (2000). *Touch the Poem.* Illus. Lisa Desimini. New York: Blue Sky.

Alarcon, Francisco X. (1998). *From the Bellybutton of the Moon and Other Summer Poems.* Illus. Maya Christina Gonzalez. San Francisco: Children's Book Press.

—— (1997). *Laughing Tomatoes and Other Spring Poems.* Illus. Maya Christina Gonzalez. San Francisco: Children's Book Press.

Asch, Frank (1998). *Cactus Poems.* Illus. Ted Lewin. San Diego: Harcourt Brace.

—— (1996). *Sawgrass Poems: A View of the Everglades.* Illus. Ted Lewin. San Diego: Harcourt Brace.

Bagert, Brod (1992). *Let Me Be . . . the Boss: Poems for Kids to Perform.* Illus. G. L. Smith. Honesdale, PA: Boyds Mills/Wordsong.

Begay, Shonto (1995). *Navaho: Visions and Voices Across the Mesa.* New York: Scholastic.

Berry, James (1994). *Celebration Song: A Poem.* Illus. Louise Brierley. New York: Simon & Schuster.

—— (1999). *Isn't My Name Magical? Sister and Brother Poems.* Illus. Shelly Hehenberger. New York: Simon & Schuster.

Bishop, Rudine Sims, ed. (1999). *Wonders: The Best Children's Poems of Effie Lee Newsome.* Illus. Lois Mailou Jones. Honesdale, PA: Boyds Mills.

Bodecker, N. M. (1976). *Hurry, Hurry, Mary Dear.* Illus. Eric Blegvad. New York: Atheneum.

—— (1974). *Let's Marry Said the Cherry.* New York: Atheneum [out of print].

Bruchac, Joseph (1996). *The Circle of Thanks: Native American Poems and Songs of Thanksgiving.* Illus. Murv Jacob. Mahwah, NJ: BridgeWater.

Burleigh, Robert (1997). *Hoops.* Illus. Stephen T. Johnson. San Diego: Harcourt Brace.

Ciardi, John (1970). *Someone Could Win a Polar Bear.* Illus. Edward Gorey. New York: Lippincott.

—— (1962). *You Read to Me, I'll Read to You.* Illus. Edward Gorey. New York: HarperTrophy.

Cullinan, Bernice E., ed. (1996). *A Jar of Tiny Stars: Poems by NCTE Award–Winning Poets.* Illus. Andi MacLeod. Honesdale, PA: Boyds Mills.

cummings, e. e. (1989). *hist whist.* Illus. Deborah Kogan Ray. New York: Crown [out of print].

Cumpian, Carlos (1994). *Latino Rainbow: Poems About Latino Americans.* Illus. Richard Leonard. Chicago: Children's Press.

Dahl, Roald (1986). *Dirty Beasts.* Illus. Quentin Blake. New York: Puffin.

—— (1982). *Revolting Rhymes.* Illus. Quentin Blake. New York: Knopf.

de Regniers, Beatrice Schenk, Eva Moore, Mary Michaels White, and Jan Carr, eds. (1988). *Sing a Song of Popcorn: Every Child's Book of Poems.* Illus. Marcia Brown et al. New York: Scholastic.

Dragonwagon, Crescent (1993). *Home Place.* Illus. Jerry Pinkney. New York: Aladdin.

Dunbar, Paul Laurence (1999). *Jump Back, Honey: The Poems of Paul Laurence Dunbar.* Illus. Ashley Bryan et al. New York: Jump at the Sun/Hyperion.

Esbensen, Barbara Juster (1997). *Words with Wrinkled Knees: Animal Poems.* Honesdale, PA: Wordsong/Boyds Mills.

Evans, Dilys (1997). *Weird Pet Poems.* Illus. Jacqueline Rogers. New York: Simon & Schuster.

Feelings, Tom (1993). *Soul Looks Back in Wonder.* New York: Puffin.

Fleischman, Paul (2000). *Big Talk: Poems for Four Voices.* Illus. Beppe Giacobbe. Boston: Candlewick.

—— (1985). *I Am Phoenix: Poems for Two Voices.* Illus. Ken Nutt. New York: Harper.

—— (1988). *Joyful Noise: Poems for Two Voices.* Illus. Eric Beddows. New York: Harper.

Fletcher, Ralph (1999). *Relatively Speaking: Poems about Family.* Illus. Walter Lyon Krudup. New York: Orchard.

Florian, Douglas (1994). *Bing Bang Boing: Poems and Drawings.* San Diego: Harcourt Brace.

—— (1997). *In the Swim: Poems and Paintings.* San Diego: Harcourt Brace.

—— (1998). *Insectlopedia: Poems and Paintings.* San Diego: Harcourt Brace.

—— (1999). *Laugh-eteria: Poems and Drawings.* San Diego: Harcourt Brace.

—— (2000). *Mammalabilia: Poems and Paintings.* San Diego: Harcourt Brace.

—— (1996). *On the Wing: Bird Poems and Paintings.* San Diego: Harcourt Brace.

Frost, Robert (1978). *Stopping by Woods on a Snowy Evening.* Illus. Susan Jeffers. New York: Dutton.

George, Kristine O'Connell (1999). *Little Dog Poems.* Illus. June Otani. New York: Clarion.

—— (1998). *Old Elm Speaks: Tree Poems.* Illus. Kate Kiesler. New York: Clarion.

Graham, Joan Bransfield (1999). *Flicker Flash.* Illus. Nancy Davis. Boston: Houghton Mifflin.

Greenfield, Eloise (1997). *For the Love of the Game: Michael Jordan and Me.* Illus. Jan Spivey Gilchrist. New York: HarperCollins.

Grimes, Nikki (1998). *A Dime a Dozen.* Illus. Angelo. New York: Dial.

—— (1994). *Meet Danitra Brown.* Illus. Floyd Cooper. New York: Mulberry.

—— (1999). *My Man Blue.* Illus. Jerome Lagarrigue. New York: Dial.

—— (1978). *Something on My Mind.* Illus. Tom Feelings. New York: Dial [out of print].

Harrison, David L. (2000). *Farmer's Garden: Rhymes for Two Voices.* Illus. Arden Johnson-Petrov. Honesdale, PA: Boyds Mills.

Hoberman, MaryAnn (1991). *Fathers, Mothers, Sisters, Brothers: A Collection of Family Poems.* Illus. Marylin Hafner. Boston: Little, Brown.

—— (1998). *The Llama Who Had No Pajama: 100 Favorite Poems.* Illus. Betty Fraser. San Diego: Harcourt Brace.

—— (1994) *My Song Is Beautiful: Poems and Pictures in Many Voices.* Boston: Little, Brown.

Holbrook, Sara (1996). *Am I Naturally This Crazy?* Honesdale, PA: Boyds Mills.

—— (1996). *The Dog Ate My Homework.* Honesdale, PA: Boyds Mills.

—— (1996). *I Never Said I Wasn't Difficult.* Honesdale, PA: Boyds Mills.

—— (1998). *Walking on the Boundaries of Change: Poems of Transition.* Honesdale, PA: Boyds Mills.

Hopkins, Lee Bennett, ed. (1969). *Don't You Turn Back: Poems by Langston Hughes.* New York: Knopf [out of print].

——, ed. (1993). *Extra Innings: Baseball Poems.* Illus. Scott Medlock. San Diego: Harcourt Brace.

——, ed. (1999). *Lives: Poems About Famous Americans.* Illus. Leslie Staub. New York: HarperCollins.

——, ed. (1988). *Side by Side: Poems to Read Together.* Illus. Hilary Knight. New York: Simon & Schuster.

——, ed. (1999). *Spectacular Science: A Book of Poems.* Illus. Virginia Halstead. New York: Simon & Schuster.

——, ed. (1984). *Surprises.* New York: HarperTrophy.

——, ed. (2000). *Yummy! Eating Through a Day.* Illus. Renée Flower. New York: Simon & Schuster.

Horton, Joan (1999). *Halloween Hoots and Howls.* Illus. Joann Adinolfi. New York: Holt.

Hubbell, Patricia (1998). *Boo! Halloween Poems and Limericks.* Illus. Jeff Spackman. Tarrytown, New York: Marshall Cavendish.

Izuki, Steven (1994). *Believers in America: Poems about Americans of Asian and Pacific Islander Descent.* Illus. Bill Fukuda McCoy. Chicago: Children's Press.

Jacobs, Leland B. (1993). *Is Somewhere Always Far Away? Poems about Places.* Illus. Jeff Kaufman. New York: Holt [out of print].

Johnson, Angela (1998). *The Other Side: Shorter Poems.* New York: Orchard.

Johnston, Tony (1996). *My Mexico~México Mío.* Illus. F. John Sierra. New York: Philomel.

Kennedy, X. J. (1997). *Uncle Switch: Loony Limericks.* Illus. John O'Brien. New York: McElderry.

Koch, Kenneth, and Kate Farrell, eds. (1985). *Talking to the Sun: An Illustrated Anthology of Poems for Young People.* New York: Metropolitan Museum of Art and Holt.

Kuskin, Karla (1994). *City Dog.* New York: Clarion.

—— (1980). *Dogs & Dragons, Trees & Dreams.* New York: HarperTrophy [out of print].

—— (1998). *The Sky Is Always in the Sky.* Illus. Isabelle Dervaux. New York: Geringer.

Larrick, Nancy, ed. (1988). *Cats Are Cats.* Illus. Ed Young. New York: Philomel.

——, ed. (1970). *I Heard a Scream in the Street: Poetry by Young People in the City.* New York: Evans.

—— (1990). *Mice Are Nice.* Illus. Ed Young. New York: Philomel.

Lauture, Denizé (1992). *Father and Son.* Illus. Jonathan Green. New York: Paperstar.

Lewis, J. Patrick (1998). *Boshblobberbosh: Runcible Poems for Edward Lear.* Illus. Gary Kelley. San Diego: Harcourt Brace.

—— (1998). *Doodle Dandies: Poems That Take Shape.* Illus. Lisa Desimini. New York: Atheneum.

—— (2000). *Freedom Like Sunlight: Praisesongs for Black Americans.* Illus. John Thompson. Mankato, MN: Creative.

Litz, A. Walton, and Christopher McGowen, eds. (1986). *The Collected Poems of William Carlos Williams: Volume I, 1909–1939.* New York: New Directions.

Livingston, Myra Cohn, ed. (1995). *Call Down the Moon: Poems of Music.* New York: McElderry [out of print].

—— (1996). *Festivals.* Illus. Leonard Everett Fisher. New York: Holiday.

——, ed. (1987). *I Like You, If You Like Me: Poems of Friendship.* New York: McElderry.

—— (1984). *Sky Songs.* Illus. Leonard Everett Fisher. New York: Holiday.

Locker, Thomas (1998). *Home: A Journey Through America.* San Diego: Harcourt Brace.

Martin, Bill, Jr., and John Archambault (1988). *Listen to the Rain.* Illus. James Endicott. New York: Holt.

Marzollo, Jean (1995). *Sun Song.* Illus. Laura Regan. New York: HarperCollins.

McCord, David (1974). *One at a Time.* New York: Little, Brown [out of print].

Merriam, Eve (1985). *Blackberry Ink.* Illus. Hans Wilhelm. New York: Morrow.

—— (1997). *Higgle Wiggle: Happy Rhymes.* Illus. Hans Wilhelm. New York: Mulberry.

—— (1996). *The Inner City Mother Goose.* Illus. David Diaz. New York: Simon & Schuster.

—— (1964). *It Doesn't Always Have to Rhyme.* New York: Atheneum.

—— (1998). *What in the World?* Illus. Barbara J. Phillips-Duke. New York: Harper Festival.

—— (1996). *You Be Good & I'll Be Night: Jump-on-the-Bed Poems.* Illus. Karen Lee Schmidt. New York: Mulberry.

Mora, Pat (1996). *Confetti: Poems for Children.* Illus. Enrique O. Sanchez. New York: Lee & Low.

Moss, Jeff (1997). *Bone Poems.* Illus. Tom Leigh. New York: Workman.

Myers, Christopher (1999). *Black Cat.* New York: Scholastic.

Myers, Walter Dean (1993). *Brown Angels: An Album of Pictures and Verse.* New York: HarperCollins.

National Museum of the American Indian, ed. (1999). *When the Rain Sings: Poems by Young Native Americans.* New York: Simon & Schuster.

Nikola-Lisa, W. (1994). *Bein' with You This Way.* Illus. Michael Bryant. New York: Lee & Low.

Nye, Naomi Shihab, ed. (2000). *Salting the Ocean: 100 Poems by Young Poets.* Illus. Ashley Bryan. New York: Greenwillow.

——, ed. (1995). *The Tree Is Older Than You Are: A Bilingual Gathering of Poems and Stories from Mexico.* New York: Simon & Schuster.

Okutoro, Lydia Omolola, ed. (1999). *Quiet Storm: Voices of Young Black Poets.* New York: Jump at the Sun.

O'Neill, Mary (1989). *Hailstones and Halibut Bones.* Illus. John Wallner. New York: Doubleday.

Oram, Hiawyn (1993). *Out of the Blue: Poems about Color.* Illus. David McKee. New York: Hyperion.

Paul, Ann Whitford (1999). *All by Herself.* Illus. Michael Steirnagle. San Diego: Browndeer.

Prelutsky, Jack (1993). *The Dragons Are Singing Tonight.* Illus. Peter Sis. New York: Greenwillow.

—— (1980). *The Headless Horseman Rides Tonight: More Poems to Trouble Your Sleep.* Illus. Arnold Lobel. New York: Greenwillow.

—— (1980). *Rolling Harvey down the Hill.* Illus. Victoria Chess. New York: Greenwillow.

Rochelle, Belinda, ed. (2000). *Words of Wisdom: A Treasury of African-American Poetry and Art.* New York: HarperCollins.

Rosen, Michael J., ed. (1992). *Home: A Collaboration of Thirty Distinguished Authors and Illustrators of Children's Books to Aid the Homeless.* Illus. Aliki et al. New York: Zolotow.

Shertle, Alice (1994). *How Now, Brown Cow?* Illus. Amanda Schaffer. San Diego: Browndeer.

Siebert, Diane (1991). *Sierra.* Illus. Wendell Minor. New York: HarperTrophy.

Silverstein, Shel (1974). *Where the Sidewalk Ends.* New York: Harper & Row.

Soto, Gary (1995). *Canto Familiar.* Illus. Annika Nelson. San Diego: Harcourt Brace.

Steptoe, Javaka (1997). *In Daddy's Arms I AM TALL: African Americans Celebrating Fathers.* New York: Lee & Low.

Stevenson, Robert Louis (1905). *A Child's Garden of Verse.* Illus. Jesse W. Smith. New York: Scribners.

Strickland, Dorothy S., and Michael R. Strickland, eds. (1994). *Families: Poems Celebrating the African American Experience.* Honesdale, PA: Boyds Mills.

Strickland, Michael R., ed. (1997). *My Own Song and Other Poems to Groove To.* Honesdale, PA: Boyds Mills.

——, ed. (1993). *Poems That Sing to You.* Honesdale, PA: Boyds Mills.

Thayer, Ernest (1901). *Casey at the Bat.* New York: Amsterdam.

Thomas, Joyce Carol (1993). *Brown Honey in Broomwheat Tea.* Illus. Floyd Cooper. New York: HarperCollins.

—— (1998). *I Have Heard of a Land.* Illus. Floyd Cooper. New York: HarperCollins.

Turner, Ann (1993). *Grass Songs.* Illus. Barry Moser. San Diego: Harcourt Brace [out of print].

Viorst, Judith (1981). *If I Were in Charge of the World and Other Worries: Poems for Children and Their Parents.* Illus. Lynn Cherry. New York: Atheneum.

Willard, Nancy, ed. (1998). *Step Lightly: Poems for the Journey.* San Diego: Harcourt Brace.

—— (1981). *A Visit to William Blake's Inn: Poems for Innocent and Experienced Travelers.* Illus. Alice Provensen and Martin Provensen. San Diego: Harcourt Brace [out of print].

Wilson, Gina (1994). *Prowlpuss.* Illus. David Parkins. Cambridge, MA: Candlewick.

Wolf, Allan (1990). *It's Show Time: Poetry from the Page to the Stage.* Asheville, NC: Poetry Alive!

Wong, Janet S. (2000). *Night Garden: Poems from the World of Dreams.* Illus. Julie Paschkis. New York: McElderry.

—— (1999). *The Rainbow Hand: Poems About Mothers and Children.* Illus. Jennifer Hewitson. New York: McElderry.

Yolen, Jane (1995). *The Ballad of the Pirate Queens.* Illus. David Shannon. San Diego: Harcourt Brace.

—— (1996). *Mother Earth, Father Sky: Poems of Our Planet.* Illus. Jennifer Hewitson. Honesdale, PA: Boyds Mills.

—— (1997). *Once Upon Ice: And Other Frozen Poems.* Illus. Jason Stemple. Honesdale, PA: Wordsong/Boyds Mills.

—— (1996). *The Originals: Animals That Time Forgot.* Illus. Ted Lewin. New York: Philomel.

—— (1996). *Sacred Places.* Illus. David Shannon. San Diego: Harcourt Brace.

—— (1995). *Water Music.* Illus. Jason Stemple. Honesdale, PA: Boyds Mills.

The Context of Children's Literature

Context refers to situation, environment, circumstance, or setting. When we are immersed in a familiar environment or context, like our home, its trappings are almost invisible to us. When someone we don't know very well comes to visit, our view changes dramatically. Suddenly, we see clutter, and every flaw is highlighted. At this point, we're looking at our place of residence through a new lens—a fresh and more critical lens. Our familiarity with our home allows us not to see its flaws. That view of our home is partly accurate, and there is nothing wrong with it—but it is not the whole picture. Our home also has the flaws and imperfections we see when we look at it through the new lens of another person's perspective. Of course, this more dispassionate and critical perspective is not the whole picture of our house either.

A similar limitation of perspective occurs in our reading; we see only part of the picture. When we read, we read through our own lens, which is fine. However, the students in our classes are not reading through our perspective; they are reading through their own lenses. As teachers, we need to try to see the literature we use in the classroom through as many lenses as we can. We need to read through the richest, most complex perspective available to us, so that, by choosing the best literature available to share with them, we can help our students do the same thing. This chapter provides tools to help you see literature more fully—not just through your familiar stance, but through fresh and more critical eyes.

In addition to widening our own lenses as readers, we also have to be aware that books written for children incorporate assumptions and world views that reflect the circumstances in which they were created—the context. For children's literature, this context includes the author's world view, the time period in which the book was written, publishing parameters at the time, contemporary notions of children's literature, and, of course, societal attitudes. In order to be conscious of what we are teaching through children's books and how these books can affect children, we must keep in mind the context in which they were written and look closely at what implied or hidden ideas these books contain. Through literature, children are taught what society values, even though those values may not be explicitly stated. It is important to be aware of all the implied messages books contain, because they may validate or change the way children see themselves and the world.

How Books Can Affect Children

Herbert Kohl (1995), who writes widely about educational issues, describes the deep impact books have on children:

> I believe that what is read in childhood not only leaves an impression behind but also influences the values, and shapes the dreams, of children. It can provide negative images and stereotypes and cut off hopes and limit aspirations. It can erode self-respect through overt and covert racism or sexism. It can also help young people get beyond family troubles, neighborhood violence, stereotyping and prejudice—all particulars of their lives that they have no control over—and set their imaginations free. (pp. 61–62)

Books validate for children that their lives are normal and that they are part of the culture. If they see dogs and cats in books, they accept them as appropriate animals to have for pets. If they see only two-parent families, they might begin to question whether something is wrong with their single-parent family. If they see only houses with white picket fences, they may come to believe that living in an apartment or in a city neighborhood is less acceptable. Even though I lived in a two-parent family, I remember thinking that something was wrong with my family because we were not like the perfect family in *Dick and Jane* stories. In that family, no one ever argued, no one ever had a temper tantrum, and no one ever worried about money. Everyone seemed happy all the time. I knew my family wasn't like that, and I worried that something was wrong with my family. Children expect the world as they know it to be represented in some of the books they read. If they see no reflections of themselves or the world they live in, they begin to wonder about themselves.

Not only does literature reflect society; it also helps shape society by suggesting that the institutions and people it shows are reflective of the norm. Children take what is written in books very seriously. They believe that books show truth—that the words would not be in print if they weren't true. Thus, if people of color are shown only in subservient roles, children internalize that view. If only women are shown doing housework, they believe that is the natural order. Children learn from books what behaviors are considered appropriate for males and females, children and adults. Books serve as a touchstone to which children compare their realities and from which they form their sense of the world. When adults select books and formulate ways to discuss books, they need to be aware that children see books as reflecting how the world really is and should be.

The views of educator, theorist, and author Louise Rosenblatt are discussed extensively in *Literature as Exploration,* first published in 1938 and reprinted in 1996. She points out that children are not aware of all the things they take away from literature or even the things they select to pay attention to. In her discussion of the interaction of the reader and the text, Rosenblatt (1996) says, "The reader is . . . immersed in a creative process that goes on largely below the threshold of awareness. . . . [The reader] is not aware of the individual responses or of much of the process of selection and synthesis that goes on as his eyes scan the page" (p. 54). Thus, teachers and adults need to find ways to make students aware of how and why they form impressions about a book.

The first step in looking at what our society values and what it teaches children through the books written for them is to examine our own assumptions and beliefs. Before we can see with a fresh or critical eye, we have to be aware of what makes up a world view and what it means to look at the world through one.

CD-ROM

To learn about the many aspects involved in using literature in the classroom, as reflected in this text's References, do a CD-ROM word search for *literature.*

Recognizing Our Own World Views

At birth, not only are we stamped with the genetic patterns of our parents, which determine our physical characteristics; we also are born into belief systems about the way people behave; what's appropriate for girls and boys; how to view people of our own race and those of other races, religions, and cultures; and what to think about people who live in a different kind of environment, such as the city, the farm, the suburbs, or the mountains. Children come to school wrapped in the amniotic sac of their culture and their family. If school validates their background by building learning around their culture and their class, they assume that this picture reflects the world. If school does not validate their background, they become aware that they are different, and they may not know how to enter into the belief system and assumptions that undergird the educational system.

When we are surrounded by people who view the world as we do, we believe that our views are natural and normal. For instance, most of us are immersed in the belief in hierarchical institutions such as school, church, and government. We view some people in these institutions as more important than others and as capable of knowing more than others. We believe that a hierarchy with one person at the top is the normal structure for institutions. At school, the principal is in charge, teachers are next in line, and students are at the bottom of the hierarchy. We call this hierarchical view of the world a "common sense" view because it is the view we know best.

The Limits of Our Ability to "See"

My world view was influenced by the books I read and what I was taught in school. I never questioned beliefs that reflected the Western view of the world. I learned that Columbus "discovered" America, never wondering why the indigenous people who already lived here didn't count. In history texts, I learned that westward expansion was a good thing because the land would be inhabited by people who were "civilized," bringing "progress" to the area. I accepted the idea that progress was measured in terms of material wealth, buildings, and technology, without examining the assumptions beneath this belief—that connections to other people, spiritual growth, and living in harmony with the earth were not important components of progress.

At that time (late 1950s), I still was not aware of the racism and sexism that were rampant in our society. In the early 1960s, when I went to college, I didn't wonder why females could not wear slacks to class at Michigan State University or why teaching, nursing, and secretarial careers were the only professions really open to women. That's just the way it was. I didn't wonder why I lived only a few miles from Detroit but never saw any people of color in my suburb. I didn't realize that I was, in fact, surrounded by racism.

Now, some 40 years later, I can look back and easily see how racism and sexism were embedded in the fabric of our society. Even the books I read as a child, I can now see, were blatantly racist. But when I read such books as the *Bobbsey Twins* series, I found nothing out of the ordinary in them. No one pointed out the racial stereotypes. I didn't "see" them with a critical perspective. For instance, in *The Bobbsey Twins in Eskimo Land,* by Laura Lee Hope, one such passage reads:

> Black Dinah, the jolly old cook of the Bobbsey family, came in from the kitchen just then with a plate of home-made cookies in her hand.
>
> [Responding to a picture Flossie had drawn] "All dat ice an' snow look like wintah, an' no mistake. An' what's dis here thing?" she asked, pointing to the igloo. "One ob dim iggles Ah hears tell about?"
>
> Flossie chuckled, and even Nan had to laugh.
>
> "Not iggle, Dinah—igloo," the taller girl corrected. (p. 2)

Although now the book's obvious depiction of the children as superior to their servant jumps out at me, I didn't notice it as a child. The demeaning dialect, which seems to be a white person's idea of how black servants would speak, didn't seem unusual to me, since I had never met anyone black and never heard any dialect other than a Midwestern Caucasian one. Nor did I notice that the only roles black people had in this series were as servants or workers in menial jobs.

The concept of racism was foreign to me as a child. I assumed that I led a "normal, average" life, not realizing that "normal" is actually based on constructs that are gradually developed by a society. We all carry around with us a set of assumptions; we see the world through the lens of these assumptions. Thus, it is very difficult to extricate ourselves from society's precepts and get a different look at the world. One intent of this chapter is to help you uncover some of your own assumptions so that you can be aware of them in your teaching. The process is like looking at your home through someone else's eyes so as to see it more freshly. But the intent is also to help you see other world views so that you can understand how people different from you might react to portrayals in books—to give you a glimpse of the racism, sexism, and classism that are sometimes present in books written for children. Our job as teachers is to reach as many of our students as possible. To do this, we need to be aware of when and why students feel shut out of a classroom or a book and the implications this feeling may have for their education and their sense of the world.

How World Views Affect Reading

Readers take from society, both consciously and unconsciously, a belief system about themselves and about their culture. This belief system creates around them a bubble through which they view the world. Because they are inside the bubble, they often are not aware of the colorings and shadings that the bubble casts on whatever they view through it. As Kathleen McCormick (1994) writes, "[Since] we read a text in our own time, not in the time in which it was written, . . . we read it with questions, anxieties and interests that come into existence because of our own particular places in history" (p. 80).

She explains further, "A text is always a site of struggle: it may try to privilege [validate] a particular reading position as 'natural,' but because readers are subjects in their own histories, they may not produce that seemingly privileged reading" (p. 69). Readers are not absolutely autonomous either. Because of this lack of autonomy, "Like the texts they read, they too are sites of struggle, caught up in cultural determinants that they did not create and in which they strive to make meaning" (p. 69). Thus, as a reader today, I often view literature through the bubble, or perspective, of being a parent. Themes of family, communication, abandonment, and sibling relationships leap out at me, even though they may be secondary to another theme.

Oftentimes teachers expect students to just look at the purpose for which the author wrote the book and not respond from their own histories. For example, if students reading *The Indian in the Cupboard,* by Lynne Reid Banks, were offended by the stereotypical portrayal of the Indian, a teacher might say that the author didn't mean anything by that portrayal and tell students not to react to things the author didn't consciously intend. The teacher might suggest that they focus on the literary elements or the story grammar and not discuss those disturbing issues, thus telling students that those issues have nothing to do with literary quality. That is what McCormick means by a privileged reading. Too often teachers expect students to read in only one way—their way. We must realize that students bring their full histories, experiences, and feelings with them when they read. If we expect students to find and create meaning in their reading worlds, we must let them start with their own experiences and responses.

Children's Literature as More Than a Story

Beneath the surface of the words and pictures, children's books contain an array of information and messages. Among the elements embedded in literature are the author's world view, societal constructs, and evidence of society's attitudes about such issues as racism, sexism, and classism.

Because all these elements are present in books, when we read books to children we are telling them what is important in the world and what to pay attention to in our culture. Through books, we are exposing them to a belief system that we have validated as important. When we share books, they assume that we value what the books emphasize. We are passing on to them ways to see themselves, other people, and the world.

The Author's World View

Literature is written by people firmly embedded in a particular culture, society, gender, race, and often religion. From the author's place at the intersection of these entities, a book is created. Authors notice things that they have learned are important; many don't see the things that their particular society does not value. The content of books directly reflects the society in which the books are produced. For instance, in *Grandpa's Town,* by Takaaki Nomura, a man and his grandson go to the bath house to enjoy the company of the other men in town. This book was published in Japan, where men bathing together is viewed as a normal activity—a view that would not prevail in an American setting. Indeed, the book is about a grandson bonding with his grandfather through an activity based on comradeship and community.

In addition to reflecting the society, authors' and artists' world views also reflect what they personally view as important enough to write about or draw. Babette Cole, for instance, loves to challenge our stereotypical views of people. In *Drop Dead,* she explodes every stilted notion we have of old people by showing Gran and Grandad as adventurous risk-takers with a great sense of humor. In *Prince Cinders,* she turns the Cinderella story on its head. The book starts with a princess looking for the prince she is enamored with and ends with Prince Cinders's big, hairy, and obnoxious brothers turning into house fairies, who spend their time doing housework. Because writers and artists draw from their own experiences, they often put women and men only in traditional roles or show only white, middle-class children. Until about 30 years ago, social and economic logistics made it difficult for women and minorities to get published, so little was written by or about them. As our culture extends authorship, this picture is changing. We need to remember, and remind our students, that all authors write from a point in time and that there is *always* a person beneath the words, a person whose attitudes and belief systems are reflected in his or her books.

Societal Constructs

Literature, like every other cultural artifact, carries embedded messages based on the constructs of the society. In Western thinking, for example, the concept of a hierarchy is used to explain the universe. The fact that those above have dominance over those lower on the ladder leads to the belief that humans have dominance over animals. But the whole idea of a hierarchy is nothing more than a theoretical construct—a concept put together to explain how the parts of the world work together and to explain who is in charge.

When we became grandparents we retired

Gran and Grandad are active, fun-loving seniors in this irreverent story by Babette Cole.
(From DROP DEAD by Babette Cole, copyright © 1996 by Babette Cole. Used by permission of Alfred A. Knopf Children's Books, a division of Random House, Inc.)

Not all cultures and societies use the same constructs to explain the universe, and many don't see the universe as a hierarchy. For instance, in the picture book *Father Sky and Mother Earth,* by Oodgeroo, an Aboriginal woman in Australia, the earth and its plants and animals are seen as entities helping each other. The book says,

> Rock created Mountains and Hills to protect his servants [Trees, Birds, Animals, Reptiles, and Insects] from the cold winds of Gale, Cyclone and Tornado. And Tree created Plants and Grass and Flowers. And Animals, Reptiles and Insects created more Animals, Reptiles and Insects. And so on. . . . And they were all very happy creating and balancing and loving and living and helping one another. (p. 16)

Vestiges of Racism, Sexism, and Classism

CD-ROM

Do a word search for *racism* to see how this issue surfaces in Invitations, References, and works by Favorite Authors.

As a country, we pride ourselves on providing opportunities for everyone and treating everyone in an equal manner. We believe that we are a classless society because movement from one class to another is possible. Yet because we each see through our own world view, it is difficult to determine how prevalent racism, sexism, and classism are in our society. And, of course, whatever is in the society at large is reflected in books. The racism, sexism, or classism found in books today is rarely intentional. However, if we don't know how to see situations and events through others' eyes, how do we recognize inherent racism, sexism, and classism? How do we know what will offend people? How do we know when others will feel that they have been wrongly or unfairly portrayed? Many times, the majority truly has no idea of what is offensive; this understanding does not come easily or all at once.

Just after I had studied stereotypes of American Indians and thought hard about *The Indian in the Cupboard*, by Lynne Reid Banks, I went to a work session of a national organization. Three of us were selecting proposals for programs about literature for an upcoming conference. One of the women in the group turned to me and said: "Can you believe it! This person wants to present a session on Southern literature and the impact that losing a war has had on the South. She claims the South is the only section of the country that has lost a war on its own soil."

I sat silent, stretching to figure out why this was offensive. Fortunately, the woman continued, "I'm sure American Indians don't feel that way, or the Mexicans who lived on and lost their land in areas like Arizona and New Mexico."

I was truly taken aback, because I had caught myself in a limited world view. History books tend to only "count" wars that involve primarily white people. No name has been given to the seizing of American Indian lands. The taking of Mexican land in the Treaty of Guadalupe-Hidalgo often isn't counted as a war on "our own land" because the land was taken from people of color.

The intent of this chapter is to uncover some of the ways in which we have been trained to "see." An important part of the process is to look at scenarios through others' eyes, just as we might look at our house through someone else's eyes. As teachers, we must keep in mind that just because something is not offensive to us does not mean it won't offend our students and their families. Remember, as McCormick tells us, that we all have different histories and experiences.

According to Audre Lorde (1992), poet and critic, "Racism/sexism/classism is the belief in the inherent superiority of one race/gender/class over all others and thereby the right to dominance" (p. 402). Racism, sexism, and classism seem to be built on expectations, selection, and power. Those who view a group through a distorted or incomplete prism have expectations about how members of that group will behave. Women might be seen as emotional, and thus disqualified from making tough decisions that must be based on a "rational" or logical approach. People in parallel cultures (a term Virginia Hamilton [in Harris, 1996] offered as a replacement for *minority cultures* because it is less hierarchical) might be seen as lazy or less intelligent, and thus disqualified from positions of power. People living in poverty might be seen as unmotivated, disorganized, and dependent, and thus not suited for positions of power. Selection comes into play because only limited instances, actions, or behaviors are selected to define these groups, from the broad array of actions individuals in these groups exhibit. Thus, the major element in racism, sexism, and classism is power—the need on the part of the people who hold power to preserve it. They disenfranchise others to keep themselves in charge. Yet people who accept racist, sexist, or classist views are not always aware that these attitudes rest on power relationships. It takes looking closely at all these isms to see the structure of power needs beneath them, since these needs are so tightly built into our society's constructs that they are practically invisible.

It is hard to get a grasp on sexism because it surrounds us and is inherent in the foundations of most aspects of our belief systems. One quick way to uncover a modicum of awareness of sexism is to select a few assumptions and expectations that we have for women and apply them to men. So imagine with me . . .

At birth he was beautiful—long lashes, symmetrical features, a full head of hair. Relatives and friends crowded around him, oohing and aahing about how handsome he was. As he grew older, he received constant attention for his looks and his outfits. "How darling! Look at those precious little buttons on his little vest. Doesn't that make him look handsome!" He liked to move and scoot after things. However, when he was quiet, just looking around or holding his stuffed animals, his parents would gush, "What a sweet, well-behaved child. Isn't he darling!"

As he grew and started to toddle around, he was curious, as all children are, picking up objects, getting into cupboards, and generally working to make sense of his world. At night, he hugged his teddy bear tight.

But the constant chorus of comments he heard from his parents told him what was important—how he looked, how docile he was, and how much he hugged his

For ideas on reducing bigotry and intolerance in schools, check out **Teaching Tolerance** at www.splcenter.org/ teachingtolerance/tt-index. html.

teddy bear. "What a good little father he will make," he heard as he walked holding his teddy bear tightly. So out of all the behaviors he displayed, his family (and society) selected the ones they found pleasing and those were the ones for which he got attention and rewards.

When he went to school, he was harshly reprimanded for any slight misbehavior and told, "I can't believe a handsome boy like you would act that way." The girls around him got to roughhouse, and all he heard from his teacher was "Girls will be girls."

He also found out it was all right for girls and their parents to make fun of boys. If a girl threw a ball poorly at her Little League game she was chastised for "throwing like a boy." Gradually he got the message: Boys couldn't do much physically; they were too clumsy and uncoordinated. He and his friends begged their parents to come to see them play ball at the park. They promised they'd come, but when they didn't think he was around, he heard them say, "The games the boys play are so slow. Girls' games are fast-paced and exciting." And parents and neighbors continued to come in droves to see the girls play.

As he grew and developed, his body became well defined and muscular. All the girls ogled and said rude things to him in the hall. When he asked them to stop, they told him they didn't mean anything by it—they were just one hundred percent all-girl and very interested in boys and their bodies. When the comments increased, he talked to his parents, who told him he should be proud to have a body that girls pay attention to—then he wouldn't have any trouble getting a woman. This seemed very important to everyone. He noticed that when the kids at school started to pair up, the boys picked by girls suddenly went up in status. His friend became "Annie's boy," and all the other boys seemed jealous of his "achievement."

When sexism is taken out of its familiar casings and shown in a different light, it appears ridiculous and shocking. Yet when the scenario is applied to a female, these same attitudes seem natural because our society has built constructs that support sexism. Of course, these constructs imply a certain "place" for men and for women, based on who is seen as most important or most powerful.

Sexism doesn't cut only one way. Males are as affected by gender expectations as females. Men are expected to take charge; to be brave, strong, athletic, rational, and responsible; and to know how to fix cars. If boys are thin and sensitive, enjoy classical music, and loathe sports, they are not easily accepted by their peers. Sexism limits choices for both sexes by making assumptions about how a person should be based solely on gender.

Just as we have used role reversal as a way to reimage and better understand sexism, we can imagine a scenario in which our current racial hierarchy is toppled. Imagine, if you will, a world in which the darker your skin, the more power you have. What expectations would people have for those with the darkest skin? What expectations would they have for people with the lightest skin? Where would you fall in this hierarchy? How would your world be different than it is now?

Or imagine reversing the way we view rich and poor people. No longer would society believe that material worth determines human worth and dignity. The rich would be seen as preoccupied with hoarding material wealth for themselves, while the poor would be seen as interested in pursuing a simple life so that all could share the earth's resources. People living simply would be elevated to a heroic status for living in a way that takes into consideration the entire community and their need for resources. Those who lived extravagantly would be viewed as selfish, concerned only with themselves and not with what is best for the world. When people in different economic situations are discussed in this way, it is easy to see that the classifications of poor and rich are defined behaviorally, not economically. But when we read of the poor or see them portrayed in the media, we may not notice that the terms *poor*, *working class*, and *underclass* hide judgmental baggage. It is important to look closely at how groups are being portrayed in order to uncover the way they are being defined.

The only way to learn how our words and actions affect people is to pay attention to how people react to us and ask them for advice and feedback. If we are to create a community of

The unearthly, celestial qualities of the story are suggested by this intriguing cover image.

(Jacket design from A WRINKLE IN TIME, by Madeleine L'Engle. Copyright © 1962, renewed 1990 by Madeleine L'Engle Franklin. Reprinted by permission of Farrar, Straus and Giroux, LLC.)

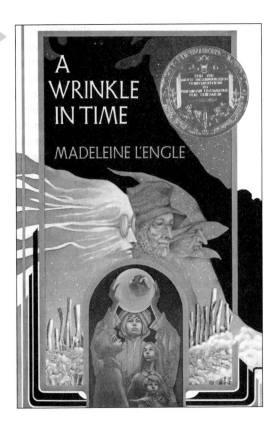

learners in our classrooms, we must be aware of and gently address the issues of racism, sexism, and classism as they arise in class. (See one way a first-grade teacher dealt with stereotypes on pages 186–187.)

Uncovering Stereotypes in Children's Books

The beliefs embedded in some texts are so prominent that we notice them even when we are not consciously looking for them. For instance, the spiritual basis of Madeleine L'Engle's *A Wrinkle in Time* would be hard to miss because of the central emphasis on good and evil. But identifying underlying beliefs in books is not always that easy. Answering the questions in the boxed feature Criteria for Evaluating the Beliefs Beneath the Writing can help the process along, making it easier to at least begin to approach the depths of the text.

If answering this set of questions for a particular book reveals extensive evidence of racism, sexism, or classism, you could then use other tools to look more closely at stereotypes and other distortions. Several other tools—boxed sets of questions on race, gender, and class—appear later in the chapter.

Recognizing Stereotypes

For those outside a culture or class, it is difficult to know what is offensive to those in it. For instance, we may not immediately understand American Indians' negative reactions to the counting book *The Ten Little Rabbits*, by Virginia Grossman and Sylvia Long, which shows rabbits dressed as American Indians performing such activities as sacred ceremonies. One way to begin to think about portrayals is to ask ourselves how we would feel if we were portrayed that way. Would we be offended if a counting book had figures of people of our race or ethnicity to count? Would we feel we were being viewed as nothing more than objects? How would Christians react if a rabbit minister or priest were administering communion to rabbit parishioners? How would they react if Mary, Joseph, and Jesus were

*For **Native American Indian Resources**, go to www.kstrom.net/isk/mainmenu.html.*

Criteria for Evaluating *the Beliefs Beneath the Writing*

As you read books, you can ask these questions to get a look at the beliefs and assumptions imbedded in the writing:

1. Who or what was included and who or what was left out of the scope of the book?

2. What information does the author assume the reader knows?

3. What attitudes are shown toward people, animals, and even the land?

4. Who has the power? How is this power shown?

5. What is shown as being important or good?

Applying the Criteria   *Evaluating the Beliefs Beneath the Writing*

The Polar Express, by Chris Van Allsburg.

1. Who or what was included and who or what was left out of the scope of the book? Upper-middle-class lifestyle is included; other socioeconomic levels are left out. Santa Claus and his relationship to Christmas are included; other celebratory traditions are left out. A white, upper-middle-class male child's experience with Christmas is included. The idea of magic and belief is included in terms of Santa Claus, while knowledge of parents as gift source is left out.

2. What information does the author assume the reader knows? The story of Christmas and Santa Claus. Familiarity with mountains and forests and wolves. Awareness of upper-middle-class lifestyle.

3. What attitudes are shown toward people, animals, and even the land? It's normal for children to question the existence of Santa Claus. Children can expect to be taken care of by adults. Adults are solicitous of children and want to be of help.

4. Who has the power? How is this power shown? Adults have the power—especially Santa Claus, who is appreciated or adored by the elves and children. The waiters on the train are not shown as having power, while the conductor is shown as being in charge. The little boy has more power or importance than the other children.

5. What is shown as being important or good? A belief in Santa Claus. Living in a big, beautiful house with rooms completely decorated and coordinated. Wearing beautiful nightclothes to bed and owning robes and slippers. Having a Christmas tree and celebrating Christmas. Getting lots of presents for Christmas. Boys are more important than girls. Girls' roles are to care for and show concern for others, so when the little boy is upset at the loss of the bell, it's only girls who respond to him. Girls are shown only in passive roles, except when they show concern for the main character. Men with swarthy complexions are shown waiting on children and are clearly servants.

place at the same time of year as Christmas might be discussed, to make children aware that other traditions exist. Children could be asked when they've been waited on and what the occasion was. The subject of who waits on people could also be broached, to broaden the view that only people of color are waitpeople. Even talking about houses—what's in them, how different people decorate them, what allows some people to afford bigger houses, and so on—can do much to allay the discomfort children may feel if they realize that their house is not nearly as grand as the one pictured. Sometimes simply raising these issues is enough to help children realize that they are not the only ones who don't have the kind of life that is portrayed in the book.

Some people might ask, "Why not let children remain innocent for a while and read stories about people who live well and enjoy life without questioning them?" Herbert Kohl (1995) answers this concern well when he points out, "There are many ways to live well, and it's important to show children that you don't have to be rich to live well, that living well is not simply a matter of being able to buy things and have other people take care of your everyday needs" (p. 25).

A more direct approach to dealing with stereotypes is demonstrated by Paula Rogovin (1998) in her book *Classroom Interviews.* In her first-grade class, she began a study on American Indian History and Culture by asking her students what they knew about American Indians. Their list included the following: Indians wear feathers, kill children, fight, dance, live in tepees, use bows and arrows, do war whoops (p. 32). Rogovin saw that the list was full of stereotypes and misinformation but did not criticize the children; instead, she asked where they got their information. They mentioned movies on television, teachers, family members, friends, and pictures. She very gently asked them, "Did you know that sometimes our information is wrong?" Many children were astounded, but she reassured them that that was not their fault because sometimes movies showed the wrong information. She explained a few aspects of the culture, telling them that although many American Indians did use bow and arrows, they used them mainly to hunt, not to kill people. "If we say that all American Indians use bows and arrows to go around killing people, that is not true. That is a stereotype" (p. 39). The students discussed this and decided that they could not believe everything they saw in the movies. From there, they watched different versions of the segment of Peter Pan showing Peter meeting the Indians. The children looked for stereotypes. One student wrote in his notebook, "Stereotypes are a kind of a lie. Like if I would say every Indian wears feathers, that would be a stereotype. And you can't use stereotypes because it hurts people's feelings. And if you told one, you would feel bad after you told it" (p. 40). Obviously, this teacher does a wonderful job of addressing issues head on and helping students not only understand stereotypes but also understand the need to question sources. Rogovin suggests that with older children, the study of misinformation and stereotyping could be extended by having them work on checking multiple sources and challenging sources of information.

Joel Taxel (1981) would agree that the kind of work Rogovin does with her students is very important because of the subconsciousness of the process. He explains: "Stereotypes, particularly with young children, do not register at the conscious level unless they are raised as an issue. Stereotypic attitudes are probably 'imprinted' at an unconscious level through repeated exposure to many books, films, television shows, and, of course, parental and peer group attitudes" (p. 15).

When we don't raise these issues, when the reading or talking is uncritical, there is always the chance that the book or movie or talk will change the way the child looks at and relates to the world. Thus, teachers must be aware of the racism, sexism, and classism in books in order to help students become aware of them and not accept the prevailing view that society seems to hold of gender, people in parallel cultures, and the poor and working class. Not talking about race, gender, and class stereotypes is just another way of perpetuating racism, sexism, and classism, since it allows the status quo to remain firmly in place. Sometimes middle-grade children do notice stereotypes, as the boxed feature Children's Voices shows.

Adults cannot effectively facilitate or encourage in young people work that they themselves have not already done. We need to have done the thinking and self-reflection about these issues before we can have genuine conversations in the classroom.

Learning from the History of Children's Literature

Part of the context of children's literature is the time period in which it was written. From the literature of each historical period, we can locate attitudes toward children, as well as attitudes toward every other aspect of life and society. By looking at what is published for children, we can see what a society thinks about who children are, what they can handle, what can be expected of them, and what is important for them to pay attention to. The purpose of this section is to look at what we can learn about children's literature from changes over the years and to think about the implications these changes have for our ability to look critically at children's literature today.

Changes in Children's Books Through the Years

Much of the early history of children's literature in the United States is grounded in the white culture. Both American Indians and blacks maintained rich oral traditions that were not part of written children's literature, for cultural and political reasons. We will look briefly at the more than two centuries of children's literature in the United States to see what kind of changes occurred as the times, attitudes, and technology changed.

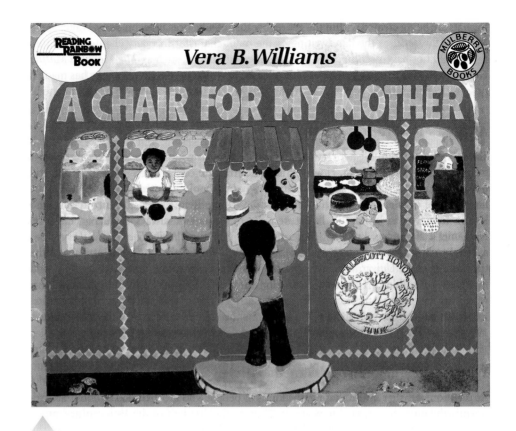

A loving working-class family and their neighborhood are painted in bold colors that suggest the vibrancy of their lives.
(From *A Chair for My Mother,* by Vera B. Williams. Used by permission of HarperCollins Publishers.)

children of color. A notable exception was *The Brownies' Book,* a magazine written for "the children of the sun" by black adults in 1920 and 1921. The goal of the magazine was to publish stories, poems, and songs that challenged racial stereotypes, built pride, and socialized black students. It was published by W. E. B. DuBois, rather than a mainstream publisher, and lasted only two years. Because it was rarely read by those beyond the target audience, white librarians and teachers were not aware of its existence. In 1996, ***The Best of The Brownies' Book,*** edited by Deanne Johnson-Feelings, was published by Oxford University Press so that the magazine's place in children's literature could be made known.

As criticism mounted in the 1970s about the roles of females in children's books, authors started to show girls as more than passive observers, thrilled just to be noticed by a male. That trend has continued, although boys are still the main characters far more often than girls. Other current trends include presenting characters with disabilities, stepparents, blended families, characters of different sexual orientation, and interracial dating, as well as matters of faith. The boxed feature Taking a Look at the Research discusses representations not often found in children's books today.

See **Books about Children with Disabilities** at *www.math.ttu.edu/~dmettler/dlit.html.*

Book Appearance

If you pick up a book printed in the 1930s or 1940s, you will at once know that it is an older book, based solely on its appearance. Color was very time-consuming to produce, so even the illustrations from this time period are in black and white.

Until recently, an illustrator would have to make a black base drawing, with three overlays for the three additional colors. It was a long, expensive process, and so books were not nearly as colorful as they are today. Even today, when a page is printed, it must go through the press once for every color used. So if a page has even a touch of red, it must go through the press once to put the red ink on and once to put the black ink on. Today four-color

Inclusion and Exclusion

Traditional representations in children's literature of an idyllic family structure have gradually given way to candid depictions of divorce, single parenting, blended families, and foster and adoptive families. Even issues of abuse and homelessness now appear occasionally in literature for children. For the most part, these books have been seen as enriching the literature selection possibilities and a welcome reflection of the variety of family structures and issues that exist in our culture today. They, indeed, give our students more authentic and meaningful text which they can relate to their own lives.

One family relationship that continues to be, for the most part, excluded is one in which there are same-gendered parents. While there are certainly children who are living in households with two moms or two dads, they are unlikely to see their families represented in classroom children's literature collections. Although books are available that depict these families, fear of censorship or teachers' personal displeasure or self-censorship is likely to keep them out of the classroom. It is hard to know how many thousands of children are living in loving families with gay or lesbian parents, siblings, or other family members but, as this act of exclusion demonstrates, "often remain invisible for the whole school experience" (Henkin, 1998, p. 81).

In young adult literature, *Am I Blue? Coming Out from the Silence,* edited by Marion Dane Bauer (1994), is a collection of original stories, by leading children's literature authors, that depict a wide range of gay and lesbian themes. In the introduction, Bauer expresses the concern of many when she speaks of the significant number of teenagers who attempt suicide because of fears associated with their gay or lesbian sexuality. Worried about the lack of information and support for these young people, she states that it is the intention of this collection "to tell challenging, honest, affecting stories that will open a window for all who seek to understand themselves or others" (p. ix).

Bauer, Marion Dane, ed. (1994). *Am I Blue? Coming Out from the Silence.* New York: HarperCollins.

Henkin, Roxanne (1998). *Who's Invited to Share? Using Literacy to Teach for Equity and Social Justice.* Portsmouth, NH: Heinemann.

(which means just about every shade, since the four colors can be combined) books are very common. Although the presses still have to make four runs, the burden is off the illustrators to make four separate layers for each page that has color. Now that modern technology, with its scanners and separators, can do the bulk of the work, producing colored picture books has become the norm. And typography has improved so much that changing a font usually just requires a click of the mouse. The downside to all this wonderful technology seems to be that the occasional author and publisher depend on impressing readers with spectacular visuals rather than the story. In years past, only stories deemed to be of excellent quality were considered worthy of the added expense of color.

Changes in Views of Children Through the Years

By looking at the kinds of books that are published for children, we can see what a society thinks children's function is. The Puritans viewed children mainly through the lens of their religious beliefs, seeing the stain of original sin on every child. They were eager to have their children lead the kind of lives that would bring them eternal salvation and saw children's learning about Puritan beliefs as the main function of childhood. There was little time for frivolous things such as games or books for entertainment (if such a thing had existed), since children had to take their salvation seriously. The only books children in the Puritan colonies had put in their hands were those that could further this otherworldly end.

One interesting aspect of the books the Puritans used to instruct children is that they did make some concessions to the way children learn best. Realizing how much more easily verse was memorized than prose, the Puritans wrote doctrine in verse for the young. *The New England Primer* was illustrated, since children were understood to like and learn from pictures.

By 1870, books for children had become much more than instructional. The shift to novels that were interesting and attractive to the young, as well as wholesome, reflected a change in views toward children. Once the overwhelmingly Puritan ethic softened, books began to focus on social behavior, since children were still seen as impressionable and not quite ready to handle books without a clear message of what was and was not acceptable in society. In the early part of the 20th century, children were expected to be purposeful and take on adult responsibilities early. Books on this side of the Atlantic reflected that somber, utilitarian approach, while fantasy and fairy tales were popular in England, where many children had a more prolonged childhood.

Today children are viewed as having psyches that must be tended to with care. We view childhood as a special time when children should not be burdened with adult responsibilities. This is a time for them to play, learn, and enjoy themselves. We understand that learning takes place in many ways, and so we try to provide children with experiences through which they can learn, such as a visit to a zoo. We know that this is a time when children develop a sense of right and wrong, and we want to provide them with good models. Today's books reflect our views of childhood, and so they nurture, console, boost self-esteem, help children see the normalcy of the experiences they go through, provide role models for them, and teach them concepts about the world in interesting ways.

Invitations

Choose several of the following activities to complete:

1. Look for good books for young people that are not written from the perspective of the virtues of individualism, competition, and capitalism. Look for books for young people that question the economic and social views of our society. If you find such books, note these qualities in your responses to them.

2. Work to unearth the assumptions on which you have built your belief system. What facts and experiences do you include in your opinions or judgments about members of the opposite sex, about people of a race different from your own, about people who belong to a different kind of church than you do, about people who have different political persuasions than you do? Can you trace the origin of these assumptions? Making your belief system explicit will not only help you understand your responses to books, but also allow you to explore your beliefs. Although these are subjects that are difficult to talk about with others, if you can find one other person in your class whom you feel you can trust, share your responses with that person. What did you learn?

3. Think back to something you read in the past that you can now see has other dimensions, such as racism or classism or sexism. Suppose you identified with the group presented in an unflattering manner in the book; how would you feel? As you read books this semester, be aware of which books make you feel like an outsider or an insider. What is it about the books that causes you to react that way?

4. Select a picture book or novel to analyze in terms of racism, sexism, or classism, using the criteria in this chapter.

5. Herbert Kohl (1995) says,

The stories we provide to youngsters have to do with personal challenge and individual success. They have to do with independence, personal responsibility and autonomy. The social imagination that encourages thinking about solidarity, cooperation, group struggle, and belonging to a caring group is relegated to minority status. Healthy community life and collective community-wide struggles are absent from children's literature and the stories most children encounter on TV, in film, or at home. (p. 62)

As you read books for this course, look at them in terms of Kohl's quote and report what you find. Which books do you think are appropriate for children? Which ones do you see as inappropriate? What can you learn from these responses about your views of children and what you think they are capable/incapable of understanding?

6. Magazines can be particularly good barometers of social change, reflecting current attitudes of the society toward children. Go to a library and look through the current year's issues of a magazine for children, noting what topics are written about in fiction and nonfiction. Or look at a series for children like the *Berenstain Bears.* Analyze how the culture has changed over the past ten years by comparing the ways gender and social issues are handled.

7. Imagine that the only artifacts you had to learn about this culture were stacks of picture books. What could you tell about this culture? What's important to us? What do we value? What is happening in the culture? Who has the power? If you have access to a special collection in your library, look through several children's books from another time period, noting all the things that are different. What view of life do these books paint?

CD-ROM

Locate other references to *culture* in Favorite Authors and References by using the word search feature.

Classroom Teaching Ideas

1. To heighten awareness of stereotypes, select one book that you know has stereotypes in it and one that does not. Read both books to your class. After students discuss how women or the aged or people in parallel cultures were portrayed differently in the books, explain to them what makes a stereotype. As the children respond to the books they read throughout the year in their book logs, ask them to notice and point out stereotypes or unfair portrayals.

2. Every time you read a book aloud to your class, as part of the follow-up discussion ask students to think about whom this book is leaving out. What people are not represented? This kind of ongoing discussion throughout the year will keep students sensitized about whom books exclude and whom they represent.

Internet and Text Resources

1. Teaching Tolerance is the site for the Southern Poverty Law Center. The mission of the center is to reduce hate, bigotry, and intolerance in schools. Find great resources at

www.splcenter.org/teachingtolerance//tt-index.html

2. Books about Children with Disabilities provides titles and sometimes brief descriptions of books that include children with CP, hearing impairments, spinal cord injuries, spina bifida, progressive illnesses, and communications disorders, as well as mental illnesses and learning disabilities. There are also links to sites featuring trade books for siblings of children with disabilities. Find it at

www.math.ttu.edu/~dmettler/dlit.html

3. Brave Girls and Strong Women Booklist is a site with annotated lists of books from small publishers. Find it at

www.members.aol.com/brvgirls/bklist.htm

4. **Books for Girls** offers booklists on topics of interest to girls. Go to

    www.girlpower.gov/girlarea/books/

5. **Children's Literature, Chiefly from the Nineteenth Century** contains pictures from early children's books, along with brief descriptions. The site would be ideal for the viewer who wants to compare themes and subject matter of earlier literature to those of present-day children's literature. Find it at

    www.sc.edu/library/spcoll/kidlit/kidlit/kidlit.html

6. **Native American Indian Resources** contains stories, art, herbal knowledge, native books, and an online bookstore. Find it at

    www.kstrom.net/isk/mainmenu.html

References

Council on Interracial Books for Children (no date). "10 Quick Ways to Analyze Children's Books for Racism & Sexism." CIBC pamphlet.

Harris, Violet (1996). "Continuing Dilemmas, Debates, and Delights in Multicultural Literature." *The New Advocate 9,* 107–122.

Harrison, Barbara, and Gregory Maguire, eds. (1987). *Innocence and Experience: Essays and Conversations on Children's Literature.* New York: Lothrop, Lee & Shepard.

Hunt, Peter, ed. (1995). *Children's Literature: An Illustrated History.* New York: Oxford University Press.

Kohl, Herbert (1995). *Should We Burn Babar? Essays on Children's Literature and the Power of Stories.* New York: New Press.

Lorde, Audre (1992). "Age, Race, Class, and Sexism: Women Redefining Difference." In Paula S. Rothenberg, ed., *Race, Class, and Gender in the United States.* New York: St. Martin's.

Marcus, Leonard S., ed. (1998). *Dear Genius: The Letters of Ursula Nordstrom.* New York: HarperCollins.

McCormick, Kathleen (1994). *The Culture of Reading and the Teaching of English.* New York: Manchester University Press.

Rogovin, Paula (1998). *Classroom Interviews.* Portsmouth, NH: Heinemann.

Rosenblatt, Louise (1996). *Literature as Exploration.* New York: Modern Language Association [1938].

Slapin, Beverly, and Doris Seale, eds. (1998). *Through Indian Eyes: The Native Experience in Books for Children.* Berkeley, CA: Oyate.

Taxel, Joel (1981). "Cultural Theory and Everyday Educational Life." Paper presented at the annual meeting of the American Educational Research Association, April 15, 1981.

Yolen, Jane, and Bruce Coville (1998). "Two Brains, One Book; or How We Found Our Way to the End of the World." *Booklinks 8,* 54–58.

Children's Books

Alcott, Louisa May (1994). *Little Women.* New York: Tor [1868].

Banks, Lynne Reid (1980). *The Indian in the Cupboard.* Illus. Brock Cole. New York: Delacorte.

Cole, Babette (1996). *Drop Dead.* London: Jonathan Cape, Random.

—— (1987). *Prince Cinders.* New York: Putman & Grosset.

Comenius, John Amos (1968). *Orbis Pictus.* London: Oxford University Press [1659].

Grossman, Virginia, and Sylvia Long (1991). *The Ten Little Rabbits.* New York: Chronicle.

Hawthorne, Nathaniel (1895). *The Scarlet Letter.* Boston: Houghton Mifflin.

—— (1837). *Parley's Universal History on the Basis of Geography.* London: Goodrich.

Hope, Laura Lee (1936). *The Bobbsey Twins in Eskimo Land.* New York: Grosset & Dunlap.

Johnson-Feelings, Deanne, ed. (1996). *The Best of the Brownies' Book.* New York: Oxford University Press.

Krauss, Ruth (1954). *How to Make an Earthquake.* Illus. Crockett Johnson. New York: Harper [out of print].

L'Engle, Madeleine (1973). *A Wrinkle in Time.* New York: Farrar, Straus & Giroux.

Lovelace, Maud Hart (2000). *Betsy-Tacy.* Illus. Lois Lenski. New York: HarperTrophy [1940, Crowell].

McMullan, Kate (1996). *Noel the First.* Illus. Jim McMullan. New York: HarperCollins.

Montgomery, Lucy Maud (1981). *Anne of Green Gables.* New York: Bantam [1908, L. C. Page].

Myers, Walter Dean (1999). *Monster.* Illus. Christopher Myers. New York: HarperCollins.

New England Primer, The (1824). Newark: Benjamin Olds [1795].

Newbery, John (1744). *A Little Pretty Pocket-Book.* Self-published.

Nomura, Takaaki (1991). *Grandpa's Town.* Trans. Amanda Mayer Stinchecum. New York: Kane/Miller.

Oodgeroo (1981). *Father Sky and Mother Earth.* Sydney, Australia: Jacaranda.

Perkins, Lucy Fitch (1917). *Belgian Twins.* Boston: Houghton Mifflin.

Rylant, Cynthia (1986). *The Relatives Came.* Illus. Stephen Gammell. New York: Simon & Schuster.

Sabuda, Robert (1999). *The Movable Mother Goose.* New York: Little Simon.

Sendak, Maurice (1963). *Where the Wild Things Are.* New York: Harper.

Smith, Janice Lee (1995). *Wizard and Wart at Sea.* Illus. Paul Meisel. New York: Harper.

Steig, William (1997). *Toby, Where Are You?* Illus. Teryl Euvremer. New York: HarperCollins.

Taylor, Theodore (1995). *The Cay.* New York: Camelot [1967, Avon Flare].

Van Allsburg, Chris (1985). *The Polar Express.* Boston: Houghton Mifflin.

Webster, Jean (1995). *Daddy-Long-Legs.* New York: Puffin [1912, Century].

Williams, Vera B. (1982). *A Chair for My Mother.* New York: Greenwillow.

—— (1984). *Music, Music for Everyone.* New York: Greenwillow.

—— (1983). *Something Special for Me.* New York: Greenwillow.

Yolen, Jane, and Bruce Coville (1998). *Armageddon Summer.* New York: Harcourt Brace.

Multicultural and International Literature

Multicultural books can be as vibrant as ***Uncle Jed's Barbershop,*** by Margaree King Mitchell, which sings with family caring and community. They can be as startlingly beautiful as ***The Dragon Prince: A Chinese Beauty & the Beast Tale,*** by Laurence Yep with Kam Mak's luminous illustrations. They can be as poignant as Allen Say's ***Emma's Rug,*** which depicts a five-year-old's fear and uncertainty. They can be as packed with fascinating information as ***Black Hands, White Sails: The Story of African-American Whalers,*** by Patricia C. McKissack and Fredrick L. McKissack. They can sing with joy, the way the illustrations by Ashley Bryan do in ***Sing to the Sun.*** They can lift us off the page with beautiful language, the way ***Meet Danitra Brown,*** by Nikki Grimes, does. They can make us laugh and cry, the way ***The Watsons Go to Birmingham—1963,*** by Christopher Paul Curtis, does.

Multicultural literature has the richness, depth, beauty, and variety of any category of literature. It is represented in every genre, including picture books, realistic and historical fiction, traditional literature, fantasy, nonfiction, and poetry.

Although multicultural literature should be integrated into the curriculum and used as other books in other genres are used, it is treated separately here so that we can closely examine books and authors who can be considered multicultural. This chapter is designed to show in concrete ways the importance of using such literature, to help you get to know what literature is available, and to encourage you to think about the issues embedded in the use of multicultural literature.

What Is Multicultural Literature?

In the broadest sense, multicultural literature could include every book because every book comes from the point of view of a culture and every book can be read from multiple points of view based on gender, socioeconomic class, ethnicity, and so on. Some ethnic groups, especially those from Europe, have had a continuous presence in children's literature. We all have heard of the Grimm brothers, Hans Christian Andersen, and the tales of King Arthur.

In the interest of diversity and equity, the focus in this chapter is on literature about and/or by historically underrepresented groups, whose faces and stories and histories are missing from much of our literature. As early as 1941, Charlemae Rollins, African American librarian and activist, raised her voice for more positive examples of blacks and black culture in children's books. This issue began to be addressed after Nancy Larrick (1965) in "The All-White World of Children's Literature" also pointed out this lack in the field. By defining multicultural literature as literature that calls attention to peoples and voices not traditionally written about or included in the body of literature most frequently taught, we can focus on filling in the part of the picture that is missing. In this country, this group is composed of people of color, including African Americans, Mexican Americans/Latinos, Asian Americans, and American Indians. This definition of multicultural literature does not include international literature, which will be addressed later in this chapter, because international literature does not focus on the issues of the multiple cultures in our nation.

Reasons for Using Multicultural Literature

Rudine Sims Bishop (1997), noted African American professor of children's literature, often talks about how literature serves as a mirror and a window for the reader. As a mirror, it shows children reflections of themselves; as a window, it shows them what other people are like. Too often children of color experience literature only as a window, while white children experience it only as a mirror. It is, of course, important that all of the children in our classrooms see people who look like them in literature, as well as people who don't look like them. Although superficial and not in itself enough, representation of their ethnicity is what children first notice when they read a book.

Benefits of Multicultural Literature for Children from Parallel Cultures

Faith Ringgold, noted artist and author, tells us on the book jacket of *The Invisible Princess* that, while reading to her granddaughters one day, she was asked why there were no African American princesses in stories. When she realized the truth in their question, she remedied the situation by writing *The Invisible Princess.* In this story, Mama and Papa Love have a child, the Invisible Princess, who saves them and the

Kam Mak's stunning illustrations make Laurence Yep's adaptation of "Beauty and the Beast" an unforgettable adventure.

(Cover art from *The Dragon Prince* by Laurence Yep. Cover art copyright © 1997 by Kam Mak. Used by permission of HarperCollins Publishers.)

other plantation slaves from their cruel master so that they can all find happiness in the Invisible Village of Peace, Freedom, and Love. This story, written in response to her grand-daughters' question, underscores the importance of seeing ourselves in representations of the world that we encounter, be it in television, books, movies, or magazines.

Philip Lee (1999), one of the founders of Lee & Low, a publishing company with a specific focus on multicultural themes, explained how this lack of representation affected him. He told of growing up in Hong Kong, where 98 percent of the population was Chinese. But because Hong Kong was then ruled by the British, "all things Anglo were better than Chinese." The commercials, the movies, and everything else surrounding him shouted out that blonde was better. Although living "in a place rich with role models, we were reminded every day that Chinese wasn't as good." As a teenager, Lee moved to California and was eager to assimilate. He even bleached his hair blonde. "How powerful," he says. "I wanted to be someone other than myself ethnically." Because he understood how important it was for children to see themselves in the media, specifically in books, and because he was conscious of what was missing, he established his company.

Benefits of Multicultural Literature for All Children

While it is easy to understand why multicultural literature is important for people in parallel cultures, sometimes it is harder to see why this literature is so vitally important for all students. The promise of multicultural literature is "not just that we will learn about other cultures but that we will learn about ourselves" (Aronson, 1996, p. 32). The achievements of others tell us something about who we are, for if others can achieve, part of the reason is that attitudes—including ours—in society have made room for this kind of achievement. Consistently reading and discussing a wide range of multicultural books has important benefits for all children.

Enjoying Good Literature

Children can enjoy multicultural literature simply because it is good literature. Good literature is a work of art that invites readers into an aesthetic or "lived through" experience. Of prime importance in selecting books is considering the literary merit of a book. Publisher Philip Lee (1999) explains that, in looking for multicultural books to publish, the first thing his company looks at is "whether or not it's a good story. Does it have believable characters, a compelling plot, and a satisfying ending—all the same elements that make any book a good read? If it doesn't read well, it won't be published." It is the literary qualities of multicultural books that have been responsible for their winning both the Newbery Award (*M. C. Higgins, the Great,* by Virginia Hamilton; and *Bud, Not Buddy,* by Christopher Paul Curtis) and Newbery Honor awards (*The Watsons Go to Birmingham—1963,* by Christopher Paul Curtis; *Yolonda's Genius,* by Carol Fenner; *Dragon's Gate,* by Laurence Yep; *The Dark-Thirty: Southern Tales of the Supernatural,* by Patricia C. McKissack; and *Somewhere in the Darkness,* by Walter Dean Myers, among others). Artistic excellence has secured the Caldecott Medal for David Diaz for *Smoky Night,* by Eve Bunting; Allen Say for *Grandfather's Journey;* Ed Young for *Lon Po Po: A Red-Riding Hood Story from China;* Leo Dillon and Diane Dillon for *Why Mosquitoes Buzz in People's Ears: A West African Tale,* by Verna Aardema, and for *Ashanti to Zulu: African Traditions,* by Margaret Musgrove, as well as several Caldecott Honor awards.

Gaining Information and Knowledge

By seeing in multicultural literature stories of the diverse citizens who live in the United States, children can gain information and knowledge. This nation has been filled with people of color from the beginning. Native American peoples have lived in what is now the United States since ancient times. Many African Americans were enslaved and brought here in the 17th century. Mexicans lived on the land that was then known as Northern Mexico and is now the Southwest of the United States. Asians came to this country in the last part of the 19th century and were largely restricted to the dangerous work of completing the Transcontinental Railroad. Since these peoples' land and/or labor helped found this country, their histories are part of America's story and their faces and stories belong in books for

At the **Multicultural Pavilion,** find research, activities, and links to other multicultural websites. Go to http://curry.edschool. virginia.edu/go/multicultural/.

CD-ROM

Use the CD-ROM database to see the many genres Laurence Yep writes in and create a list of his books.

CD-ROM

Find lists of award-winning books on the CD-ROM.

children. Using multicultural literature helps children understand that being American is a matter of where one was born or one's legal status, not how one looks. Through books, we can give children access to the whole picture, showing them that there are Asian Americans, Latinos, African Americans, and American Indians who are part of America's history and who contribute today to this country's beliefs, identity, and values.

Expanding World Views

The varying perspectives offered by multicultural literature can expand children's world views. Many students are not aware that there is more than one way to view the world, people, and events. Multicultural literature helps them understand the existence of multiple viewpoints in very concrete ways. Stories like *Home to Medicine Mountain,* by Chiori Santiago, and *My Name Is SEEPEETZA,* by Shirley Sterling, show American Indian children's reactions to being forced by law to attend schools that sought to erase their native culture. In these books, we also see the point of view of the people who ran these schools.

Through experiencing such books, children discover viewpoints other than the EuroAmerican one. They learn that there is never only *one* story—one objective or true way to look at things. To any given issue or event, we each bring our cultural background and experiences and point of view. One way to help students see this is to use several books on Christopher Columbus's landing in the Americas. Most show the story from Columbus's point of view, but an increasing number—including Michael Dorris's *Morning Girl*—tell the

Readers are taken as far back as 1500 for glimpses of the various peoples who inhabited the place now called Texas.

(From VOICES OF THE ALAMO by Sherry Garland, illustrated by Ronald Himler. Illustration copyright © 2000 by Ronald Himler. Reprinted by permission of Scholastic Inc.)

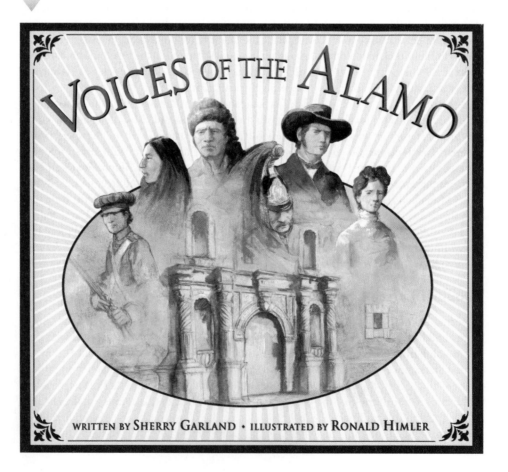

story of Columbus's landing from the point of view of the native people on the shore. By reading Sherry Garland's picture book *Voices of the Alamo,* children can hear the many voices of people over time who inhabited the area where the Alamo was built, and then perhaps talk about the range of views and why there is a difference in the way people think.

Appreciating Cultural Diversity

Through multicultural literature, children can develop an appreciation of and respect for cultural diversity. Children who are members of the majority have always found mirrors in books. Too often they have not been exposed to the views of people of color. Thus, they cannot discover views they can respect, admire, and love. Rudine Sims Bishop (1992) explains that, when they see only people like themselves in books, they get an "exaggerated sense of their own importance. . . . [They are also] denied the benefits of books as windows onto worlds and people different from, and yet similar to, themselves" (p. 20). Thus, they do not have opportunities to develop "a full understanding of what it means to be human, of their connections to all other humans in a world populated by a wide variety of people and cultures" (p. 20).

What better way to address this than by reading multicultural literature? Valerie Flournoy's *The Patchwork Quilt,* illustrated by Jerry Pinkney, shows the centrality of the family reflected in the work on the quilt. *Tea with Milk,* by Allen Say, demonstrates the difficult choice a young Japanese American woman has to make about her future. Gary Soto's *Chato's Kitchen,* an amusing story about a cat who invited a family of mice to dinner, captures the flavor of life in East L.A. culture. A novel with an American Indian as the main protagonist is Joseph Bruchac's *The Heart of a Chief.* Sixth-grader Chris Nicola is shown as a fully developed character concerned about a wide variety of issues, including the stereotyping of American Indians. It takes courage, but he works to help his fellow classmates understand how he feels. In response to a fellow classmate's question about Thanksgiving, he says, "It's kind of funny in a grim way" (p. 109). He goes on to ask his classmates to "Think of what it's like for an Indian kid to go to a school where they're dressing the other kids up in phony Indian costumes with eagle feather headdresses made of paper and cardboard. You feel like they're making fun of your whole culture" (p. 109).

Pat Mora (1998), Latina author and poet, says we need to put literature to work as an art form "that moves readers to hear another human's voice, and thus to experience the doubts, fears, and joys of a person who may not look or sound at all like us" (p. 283).

Another aspect of diversity that can be celebrated through multicultural literature is language diversity or bilingualism. With the growing number of Spanish-speaking people in this country, books are beginning to be published with the story or poems in both Spanish and English. One such picture book for older readers is *It Doesn't Have To Be This Way: A Barrio Story,* by Luis J. Rodríguez. The poetry of Francisco X. Alarcon (see Chapter 5) and Gary Soto is often published in both languages, side by side on the page. Other books are enriched by the inclusion of phrases or vocabulary in the language of the culture being written about. Julia

W

Use *Bilingual Books for Children* as a resource. Find it at www.ala.org/alsc/bilingual_ books_for_children.html.

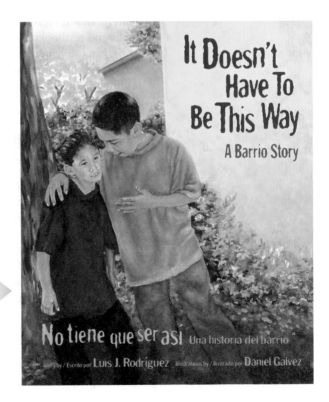

This is a compelling story, written in both Spanish and English, of a young boy's encounter with the world of gangs, a world the author knows firsthand.

(*It Doesn't Have To Be This Way: A Barrio Story/No tiene que ser así: Una historia del barrio,* story by Luis J. Rodríguez and illustrations by Daniel Galvez. Reprinted with the permission of the publisher, Children's Book Press, San Francisco, CA. Story copyright © 1999 by Luis J. Rodríguez. Illustrations copyright © 1999 by Daniel Galvez.)

Cynthia Leitich Smith, a mixed-blood member of the Muscogee (Creek) Nation, features contemporary Indian life in both her picture book and her first novel.

Virginia Driving Hawk Sneve, Rosebud Sioux author, writes in a quiet, uncomplicated manner. In addition to writing Native American folk tales, she has produced a series of books called *First American Books,* which explain the background of many native nations.

Clifford Trafzer (Richard Red Hawk), author, writes mainly nonfiction for older readers, although he does have a few books for early elementary children.

Asian American

Sook Nyul Choi, Korean American author, writes poignant, moving novels and picture books based on her experiences in escaping from Japanese rule and being an immigrant in a new country.

Yangsook Choi, Korean American illustrator, captures the mood and period of the books she illustrates. She paints spare yet elegant pictures, in colors ranging from vivid to muted.

Sheila Hamanaka, Japanese American artist and author, writes picture storybooks, nonfiction, and folk tales. Her dramatic, vibrant illustrations are done in watercolor, oil, and even paper collage.

Minfong Ho, Thai American author, writes charming rhythmic poems, as well as picture books and novels based on experiences in Thailand and Cambodia.

Benrie Huang, Taiwan-born artist, has illustrated more than twenty-five picture books. Her illustrations are often rounded and soft-toned, and her compositions offer a variety of perspectives.

Dom Lee, Korean American illustrator, is known for his evocative illustrations. Expressive faces, often done in sepia tones, give his pictures the quality of old photographs.

Huy Voun Lee, Cambodian illustrator and author, is known for her masterful use of pattern. She creates visually captivating illustrations with cut-paper collage and rich details.

Jeanne M. Lee, Chinese American author and illustrator, often retells tales and illustrates them in brilliant colors with stylized drawings.

Marie G. Lee, Korean American author, writes sensitive stories about adjusting to life in a new country and surviving as an ethnic minority.

Grace Lin, Chinese American illustrator, is known for her lively, color-saturated paintings.

Ken Mochizuki, Japanese American author, has written award-winning picture books dealing with the racism that Japanese Americans have had to face.

Lensey Namioka, Japanese American author, writes poignant, funny stories dealing with family situations, which often involve conflict over the pull of two cultures.

Ching Yeung Russell, Chinese American author, writes loosely autobiographical novels and picture books that are filled with rich cultural details of China in the 1940s.

Allen Say, Japanese American author and illustrator, focuses mainly on picture books. He began as an illustrator of others' work but now writes and illustrates his own books.

Chris Soentpiet, Korean-born illustrator, creates richly detailed, dramatic illustrations that are beautifully lit and strongly realistic.

Yoshiko Uchida, Japanese American author, writes lively stories, which often portray the pain of rejection as well as the spirit of determination.

Janet Wong, Chinese Korean American poet, touches the heart of human experience with her sometimes funny, sometimes sarcastic, always sensitive poems.

Paul Yee, Chinese Canadian author, writes hard-hitting, honest short stories, novels, and picture books, which often focus on aspects of life as an ethnic minority.

Laurence Yep, Chinese American author, is a prolific storyteller who writes beautifully in many genres, including realistic and historical fiction, fantasy, picture books, and short stories.

Ed Young, Chinese American illustrator, has won the Caldecott Medal for his complex use of color and shadow. His impressionistic compositions capture the emotional content of the scenes.

Latino/Chicano

Alma Flor Ada, Cuban American author, captures the authentic flavor of Latin culture in her folk tales, poetry, and novels. She also writes picture books based on inventive versions of fairy tales.

Francisco X. Alarcon, award-winning Chicano poet and educator, has written three collections of seasonal poems for young people, all of which are playful, moving, and inspirational.

Rodolfo Anaya, Mexican American author and renowned storyteller, although mainly a writer for adults, also writes lyrical folk tales and picture books for children.

Lulu Delacre, Puerto Rican American author, writes evocative, often touching stories, well integrated with cultural details.

David Diaz, Mexican American illustrator and Caldecott winner, is known for his use of bold colors, his innate sense of design, and his naive-style incandescent illustrations.

Carmen Lomas Garza, renowned Chicana illustrator, often uses cut-paper art in her vibrant narrative paintings, which sing out with pride in her Mexican American heritage.

Susan Guevara, illustrator, creates paintings that beg to be pored over for their detailed, richly colored depictions.

Juan Felipe Herrera, a bilingual poet and picture book author, writes poetry that can be understood more with the heart than with the head and lyrical prose that often speaks to the new immigrant experience.

Nicholasa Mohr, Puerto Rican American author, touches the heart of Puerto Rican pride with her many novels about growing up.

Pat Mora, Latina author, writes picture books, poetry, and novels that sparkle with love and respect for her Mexican heritage.

Luis J. Rodríguez, Chicano author, has turned to writing children's books. His books about what an immigrant child faces have a strong sense of immediacy.

Enrique O. Sanchez, illustrator, uses warm glowing colors and stylized figures, which make his work eye-catching and evocative.

Gary Soto, Mexican American author, writes poetry, short stories, picture books, and novels evocative of his experiences in the Mexican American community.

(1997) says, "When a child at a bookstore where I was giving a reading asked me, 'You are Jewish, so how come you can write *Hark! A Christmas Sampler*?' I answered: 'I have written murder mysteries, too'"(p. 289).

Rudine Sims Bishop (1992) believes, "The issue of perspective—when evaluating books about people of color—is often over-simplified to the question of whether whites can or should write about people of color" (p. 31). She points out that this issue is made more complicated by the subtle way attitudes are formed and synthesized in each of us: "Unfortunately, writers who are members of non-dominant groups are not immune from having absorbed some of the negative attitudes held about their own group by others, and these stereotypic attitudes towards their own group will be reflected in their work" (p. 31). Bishop suggests, "Some white writers, from their own vantage point, can create works about blacks that are positive and noteworthy" (p. 31). For her, "The race of the author is not the point—the perspective of the author is what matters" (p. 31). Ultimately, the success of a book will be determined by "how effectively it succeeds in fulfilling the author's purpose or in satisfying the readers' needs" (p. 31).

Philip Lee (1999), publisher, agrees with Bishop: "The ethnicity of the authors and artists is an important factor, but by no means do we feel that it is a requirement." Lee & Low has published multicultural stories by authors and illustrators from both within and outside the culture of the story. In an interview with Sloan (1999), Lee says, "Our experience has shown us that the same background authors/artists can often bring an additional personal identification to the story. However, it would be wrong to assume that they are automatically experts in their ethnic heritage" (p. 30).

Lee offers *Baseball Saved Us* as an example. Author Ken Mochizuki, a Japanese American born and raised in Seattle, had parents who were sent to the internment camp in Minidoka, California. Since "he was not born until after their internment, he had to spend a great deal of time researching historical articles and interviewing members of the Japanese American baseball league to achieve a historically authentic story in spite of his ethnic heritage" (p. 30).

Lee explains that the illustrator, Dom Lee, was selected not only because of his powerful imagery but also because he is a big sports fan. Being from Korea, he knew little about the internment history. "So he too went searching for factual materials, working with the Baseball Hall of Fame and studying the photographs of Ansel Adams, who was the only person officially allowed to take pictures of the camps" (p. 30). After Lee received Ken's manuscript and Dom's sketches, he contacted former internees in the New York area for fact-checking. They were able to offer comments that led to changes in the text and the art. "Clearly, even with an all Asian American team of a Japanese American author, a Korean American illustrator, and a Chinese American editor, we had to do extensive research to ensure the authenticity of *Baseball Saved Us*" (p. 30). The resulting story was not only an Asian American story but also a sports story.

According to Susan Stan (1999), a children's literature expert who has done research on international books, few of the children's books coming out of Russia and China would be considered appropriate for sale in this country, largely because political conditions there dictate that books be published to instruct or indoctrinate. Little literature comes from Africa and India because the multiple languages and lower literacy rates make it difficult to internally support the costs of publishing. Since "the size of the book buying market, the literacy rates, the reading habits of a people, and the wealth of the nation are all critical factors in supporting an ongoing indigenous publishing program, publishing any children's books seems to be an impossible task wherever some or many of these elements are missing" (Stan, 1999, p. 171).

Another concern Stan addresses is that international fare is not reflective of the world's literature for children, since "most of the children's literature from outside our borders comes from places with people who see the world much as we do and is then edited to conform even more strictly to our world view" (p. 175). Fortunately, such a tendency has not prevented some distinctly "other" books from making it into publication, such as **Pheasant and Kingfisher,** by Catherine Helen Berndt; **The Friends,** by Kazumi Yumoto; **Linnea in Monet's Garden,** by Christina Björk; **The Red Comb,** by Fernando Picó; and **Winter Rescue,** by W. D. Valgardson. These books "do not repackage the world into a form most comfortable for American readers but take them on new journeys into unfamiliar and exciting territories" (p. 176).

Kane/Miller, a publisher specializing in translated children's books, does offer books from distinctly different points of view and books that describe life in the present in a foreign country, but these are a small part of their total offerings. The company carries books from Australia, Belgium, Bolivia, Brazil, Canada, England, France, Germany, Ghana, Italy, Japan, the Netherlands, Norway, the Philippines, Spain, Sri Lanka, Sweden, and Venezuela. When a book is translated, Kane/Miller takes care to keep the foreign flavor of the book instead of Americanizing it. Ken Miller (2000), one of the publishers, explained that when the book **Brush,** by Pere Calders, was published in England, the publishers there changed the name of the dog to Scamp and the name of the little boy to Joey. Kane/Miller kept the original names of Turco and Little Sala.

Which International Books Get Selected?

To see what is available in international literature, many publishers go to the big, international book fairs that take place in Frankfurt, Germany; Bologna, Italy; and Harare, Zimbabwe. According to Carl Tomlinson (1999), who has done extensive work on international literature, the negotiation and bidding for rights to publish books begin at these fairs. Given the extra expense to the publisher of translating a book written in another language, editors want to be sure that the books they sign will appeal to readers here. According to Hoyle (1994), often the jacket is changed to make the book more marketable in the United States; sometimes new interior illustrations are drawn as well. Publishing books from other countries involves risk on the part of publishers, since historically translated books have not sold well in this country.

First published in Spain, this story shows how Little Sala deals with his family's decision to get rid of his dog, who chews everything in sight.

(From *Brush* by Pere Calders, illustrated by Carme Solé Vendrell. American text copyright © 1986 Kane/Miller Book Publishers. All rights reserved. Used by permission of Kane/Miller Book Publishers.)

What do publishers look for in international literature? Generally speaking, according to Stan (1999), American publishers are most likely to publish international books that have won awards in their country of origin—books that can be considered "the best." They also look for universal story lines and generic settings that could be construed as American. Kane/Miller often selects books that would not normally be published here because our culture avoids discussion of the topics written about. For instance, because American publishers are squeamish about publishing books discussing body parts or body functions, Kane/Miller carries the series from Japan called *My Body Science,* with such titles as **The Holes in Your Nose** and **All About Scabs,** by Genichiro Yagyu. They also publish the Australian book **Welcome With Love,** by Jenni Overend, in which a family helps Mom deliver her baby at home.

Another Kane/Miller book, **Good Bye Rune,** by Marit Kaldhol, deals with the difficult emotions of grief and sorrow. This book handles these disturbing subjects with honesty and love. Harcourt Brace translated and published **Rose Blanche,** by Roberto Innocenti and Christophe Gallaz, which shows a young child becoming aware of the hunger in the concentration camps and reacting to that need. The harsh realities shared in these two books are not often found in books for children written and published in the United States. Perhaps as teachers, librarians, and parents demand more books that face tough issues and the difficult parts of history, authors will write such books and publishers will publish them.

Invitations

Choose several of the following activities to complete:

1. In your notebook, list the children's trade books (non-textbooks) you remember reading as a child. How many of those books were written by or about someone from another ethnic group or culture? What does this suggest to you? Share your results in a small group. Read the statements made by children in the boxed feature Children's Voices on page 205. Do any surprise you?

2. In your notebooks, explore why you think it's important to use multicultural literature in the classroom. What concerns or questions do you have? After discussing these topics in small groups, return to your notebooks and reflect on what you discovered through the discussion.

3. Form a small group and have each member choose a different multicultural group. After reading five novels or picture books about your multicultural group, create an annotated bibliography of your reading. Make copies for your group. When you share the annotations, discuss what you have learned through your reading.

4. Read three multicultural novels from different cultures and evaluate them using the criteria listed in this book. Share the results with your group.

CD-ROM

To see examples of how to use the strategy of listing, search Invitations and Classroom Teaching Ideas for the word *list* or *listing.*

5. Find ten multicultural picture books on the same culture. Rank them from 1 to 10, with 1 being the best. Form a group with students who have read books on other cultures. Share your favorite three books, using criteria discussed in this chapter to explain why they are the most successful.

6. In a small group, create a readers theater presentation for a favorite multicultural novel. Share it with the class.

7. Read ten international picture books, and then choose your favorite to read aloud to a small group. In your notebook, discuss what you learned from this experience.

Traditional or Folk Literature

e learn through stories, just as we learn through our experiences in life. Sometimes stories are easier to learn from than real-life situations because stories offer more distance from the experience. We can see ourselves and our actions in the characters and the problems they encounter, and yet we have enough distance that we feel safe in exploring the difficulties these make-believe characters confront.

Folk literature speaks to universal experiences of what it means to be human. These seemingly simple stories allow us to reexperience, on a psychological level, universal issues in our lives. In *Tell Me a Tale: A Book about Storytelling,* Joseph Bruchac (1997), storyteller, author, and poet, explains

what these kinds of stories have meant to him: "Few things have helped me understand the world better than a good story.... Stories helped me grow, and stories helped me gain insight...., Stories helped me overcome my problems and stories taught me many things: that I didn't have to be ashamed when I was afraid, that I could learn to be brave, that there were times for sorrow and times for joy, that things were always going to change and that some things—like love and courage, hope and faith—were unchanging" (p. xi).

The stories Bruchac learned so much from are the folk stories he heard as he was growing up. He says, "Stories, like trees, have roots. They are rooted in our words and in our world" (p. 5).

Through Tasuku we learn that we can never be invulnerable, that there is always something or someone who has power over us.

Tsubu, the Little Snail, by Carol Ann Williams, another non-Japanese writer, is the story of a childless elderly couple who pray for a son. The Water God sends them a snail boy, who grows up to marry a noble's daughter. One day she loses him on the way to the spring festival. Because her love causes her to search everywhere without caring what anyone thinks of her, when she finds him later that day, his shell cracks and the son of the Water God emerges. The author tells us in her note that, although the details in this tale vary, the message always stays the same: "Life is sacred. No matter how insignificant it may seem, it is to be loved and respected. It is also a source of joy." The origins of this story are in Shintoism, with its "emphasis on recognizing the fundamental mystery at the heart of all things."

Since cultures reflect their values and concerns in their stories, we see both universal and unique characteristics of cultures in their folk tales. These Japanese folk tales give us hints about some of the important aspects of the Japanese culture as three Anglo writers and one Japanese writer see it.

American Indian Folk Tales

One of the best ways to learn about the native peoples of America is through the abundance of culturally authentic American Indian folk tales that exist today. The multitude of nations that make up the group referred to as American Indians, while certainly not all the same, do have some beliefs in common.

CD-ROM

Search the CD-ROM database for other books by Joseph Bruchac.

On the front cover flap of *Between Earth and Sky: Legends of Native American Sacred Places,* Joseph Bruchac, an Abenaki writer, talks about American Indian traditions. He states that in American Indian tradition, "All is sacred and legends exist to help us understand our lives. Stories from the land speak to us, can tell us of wisdom, can tell us of power, can tell us of the world that surrounds us. Listen." In this book, through the guidance of his uncle and the retelling of various American Indian legends, a young boy learns that everything living and inanimate has its place and should be considered sacred and given respect. The notes offer a clear idea of some essential values within the cultures and give us a measure of how representative the book is of the cultures.

Paul Goble, although not American Indian, writes with knowledge and reverence about their cultures and beliefs. In *Her Seven Brothers,* he retells the Cheyenne legend in which a girl and her seven chosen brothers become the Big Dipper. It tells us, "In the old days . . . there were more people who understood animals and birds." The young girl and her younger brother understand animals. This story about giving and being in touch with the spirit reflects a culture that validates and respects such communication. The collecting of possessions is not emphasized, as the people are shown living in tepees with their dogs and a few minimal possessions. This type of story is often viewed as an explanation tale, which tells how something happened; but looking closely, we see that it is also a story about living and what is valued in life.

Antelope Woman: An Apache Folktale, by Michael Lapaca, reveals why Apaches honor all things great and small. Lapaca, both the artist and the author, makes use of his cultural roots (Apache, Hopi, and Tewa) and artistic training to develop stories filled with the beautiful designs and patterns found in pottery and basketry in the Southwest.

Shingebiss: An Ojibwe Legend, retold by Nancy Van Laan, a nonnative author, teaches the power of perseverance and resourcefulness through the story of a duck in the cold North. This duck bravely challenges the Winter Maker and manages to find enough food to survive. The Author Notes once again give us important information. Van Laan says that the Ojibwe "perceive nature to be their teacher. They closely watched birds and animals to see how to survive the harsh climate. They believe every living thing imparts a sacred teaching."

These few stories about American Indians reflect reverence toward the earth and animals and a belief in a spiritual power. They offer a sense of some of the values held by American Indian peoples, as well as a glimpse at how they view the world.

Shingebiss, known for his determination and grit, is given a very definite look through the lines of the woodcuts.

(Cover, from SHINGEBISS by Nancy Van Laan. Jacket art © 1997 by Betsy Bowen. Reprinted by permission of Clarion Books/Houghton Mifflin Company. All rights reserved.)

Comparing Versions of a Folk Tale

Many of the folk tales written today are based on past stories or songs. Every writer and every illustrator make choices about what to emphasize in the tales they write and illustrate. The choices they make may alter the tale slightly or change it a great deal, depending on how they interpret the plot, characters, setting, theme, and structure. Comparing two versions of the same tale can yield interesting insights; the boxed feature Criteria for Evaluating More Than One Version of the Same Tale provides the criteria for doing so.

In the boxed feature Applying the Criteria: Evaluating Two Versions of a Yiddish Folk Tale on page 236, two folk tales are then compared. Both use as sources Yiddish songs the authors heard as young children. Steve Sanfield's **Bit by Bit** is based on the song "If I Had a Little Coat," while Simms Taback's **Joseph Had a Little Overcoat,** a 1999 Caldecott Honor Medal winner, is based on the song "I Had a Little Overcoat." Both tell the tale of a man who is able to make something out of little by transforming a cherished worn-out overcoat into other pieces of clothing. As each item becomes worn out, the man transforms it into something new, until eventually he is left with nothing material, but he has the ability to make art by retelling his experience through story. While the two tales have only slight variations in plot, the differences in characters, setting, theme, and structure show how much an individual author's or illustrator's unique approach alters a common folk tale.

𝒞riteria for Evaluating *More Than One Version of the Same Tale*

1. **Plot.** What is the sequence of events in the story? Do the plots differ? How might the different versions appeal to children of different ages?

2. **Characters.** How are the characters portrayed? What details (either visual or textual) contribute to the characterization? Are there any differences that change our understanding of the characters?

3. **Setting.** Where does the story take place? What do you learn about the culture from the details of the setting? Is this different for the tales being compared?

4. **Theme.** What is the message? What values are shown as important? Is the theme the same in each version?

5. **Style or language.** What do you notice about how the writer uses language? How does it differ in each tale?

6. **Structure.** What is the framework from which the story is narrated? Is it a simple chronological retelling, or does it have a more complex structure, such as a story within a story, flashbacks, or multiple narrators?

7. **Visual elements.** How is the art used to develop, contribute to, and extend the story? Is it done differently in the different versions?

GAIL CARSON LEVINE

Ella Enchanted

Ella's mysterious smile invites readers to uncover her secret. (Cover art from *Ella Enchanted* by Gail Carson Levine. Used by permission of HarperCollins Publishers.)

Females in Fairy Tales

Fairy tales written about other times and places often portray male and female figures in stereotypical ways, showing females as subservient and passive. Thus, teachers and parents sometimes hesitate to use them for fear of diminishing what a little girl thinks she can accomplish. As more and more research is done on tales around the world, writers are unearthing tales that feature strong and even daring women. One such tale is ***Rimonah of the Flashing Sword: A North African Tale,*** by Eric A. Kimmel, an Egyptian version of "Snow White." When Rimonah is taken by the huntsman to be killed, she escapes and goes to live with the Bedouin in the desert, where she becomes skilled with the dagger and sword. When her stepmother pursues her, Rimonah cleverly escapes. The second time she is not as lucky and is plunged into a deep sleep, only to be awakened by a prince. This story emphasizes how fearless and brave Rimonah is.

In ***Clever Katya: A Fairy Tale from Old Russia,*** by Mary Hoffman, Katya is portrayed as a clever child able to solve the Tsar's riddles. This not only helps her father but ultimately is beneficial to her. In the Author's Note, Hoffman tells us that originally this tale was called "The Wise Little Girl" and featured a nameless heroine. Hoffman explains that she likes the story because "the weak get the better of the strong, the child of the adult, and the female of the male." She further notes that the three tasks set by the Tsar are consistent with the tradition in folklore of using the number three.

Another book about an active female who does her own problem solving is ***Count Silvernose: A Story from Italy,*** by Eric A. Kimmel. This girl is the oldest and least pretty of three daughters, but smart and clever. When her two sisters are left for dead in Count Silvernose's castle, she goes to his home as a servant and not only rescues her sisters but also manages to get rid of the evil Count Silvernose.

Children have very strong feelings about fairy tales, as their comments in the boxed feature Children's Voices indicate. On your own, examine the messages about males in fairy tales. How are they characterized? What are they admired for?

See **Cinderella Variants** to find more than 100 variants of the fairy tale at www.acpl.lib.in.us/ Childrens_Services/cinderella.html.

 Tall Tales

Tall tales are very much a part of the American folk tradition. They may be based on a real person whose exploits are exaggerated or on someone totally imaginary. Characters include Paul Bunyan, Johnny Appleseed, Pecos Bill, Joe Magarak, and the Swamp Angel. Although tall tales may be wild, humorous, exaggerated stories, they contain a kernel of truth. While making us laugh, they also show us what it means to be quick-witted or brave and how to overcome adversity. The truths contained in these tales are more significant than how real or fictional a particular story is.

Tall tales generally share the characteristics shown in the boxed feature Criteria for Identifying Tall Tales on page 244. Examples of these characteristics taken from several tales are shown in the boxed feature Applying the Criteria: Identifying Characteristics of Tall Tales.

As with other forms of traditional literature, background notes provided by the authors are valuable for understanding the times and conditions that gave birth to tall tales. In ***Mike Fink,*** Steven Kellogg explains that extraordinary strength was needed to work on keelboats

Children's Voices

On reading fairy tales . . .

I like "Cinderella" because I like her dress. —Taylor, 2nd grade

My favorite is "Once Upon a Time." They're my favorite, with "Sleeping Beauty" and other girl stuff. —Elizabeth, 2nd grade

I like "Jack and the Beanstalk" because it is weird that Jack can hold on the stalk and not fall off. —Kate, 3rd grade

I like "Peter Pan." It has magic. —Richard, 3rd grade

When I was little, I read stories like "Cinderella," "Snow White," "Hansel and Gretel." What I like about "Cinderella" is that Cinderella went into a carriage and went off with the prince. What I like about "Snow White" is that she sang and danced with animals. What I like about "Hansel and Gretel" is that they came to their cottage with jewelry. —Jayne, 4th grade

I read them to my sister and for myself, once in a while. Everyone has to fantasize. —Craig, 6th grade

In them, the good guy always wins and the bad guy always gets what he deserves, so they always make you feel good. —Alison, 6th grade

I like to read fairy tales because they let me know I can dream. —Patrice, 6th grade

The sweet princess would always get her prince. —Tessa, 7th grade

I like fairy tales with a weird twist at the end. —Hailey, 7th grade

I used to like fairy tales but now they are too babyish. —Becky, 7th grade

They are always too farfetched to be remotely true. —Natalie, 7th grade

They always seem to turn out perfect. It was comforting when I was little. —Aaron, 7th grade

Fairy tales always have to do with cool things like magic, animals, and people. They always end with a happy ending, and begin with once upon a time. I like them. —Katie, 7th grade

I remember reading fairy tales when I was little. They each had a moral and gave you something good to read about. —Carolyn, 7th grade

I remember them when I was little reading them and pretending I was in it. —Hanna, 7th grade

I don't read many fairy tales anymore, but I did when I was younger. I really liked them and every so often I will take them off my bookshelf and read them. I enjoy reading them because they are so magical and make-believe, so they are fun to read. —Julia, 7th grade

I remember writing fractured fairy tales after reading them. I did like them because they were so fun to listen to and read. —Dustin, 8th grade

Individual Aspects of Mythology

In her introduction to **Mythical Birds & Beasts from Many Lands,** Margaret Mayo tells us that for thousands of years people have believed that fabulous birds and beasts exist. They've told stories about the animals' special power, appearance, and realms. This collection includes tales of the European unicorn, the North American thunderbird, the Chinese dragon, and the Aztec-inspired feathered snakes. It is interesting to look at what characteristics various cultures give their beasts, how they interact with the beasts, and what the beasts do or give to the cultures.

The One-Eyed Giant: And Other Monsters from Greek Myths, by Anne Rockwell, devotes two pages to each kind of monster, including the Cyclopes, Medusa, the Minotaur, and the Centaur. Aliki's **The Gods and Goddesses of Olympus** is the story of how the "awesome Olympians earned their thrones on Olympus." The lovely pictures and the clearly written text make this a good introduction to the major Greek gods.

These books and more are in the folklore section of the library. Browse through them and see what discoveries you make.

Heroes in Folk Literature

Folk tales, fairy tales, tall tales, fables, and myths often portray heroes. The hero's journey has been described in literature throughout the ages. Often it is part of a coming-of-age story in which a young person leaves home to find himself or herself. This is a common theme in stories, probably because each of us must take this journey. Whether or not we physically leave home, we must separate from our parents, look within ourselves, and figure out what values or beliefs are truly our own.

Joseph Campbell (1988), a famous author who writes about myths and legends, calls this part of life the hero's journey. That journey, which is like a circle, starts out when a young man or woman leaves home to seek his or her fortune. Along the way, obstacles arise. The hero or heroine overcomes these obstacles, learns from the experience, and then continues on. Eventually the hero or heroine returns home, strengthened by the experience and ready to help his or her family and people. In his explanation of Campbell's cycle, Bruchac (1997) says:

Most stories about heroes or heroines have these four parts:

Departure.

Difficulty—faces obstacles, hardships including evil people, threats by monsters, and abandonment.

Discovery—finds a way to overcome obstacles. Doing this, he or she gains power or is given a special gift.

Return—the hero or heroine goes back home, often using what he or she has gained to help the people. (p. 45)

We all have different definitions of what makes a person or an action heroic. The boxed feature Characteristics of a Hero summarizes what Joseph Campbell (1988) says about heroes in Chapter 5 of *The Power of Myth,* to help you look at the array of characteristics considered heroic.

The hero cycle appears in such stories as Eric A. Kimmel's **Count Silvernose,** Mary Hoffman's **Clever Katya: A Fairy Tale from Old Russia,** Carol Ann Williams's **Tsubu, The Little Snail,** and even Paul Zelinsky's **Rapunzel.** People in the legends of William Tell,

Characteristics of a Hero

The following characteristics are adapted from Joseph Campbell (1988):

- A hero gives his or her life to something bigger than himself or herself—some higher end.

- A hero performs a courageous act, either physical or spiritual.

- A hero is usually someone from whom something has been taken or who feels there's something lacking in the normal experience available or permitted to members of his or her society.

- A hero embarks on a series of adventures to recover what is lost or to discover some life-giving information.

- A hero usually moves out of the known, conventional safety of his or her own life to undertake a journey.

- A hero undergoes trials and tests to see if he or she has the courage, the knowledge, and the capacity to survive.

- A hero has to achieve something.

- A hero's journey usually consists of a departure, a fulfillment, and a return.

Robin Hood, and King Arthur have many of the characteristics of heroes. As you read traditional literature, look for evidence of the hero cycle and the characteristics considered heroic.

Evaluating Traditional Literature

Each genre has unique qualities that make it necessary to alter or add to the criteria used to evaluate other books. In Chapter 2, the text of books is evaluated mainly in terms of plot, characters, setting, theme, style or qualities of writing, emotional impact, imaginative impact, and vision. Some of these criteria do not play as important a part in traditional literature, however, since plots are usually linear and one-dimensional, characters are often stereotypical and flat, and the setting is "long ago." One additional element that is important in traditional literature is a respect for and understanding of the culture being written about. The text must be truthful and faithful to the original story. With folk tales, we must think about whether there is anything that would embarrass or hurt a child of that culture and whether or not the book fosters cultural stereotypes. This element will be called respect for the culture.

The visual aspects of a book should be looked at in terms of the four questions in Chapter 2:

1. Does it delight and involve you?

2. Does the artist pick moments that are highly visual?

3. Does the artwork enhance the author's words?

4. Is there variety in the work in terms of perspective and composition?

But accurate representation of the people and culture is also essential. Oftentimes illustrators of books on American Indians show a mishmash of "generic Indian" designs, oblivious to the fact that there are many American Indian nations, each with its own designs and traditions. It is always easier to trust in the authenticity of the book when the illustrator and author talk about the ways they've worked to be true to the culture. In the boxed feature Criteria for Evaluating Traditional Literature on page 252, this artistic element is called accurate visual representation.

7. **Cinderella Variants** lists more than 100 variants of the fairy tale. Find it at

www.acpl.lib.in.us/Childrens_Services/cinderella.html.

To find Little Red Riding Hood variants, use the same address but change "cinderella" to "redridinghood."

8. **Aadizookaanag—Traditional Stories, Legends, and Myths** is a lovely site with stories from the cultures of indigenous peoples. Find it at

www.kstrom.net/isk/stories/myths/html/

9. **Folklore and Mythology Electronic Texts** provides oodles of complete texts. Find it at

www.pitt.edu/~dash/folktexts.html/#1

10. **Aesop Fables Online Collection** provides texts of over 600 fables! Go to

www.aesopfables.com

11. **AbsoluteWhootie: Stories to Grow By** contains a selection of fairy tales and folk tales from around the world that speak to such themes as courage, justice, and kindness. Go to

www.storiestogrowby.com

References

Bruchac, Joseph (1997). *Tell Me a Tale: A Book about Storytelling*. San Diego: Harcourt Brace.

Campbell, Joseph (1988). *The Power of Myth*. New York: Doubleday.

Emrich, Duncan (1972). *Folklore on the American Land*. Boston: Little, Brown.

Ford, Clyde (2001). Speech at Spring Conference of National Council of Teachers of English. Birmingham, Alabama, March 29–31.

McDermott, Gerald (1999). "Traditional Fantasy in Picture Books." IRA Annual Convention. San Diego, May 2–7, 1999.

Children's Books

Aesop (1967). *Aesop's Fables*. Illus. Arthur Rackham. New York: Franklin Watts.

Aliki (1994). *The Gods and Goddesses of Olympus*. New York: HarperCollins.

Bornstein, Harry, and Karen L. Saulnier, eds. (1992). *Nursery Rhymes from Mother Goose: Told in Signed English*. Illus. Patricia Peters. Signline drawings by Linda C. Tom. Washington, DC: Kendall Green.

Brill, Marlene Targ (1998). *Tooth Tales from around the World*. Illus. Katya Krenina. Watertown, MA: Charlesbridge.

Bruchac, Joseph (1996). *Between Earth and Sky: Legends of Native American Sacred Places*. Illus. Thomas Locker. San Diego: Harcourt Brace.

Climo, Shirley (1994). *Stolen Thunder: A Norse Myth*. Illus. Alexander Koshkin. New York: Clarion.

Cole, Joanna, ed. (1989). *Anna Banana: 101 Jump-Rope Rhymes*. Illus. Alan Tiegreen. New York: Morrow.

Cole, Joanna, and Stephanie Calmenson (1990). *Miss Mary Mack and Other Children's Street Rhymes*. Illus. Alan Tiegreen. New York: Morrow.

Craft, M. Charlotte (1996). *Cupid and Psyche*. Illus. K. Y. Craft. New York: Morrow.

Delacre, Lulu (1996). *Golden Tales: Myths, Legends, and Folktales from Latin America*. New York: Scholastic.

Doucet, Sharon Arms (1997). *Why Lapin's Ears Are Long: And Other Tales from the Louisiana Bayou*. Illus. David Catrow. New York: Orchard.

Emerson, Sally, ed. (1988). *The Nursery Treasury: A Collection of Baby Games, Rhymes and Lullabies*. Illus. Moira MacLean and Colin MacLean. New York: Doubleday.

Evetts-Secker, Josephine (1999). *The Barefoot Book of Mother and Son Tales*. Illus. Helen Cann. New York: Barefoot.

Furlong, Monica (1998). *Robin's Country*. New York: Knopf.

Goble, Paul (1988). *Her Seven Brothers*. New York: Bradbury.

Goldin, Barbara Diamond (1999). *Journeys with Elijah: Eight Tales of the Prophet*. Illus. Jerry Pinkney. San Diego: Harcourt Brace.

Hamilton, Virginia (1995). *Her Stories: African American Folktales, Fairy Tales, and True Tales*. Illus. Leo Dillon and Diane Dillon. New York: Blue Sky/Scholastic.

—— (1991). *In the Beginning: Creation Stories from Around the World*. Illus. Barry Moser. San Diego: Harcourt Brace [1988].

—— (1985). *The People Could Fly: American Black Folktales*. Illus. Leo Dillon and Diane Dillon. New York: Knopf.

—— (1997). *A Ring of Tricksters: Animal Tales from America, the West Indies, and Africa.* Illus. Barry Moser. New York: Blue Sky/Scholastic.

Hayes, Barbara (1998). *Folk Tales and Fables of the Middle East and Africa.* Illus. Robert R. Ingpen. New York: Chelsea.

Hoffman, Mary (1998). *Clever Katya: A Fairy Tale from Old Russia.* Illus. Marie Cameron. New York: Barefoot.

Isaacs, Anne (1994). *Swamp Angel.* Illus. Paul O. Zelinsky. New York: Dutton.

Johnson, David A. (1998). *Old Mother Hubbard: A Nursery Rhyme.* New York: McElderry.

Johnson, Janet P. (1998). *Keelboat Annie: An African American Legend.* Illus. Charles Reasoner. Mahwah, NJ: Troll.

Kellogg, Steven (1992). *Mike Fink.* New York: Morrow.

—— (1984). *Paul Bunyan.* New York: Morrow.

—— (1995). *Sally Ann Thunder Ann Whirlwind Crockett.* New York: Morrow.

Kimmel, Eric A. (1996). *Count Silvernose: A Story from Italy.* Illus. Omar Rayyan. New York: Holiday.

—— (1995). *Rimonah of the Flashing Sword: A North African Tale.* Illus. Omar Rayyan. New York: Holiday.

Lapaca, Michael (1996). *Antelope Woman: An Apache Folktale.* Flagstaff, AR: Northland.

Lester, Julius (1990). *Further Tales of Uncle Remus: The Misadventures of Brer Rabbit, Brer Fox, Brer Wolf, the Doodang, and Other Creatures.* Illus. Jerry Pinkney. New York: Dial.

—— (1994). *John Henry.* Illus. Jerry Pinkney. New York: Dial.

—— (1999). *When the Beginning Began: Stories about God, the Creatures, and Us.* Illus. Emily Lisker. San Diego: Silverwhistle.

Levine, Gail Carson (1997). *Ella Enchanted.* New York: HarperCollins.

Lobel, Arnold (1980). *Fables.* New York: Harper.

Martin, Rafe (1996). *Mysterious Tales of Japan.* Illus. Tatsuro Kiuchi. New York: Putnam.

—— (1992). *The Rough-Face Girl.* Illus. David Shannon. New York: Putnam.

Mayo, Margaret (1997). *Mythical Birds & Beasts from Many Lands.* Illus. Jane Ray. New York: Dutton.

McDermott, Gerald (1974). *Arrow to the Sun: A Pueblo Indian Tale.* New York: Viking.

—— (1993). *Raven: A Trickster Tale from the Pacific Northwest.* San Diego: Harcourt Brace.

—— (1999). *The Stonecutter: A Japanese Folk Tale.* New York: Econo-Clad [1975, Viking].

McKinley, Robin (1978). *Beauty: A Retelling of the Story of Beauty & the Beast.* New York: Harper & Row.

Mutén, Burleigh (1999). *Grandmothers' Stories: Wise Woman Tales from Many Cultures.* Illus. Sian Bailey. New York: Barefoot.

Napoli, Donna Jo (1996). *Zel.* New York: Dutton.

Opie, Iona, ed. (1996). *My Very First Mother Goose.* Illus. Rosemary Wells. Cambridge, MA: Candlewick.

Opie, Peter, and Iona Opie, eds. (1992). *I Saw Esau: The Schoolchild's Pocket Book.* Illus. Maurice Sendak. New York: Walker.

Osborne, Mary Pope (1991). *Favorite Greek Myths.* Illus. Troy Howell. New York: Scholastic.

Patz, Nancy (1983). *Moses Supposes His Toeses Are Roses and Seven Other Silly Old Rhymes.* San Diego: Harcourt Brace.

Polacco, Patricia (1995). *Babushka's Mother Goose.* New York: Philomel.

Pullman, Philip (1999). *I Was a Rat.* New York: Knopf.

Rockwell, Anne (1996). *The One-Eyed Giants: And Other Monsters from Greek Myths.* New York: Greenwillow.

Sanfield, Steve (1995). *Bit by Bit.* Illus. Susan Gaber. New York: Philomel.

Say, Allen (1974). *Under the Cherry Blossom Tree: An Old Japanese Tale.* New York: Houghton Mifflin.

Schwartz, Alvin (1972). *A Twister of Twists, a Tangler of Tongues.* Illus. Glen Rounds. New York: Lippincott.

Stanley, Diane (1995). *Petrosinella: A Neopolitan Rapunzel.* New York: Dial.

Taback, Simms (1999). *Joseph Had a Little Overcoat.* New York: Viking.

Van Laan, Nancy (1997). *Shingebiss: An Ojibwe Legend.* Woodcuts by Betsy Bowen. Boston: Houghton Mifflin.

Walker, Paul Robert (1995). *Giants! Stories from Around the World.* Illus. James Bernardin. San Diego: Harcourt Brace.

Walker, Richard (1998). *The Barefoot Book of Trickster Tales.* Illus. Claudio Muñez. New York: Barefoot.

Williams, Carol Ann (1995). *Tsubu, the Little Snail.* Illus. Tatsuro Kiuchi. New York: Simon & Schuster.

Wolfson, Margaret Olivia (1996). *The Marriage of the Rain Goddess: A South African Myth.* Illus. Clifford Alexander Parms. New York: Marlow.

Wood, Audrey (1996). *The Bunyans.* Illus. David Shannon. New York: Blue Sky/Scholastic.

Yolen, Jane (2000). *Not One Damsel in Distress: World Folktales for Strong Girls.* Illus. Susan Guevara. San Diego: Starwhistle.

—— (1998). *Pegasus, the Flying Horse.* Illus. Li Ming. New York: Dutton.

—— (1995). *A Sip of Aesop.* Illus. Karen Barbour. New York: Blue Sky/Scholastic.

Young, Ed (1989). *Lon Po Po: A Red-Riding Hood Story from China.* New York: Philomel.

—— (1992). *Seven Blind Mice.* New York: Scholastic.

Zelinsky, Paul (1997). *Rapunzel.* New York: Dutton.

Realistic and Historical Fiction

eer pressure. Choices. Divorce. Friendship. Death of a pet. Death of a grandparent. Moving. Loss of friends. Sibling rivalry. Survival in the wilderness. Falling in love. Solving a mystery. Overcoming adversity. Sports adventures. Family closeness. Coping with disabilities. Adoption. Problems with growing up. Although these topics appear unrelated, explorations of these themes set in contemporary times are grouped together under the umbrella term *realistic fiction* because they deal with real-life issues children experience. Books in this genre are often avenues for understanding one's own situation, meeting people who are similar to people one knows, and seeing how other people negotiate their lives. The focus on life's experiences makes this genre very appealing to children, who are eager to learn more about people and how they handle life's situations. This chapter will deal separately with historical fiction because, although it is a kind of realistic fiction, its emphasis on accuracy and authenticity raises different issues.

What Is Realistic Fiction?

The classification *realistic fiction* is assigned to stories that are convincingly true to life and that help children examine their own lives, empathize with other people, and see the complexity of human interaction. But exactly what does *real* mean and how real can realistic fiction be? When students are asked to assess this genre in terms of how realistic it is, they often respond only in terms of their own experiences, claiming that people they know don't act that way. Oftentimes they judge realism by imagining their friends and family in the roles of the characters. Behavior that is realistic to one person may seem far fetched to others. Gordon Korman (2000) says that he often begins stories with a real event and yet that tends to be the part of the story that seems unbelievable. He tells about visiting a school where a first-year teacher was teaching his students where their food comes from by having them raise a chicken in class, feed it, take it home on weekends, and then eventually have it killed and eat it. Korman could immediately see the problem with this "lesson plan"—the children would become too attached to the chicken to want to eat it. When he put this incident in one of his books and invented the rest of the story, readers complained that the chicken incident didn't seem realistic!

How real is too real if this genre is supposed to mirror real life? First of all, since moving the story along is the primary consideration, much of real life must be left out. Readers usually don't need to see in detail the showering, dressing, eating, and hygienic habits of characters. A more controversial issue is the realism of topics in realistic fiction. Should children read about death, cancer, and AIDS? Should they read about violence and abuse? Should they read about corruption and cruelty? Should they read about diverse families, such as families with two mothers or two fathers? Today all of these issues are being written about, but some parents don't want their children exposed to such realism (see the discussion on censorship later in this chapter). One standard that seems to permeate children's realistic stories is whether the ending offers hope or is uplifting in some way. Robert Cormier has been criticized because his books for older readers seem not to offer hope. Writers for younger children almost always hold out hope. Betsy Byars (2000) said, "I could never write anything that depresses me." She is an irrepressible person, however, who by nature seems to see the positive side of things, and that is reflected in her books even though they deal with tough issues. At bottom, then, realistic fiction is a genre that deals with the experientially true, tempered by both the author's view of life and what the public will accept.

The Appeal of Realistic Fiction

Realistic fiction is a genre of great appeal, as evidenced by the large number of Newbery Awards given to realistic fiction books. We like to meet other people whom we can relate to, whom we can learn from, and whom we can laugh with. Realistic fiction is appealing and valuable to children for a variety of reasons:

1. They can learn about human behavior and how people interact and get along with each other.

2. They can laugh with others in books and learn to laugh at themselves a little.

3. They can meet people who are experiencing the same feelings and emotions that they are and use these characters' experiences as a guide in handling challenges in their own lives, such as death, divorce, and moving.

4. They can learn about people who have different experiences and living conditions and thus can see that the whole world does not live as they do.

5. They can participate vicariously in events and activities that they may never actually experience, such as living in the woods, fighting for their homes, or climbing a mountain.

6. They can find out what it's like to live in another place, such as Appalachia, New York City, or the Cholistan Desert in Pakistan.

7. They can take an active part in solving a mystery and feel that they are helping to change the balance in the world between good and evil.

8. They can be delighted by heartwarming and life-affirming stories and good writing.

Types of Realistic Fiction

Realistic fiction is a broad category that includes many kinds of books. Among the most popular are adventure stories, animal stories, family stories, growing-up stories, books on social issues, humor, mysteries, romances, school stories, and sports stories. Children have definite ideas on the kinds of realistic fiction they prefer, as the boxed feature Children's Voices shows (see page 262).

Adventure Stories

Many people love the idea of adventure—of participating in an event or undertaking marked by risk or excitement. For some, going on a roller coaster and believing life will end momentarily is enough adventure. Other people actually go white water rafting or parasailing or mountain climbing. Most of us, however, would rather read about others participating in adventures. Then, from the safety of our own homes, we can watch others undertake dangerous adventures, witnessing vicariously as they fight wars or survive in the wilderness.

Gary Paulsen writes compelling adventures of survival, such as **Hatchet** and **Canyons.** Will Hobbs puts readers squarely in the center of dangerous situations in **Far North, Ghost Canoe,** and **Downriver. The Shark Callers,** by Eric Campbell, pits the protagonists against a massive tidal wave in shark-infested waters.

Adventure involving risks is largely absent from early readers mainly because many young children cannot separate themselves from the characters and thus find adventure stories too frightening. However, chapter-book adventures do exist, including **The Righteous Revenge of Artemis Bonner,** by Walter Dean Myers, in which a young man goes West to avenge the murder of his uncle, and the **Danger Guys** series. In **Danger Guys and the Golden Lizard,** by Tony Abbott, the protagonists engage in mildly risky adventures, facing dangerous Land Rover rides, a plane crash in the jungle, and the jaws of an alligator.

Animal Stories

Almost every child has had positive experiences with animals and loves to read stories that have animals in them. We love animals because they are soft to pet, respond to us with soulful looks, and live totally in the present, allowing play and fun to take precedence in their lives. We believe that our own animals care deeply about us and are very attuned to us. We love their loyalty, their patience, their wish to spend as much time as possible with us. They make us feel special and needed. We recognize that our animals need us, too,

Go to **Book Lists at the RT Library** to find lists of books about school, survival, and more at www.gti.net/rocktwp/ booklist.html.

Nathan and Lighthouse George paddle through treacherous waters, both literally and metaphorically, in this mystery adventure.

(From *Ghost Canoe* by Will Hobbs. Cover art copyright © 1997. Used by permission of HarperCollins Publishers.)

On realistic fiction . . .

I like books that can really happen but don't. Realistic books are easier to think about, understand, and have feelings for. But if they really haven't happened, authors can add anything they want as they go along.
—Jennifer, 7th grade

I like to read realistic fiction that has happened or can happen. It's neat to put yourself in characters' shoes and knowing what you did in the book could really happen.
—Kelli, 7th grade

I like to read about real life because I like to compare my life to the character's.
—Luis, 7th grade

I like to read about characters that are in trouble and are trying to get out of their situation. —Katie, 7th grade

On adventure books . . .

Gary Paulsen is my favorite author. He writes a lot of adventure novels that keep you on the edge of your seat and make you feel lucky you don't have to go through what the characters go through. —Michael, 7th grade

I like something adventurous or with a twist at the end or something that tells about kids my age with problems that relate to mine. —Hailey, 7th grade

In survival stories it's interesting how they do the things they do like survival skills and different tactics, also some things they learn from mistakes. —Ben, 7th grade

Gary Paulsen in **Hatchet**, **Brian's Winter**, **The River**, *and* **Brian's Return** *brilliantly describes nature, Brian's activities in the woods, and how he lives.* —Matt, 8th grade

On humor . . .

My favorite author is Roald Dahl because he is funny and seems like he knows how to end a book or when to end a book. —Keith, 7th grade

If I were to remember anything out of a book it would be the part that makes me laugh. —Brittany, 7th grade

I like funny books read aloud to me. —Derrick, 7th grade

On mystery . . .

I like Nancy Drew books because they are exciting and scary. —Shelby, 3rd grade

I like dramas and mysteries. I like the suspense and outcomes. —Erin, 7th grade

I like mysteries because you never know what's going to happen. —Jenny, 7th grade

I like mysteries to be read to me. —Michael, 7th grade

On sports books . . .

I like sports books because I play sports and I like to keep up to date on facts about sports players and sports. —Billy, 7th grade

On my own I like to read sports books because I play sports and they are interesting to me. —Madison, 7th grade

and we give them our time and are generous in ways that we might not be with siblings. For all these reasons, we have a passion for animal stories.

You may remember reading an animal story that tugged at your heartstrings or made you cry. Every time I read **Where the Red Fern Grows,** by Wilson Rawls, to my middle school students, I cried when Old Dan and Little Ann died. Maybe you remember **Sounder,** by William H. Armstrong; **Shiloh,** by Phyllis Reynolds Naylor; or **Stone Fox,** by John Reynolds Gardiner.

Realistic animal stories are written even for the youngest readers. **Biscuit,** the first title in an early reader series by Alyssa Satin Capucilli, features a darling yellow puppy who doesn't want to go to bed yet. Chapter books featuring animal stories include **A Dolphin Named Bob,** by Twig C. George; **Tornado,** by Betsy Byars; and **There's an Owl in the Shower,** by Jean Craighead George.

Family Stories

Sometimes family stories are called problem novels because they often deal with family problems such as divorce. Students enjoy reading about other people experiencing the same things they are. They get to see how others handle these things and, most of all, know that they are not the only ones in the world who are dealing with this issue or feeling this way. Students respond to family books because they can see that the characters experience feelings of confusion, insecurity, anger, and loss and then adjust.

Dear Mr. Henshaw, by Beverly Cleary, shows children coping with the emotional loss caused by divorce. Many books deal with several themes at once. In **The World of Daughter Maguire,** by Sharon Dennis Wyeth, Daughter is trying to understand what being biracial means as she copes with her parents' potential divorce. **Plain City,** by Virginia Hamilton, shows the main character dealing with being biracial as well as accepting that her father was psychologically damaged. The stories of Cynthia Voigt, in such books as **Homecoming,** focus on Dicey and her brothers and sisters as they cope with a mentally ill mother and an absent father. In **Belle Prater's Boy,** by Ruth White, the boy must cope with the disappearance of his mother as his cousin learns to accept the death of her father. **Joey Pigza Loses Control,** by Jack Gantos, focuses on the antics of Joey, a hyperactive child, when he comes to visit his grandmother and alcoholic father for the summer. Laurence Yep's **Child of the Owl** portrays twelve-year-old Casey learning to appreciate her Chinese heritage when she's sent to live with her grandmother in Chinatown because her father's illness prevents him from caring for her.

Growing-Up Stories

Growing-up stories portray the struggles young people go through with friends, identity, and ethical issues. Beverly Cleary's **Ramona** stories, Lois Lowry's **Anastasia Krupnik,** and Christopher Paul Curtis's **The Watsons Go to Birmingham—1963** are among the best known and loved. **The Baby-Sitters Club** series, by Ann M. Martin, showcases friendship and the issues of being part of a group. **Wringer,** by Jerry Spinelli, poignantly portrays a young boy dealing with peer and community pressure to kill pigeons as part of a community fund-raising event. **The Great Gilly Hopkins,** by Katherine Paterson, shows young Gilly trying to understand what family is as she moves in and out of foster home experiences. **Maniac Magee,** by Jerry Spinelli, tells of the growing-up years of Maniac, after the death of his parents, when he

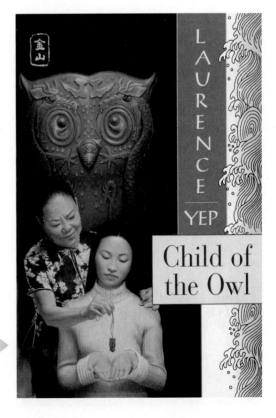

Paw Paw's affection for her granddaughter and patience in teaching her about their Chinese culture permeate this story, which focuses on Casey's adjustment to living away from her father.
(Cover art from *Child of the Owl* by Laurence Yep. Used by permission of HarperCollins Publishers.)

becomes something of a hero because of his unusual feats. For many children, growing up includes dealing with the death of someone close to them. *Walk Two Moons,* by Sharon Creech, shows Salamanca coming to accept the death of her mother. In *Crazy Lady!,* by Jane Leslie Conly, a young boy is coping with the death of his mother as he learns how to accept a mentally retarded boy.

Growing up also includes dealing with sexuality. The ever-popular *Are You There God? It's Me, Margaret,* by Judy Blume, talks about girls' body changes. In *The Goats,* by Brock Cole, two young people are confronted with their own sexuality when they are stripped and left on an island by other campers. Other books look at understanding one's sexual identity. *Annie on My Mind* and *Good Moon Rising,* both by Nancy Garden, are stories of girls coming to accept their homosexuality.

Other growing-up stories tell of the impact of moving to a different city or country. In Naomi Shihab Nye's *Habibi,* the Arab American protagonist moves from the United States to Israel, where she deals with cultural and language changes and sees evidence of prejudice and hatred.

Books on Social Issues

CD-ROM

To find authors who write about social issues, search Favorite Authors for the key word *issues*.

Some realistic fiction deals with issues beyond the scope of everyday family interactions. These issues include abuse, alcoholism, drug use, homelessness, homophobia, poverty, racism, sexism, and violence. More resources than the family itself can provide are required to address these issues, which have societal implications.

Books that deal with the gritty theme of family abuse include *I Hadn't Meant to Tell You This* and *Lena,* by Jacqueline Woodson; *Uncle Vampire,* by Cynthia D. Grant; *Max the Mighty,* by Rodman Philbrick; *When She Hollers,* by Cynthia Voigt; and *What Jamie Saw,* by Carolyn Coman. In *Freak the Mighty,* by Rodman Philbrick, Max has to come to terms with witnessing his father killing his mother.

The plight of a homeless father and his son is seen in Eve Bunting's picture book *Fly Away Home.* In Jacqueline Woodson's *From the Notebooks of Melanin Sun,* Melanin, a high school boy, is trying to figure out what it means to him to have a lesbian mom. Woodson's *If You Come Softly* deals with parent issues, school issues, and ultimately the violence in our society, through the love story of Jeremiah and Ellie. The persistence of racism is confronted in Suzanne Fisher Staples's *Dangerous Skies.* Coping with being the only Korean family in town is depicted in Marie G. Lee's *Necessary Roughness. Bearstone,* by Will Hobbs, shows Cloyd trying to hold onto his Native American culture as he moves from foster home to foster home.

Humor

Michael Cart (1995), writer and critic, claims, "Humor is the Rodney Dangerfield of literary forms: It gets no respect" (p. 1). Yet, according to Barbara Elleman (2000), scholar and critic, "Funny picture books are not only good for kids but encourage them to think creatively and read more." She believes that because children's lives are often so structured, they are taught things step by step. Humor helps them think outside the box and do such things as play with words: "Giggles can affect children in many positive ways." Dan Gutman (2000), creator of witty and entertaining books for middle grade readers, echoes some of Elleman's concerns: "Kids want to laugh, but comedy gets a bad rap. People assume it doesn't require much work and is not of high quality." Gordon Korman

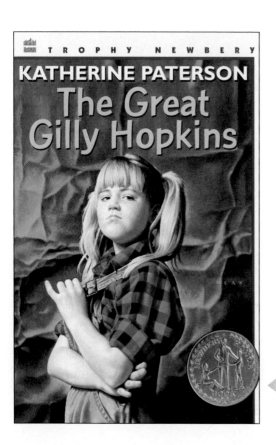

It takes a special person to understand and penetrate the tough exterior that Gilly Hopkins presents to the world.

(Cover art from *The Great Gilly Hopkins* by Katherine Paterson. Used by permission of HarperCollins Publishers.)

(2000), writer of humorous novels such as *The Chicken Doesn't Skate,* points out that a funny book is usually the one book that will turn reluctant readers into readers. Another writer of humor, Paula Danziger (1999), explains that she deals with "serious issues and uses comedy to make those issues more bearable.... Humor is touching.... It gets close to feelings. It can make us feel better—almost like a caress of understanding—or it can really hurt—like a stiletto in your heart" (p. 29). Betsy Byars writes about growing-up issues in extraordinarily funny ways in such books as *Bingo Brown and the Language of Love.*

Humor abounds in picture books such as Margie Palatini's *Moosetache, Ding Dong Ding Dong,* and *Piggie Pie!;* Babette Cole's *The Trouble with Mom;* and David Wisniewski's *Tough Cookie* and *The Secret Knowledge of Grown-Ups.* Early readers such as *A Know-Nothing Birthday,* by Michele Sobel Spirn, and *Wizard and Wart at Sea,* by Janice Lee Smith, let kids laugh as they read. Chapter books that will keep kids chuckling and reading include *The School Bus Driver from the Black Lagoon,* by Mike Thaler; *Play Ball, Amelia Bedelia,* by Peggy Parish; *The Time Warp Trio,* by Jon Scieszka; and *The Shrinking of Treehorn,* by Florence Parry Heide. Chris Lynch's *Babes in the Woods: The He-Man Women Haters Club #3* and Paula Danziger's *Amber Brown* series bubble over with humor. Other writers of humorous books include Judie Angell, Beverly Cleary, Ellen Conford, Helen Cresswell, Louise Fitzhugh, Stephen Manes, Barbara Park, Daniel Pinkwater, Barbara Robinson, and Barbara Wersba.

Mysteries

From the *Nancy Drew* and *Hardy Boys* series to today's crop of whodunnits, young people love mysteries. Part of the thrill of mystery reading is trying to figure out who did it before the characters do. This kind of book requires active reading and thinking and evaluating, as the reader must decide which clues are worth paying attention to.

This kind of book demands a lot of the author, too. Betsy Byars (2000), who won an Edgar Award for one of her mysteries, says, "Mysteries are the most structured of the genres to write." When she writes mysteries, she draws an actual map. Jean Lowry Nixon (2000) explains that making young detectives realistic is at the core of writing mysteries for young people. The young person has to be a believable character and have a strong motive to want to solve the mystery. Kids like to know that kids are clever enough to pick up a clue that police miss. Nancy Werlin (2000) believes that the world of the mystery is highly moral, with its emphasis on right and wrong, good and evil: "The world of mystery says the truth must be found and right must be restored." Byars offers another reason for the popularity of mysteries. She feels that detective stories are "one way we can deal with violent death—we can make sense of it with human intelligence." Perhaps this explains why the genre is so popular with children.

Many early reader books, such as *Detective Dinosaur: Lost and Found,* by James Skofield, introduce children to the genre. These are followed up by chapter books such as Betsy Byars's *The Seven Treasure Hunts;* the *Chet Gecko* mysteries, by Bruce Hale, such as *The Chameleon Wore Chartreuse;* the *Sammy Keyes* books, by Wendelin Van Draanen, such as *Sammy Keyes and the Hotel Thief;* the *Encyclopedia Brown* series, by Donald J. Sobel, such as *Encyclopedia Brown Solves Them All;* and the *Carmen Sandiego* mystery series, published by HarperTrophy. Other mysteries include *The Westing Game,* by Ellen Raskin; *The Case of the Lion Dance,* by Laurence Yep; and *Mr. Was,* by Pete Hautman. If students like mysteries, refer them to authors such as Jay Bennett, Lois Duncan, and Jean Nixon Lowery.

Romances

Everyone wants to be cared about. In about sixth or seventh grade, some boys and girls start wanting attention that takes on romantic overtones. They want someone to care for them in a special way. At this age, the search for romance is often played out, especially for girls, in romance novels. The *Sweet Valley High* series, with over 100 titles, is often the first kind of romance novel girls read. The focus of these novels is on how important it is for a girl to be accepted by a boy. More developed romance novels usually use romance as the frame for the story, while the protagonist deals with other issues.

W

*Find plans for using mysteries in the classroom at **Kids Love a Mystery.com** at http:// mysterynet.com/learn*

CD-ROM

If you like *mysteries* because they are *compelling,* do a word search in Favorite Authors for either word to find the names of more authors who write compelling stories/mysteries.

In *The Melinda Zone,* by Margaret Willey, Melinda is working out her feelings about her relationship with each of her divorced parents as she gets involved with Paul. It isn't the end of the story when Paul asks her out; it's the beginning. In *Thwonk,* by Joan Bauer, growing-up issues are embedded in a hilarious story of a girl who makes her dreamboat fall in love with her and then realizes what a bore he is. *Motown and Didi,* by Walter Dean Myers, is the story of two teens struggling with family issues but finding strength in the caring of the other person. In *Whistle Me Home,* by Barbara Wersba, Noli and TJ seem like soul mates until Noli finally realizes that TJ is gay. She has to figure out whether a relationship without romance is doable for her. These four novels have multiple plot lines, well-developed characters, and substantial themes within the romance format.

School Stories

Because children spend at least six hours each weekday in school, they have intimate knowledge of the setting and the workings of school. They love to hear school stories, which tend to be humorous and show characters doing things they might like to do. One popular picture book is *Miss Nelson is Missing,* by Harry Allard, which shows how one teacher dealt with an unruly class. Early readers such as *Arthur's Back to School Day,* by Lillian Hoban, calm students' fears of returning to school. Patricia Reilly Giff's chapter books, *The Kids of the Polk Street School,* offer stories of school experiences—such as losing library cards and making friends in *Say "Cheese."* Douglas Evans's *The Classroom at the End of the Hall* exaggerates events in a third-grade classroom. Andrew Clements's *Frindle* and *The Landry News* are humorous stories of fourth- and fifth-graders and their amazing undertakings. Many of Gordon Korman's humorous books are set in school, such as *Beware the Fish!* in which the students take action when they hear their school may close.

Sports Stories

Sports books are stories much like any other realistic story except that the framework on which the story is based is a sport instead of a mystery or a romance or an adventure. One chapter-book series popular with kids is Bruce Brooks's *The Wolfbay Wings,* about a hockey team. Embedded in stories such as *Barry* are traditional growing-up issues, such as getting good grades and being part of a team. The coaches in these books are pretty low key and encourage the kids to enjoy playing.

Another popular sports writer for younger kids is Matt Christopher, who is known for his fast-paced, action-packed stories, such as *The Kid Who Only Hit Homers.* Will Weaver's sports stories for older readers are meaty and satisfying. His baseball series about Billy Baggs, which includes *Striking Out, Hard Ball,* and *Farm Team,* has won many awards. John H. Ritter's baseball novels offer older readers a look at societal and family issues. In *Choosing Up Sides,* Luke has to decide whether his left-handedness is a mark of the devil, as his preacher father believes, or a gift for powerful pitching, as his uncle believes. In *Over the Wall,* the angry Tyler learns much about the Vietnam War and about healing in his bid to make the Little League All-Stars.

Using the sports story format to move his stories forward, Will Weaver focuses on father-son relationships and their importance to the mental and emotional health of the son.

(Cover art from *Hard Ball* by Will Weaver. JACKET ART © 1998 BY MICHAEL KOELSCH. JACKET © 1998 BY HARPERCOLLINS PUBLISHERS. Used by permission of HarperCollins Publishers.)

Using sports as a frame, David Klass writes compelling stories in such novels as **Wrestling with Honor** and **Danger Zone,** which are packed with issues of growing up and identity. Chris Lynch also has sports books for older readers, including **Iceman** and **Shadow Boxer,** both of which deal with family and relationship issues. Well-written books such as these can oftentimes lure otherwise reluctant readers into pleasurable reading experiences.

Themes and Formats of Realistic Fiction

Realistic fiction—whether in the form of picture books, chapter books, or novels—is packed with themes. Sometimes it's helpful to think about realistic fiction in terms of themes if you want to bring to your class books that can reach students going through a specific experience, such as the death of a loved one. Themes can also be the umbrella with which to focus a unit. In the boxed feature A Sampling of Realistic Fiction on page 268, books related to various themes are described.

It is also useful to think of realistic fiction in terms of narrative voice, to ensure that students are exposed to a variety of formats. Although first and third person still predominate in realistic fiction, contemporary authors have devised creative ways to use these voices.

First-Person Narrative

In fiction, events are frequently shown through the eyes of a narrator. Although this approach precludes the author from showing anything that the narrator does not either experience or have someone else tell her or him, there is an immediacy and closeness to events when one person is telling the story. Readers can identify with narrators, since they know exactly how they think and feel. In Paula Danziger's **Amber Brown Sees Red,** the first page says, "I, Amber Brown, am going through a growth spurt. Either that or the mirror's getting smaller." Some authors intersperse letters into a first-person account in order to hear from another character, as Patricia MacLachlan does in **Sarah, Plain and Tall.** Other times the entire story is told through letters or diary entries.

Third-Person Narrative

When a story is told in the third person, we can see the broad sweep of the story right away because we don't have to wait for the first-person narrator to show it to us. In Florence Parry Heide's **The Shrinking of Treehorn,** we hear immediately that something unusual is happening to the main character, Treehorn: "The first thing he noticed was that he couldn't reach the shelf in his closet that he had always been able to reach before, the one where he hid his candy bars and bubble gum" (p. 2).

Alternating or Multiple Narrators

To give readers access to two points of view, some writers choose to alternate viewpoints from chapter to chapter. Margaret Willey's **Facing the Music** alternates between fifteen-year-old

Palmer cannot admit to his own family, let alone his friends, how much he abhors the yearly town activity that so many approach with joy and relish.
(Jacket art for *Wringer* by Jerry Spinelli. JACKET ART COPYRIGHT © 1997 BY CLIFF NIELSEN. JACKET COPYRIGHT © 1997 BY HARPERCOLLINS PUBLISHERS. Used by permission of HarperCollins Publishers.)

for their own grief. The message that appearance pales in comparison to the substance of a person is important for all readers.

7. **Imaginative impact.** So much is left unsaid that readers can imagine many scenarios involving the characters. The open-endedness evokes many questions. What will happen with the cave the Fingers family is digging? Will they discover something underground that will halt their progress? How is the uncle who was in Vietnam doing? What does the Fingers family do to embrace him? Will Aunt Patty change as a result of her experience with her nieces?

8. **Vision of the author.** The author shows the deep connections that unite people. She knows that children can be cruel to each other, especially if they've been brought up to believe that they are somehow better than other people. She also knows the immense capacity children have to be kind and connected with each other. Although we see many gossipy, curious neighbors who find a reason to come over to the cul-de-sac to get a glimpse of the children on the roof, the author deals with them in a kind way, implying that they are lonely or have little to do. The author focuses on the positive in people while acknowledging the negative. Her view of the world is refreshing.

9. **Realistic elements.** The wisdom in this story, often conveyed through the words of Willa Jo, makes it seem very realistic. When Aunt Patty is overly concerned about finding friends for her nieces, Willa Jo thinks: "She didn't seem to know that friends aren't something one person picks out for another, like flowers at a shop" (p. 38). The girls' reactions when their aunt outfits them in clothes of her choice remind me of my own children's incredulousness when I tried to pick out something I thought they should like to wear. People's reactions to the fact that Little Sister didn't speak after the death of Baby also seem very realistic. Most characters, in their frustration with not being able to help Little Sister, think she should be shocked out of it or put in situations where she will be forced to speak. Judging people on outward appearances is fairly typical of most of us. Aunt Patty concludes that the Fingers children are not suitable to play with because of the appearance of their house and the fact that they are allowed to play in the dirt. This author appears to be a very good student of life, watching people and capturing their attitudes and beliefs in the story.

---

with the Forty-Niners, or choke through a dust storm during the Great Depression. Readers can go skinny-dipping with President John Quincy Adams in a chilly Potomac River at dawn, catch Teddy Roosevelt's children in the act of climbing lampposts in Lafayette Square, smell the sweat of youngsters helping their parents fell trees for their new homestead in the territories, and even listen in on their complaints. Historical fiction sets a story within the overview of an earlier period, emphasizing extraordinary events or historical figures, or just gives a feeling for what life could have been like in "the good old days." (Karr, 2000, p. 30)

At **Children's Library**, *find a series of websites on different aspects of historical fiction. Go to www.boulder.lib.co.us/ youth/booklists/booklists_ historical.html.*

At its best, historical fiction is both good fiction and good history. There is general agreement about what makes good fiction: a compelling plot, well-developed characters, important themes, a setting readers can easily enter, and writing that makes the story flow effortlessly. There are, however, different views about what makes good history (Is point of view a factor? Is there such a thing as objectivity?) and what kind of history school children should be exposed to (some want children to hear only about the positive aspects of our past). Wendy Saul (in Meltzer, 1994) reminds us that professional historians encourage students to reflect on the following key issues: What is worth knowing? Who is a reliable source? What facts in a given document are emphasized or ignored? Whose sense of "normal" is evident in the description or re-creation of events? Whose values? Whose perceptions of time? Whose perceptions of pleasure or pain?

This sense of inquiry has not always been apparent in historical fiction for children. Jean Fritz (1998) said that when she started writing historical fiction, children were to be "protected from grimness of present or past. History didn't require original research. Stories were told in general ways." As a result, the stories that were written often came across as lifeless and smacked of sameness. Only the positive qualities of a historical figure were revealed. Children were not given a chance to see that heroes could grow through mistakes. In an effort to make this historical fiction interesting, writers used dialogue. But all the characters sounded like the "good" boy next door when they were given words to say. Fritz refused to put in dialogue she couldn't absolutely document. She could document that Paul Revere said "damn," and so she used it in her book about him. One boy wrote to tell her that this was the first history book he believed! Fritz believes that historical fiction writers today show more respect for children, for research, and for accuracy. Much of the historical fiction written today is lively, intriguing, suspenseful, and full of people readers can connect to, flaws and all.

What historical fiction is depends on who is defining it. For school children, the past is any year before they were born; it may even include the years they were babies and toddlers. For adults, the present stretches much further back; almost no one views the years they themselves were school children as "historical" ones. Books published or set in a time period 25 or more years ago have often been moved into the category of historical fiction simply because children today have no awareness or memories of those times.

The Appeal of Historical Fiction

Historical fiction is filled with dramas and adventures of people in times past. What can children get out of historical fiction that they can't get from the study of textbook history? Why are children interested in reading historical fiction?

Historical fiction can enrich the lives of readers by helping them do the following:

1. Vicariously experience events and feelings as they were experienced by the people of the time.

2. Understand that there are universal truths, such as the need to be loved and cared for.

3. See that people not only had different clothing and living conditions but also had different beliefs—for example, that children were the property of their parents and that disfigured or handicapped people were to blame for their condition.

4. See many interpretations of the same period in history and understand that people view events from their own point of view, embedded in their own circumstances. For example, Patriots and Tories viewed the Revolutionary War very differently and would write about it in different ways.

5. Discover core values in the lives of others, as well as see examples of many people of courage.

6. Understand the prejudices and biases of another time period and thereby have more insight into our own society.

7. See what they have in common with people in other times and realize that all people have problems and challenges.

8. Develop an awareness that when and where people live influences who they are.

9. Satisfy their curiosity about the past by becoming involved in well-written, compelling stories.

10. Experience in an immediate and compelling way historical events or details that otherwise might seem boring and academic.

Children have definite views on the value of historical fiction, as the boxed feature Children's Voices indicates (see page 276).

story by Patricia and Fredrick L. McKissack, tells of a Christmas celebration on a pre–Civil War plantation. **Drummer Boy: Marching to the Civil War,** by Ann Turner, and **Pink and Say,** by Patricia Polacco, are both set in the Civil War. Elizabeth Fitzgerald Howard's **Virgie Goes to School with Us Boys** is the story of a Quaker school for black children after the Civil War. Allen Say's **Grandfather's Journey** is one immigrant's experience of coming to this country in the early part of the 20th century. **Baseball Saved Us,** by Ken Mochizuki, tells of the Japanese internment camps during World War II. **If a Bus Could Talk: The Story of Rosa Parks,** by Faith Ringgold, describes the beginning of the civil rights movement. Picture books can be found on many topics in history. For more examples, take a look at the boxed feature A Sampling of Historical Fiction Picture Books.

A Sampling of Historical Fiction Picture Books

Ancient Egypt

Bunting, Eve. *I Am the Mummy Heb-Nefert.* Illus. David Christiana.
A mummy on display in a museum recalls her past life in ancient Egypt as the lovely wife of the pharaoh's brother.

Columbus's landing

Yolen, Jane. *Encounter.* Illus. David Shannon.
A Taino boy on the island of San Salvador recounts the landing of Columbus and his men in 1492.

Pre–Civil War

Hooks, William H. *Freedom's Fruit.* Illus. James Ransome.
Based on a tale told to the author as he was growing up in rural North Carolina, this story is about Mama Marina, a slave woman and conjurer who casts a spell on her daughter in order to earn her freedom by fooling her master.
Hopkinson, Deborah. *Birdie's Lighthouse.* Illus. Kimberly Bulcken Root.
When her father becomes ill during a severe storm off the coast of Maine in 1855, ten-year-old Birdie keeps the light burning.
———. *Sweet Clara and the Freedom Quilt.* Illus. James Ransome.
A young slave stitches a quilt with a map pattern, which guides her to freedom in the North.
Siegelson, Kim L. *In the Time of Drums.* Illus. Brian Pinkney.
Mentu, an American-born slave boy, watches his beloved grandmother, Twi, lead the insurrection at Teakettle Creek of the Ibo people arriving from Africa on a slave ship. This lyrically told tale speaks strongly of the desire for freedom in every human soul.
Turner, Ann. *Nettie's Trip South.* Illus. Ronald Himler.
A ten-year-old northern girl visits Richmond, Virginia, and encounters the awful realities of slavery when she sees a slave auction.
Van Leeuwen, Jean. *Nothing Here But Trees.* Illus. Phil Boatwright.
A pioneer family carves out a new home amidst the densely forested land of Ohio in the early 19th century.

Post–Civil War

Bradby, Marie. *More Than Anything Else.* Illus. Chris K. Soentpiet.
In this story, based on an early incident in the life of Booker T. Washington, we see him working in the salt mines with his father and dreaming about the day he can learn to read.
Lester, Julius. *Black Cowboy Wild Horses: A True Story.* Illus. Jerry Pinkney.
Bob Lemmons, a former slave, displays his legendary tracking skills as he singlehandedly brings in a herd of mustangs.

Late 19th century

Bunting, Eve. *Train to Somewhere.* Illus. Ronald Himler.
In this poignant, beautifully done story set in the late 19th century, Marianne travels westward on the orphan train in hope of being placed with a caring family.
Howard, Ellen. *The Log Cabin Quilt.* Illus. Ronald Himler.
When Elvirey and her family move to a log cabin in the Michigan woods, something even more important than granny's quilt pieces makes the new dwelling home. The hard work involved in raising a cabin and moving to a new area is emphasized.
Kalman, Esther. *Tchaikovsky Discovers America.* Illus. Laura Fernandez and Rick Jacobson.
A fictional little girl, Jenny, writes to her best friend about her meetings with Tchaikovsky when he comes to America in 1891. The illustrations show details of life at this time, and we get glimpses of Tchaikovsky and what he did on this documented trip to America.
Lasky, Kathryn. *She's Wearing a Dead Bird on Her Head!* Illus. David Catrow.
This is a fictionalized account of the activities of Harriet Hemenway and Minna Hall, founders of the Massachusetts Audubon Society, a late-19th-century organization that would endure and have an impact on the bird-protection movement.
Levitin, Sonia. *Nine for California.* Illus. Cat Bowman Smith.
Amanda, along with her four siblings and her mother, travels by stagecoach from Missouri to California to join her father. In this funny, heartwarming tale, mother saves the day whenever crises arise.

Turner, Ann. *Dakota Dugout.* **Illus. Ronald Himler.**
A grandmother describes to her granddaughter life in a sod house on the Dakota prairie, sharing the joys as well as the difficulties.

——. *Red Flower Goes West.* **Illus. Dennis Nolan.**
On the journey to California, a family nurtures the one thing Mother would not leave behind—a red geranium from her own mother's garden. As it survives river crossings and wagon jouncings, it becomes symbolic of the family's ability to survive.

Early 20th century

Hall, Donald. *The Milkman's Boy.* **Illus. Greg Shed.**
After 1915, people stopped keeping cows in their backyards and depended on horse-drawn wagons to deliver fresh milk to them. This story shows what it took for one family to maintain its milk delivery service.

Lasky, Kathryn. *Marven of the Great North Woods.* **Illus. Kevin Hawkes.**
To keep him away from the influenza epidemic of 1918, a young boy is sent to a logging camp in Duluth, Minnesota, where he finds a special friend.

Lee, Milly. *Earthquake.* **Illus. Yangsook Choi.**
Following the earthquake of 1906, a Chinese American family hurrying from its San Francisco home meets others trying to make their way to safety.

Littlesugar, Amy. *Tree of Hope.* **Illus. Floyd Cooper.**
Florrie's parents both work hard at menial jobs to make ends meet during the Great Depression. Florrie wishes that the Lafayette Theater in Harlem would reopen so that her Daddy could reach his dream and act again.

Moss, Marissa. *True Heart.* **Illus. C. E. Payne.**
This story, based on the history of women who worked on the railroad, tells of a young girl at the turn of the century who accomplishes her dream of becoming an engineer when the male engineer is injured and can't drive his train.

World War II

Borden, Louise. *The Little Ships: The Heroic Rescue at Dunkirk in World War II.* **Illus. Michael Foreman.**
A young English girl and her father take their fishing boat and join scores of other civilian vessels crossing the English Channel to rescue Allied troops stranded on the beach at Dunkirk by Nazi fire.

Hunter, Sara Hoagland. *The Unbreakable Code.* **Illus. Julia Miner.**
A young Navajo boy does not want to leave the reservation when his mom marries a man from Minnesota. His grandfather shows the quiet pride of a Navajo code talker as he explains to his grandson how the Navajo language, faith, and ingenuity helped win World War II. He reminds his grandson that he, too, has something to take off the reservation—the unbreakable code.

Lee, Milly. *Nim and the War Effort.* **Illus. Yangsook Choi.**
Nim, a little Chinese American girl, works hard collecting newspapers for the war effort so that she can prove herself as she proves her loyalty.

In historical fiction picture books, the illustrator carries much of the burden of telling the story. E. B. Lewis (2000), artist and illustrator, says that the "author provides the seed while the artist is the sun needed to make the story grow." The drawings must be accurate if the illustrator is to contribute effectively to the story and its authenticity. Lewis explains the extensive research he undertakes for each book he illustrates, not only researching the geography of a place in the picture collections of the library but actually going to Ethiopia when he couldn't envision the setting. He says, "I want kids to be transported to other places through the perfect match of text and image."

Authenticity sometimes presents unusual problems for illustrators of historical picture books. Philip Lee (1999), book publisher, explained the dilemma Dom Lee faced in illustrating **Baseball Saved Us,** by Ken Mochizuki. Through researching the Japanese internment camps, Lee found that the guards at these camps actually wore old World War I uniforms, even though the internment occurred during World War II. The artist and publisher had to decide whether to be totally accurate at the expense of confusing their readers. They decided to use World War II uniforms for the sake of clarity.

Historical Fiction Series Books

Series books have become some of the most popular books of historical fiction among children and have spurred an interest in historical fiction. Children seem to like the predictability of the diary format and the guarantee that the book will get them in touch with another time in this country's history through the eyes of a person their age. *Dear America,* one popular series, includes books by many of this country's best writers, such as Ann

Rinaldi, Kristina Gregory, and Kathryn Lasky. Books in this series about people of different ethnicities are often written by authors of that ethnicity, such as Laurence Yep and Walter Dean Myers.

Children tend to think of these stories as "real." Oftentimes it is difficult to even find out whether or not these series books are fiction. Early volumes in the *Dear America* series and currently published volumes in the *American Diaries* series only indicate in small print on the copyright page that the book is fiction. (Now the *Dear America* series does have on the cover page an indication that the character is fictional.) Although generally well written, historical fiction series books are sometimes packaged in misleading ways, so readers believe that they are reading an actual diary of a child who lived in the time period of the book. Most of these books do not list sources from which the author drew, and none of them have acknowledgments or an author's note about the process of writing the book. In spite of these factors, these books have stimulated interest in reading historical fiction and usually give readers a good look at other times and places.

The Dear America series has its own website. Dear America: Official Website is at www.scholastic.com/ dearamericaindex.htm.

The Challenges of Writing Historical Fiction

Since writers of historical fiction focus on the events and issues of distant time periods, not only do they have the job of writing a compelling story, they have the additional task of doing sufficient research to make their stories authentic and lively. They can't get carried away and bury the story under the weight of all they've learned. They have to be judicious in the selection of the details. They have to decide whether they need to add characters, change the ages of characters, and combine events that happened in diverse places. They face the challenging job of making sense out of all their research. After all, the primary sources they use do not all represent one consistent view nor do they necessarily suggest the meaning beneath the events. The responsibilities of historical fiction writers are numerous.

Researching

What does it take to gather information for a story? Katherine Ayres says in an author's note of her research for **North by Night: A Story of the Underground Railroad,** "To help me write Lucinda's letters and those of young men who admire her, I read real letters of young courting couples." Next she studied slavery from Northern and Southern perspectives, using original slave narratives and abolitionists' writing. "I found a book with yellowing pages, written in 1856, about fugitive slaves who escaped to Canada. I read newspapers' reward notices for runaway slaves." She also visited the tombstone of a four-year-old slave child.

In writing the story of **Trouble's Daughter: The Story of Susanna Hutchinson, Indian Captive,** Katherine Kirkpatrick even had to learn about another language. Her activities during the three years she spent writing the book included "listening to Lenape language tapes, auditing a college course in archaeology, reading Dutch documents in translation, finding old maps, and hiking and kayaking through the area" (p. 244).

Stories of more recent times often rely heavily on other people's memories. In the acknowledgments to **Dave at Night,** which is set in the 1920s, Gail Carson Levine gives thanks to

> Irving Aschheim for sharing the bounty of his encyclopedic memory; to Michael Stall and Hyman Bogen for helping me understand asylum life; to Jim Van Duyne for explaining the mysteries of classic luxury cars; to Steve Long of the Tenement House Museum for answering my questions about the Lower East Side and for directing my research into productive channels; to Kenny Dasowitz of the New York Transit Museum for telling me about travel by trolley and train in a younger New York City; to Nedda Sindin for her help with Yiddish and for her memories of New York City in the twenties . . . .

The stories of authors' research paths often parallel the stories they uncover.

Cynthia DeFelice (1998), writer of historical fiction, likens research to a skeleton that the author fleshes out to create an historical novel: "A skeleton without blood and muscle and skin is not a complete human being; but without the bones, the rest has no form or strength" (p. 30). She goes on to explain, "Facts alone don't make a story; yet historical fiction that isn't based on fact simply won't stand up" (p. 30). Jill Paton Walsh (in Harrison and Maguire, 1987), writer of many novels of historical fiction, enjoys the research. She believes that the past is more accessible than the present: "You can read private letters and diaries, which would be intolerable conduct toward your contemporaries. It is nearly as intolerable to eavesdrop and certainly intolerable to put real people directly into your books" (p. 269). Thus, we can access the past through the library, while we are isolated in the present.

Keeping the Story First

When writers engage in research, they find out much more than they could ever use in a single story. In a conversation about his book *Heart of a Jaguar,* the story of a Mayan boy in the 13th century, Marc Talbert explained that his first draft was so full of history and facts that it was hard to see the story (personal interview, November 1995). His editor reminded him not to write a complete history of the Mayan people but to focus on what was necessary to tell the story of this young boy and his decision to be sacrificed.

Elizabeth George Speare (in Sipe, 1997) explains that every detail in historical fiction must do double duty: "It must not only add to the reader's sense of the historical setting but also contribute to the story" (p. 247). Writers of historical fiction are not historians, who can consider an exhaustive number of causes for a historical event and range over a huge geographical area, analyzing large, complicated events. Fictional text often deals in miniatures, which imply or symbolize larger social and cultural forces, as when the interactions of a few characters indicate a broad societal theme.

Lois Lowry (in Sipe, 1997) says she "can't write well about 'huge events' such as World War II" (p. 252); but she can find the details of everyday life which exemplify and evoke these events in such novels as *Number the Stars.* Fiction streamlines and simplifies so that the plot is clear and easy to follow and reaches a satisfying resolution.

Distinguishing Facts from Fiction

Authors such as Mildred Pitts Walter make very clear to readers which parts of their story are fact and which are fiction. In a Historical Note at the end of *Second Daughter: The Story of a Slave Girl,* Walter says that the sister Bett in the story is fictional. She also explains that she uses slave names that existed in records, but for most slaves no record of names was found. Although she included in her story the names of actual outstanding black contemporaries of the main character Elizabeth, she has "no indication that they ever met" (p. 213). Carolyn Meyer, in *Where the Broken Heart Still Beats,* took "the key facts of the history of Cynthia Ann Parker and used them as a framework on which to fashion the story of her life, as it could have been. Lucy Parker, her brothers and sisters, and her journal are my fictional inventions" (p. 194).

Creating Meaning in Events

Like historians, writers of historical fiction not only *see* meaning in events and chains of events, they also *create* meaning. Joyce Hansen (in Sipe, 1997), writer of historical fiction, believes that the writer must impose her own interpretation and actively construct history. She writes of finding much contradictory information in the historical records and learning that "history is made up of individual stories shaded by individual perceptions and experiences" (p. 246). Thus, it was necessary for her to take authorial responsibility for the shape of her story, in the same way a historian would.

In general, according to Sipe (1997), authors seem to accept history as a construction and go on to debate the degree to which history may be flexibly interpreted to meet the needs of the present. One debate centers around the way females in past times are portrayed.

fictional ones. Whether because of the publisher's decision or the author's, many books meant for elementary children simply do not contain information on authenticity, and we cannot be expected to know so much about each time period that we can spot inauthenticity. If in doubt about the historical accuracy of a book, consult book reviews in journals or on the Internet. Sometimes you just have to trust your own instincts and assume that you can spot obvious inaccuracies. If the language seems too modern or strained, if characters seem like today's youth in old-fashioned clothes, if the history is smothering the story, this is probably not a book you should share with your class.

It is delightful to find author's notes and other indications of how authors went about constructing the story, what details they changed or added, and how they dealt with the language issues; it is unfortunate that that information is not always available. But the fact that there is not enough information in the book to address the first two evaluative criteria in the boxed feature Criteria for Evaluating Historical Fiction does not mean that a book is unfit for use. Publishers seem more willing to publish explanatory material than ever before, and I hope this trend continues because such information enriches the experience the reader has with the book.

As the evaluation in the boxed feature Applying the Criteria: Evaluating Historical Fiction shows, the book *The Road to Freedom: A Story of the Reconstruction,* by Jabari Asim, does not meet all the criteria. Yet the book is still a good choice for classroom use, because the issues in the book are very worthy ones and the book is well written. Almost nowhere else do we hear the voices of ex-slaves and experience the day-to-day difficulties of their lives. The lack of sources could be dealt with by challenging students to find resources that verify the information in the book, by either looking on the Internet, going to the library, or contacting the author.

Criteria for Evaluating *Historical Fiction*

1. Is fact distinguished from fiction?

2. From the inside jacket flap, acknowledgments, or author's note, can you get a sense of the research the author did and learn what sources were used?

3. Do the action and plot develop out of the time period? If the book could be set in any other time period with the same conflicts present, it's not historical fiction.

4. Do the characters jump to life and make the reader feel connected to them? Do they express attitudes and beliefs consistent with the time period?

5. Are the historical setting and events woven into the story in seamless ways, or do the characters spout history lessons?

6. Are the themes significant ones?

7. Does the writing bring the story to life?

8. Is the story authentic in language, details, and spirit of the times?

Applying the Criteria *Evaluating Historical Fiction*

The Road to Freedom: A Story of the Reconstruction, by Jabari Asim. I chose this book, which has not been scrutinized by critics, in order to mimic the situation many teachers will be in when they are selecting historical fiction for their classes.

Synopsis: Ezra Taplin is ten when the Union soldiers arrive at the North Carolina plantation to set him, his father, and the rest of the slaves free. These soldiers force the ex-slaves to go to Roanoke to be resettled and to work for the Union army. At the end of the war, Ezra and his dad go to Charleston, where there is a settlement of blacks who were born free. One of this group, Thaddeus Cain, is willing to help the Taplins establish a new life.

1. **Is fact distinguished from fiction?** No. Nowhere in this book, one of the series called *Jamestown's American Portraits,* is there any indication that it is fiction. On the back cover, along with a picture of the author, is the information that he is a poet, critic, and fiction writer. No mention is made of what parts of the story were based on fact.

2. **From the inside jacket flap, acknowledgments, or author's note, can you get a sense of the research the author did and learn what sources were used?** No. Nothing is mentioned about sources. There are, however, five pictures from the time of the story, including a picture of black troops in uniform, two pictures of the ruins of cities in South Carolina, and a picture of Frederick Douglass. In the story are passages from Douglass's writings, as well as excerpts from black newspapers, which I take as indications that much research was done. Also, the descriptions of the city, how the ex-slaves lived, and the issues they were concerned with seem to be steeped in research because they appear accurate.

3. **Do the action and plot develop out of the time period?** The action and plot come out of the time period because they relate to the struggle of ex-slaves to find a way to make a living as they deal with the racist and repressive "Black Codes." Also, we see how many people place ads in black newspapers, hoping to find relatives who had run away or been sold away. The only part of the plot line that strained credibility a bit was on the very last page, when Ezra's mother, who had been gone since he was two, pulled up in a wagon and the family was reunited. While this event is within the range of the possible, it just seems to make the ending too pat.

4. **Do the characters jump to life and make the reader feel connected to them? Do they express attitudes and beliefs consistent with the time period?** The story is told through the eyes of Ezra, a likable boy. While I could get a good sense of Ezra's father, Thaddeus Cain, and his friend Cinda, I didn't feel closely connected to any of the characters. The characters, however, did seem to express attitudes and beliefs of the time period. It was hard to read about how thrilled Ezra was when a white man first spoke kindly to him. He reveled in his feelings of acceptance. Because this is a period not often written about from the point of view of the freed slaves, I had never thought about how deeply many slaves internalized the belief that they were inferior. The other attitude that seemed consistent with the times was the insistence of some Southern whites that they would never accept blacks as equals. This story showed how very difficult each step of "emancipation" was.

5. **Are the historical setting and events woven into the story in seamless ways, or do the characters spout history lessons?** Throughout the book, the events are woven into the story very tightly. The only time a character had the burden of "telling" history was in the second chapter from the end, when Ezra summarized in about four pages all the actions blacks in southern states were taking to resist the discrimination and oppression of those who did not view blacks as equals.

6. **Are the themes significant ones?** Yes. This story makes evident what the struggle for freedom involved. The information on the struggles of blacks at the time is rarely mentioned in other books I've read. Themes of inferiority versus superiority, speaking up in the face of oppression and death, and importance of family to a people who had been at the mercy of their masters all make this book a provocative one.

7. **Does the writing bring the story to life?** I found the writing to be excellent. The device of opening the book with an old man looking back on his early days of freedom is effective. The language, rich with description, allowed me to see the farm, the island, and the city.

8. **Is the story authentic in language, details, and spirit of the times?** The story seems very authentic, even though this is not a view of the Reconstruction period that we hear often. It is especially interesting to see how the author handled the language issue, since he was writing from the point of view of an uneducated ex-slave. Much of the narration is in the mind of the narrator, and that is written in standard English. Dialect is used only in dialogue and only if the character spoke in dialect. Thaddeus Cain, a very educated black man, speaks in standard English. The author never uses the word *nigger,* but instead has Northern troops refer to black males as *boys* or *coloreds.* The language choices the author made work for this book, as they involve us in the burning equity issues of the time.

Favorite Authors of Realistic and Historical Fiction

Since more books are written in the genre of realistic and historical fiction than in any other, I have had to limit my list of favorite authors. To do otherwise would be to create an unwieldy list, which would not be as useful.

Favorite Authors of Realistic and Historical Fiction

Joan Bauer often focuses on the growing-up experiences of memorable female characters, whom readers get to know well through details, dialogue, and humor.

Marian Dane Bauer writes stories for the younger set that are sensitive, evocative, and unforgettable. She involves her characters in some of life's biggest challenges, such as dealing with divorce and death.

Judy Blume continues to delight readers with tales of growing up, puberty, and coping with siblings. Always laced with humor, her stories keep the reader involved.

Betsy Byars's exuberance for life comes through in her stories for children. While she often writes about sensitive issues, she does so with humor and honesty.

Beverly Cleary writes with clarity, sensitivity, and humor. She tackles many of the prickly issus of childhood with aplomb.

Carolyn Coman gets inside the minds of her characters, sharing their fears, doubts, and hopes in sensitively written books marked by excellent dialogue.

Bruce Coville's warmth, humor, and sensitivity come bursting through in all of his books. His choices of themes and situations demonstrate his deep understanding of the world of the child.

Christopher Paul Curtis writes with humor and compassion. By putting endearing characters in memorable situations, his books bring to light social issues such as racism and discrimination.

Paula Danziger specializes in using humor to capture and keep readers' attention in her sensitive stories of growing up.

Lois Duncan writes compelling mysteries that often have a touch of the supernatural in them.

Paula Fox writes with honesty and clarity about issues that face young readers. Her characterization is especially notable; readers feel a deep empathy for characters facing issues such as loss and lack of courage.

Nancy Garden creates layered stories that ring with emotional honesty as characters face challenging issues such as accepting their own sexuality.

Patricia Reilly Giff offers her young readers a wide range of reading experiences. Her tales of school experiences are humorous and sensitive; her stories of earlier times are evocative and memorable.

Cynthia D. Grant writes powerful novels dealing with social issues such as abuse. Her strong characterization and compelling plot lines bring these issues home to the reader.

Margaret Peterson Haddix, a versatile writer who is as comfortable writing fantasy as she is writing realistic fiction, creates stories with strong plots and memorable characters.

Virginia Hamilton, a writer in almost every genre, creates mysteries and growing-up stories with intriguing plot lines and characters with depth.

Will Hobbs crafts amazing adventure/survival stories, which demonstrate his familiarity with the wild and his skill in making readers care about characters.

Gordon Korman, one of the funniest writers around, creates deliciously involving stories, often about kids getting into trouble.

Julius Lester, a master wordsmith, uses his love of language to bring historical and realistic tales to life.

Gail Carson Levine, a highly inventive writer who constantly amazes her readers with the variety in her works, is noted for involving plot lines, the ability to create memorable settings, and characters who jump to life.

Jean Nixon Lowery is a master crafter of spellbinding mysteries. Her young detectives are provided with both a motive and the resources for an investigation, and her plots are ingenious in their twists and turns.

Lois Lowry exhibits a capacity to write on a wide range of topics and in several genres. Some of her books for young readers humorously explore issues of family life, while others more soberly explore issues in society.

Carolyn Meyer writes both historical and realistic fiction in which characters jump to life, their issues become our issues, and the settings are well drawn.

Walter Dean Myers, a writer in many genres, writes with honesty, an ear for dialogue, compassion for his characters, and a sensitivity to issues of importance to his audience.

Lensey Namioka creates endearing characters and interesting plot lines. She offers readers an inside view of life in the homes of Chinese American children, as her characters deal with issues of childhood and acceptance.

Phyllis Reynolds Naylor is difficult to categorize as a writer because she writes so many different kinds of books. But whether she's writing about an endearing dog or travel through time, her plot development is superb, her characters are memorable, and her themes keep swirling through the reader's head long after the book is finished.

Katherine Paterson writes so beautifully that many of her books have become children's classics. She evokes settings readers can relate to, characters they care about, and plots that become etched in their minds.

Gary Paulsen is a master at crafting words that quickly involve the reader in the world of his characters. His plots, which often focus on adventure and survival, keep readers on the edge of their seats.

Richard Peck writes effectively for a range of ages. Whether he is writing a mystery, a time travel story, or a story about a sensitive social issue, he has a great ear for dialogue and an ability to capture the foibles and joys of human behavior.

Daniel Pinkwater's sense of humor and the absurd permeates his hilarious stories, which often have serious themes at the core.

Kathryn Reiss weaves us into the worlds she creates through her words. Her plot lines are fascinating, her ability to evoke a particular time period is outstanding, and her characters deal with issues that become real to readers.

Ann Rinaldi writes historical fiction so realistically that the reader feels part of the time and connected to the characters. Her research is notable, and she always provides engrossing plot lines.

Jerry Spinelli is a master storyteller who remembers being a kid and writes compellingly about the many aspects of childhood and adolescence. Humor is part of all his

books, although he writes stories with many different tones.

Suzanne Fisher Staples specializes in stories with compelling plots, well-developed characters, and easily entered settings, often in other countries. Much of the material for her novels was gathered during her time as a wire service correspondent in India.

Cynthia Voigt creates characters who resonate with readers, issues that readers care about, and compelling plot lines that keep readers reading. Her use of language is notable.

Virginia Euwer Wolff writes in a fresh way, often taking risks in format (prose poem, multiple points of view) to achieve the effect she is after. Her plots are fascinating, her language is beautiful, the issues she tackles are memorable, and her characters are ones that remain with us long after the book is finished.

Jacqueline Woodson knows how to touch the heart as she crafts stories with characters we care passionately about, issues that strike a chord in us, and plots that involve us.

Laurence Yep is another author who writes in many genres. His stories of children learning about their Chinese heritage are wonderful, as are his stories of historical fiction.

Invitations

Choose several of the following activities to complete:

1. Have each member of your small group choose a different theme in realistic fiction—for example, death, family, pets, fears, or friendship—and find ten picture books on the topic. Rank the books from 1 to 10, with 1 being the best. What criteria influenced your ratings? Share your reactions to the top two or three books with your group. What aspects of the theme does each explore?

2. Choose a controversial topic—for example, abuse, violence, or homosexuality—and read a novel that explores that theme. In your notebook, discuss why you would or would not use this novel with students. What are the literary and thematic merits of the

Lewis, E. B. (2000). "Getting the Details Right: Creating Illustrations for Books Set in Other Times and Places." IRA Annual Convention, Indianapolis, Indiana, April 30–May 5, 2000.

MacLeod, Anne Scott (1998). "Writing Backward: Models in Historical Fiction." *HornBook Magazine,* Vol. 74, No. 1, pp. 26–33.

McGillis, Roderick (1995). "R. L. Stine and the World of the Child Gothic." *Bookbird 33,* 15–21.

Meltzer, Milton (1994). *Non-Fiction for the Classroom.* New York: Teachers College.

Nixon, Jean Lowry (2000). "President's Symposium on Mystery Through Literature." IRA Annual Convention, Indianapolis, Indiana, April 30–May 5, 2000.

Sipe, Lawrence (1997). "In Their Own Words: Authors' Views on Issues in Historical Fiction." *New Advocate 10,* 243–258.

Stewig, John (1994). "Self-Censorship of Picture Books about Gay and Lesbian Families." *The New Advocate 7,* 184–192.

Werlin, Nancy (2000). "President's Symposium on Mystery Through Literature." IRA Annual Convention, Indianapolis, Indiana, April 30–May 5, 2000.

Children's Books

Abbott, Tony (1996). *Danger Guys and the Golden Lizard.* Illus. Joanne Scribner. New York: HarperTrophy.

Aliki (1998). *Marianthe's Story: Painted Words/Spoken Memories.* New York: Greenwillow.

Allard, Harry (1985). *Miss Nelson is Missing.* Illus. James Marshall. Boston: Houghton Mifflin.

Armstrong, William H. (1969). *Sounder.* Illus. James Barkley. New York: Harper & Row.

Asim, Jabari (2000). *The Road to Freedom: A Story of the Reconstruction.* Lincolnwood, IL: Jamestown.

Avi (1991). *Nothing But the Truth.* New York: Orchard.

Ayres, Katherine (1998). *North by Night: A Story of the Underground Railroad.* New York: Delacorte.

Barrett, Tracy (1999). *Anna of Byzantium.* New York: Delacorte.

Barron, T. A. (2000) *Where Is Grandpa?* Illus. Chris K. Soentpiet. New York: Philomel.

Bauer, Joan (1995). *Thwonk.* New York: Delacorte.

Beatty, Patricia (1987). *Charley Skedaddle.* New York: Morrow.

Blos, Joan W. (1979). *A Gathering of Days: A New England Girl's Journal, 1830–32.* New York: Aladdin.

Blume, Judy (1970). *Are You There God? It's Me, Margaret.* Englewood Cliffs, NJ: Bradbury.

Borden, Louise (1997). *The Little Ships: The Heroic Rescue at Dunkirk in World War II.* Illus. Michael Foreman. New York: McElderry.

Bradby, Marie (1995). *More Than Anything Else.* Illus. Chris K. Soentpiet. New York: Orchard.

Brooks, Bruce (1999). *Barry (Wolfbay Wings #11).* New York: Laura Geringer.

Bunting, Eve (1991). *Fly Away Home.* Illus. Ronald Himler. New York: Clarion.

—— (1997). *I Am the Mummy Heb-Nefert.* Illus. David Christiana. San Diego: Harcourt Brace.

—— (1994). *The In-Between Days.* New York: HarperTrophy.

—— (1996). *SOS Titanic.* San Diego: Harcourt Brace.

—— (1996). *Train to Somewhere.* Illus. Ronald Himler. New York: Clarion.

Byars, Betsy (1991). *Bingo Brown and the Language of Love.* Illus. Cathy Bobek. New York: Puffin.

—— (1991). *The Seven Treasure Hunts.* Illus. Jennifer Barrett. New York: HarperTrophy.

—— (1996). *Tornado.* Illus. Doron Ben-Ami. New York: HarperTrophy.

Campbell, Eric (1993). *The Shark Callers.* San Diego: Harcourt Brace.

Capucilli, Alyssa Satin (1996). *Biscuit.* Illus. Pat Schories. New York: HarperCollins.

Christopher, Matt (1972). *The Kid Who Only Hit Homers.* Illus. Harvey Kidder. Boston: Little, Brown.

Cleary, Beverly (1983). *Dear Mr. Henshaw.* Illus. Paul O. Zelinsky. New York: Dell.

Clements, Andrew (1996). *Frindle.* Illus. Brian Selznick. New York: Aladdin.

—— (1999). *The Landry News.* Illus. Salvatore Murdocca. New York: Simon & Schuster.

Cole, Babette (1983). *The Trouble with Mom*. London: Windmill.

Cole, Brock (1987). *The Goats*. New York: Farrar, Straus and Giroux.

Collier, James Lincoln, and Christopher Collier (1974). *My Brother Sam Is Dead*. New York: Scholastic.

—— (1994). *With Every Drop of Blood: A Novel of the Civil War*. New York: Delacorte.

Coman, Carolyn (1993). *Tell Me Everything*. New York; Farrar, Straus and Giroux.

—— (1995). *What Jamie Saw*. Arden, NC: Front Street.

Conly, Jane Leslie (1993). *Crazy Lady!* New York: HarperTrophy.

Couloumbis, Audrey (1999). *Getting Near to Baby*. New York: Putnam.

Coville, Bruce (1996). *My Grandfather's House*. Illus. Henri Sorensen. New York: Bridgewater.

Creech, Sharon (1994). *Walk Two Moons*. New York: HarperCollins.

Curtis, Christopher Paul (1995). *The Watsons Go to Birmingham—1963*. New York: Delacorte.

Cushman, Karen (1994). *Catherine, Called Birdy*. New York: Clarion.

Danziger, Paula (1997). *Amber Brown Sees Red*. Illus. Tony Ross. New York: Putnam.

Davis, Ossie (1992). *Just Like Martin*. New York: Simon & Schuster.

Dorris, Michael (1992). *Morning Girl*. New York: Hyperion.

—— (1996). *Sees Behind Trees*. New York: Hyperion.

Draper, Sharon M. (1997). *Forged by Fire*. New York: Simon & Schuster.

Dyer, T. A. (1981). *A Way of His Own*. Boston: Houghton Mifflin.

Evans, Douglas (1996). *The Classroom at the End of the Hall*. Illus. Larry Di Fiori. Arden, NC: Front Street.

Fenner, Carol (1995). *Yolonda's Genius*. New York: McElderry.

Fleischman, Paul (1993). *Bull Run*. Illus. David Frampton. New York: HarperCollins.

—— (1997). *Seedfolks*. Illus. Judy Pedersen. New York: HarperCollins.

Flournoy, Valerie (1985). *The Patchwork Quilt*. Illus. Jerry Pinkney. New York: Dutton.

Forbes, Esther (1943). *Johnny Tremain*. Illus. Lynn Ward. Boston: Houghton Mifflin.

Gantos, Jack (2000). *Joey Pigza Loses Control*. New York: Farrar, Straus & Giroux.

Garden, Nancy (1982). *Annie on My Mind*. New York: Farrar, Straus & Giroux.

—— (1996). *Good Moon Rising*. New York: Farrar, Straus & Giroux.

Gardiner, John Reynolds (1980). *Stone Fox*. New York: HarperCollins.

Garland, Sherry (1995). *Indio*. San Diego: Harcourt Brace.

—— (1993). *The Lotus Seed*. Illus. Tatsuro Kiuchi. San Diego: Harcourt Brace.

—— (1992). *Song of the Buffalo Boy*. San Diego: Harcourt Brace.

George, Jean Craighead (1974). *Julie and the Wolves*. New York: HarperTrophy.

—— (1995). *There's an Owl in the Shower*. Illus. Christine Herman Merrill. New York: HarperTrophy.

George, Twig C. (1996). *A Dolphin Named Bob*. Illus. Christine Herman Merrill. New York: HarperTrophy.

Giff, Patricia Reilly (1997). *Lily's Crossing*. New York: Delacorte.

—— (1985). *Say "Cheese."* Illus. Blanche Sims. New York: Dell.

Glenn, Mel (1996). *Who Killed Mr. Chippendale? A Mystery in Poems*. New York: Dutton.

Grant, Cynthia D. (1993). *Uncle Vampire*. New York: Atheneum.

Greene, Bette (1999). *Summer of My German Soldier*. New York: Puffin [1973, Dial].

Haddix, Margaret Peterson (1997). *Don't You Dare Read This, Mrs. Dunphrey*. New York: Aladdin.

Hale, Bruce (2000). *The Chameleon Wore Chartreuse: A Chet Gecko Mystery*. San Diego: Harcourt Brace.

Hall, Donald (1997). *The Milkman's Boy*. Illus. Greg Shed. New York: Walker.

Hamilton, Virginia (1993). *Plain City*. New York: Blue Sky/Scholastic.

—— (2000). *Over the Wall.* New York: Philomel.

Rostkowski, Margaret I. (1999). *After the Dancing Days.* New York: Econo-Clad [1985, Harper & Row].

Ruby, Lois (1994). *Steal Away Home.* New York: Macmillan.

Russell, Ching Yeung (1999). *Child Bride.* Illus. Jonathan T. Russell. Honesdale, PA: Boyds Mills.

Rylant, Cynthia (1992). *Missing May.* New York: Orchard.

Sachs, Marilyn (1997). *Another Day.* New York: Dutton.

Sappéy, Maureen Stack (1999). *Letters from Vinnie.* Asheville, NC: Front Street.

Say, Allen (1997). *Allison.* Boston: Houghton Mifflin.

—— (1993). *Grandfather's Journey.* Boston: Houghton Mifflin.

Scieszka, Jon (1991). *The Time Warp Trio: Knights of the Kitchen Table.* Illus. Lane Smith. New York: Puffin.

Siegelson, Kim L. (1999). *In the Time of Drums.* Illus. Brian Pinkney. New York: Hyperion.

Skofield, James (1996). *Detective Dinosaur: Lost and Found.* Illus. R. W. Alley. New York: HarperTrophy.

Smith, Janice Lee (1995). *Wizard and Wart at Sea.* Illus. Paul Meisel. New York: HarperCollins.

Sobel, Donald J. (1968). *Encyclopedia Brown Solves Them All.* Illus. Leonard Shortall. New York: Scholastic.

Spinelli, Jerry (1990). *Maniac Magee.* Boston: Little, Brown.

—— (1997). *Wringer.* New York: HarperTrophy.

Spirn, Michele Sobel (1998). *A Know-Nothing Birthday.* Illus. R. W. Alley. New York: HarperTrophy.

Staples, Suzanne Fisher (1996). *Dangerous Skies.* New York: Farrar, Straus & Giroux.

—— (2000). *Shiva's Fire.* New York: Farrar, Straus & Giroux.

Steig, William (1998). *Pete's a Pizza.* New York: HarperCollins.

Stewart, Sarah (1997). *The Gardener.* Illus. David Small. New York: Farrar, Straus & Giroux.

Talbert, Marc (1995). *Heart of a Jaguar.* New York: Simon & Schuster.

—— (1995). *A Sunburned Prayer.* New York: Simon & Schuster.

Taylor, Mildred D. (1976). *Roll of Thunder, Hear My Cry.* New York: Dial.

Temple, Frances (1996). *The Beduins' Gazelle.* New York: HarperTrophy.

—— (1994). *The Ramsay Scallop.* New York: HarperTrophy.

Thaler, Mike (1999). *The School Bus Driver from the Black Lagoon.* Illus. Jared Lee. New York: Avon.

Turner, Ann (1985). *Dakota Dugout.* Illus. Ronald Himler. New York: Macmillan.

—— (1998). *Drummer Boy: Marching to the Civil War.* Illus. Mark Hess. New York: HarperCollins.

—— (1987). *Nettie's Trip South.* Illus. Ronald Himler. New York: Macmillan.

—— (1999). *Red Flower Goes West.* Illus. Dennis Nolan. New York: Hyperion.

Van Draanen, Wendelin (1998). *Sammy Keyes and the Hotel Thief.* New York: Knopf.

Van Leeuwen, Jean (1998). *Nothing Here But Trees.* Illus. Phil Boatwright. New York: Dial.

Vick, Helen Hughes (1993). *Walker of Time.* Tucson, AZ: Harbinger.

Voigt, Cynthia (1981). *Homecoming.* New York: Atheneum.

—— (1994). *When She Hollers.* New York: Scholastic.

Walter, Mildred Pitts (1996). *Second Daughter: The Story of a Slave Girl.* New York: Scholastic.

Watkins, Yoko Kawashima (1994). *My Brother, My Sister, and I.* New York: Bradbury.

—— (1986). *So Far from the Bamboo Grove.* New York: Lothrop, Lee & Shepard.

Weaver, Will (1995). *Farm Team.* New York: HarperTrophy.

—— (1998). *Hard Ball.* New York: HarperCollins.

—— (1993). *Striking Out.* New York: HarperTrophy.

Wersba, Barbara (1997). *Whistle Me Home.* New York: Holt.

Whelan, Gloria (1995). *Once on This Island.* New York: HarperCollins.

White, Ruth (1996). *Belle Prater's Boy.* New York: Farrar, Straus & Giroux.

Willey, Margaret (1996). *Facing the Music.* New York: Delacorte.

—— (1993). *The Melinda Zone.* New York: Bantam.

Williams, Carol Lynch (1998). *If I Forget, You Remember.* New York: Delacorte.

Wisniewski, David (1998). *The Secret Knowledge of Grown-Ups.* New York: Lothrop, Lee & Shepard.

—— (1999). *Tough Cookie.* New York: Lothrop, Lee & Shepard.

Wolff, Virginia Euwer (1998). *Bat 6.* New York: Scholastic.

—— (1993). *Make Lemonade.* New York: Holt.

Woodson, Jacqueline (1995). *From the Notebooks of Melanin Sun.* New York: Blue Sky/Scholastic.

—— (1994). *I Hadn't Meant to Tell You This.* New York: Bantam Doubleday Dell.

—— (1998). *If You Come Softly.* New York: Putnam.

—— (1995). *Lena.* New York: Delacorte.

Wyeth, Sharon Dennis (1995). *Always My Dad.* Illus. Raúl Colón. New York: Knopf.

—— (1994). *The World of Daughter Maguire.* New York: Delacorte.

Yep, Laurence (1998). *The Case of the Lion Dance.* New York: HarperCollins.

—— (1977). *Child of the Owl.* New York: HarperCollins.

—— (1993). *Dragon's Gate.* New York: HarperCollins.

Yin (2001). *Coolies.* Illus. Chris K. Soentpiet. New York: Philomel.

Yolen, Jane (1988). *The Devil's Arithmetic.* New York: Viking.

—— (1992). *Encounter.* Illus. David Shannon. San Diego: Harcourt Brace.

Modern Fantasy and Science Fiction

Fantasy connects well to the lives and the play of children. Children go in and out of worlds of make-believe, in which animals and toys talk and in which they become something other than themselves. Oftentimes their fantasy life is as real to them as their real life. Children don't have a difficult time believing in fantasy because they recognize that the world has many unseen elements—feelings, wonder, tensions, dreams, fears, hopes, wishes, and longings. Magic seems natural to them, a way to go beyond the boundaries of their very small worlds. It is no wonder they love books filled with little people, talking animals, and live toys, such as *The Borrowers,* by Mary Norton; *Alice in Wonderland,* by Lewis Carroll;

Charlotte's Web, by E. B. White; *The Complete Tales & Poems of Winnie-the-Pooh,* by A. A. Milne; *The Wind in the Willows,* by Kenneth Grahame; *Raggedy Anne Stories,* by Johnny Gruelle; *The Wonderful Wizard of Oz,* by L. Frank Baum; and *The Tale of Peter Rabbit,* by Beatrix Potter. These stories speak of their deepest hopes, dreams, emotions, and fears and take them to exciting and new places. Fantasy provides a vision that other genres don't offer.

Authors of fantasy are well aware of the existence of wonder, that "great excitement that is a mixture of astonishment and delight" (Cooper, in Harrison and Maguire, 1987). Yet most children abandon fantasy when adults stop reading to them. Then they mainly read realistic fiction and informational books—perhaps trying to figure out how to get along in the world, how to crack those seemingly secret codes of behavior so that they can be accepted by others. Sometime in middle school many students find or rediscover that part of themselves that believes in the vision fantasy offers, and they begin reading *The Dark Is Rising* series, by Susan Cooper; *The Chronicles of Narnia,* by C. S. Lewis; and *The Chronicles of Prydain,* by

Lloyd Alexander. They allow the smoldering embers of their love of fantasy to burst back into flame.

Because fantasy can enrich the early lives of children, it is important to think about your own attitudes about fantasy, which you will bring to the children you teach. Are you comfortable with fantasy, or do you believe it is silly? Do you think it is a genre all children can enjoy? In my 30 years in the classroom, I have found that teachers' attitudes toward books and materials have a very real impact on the way children respond. By finding books in this genre that you can actively enjoy along with your students, you'll give your students an opportunity to find joy in this genre too. Some children explain how they view fantasy in the boxed feature Children's Voices.

What Is Fantasy?

W

*For information and surprises, go to **The Wonderful Wizard of Oz Website** at www.eskimo.com/~tiktok/index. html.*

Lloyd Alexander (in Harrison and Maguire, 1987), notable fantasy writer, gives a simple, straightforward definition of fantasy: "If the work contains an element of the impossible (at least as we currently understand the world), we classify it as fantasy; . . . if its events could indeed physically happen in the real world, we classify it as realism." He adds, however, that such classification is "simply a categorical convenience" (p. 195). Alexander's definition confirms that genres slide together, making it difficult to separate them. Events that seem very real may cause one person to identify a book as realistic, while others would categorize it as fantasy because it includes talking animals, which are viewed as an impossibility. Even novels that take us way back in time can seem real, probably because the writers make the transition seem so effortless with their vivid descriptions.

The genre of fantasy includes high fantasy, time travel, magic in everyday life, fantastical worlds, animals that talk and think, battles of good against evil, and even historical fantasy. The characteristics that distinguish one kind from the other are important only because they provide an indication of what kind of experience you'll have with that kind of book. Do you like having one foot in the real world and one foot in the world of magic and seeing how the two worlds exist side by side? Do you want to go to fresh, new worlds, where you can see how they organize their society, what customs they have, and what they consider "normal" and thus see our own world in much clearer ways? Do you like to get involved in time slips, in which one character goes to another time? Do you like to wonder whether people in eras before or after us are speaking to us? Do you enjoy the feeling of being able to do something few other people can

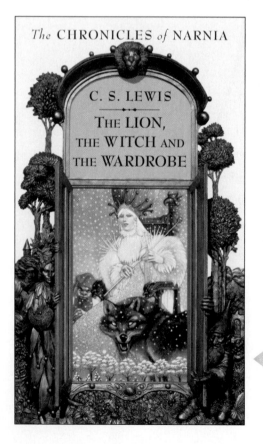

The Lion, the Witch and the Wardrobe, one of the best-loved of **The Chronicles of Narnia,** takes children into the heart of Narnia, where the forces of good and evil are at odds.
(Cover art from *The Lion, the Witch and the Wardrobe* by C. S. Lewis. COVER ART COPYRIGHT © 1994 CHRIS VAN ALLSBURG. COVER COPYRIGHT © 1994 BY HARPERCOLLINS PUBLISHERS. Used by permission of HarperCollins Publishers.)

Children's Voices

On fantasy . . .

It leaves you with wonder. —Jonah, 6th grade

It sparks your imagination and gives you the feel for creativity. —Allison, 7th grade

I love the fact that anything can happen. —Elizabeth, 7th grade

I guess I'm somewhat of a dreamer. Fantasy worlds are perfect without problems and troubles. —Carlyn, 7th grade

It gives you a chance to "escape reality." You can really use your imagination. —Julie, 7th grade

They take me to a whole different world and my imagination can think of anything. They take me away from all my thoughts and problems. —Joseph, 7th grade

I like fantasy because of how they [heroes] do what they do and fight against unbeatable odds. —Sam, 7th grade

These types of books bring me to another world. In this world I'm anyone I want to be. I can imagine a different time and place. Fantasy also gets my imagination going. —Georgia, 8th grade

I enjoy fantasy because I sometimes like to picture myself anywhere but in the world today. —Liz, 8th grade

Brian Jacques is one of my favorite authors because his stories are woven together with information they give. I also like J. K. Rowling because she does not give information if it is not part of the story. —Brian, 8th grade

*In **Mossflower** there's a badger named Bella. She's a leader. She protects her people. So do I.* —Amie, 8th grade

*I like **Harry Potter.** They have a lot of adventure and it really has some heart-throbbing moments.* —Steven, 4th grade

J. K. Rowling is my favorite author because of her immense use of detail, her funny yet serious way of telling the story. —Annie, 6th grade

*I thought that **Harry Potter's** Hermione was an awful lot like me. That was a light, fun read and I will always be jealous of the characters.* —Sara, 7th grade

On horror . . .

***Goosebumps** books are "funny-scary and quick and easy to read. I can finish one in an hour. . . . When you read **Goosebumps,** you can talk to other children who've read them and find out that they're scared about things, too. Also when you read about monsters and ghosts, you imagine what they look like in your mind even though you've never seen them in the real world, so you really have to use your imagination. This is a good thing."* —Rachel (cited in Rud, 1995/1996, p. 24)

*I like scary books such as **Fear Street, Terror Academy,** and **Goosebumps.*** —Jon, 7th grade

I read horror mostly because I love the way you get so involved in the story that you can't put it down. To me, I feel I'm actually in the story. —Katie, 7th grade

do, such as talk to animals, transport yourself from one place to another through a magic spell, or become part of the world of toys? All of these kinds of experiences are available through the magical genre called fantasy.

The Appeal of Fantasy

Find out more about this popular series at the **Harry Potter** page on Scholastic's website. Go to www.scholastic.com/harrypotter/home.asp.

Whether they acknowledge it or not, most people appreciate fantasy. Why else would they go in droves to see such movies as *Star Wars, Jurassic Park, Close Encounters of the Third Kind,* and *ET*? Why else would hotels have no thirteenth floor? Why else would newspapers print daily horoscopes? Why else would J. K. Rowling's **Harry Potter** books be at the top of the bestseller list week after week, month after month? Because our society sees reason as the opposite of and more desirable than emotion, however, people are often apologetic about their love of the magical and mysterious. They think of fantasy as an add-on, an extra, almost an unneeded appendage in their lives. After all, Freud, the grandfather of psychology, believed that fantasy was an escape from real life, and this theory worked its way into popular thought. Freud would certainly not consider fantasy to be of any essential importance. Luckily, some of his successors have taken issue with his theory about fantasy and demonstrated its positive aspects.

Fantasy can channel actions into the verbal rather than the physical. Psychologist Melanie Klein explains that when life appears futile and meaningless, creative activity reduces mental stress (in Harrison and Maguire, 1987, p. 54). Bruno Bettelheim (in Harrison and Maguire, 1987, p. 55) says that children under stress are able to battle through their problems only if they can fantasize about future achievements—even in an exaggerated and improbable way. If a child for some reason is unable to imagine her or his future optimistically, arrested development results. Jerome L. Singer (in Harrison and Maguire, 1987, p. 54) points out that the low-fantasy child reveals much action and little thought; the high-fantasy child is more highly structured and creative and tends to be verbally, rather than physically, aggressive. Stimulating children's minds through fantasy can help them cope with issues in their lives in imaginative, not physical, ways.

Fantasy can help fuel hope. Imagination helps us to hope, to envision things as they could be. If we could see only who we are now and how we live now, without imagining how things could be different, we would be without hope. If we saw only bleakness and despair around us, how would we know there could be another kind of existence if our imagination didn't let us fly above our present reality and see possibilities? In such books as **Howl's Moving Castle,** by Diana Wynne Jones, we see the hero's journey, the tests she survives, and her return. Seeing ourselves as the hero gives us hope that we too can accomplish wonderful feats.

Fantasy can make a difference in the way we see things. As people age, they tend to become deadened to their surroundings, even taking the beauty of nature for granted. Think about how differently young children and adults take a walk. Adults stroll along, while young children leave nothing unexplored. They look and question. They know that the world is filled with amazing information, and their curiosity drives them. They believe that almost anything is possible. By providing literature that stretches the imagination, we can perhaps help children retain their curiosity, keeping their minds flexible so that they'll be willing to stretch

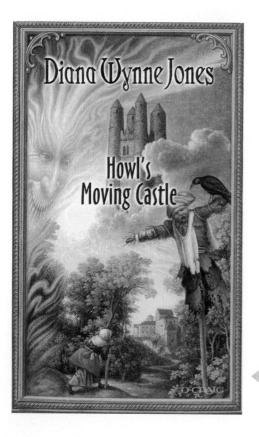

In this warm-hearted, witty fantasy, Sophie, turned into an old woman by a witch, finds that seeking her fortune involves bargaining with the heartless Wizard Howl. (Cover art from *Howl's Moving Castle* by Diana Wynne Jones. Used by permission of HarperCollins Publishers.)

out and grab concepts that seem just out of reach. Keeping the imaginative muscles flexed helps children think about familiar things in unaccustomed ways.

Fantasy can help us grapple with the essential questions of the universe, for which there are no observable answers. Some people turn to fantasy because it taps into their deep inner longing to understand phenomena that science and religion have been unable to explain to everyone's satisfaction. Erich Fromm suggests (in Harrison and Maguire, 1987) that acceptance and understanding of this other world are contained in the subconscious mind, which he calls the storehouse of a "forgotten language . . . the common origin of dream, fairy tales, and myth" (p. 178). It has been suggested that this subconscious mind Fromm alludes to, which we carry around within us and sometimes let ourselves experience, may be a genetic intelligence of things the human race has known since the earliest days. As Natalie Babbitt (in Harrison and Maguire, 1987) describes it, "true fantasy" is not a new creation but "is distilled and interpreted—from impressions that go far back into prehistory, impressions that, so far as we can tell from the study of folktales, are common to us all whatever our age and nationality" (p. 174). Babbitt believes this other world that is deep within our subconscious will always be somewhere; because no matter how we may try to deny it, our need for it is large. Patricia Lee Gauch (1994) writes that the creation of the best fantasy involves probing the wisdom of "that dark and secret place in the human psyche," as well as using the intellect. "Fantasies have common recurring elements because the terrain of the human psyche is universal, or, as Jung argued, 'the journey reflects a collective human experience'" (p. 162). Given that we all have to answer the same essential questions about our lives, Gauch says, "If literature does, in fact, provide a map for living, there is no map more powerful for the developing individual, more full of humanity, than fine fantasy" (p. 166).

Fantasy can help empower us to become who we wish to be. Especially in quest or high fantasy, we live through the trials of the heroes; we experience their decision making and the consequences of those choices. We hurt when they hurt, we are thrilled when they are thrilled; we are defeated when they are defeated; and we are victorious when they are victorious. This kind of fantasy asks us to go within, to dwell in those shadowy places in our heart and mind. Through fantasy, we can get to know ourselves better: what we're capable of, what fears hold us back, what we'd like to accomplish, what things are near and dear to our heart, and what issues we're willing to take a stand on. In this age of media scrutiny, when all the blemishes of contemporary and historical heroes are publicized, children need to see figures of heroic dimension. Fantasy can help empower them to be the people they want to be by giving them models for facing their deepest fears and accepting challenges they aren't sure they're capable of. By inhabiting this inner territory, we can all become more aware of that which we are capable of.

Fantasy can help us learn about and understand people. Bruce Coville's **Jennifer Murdley's Toad** provides an excellent illustration of what judging people on their appearance can bring. Through magic and humor, Coville shows that the worth of a person rests on much more than his or her outer covering or body. Children like books that help them understand the complexities of human behavior so that they can be more successful in negotiating their way through life.

Fantasy can allow us to vicariously have experiences that make us special. When students read stories of magic in everyday life, they can envision something exciting happening to them—such as getting a talking dog. This makes them special, giving people a way to relate to them and recognize in them qualities that they had never seen. Fantasy helps readers to feel deep inside, "if only someone really knew me, knew all the exciting thoughts and ideas I have, knew how much fun I could be." When the characters in Edward Eager's **Knight's Castle** become little people along with Roger's toy soldier, they are called on to display the kind of courage and inventiveness that most children are never called on to display. They have found a way to demonstrate who they really are and who they can be. In our ordinary-seeming lives, we often feel that we don't have a chance to show our promise or true ability.

Fantasy can reveal truths about life. At the core of much fantasy literature lies a gleaming nugget of truth, which is obscured in our regular world. Being in an imaginary world has the effect of lifting us up above our world so that we can clearly see these nuggets, which are usually covered by our fears or by the blinders we develop within a culture.

Lyra learns some uncomfortable truths about life as she journeys to the North to solve the mystery of the missing children.

("Cover illustration" by Eric Rohmann, copyright © 1996 by Eric Rohmann, from THE GOLDEN COMPASS by Philip Pullman. Used by permission of Alfred A. Knopf Children's Books, a division of Random House, Inc.)

Because our society is not comfortable with the idea of death, we tend to fear it and miss the truths death holds. *Tuck Everlasting,* by Natalie Babbitt, in which one family lives forever, asks readers to think about the purpose of dying—how it fits into the natural order of things and is part of the rhythm of life. Readers of **The Golden Compass,** by Philip Pullman, might question whether religious organizations could be involved in far-reaching schemes to protect their own power at the expense of the people.

Fantasy can make life more diverting and interesting. Reading fantasy takes us away from the humdrum of daily existence and gives us interesting things to think about. It provides an escape when we need one. Who wouldn't rather live in a world peopled by flying dragons or wizards-in-training? Who wouldn't rather be neutralizing the "threads" spewed by the Red Star so as to save the world from fires and great destruction? Who wouldn't rather be able to see what mere Muggles cannot? Given how many alternatives we have in our complex society, sometimes it's restful to go to a world where the hero has more clear-cut choices. Fantasy can lull and enfold us if we let ourselves inhabit that secret place within—that place that wants to believe.

The Centrality of Imagination

Fantasy is certainly not the only genre that stimulates the imagination. But since imagination is the key ingredient in this genre, this is a good place to look at the importance of imaginative thinking. Maxine Greene (1995), educator and philosopher, explains that imagination makes empathy possible. It allows us to make "the leap across the boundaries of our own lives and into someone else's shoes" (p. 3). It lets us put aside the familiar and make the unfamiliar real. For a moment, we can feel what it's like to live in a different place and time and see the world in a different way. As a little girl reading **Raggedy Ann Stories,** by Johnny Gruelle, and hearing what dolls talked about when out of sight of humans, I felt such empathy for my dolls that I began to make room for them in my bed at night so that they wouldn't feel neglected.

Imagination allows us to see openings through which we can move, to envision possibilities, and to explore the unknown. As a child, I was startled by the fantastical ways in which the main character of **The 21 Balloons,** by William Pène du Bois, conceived of and built hot-air balloons. One balloon had a little basket house beneath, another was a balloon merry-go-round, and another was a life raft designed to help a group of people escape from a volcanic island. This book nudged me to think about the world as I had never envisioned it before and made me aware that there were ways of seeing other than my own.

Only through imagining can one break with fixed views and see past the supposedly objective and real. To find new orders in experience, we must be able to see beyond the normal or conventional so that we can form notions of what can be or should be. Thus, imagination is at the core of learning that goes beyond the self. Imagination lets us see things that are not in our lives but could be; it lets us envision new ways of thinking and doing things. After reading **Mary Poppins,** by P. L. Travers, I wanted so much to be able to move through space as Mary did. I wondered how a mere umbrella could propel Mary upward and move her anywhere she wanted to go. I was sure there must be some device that could move humans through space the way Mary moved. I was intrigued by what I had never thought of before. Imagination took me not only beyond the boundaries of my own neighborhood and experience, but also beyond the boundaries of my own ways of thinking.

Imagination isn't a luxury but a necessity. It is needed everywhere. Changes in medicine, education, law, physics, and technology all begin with seeing things in new ways. Imagination helps us meet new challenges and devise workable solutions to problems in our society. "We have to be able to conceive of things in new ways, to think 'outside the box' and not be tied to the way things are presently. Without this capacity, little forward change would happen in our world" (Greene, 1995, p. 36). Greene reminds us that too often we view imagination as something superfluous, not realizing its essential value for all children. Imagination teaches creative thinking. It opens windows in the actual, shedding a kind of light and allowing children to see new perspectives. Imagination feeds one's capacity to feel one's way into another's vantage point. It promotes curiosity and adaptability, qualities that help us survive.

By freeing the imagination, fantasy can help children face reality with more creativity and spontaneity of thought. Stimulating and unleashing the imagination is an important part of children's education, and the use of fantasy can engage them in the very serious work of releasing the imagination.

Kinds of Fantasy

When you hear the term *fantasy,* you may think of imaginary worlds in which the forces of good fight the forces of evil or you may think of dragons and queens and castles. Yet these elements are mainly associated with high fantasy, which is only one of the many kinds of fantasy written today. The goal of this section is to give you a glimpse of the kinds of treats that exist within each of the very different categories of fantasy.

Magic in Everyday Life

Stories about magic taking place in our familiar, everyday world generally are devoid of the lofty fight for good and evil and usually include humor and zaniness. Bruce Coville's **Magic Shop** books (**Jeremy Thatcher, Dragon Hatcher; Jennifer Murdley's Toad;** and **The Skull of Truth**), which are laced with humor as well as serious undercurrents, have wide appeal to upper elementary school children and make good read-alouds. One involves a dragon, another has a talking toad, and the third features a skull that casts spells. The appearance of these animals/objects has dramatic and very humorous effects on the children who find them. Another humorous, wacky series is **Freaky Friday,** by Mary Rodgers, in which bizarre events occur, such as a child turning into his own father. Roald Dahl writes humorous, fantastic adventures, such as **Charlie and the Chocolate Factory.** Diane Duane's **Wizardry** series, including **Deep Wizardry,** will also enthrall children because its young characters acquire special powers, with fascinating and often humorous results. Also included in this category are talking animal books such as **Smart Dog,** by Vivian Vande Velde; **Bunnicula: A Rabbit-Tale of Mystery,** by Deborah Howe and James Howe; and **Dr. Dolittle: A Treasury,** by Hugh Lofting.

Books with a more serious tone that tell of unusual things happening right around us include **Tuck Everlasting,** by Natalie Babbitt; **Charlotte's Web,** by E. B. White; and **James and the Giant Peach,** by Roald Dahl. Books in which toys come to life, every child's dream, include **Raggedy Ann Stories,** by Johnny Gruelle, and **The Velveteen Rabbit,** by Margery Williams, a perennial favorite.

Some books have distinctive structures that make them hard to categorize. **Harry Potter and the Sorcerer's Stone** and the rest of J. K. Rowling's series are such books. The story begins in everyday England, but when Harry turns eleven he is escorted to a school for wizards, Hogwarts. I question whether this world filled with magic is in another dimension that Muggles (nonbelievers in magic) don't have access to or whether Muggles don't have access to this world simply because they don't know how to see it and don't believe it can exist. So the question for me in categorizing this book is whether or not it takes place in our everyday world. Another book difficult to categorize is **Skellig,** by David Almond. Although the story

transplanted brains of fourteen-year-olds rule the world. They are directed by the Overlord, who is power hungry and will destroy and mutilate to achieve his ends.

Themes in Science Fiction

Much science fiction takes readers to new frontiers and new dimensions of experience. In *Twenty Thousand Leagues Under the Sea,* Jules Verne, one of the first science fiction writers, imagined a vessel navigating under the sea. Much of what he wrote about was realized in the 20th century. Although, at this point in society's development, many people are skeptical about new frontiers, perhaps what was written about in the 20th century will be realized in the 21st century. Several threads, or themes, appear frequently in science fiction, reflecting dreams about what this world could become.

Expanding Views of What People Can Do

Some stories encourage us to think about potential—what kinds of mental communication we're capable of, how powerful our minds could be, whether we limit people with our expectations of them, whether we could live forever or for much longer time periods, whether we could ever fly or move from place to place using only our minds. By showing humans creating, inventing, and achieving in other times and other worlds, science fiction expands our view of what humans are capable of.

In Virginia Hamilton's *Justice Cycle,* a trilogy that begins with *Justice and Her Brothers* (and was reprinted in 1998), four teenagers learn how to develop their psychic powers. They learn to mind trace (communicate telepathically), mind jump (project themselves through space by using their minds), and even use the power of their minds to vector to the surface of another planet in order to bring forth the water they sense is 70 feet beneath the surface. This story shows us that young people are very capable in important ways.

In Nancy Farmer's *The Ear, the Eye, and the Arm,* three men whose mothers were affected by plutonium have special abilities that enable them to be excellent detectives. This book makes the reader wonder whether mutations will yield extraordinary human abilities.

Confronting Ecological Issues

What are we doing to this planet? Some science fiction looks back on a nearly destroyed world and shows how the universe evolved since the time of chaos. The movie *Planet of the Apes* is one example. Monica Hughes's *The Crystal Drop* takes readers to the near future, when the most precious commodity is water! Peter Dickinson's *Eva* is set in a world where most of the forests and jungles are gone, a direct result of humankind's actions. By presenting stark images of what a future world could be like, these books encourage a close look at what we are doing physically to our planet.

Challenging Assumptions About Animals or Other Life Forms

In Peter Dickinson's book *Eva,* Eva, whose brain was implanted in the body of a chimp after a terrible car accident, makes an impassioned plea for humane treatment of the animals of the world. As a chimp who can "speak" by typing on a keyboard, she lets scientists know animals' reactions to the way they are viewed as "Other" and caged and experimented on. This book challenges current notions of how animals should be used by humans.

In this compelling story, the mental and psychic abilities of Justice and her brothers hint at what humans are really capable of.

(Cover art from JUSTICE AND HER BROTHERS by Virginia Hamilton. Cover art copyright © 1998 by Scholastic Inc. Reprinted by permission of Scholastic Inc.)

Other books put humans face to face with aliens, causing them to question their assumptions about themselves and the aliens. **The Mudhead,** by Josephine Rector Stone, and **The Golden Aquarians,** by Monica Hughes, put humans on distant planets, where they assume they have the right to do as they please. The humans discount living entities native to the planet because they view them as inferior to humans. Both stories bring the reader to the realization that alternative life forms can be compassionate, intelligent creatures and that it is the humans who are the aliens.

Challenging Ideas and Values of Society

The enormously popular **The Giver,** by Lois Lowry, paints a picture of a society seemingly without violence, where everyone has meaningful work and perfect relationships and no confrontations occur. This harmony has been achieved through a sameness that pervades the society, leaving no color, no unique dress styles, no specialness. Lowry shows us in chilling ways what this kind of society costs in terms of the human spirit and freedom. She challenges the belief that we would be happy if we were all the same. Since children seek acceptance by their peers, a book about the dangers of total sameness would be particularly provocative for them.

In Madeleine L'Engle's **A Wrinkle in Time** trilogy, the children travel to a planet where the eyeless inhabitants can "see" better than the children do. The story implies that there is more to truly seeing than the physical eye and makes readers question how much they really see.

Evaluating Fantasy and Science Fiction

Although fantasy and science fiction can be evaluated much like any other genre, there is one issue that is of special importance—how the writer gets us to suspend disbelief and enter the new world. Thus, believability in plot, characters, and setting needs to be looked at closely. Patricia Lee Gauch (1994), author and editor, says, "The building blocks of that [new] world need to be firmly set in our own world" (p. 164). In other words, the book must give us concrete details so that we can see specifically what the new world looks like. It must "burst with life at every turn—sensory life; life in the small, not merely the general; sensory life, the filaments of which attach themselves to our own experience; life arranged in a peculiarity of detail, not a generality" (p. 164). In the boxed feature Applying the Criteria: Evaluating a Fantasy, I evaluate **Harry Potter and the Sorcerer's Stone,** by J. K. Rowling, which is used frequently in upper elementary school.

Applying the Criteria *Evaluating a Fantasy*

1. ▶ **Plot.** Science fiction and fantasy are generally heavy on plot, and this is certainly the case with the **Harry Potter** books. The intertwined plot lines offer complexity and keep the interest of the reader. We wonder how Harry will find out he is a wizard, who Nicolas Flamel is, when Voldevort will show himself, if Harry's team will win Quidditch, and why Snape wants to jinx Harry. The pace is brisk throughout the book, with enough action and foreshadowing to keep readers turning the pages. We're drawn into the plot when we read, "There was nothing about the cloudy sky outside to suggest that strange and mysterious things would soon be happening all over the country" (p. 2). The plot line is believable because the author meticulously lays the groundwork with details. The very still cat sitting on the wall outside the Dursleys' turns into a person of magic; we know right away that people in this story will have special powers. In interviews, Rowling says that she knew every detail of the world she created, down to the banking system and mail system, before she wrote a single word of the story. Another wonderful thing about this plot line is that many of the tensions of the story are dissolved and

(continued)

L'Engle, Madeleine (1986). *Many Waters*. New York: Farrar, Straus & Giroux.

—— (1973). *A Wind in the Door*. New York: Farrar, Straus & Giroux.

—— (1962). *A Wrinkle in Time*. New York: Farrar, Straus & Giroux.

Levitin, Sonia (1999). *The Cure*. San Diego: Silver Whistle.

Levy, Elizabeth (1979). *Frankenstein Moved in on the Fourth Floor*. Illus. Mordicai Gerstein. New York: Harper & Row.

Lewis, C. S. (1950). *The Lion, the Witch and the Wardrobe (The Chronicles of Narnia)*. Illus. Pauline Baynes. New York: Macmillan.

Lofting, Hugh (1967). *Dr. Dolittle: A Treasury*. New York: Lippincott.

Lowry, Lois (1993). *The Giver*. Boston: Houghton Mifflin.

Lunn, Janet (1983). *The Root Cellar*. New York: Scribner.

McCaffrey, Anne (1979). *Dragondrums*. New York: Atheneum.

McKinley, Robin (1982). *The Blue Sword*. New York: Greenwillow.

—— (1985). *The Hero and the Crown*. New York: Greenwillow.

—— (1994). *A Knot in the Grain and Other Stories*. New York: Greenwillow.

Melling, Orla (1996) *The Singing Stone*. Toronto: Viking Kestrel.

Milne, A. A. (1926). *The Complete Tales & Poems of Winnie-the-Pooh*. London: Methuen.

Morgan, Jill (1996). *Blood Brothers*. New York: HarperTrophy.

Naylor, Phyllis Reynolds (1981). *Faces in the Water (York Trilogy)*. New York: Atheneum.

—— (1981) *Footprints at the Window (York Trilogy)*. New York: Atheneum.

—— (1980). *Shadows on the Wall (York Trilogy)*. New York: Atheneum.

Nix, Garth (1997). *Shade's Children*. New York: HarperCollins.

Norton, Mary (1952). *The Borrowers*. Illus. Diana Stanley. London: Dent.

O'Brien, Robert C. (1971). *Mrs. Frisby and the Rats of NIMH*. New York: Atheneum.

Park, Ruth (1982). *Playing Beatie Bow*. New York: Atheneum.

Pearce, Philippa (1992). *Tom's Midnight Garden*. New York: HarperCollins.

Peck, Richard (1983). *The Dreadful Future of Blossom Culp*. New York: Delacorte.

Pfeffer, Susan Beth (1988). *Rewind to Yesterday*. Illus. Andrew Glass. New York: Delacorte.

Pinkwater, Daniel (1979). *Alan Mendelsohn: The Boy from Mars*. New York: Dutton.

Potter, Beatrix (1934). *The Tale of Peter Rabbit*. Akron, OH: Saalfield [1st American edition, Harcourt Brace, 1953].

Pullman, Philip (1996). *The Golden Compass*. New York: Knopf.

Reiss, Kathryn (1993). *Dreadful Sorry*. San Diego: Harcourt Brace.

Rodgers, Mary (1972). *Freaky Friday*. New York: HarperCollins.

Rowling, J. K. (1998). *Harry Potter and the Sorcerer's Stone*. New York: Scholastic.

Service, Pamela F. (1990). *Under Alien Stars*. New York: Atheneum.

Sleator, William (1988). *The Duplicate*. New York: Dutton.

—— (1981). *Green Futures of Tycho*. New York: Dutton.

—— (1984). *Interstellar Pig*. New York: Dutton.

—— (1985). *Singularity*. New York: Dutton.

Stone, Josephine Rector (1980). *The Mudhead*. New York: Atheneum.

Travers, P. L. (1934). *Mary Poppins*. Illus. Mary Shepard. London: Howe.

Turner, Megan Whalen (2000). *The Queen of Attolia*. New York: Greenwillow.

—— (1996). *The Thief*. New York: Greenwillow.

Vande Velde, Vivian (1999). *Never Trust a Dead Man*. San Diego: Harcourt Brace.

—— (1998). *Smart Dog*. San Diego: Harcourt Brace.

Verne, Jules (1995). *Twenty Thousand Leagues Under the Sea*. New York: Puffin [1899].

Vick, Helen Hughes (1993). *Walker of Time*. Tucson, AZ: Harbinger.

White, E. B. (1952). *Charlotte's Web*. New York: Harper.

Williams, Margery (1998). *The Velveteen Rabbit.* Philadelphia: Running [1922].

Yolen, Jane (1988). *The Devil's Arithmetic.* New York: Viking Kestrel.

—— (1996). *Hobby: The Young Merlin Trilogy.* San Diego: Harcourt Brace.

—— (1997). *Twelve Impossible Things Before Breakfast.* San Diego: Harcourt Brace.

Yolen, Jane, and Martin H. Greenberg (1995). *The Haunted House: A Collection of Original Stories.* Illus. Doron Ben-Ami. New York: HarperCollins.

Yolen, Jane, Martin H. Greenberg, and Charles G. Waugh, eds. (1986) *Dragons and Dreams.* New York: Harper & Row.

Nonfiction Books

Some people wrinkle up their noses at the mention of nonfiction, remembering flat textbook-like books. Others are happy to hear that it's an acknowledged genre in children's literature. Today's nonfiction crackles with life. The illustrations are vibrant and powerful, the language is rich and compelling, and the subjects are varied and fascinating. Nonfiction, or informational, books are some of the most exciting and stimulating books in the field of children's literature. They intrigue, fascinate, compel, engage, and occasionally shock young readers, motivating them to want to learn more. They often draw students to question information in new ways. Amy McClure (1998) explains children's reactions to the rich-

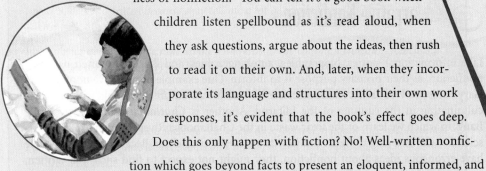

ness of nonfiction: "You can tell it's a good book when children listen spellbound as it's read aloud, when they ask questions, argue about the ideas, then rush to read it on their own. And, later, when they incorporate its language and structures into their own work responses, it's evident that the book's effect goes deep. Does this only happen with fiction? No! Well-written nonfiction which goes beyond facts to present an eloquent, informed, and well-crafted discussion of those facts can generate these same involved enthusiastic responses" (p. 39).

As very young children learn to read, they also read to learn. They are hungry for information about the world. They will happily read nonfiction to acquire information, to satisfy their curiosity, to comprehend the world more fully, to understand new concepts, to make connections to their lives and their learning, and to have fun! Kevin Spink (1996) points out that we often view reading as being informative *or* pleasurable, forgetting that it can be both. He explains that his first-graders "turn to informational books and magazines with a fervor and

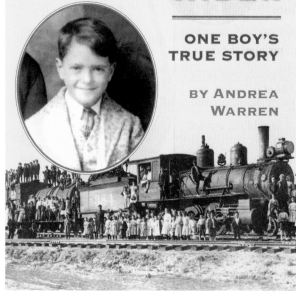

In this book of narrative nonfiction, autobiography is blended with informational writing to create an unforgettable tale.
(Cover from ORPHAN TRAIN RIDER by Andrea Warren. Copyright © 1996 by Andrea Warren. Reprinted by permission of Houghton Mifflin Company. All rights reserved.)

2. **Cartoon format.** *"Why Was I Adopted?,"* written by Carole Livingston and illustrated by Arthur Robins, explains adoption in a straightforward manner, using whimsical cartoonlike drawings to make a serious topic seem less scary.

3. **Photo story.** *A Forever Family,* by Roslyn Banish, tells the true-life story of eight-year-old Jennifer Jordan-Wong's adoption by a family after four years of living as a foster child with many families. The book relies on the photos as much as the short text to tell the story.

4. **Interviews.** In *How It Feels to be Adopted,* Jill Krementz, award-winning photographer and writer, shows the complexity of adoption issues by interviewing 19 adopted children and their families. The interview format allows readers to see a wide range of responses to one issue.

5. **First-person narrative.** *Orphan Train Rider: One Boy's True Story,* by Andrea Warren, uses photos, text, and first-person narrative to tell the gripping story of seven-year-old Lee, who was put on an orphan train with his three-year-old and five-year-old brothers. In alternating chapters, the author tells the history of orphan trains and the story of Lee, who was put on the train with no knowledge of what was happening. This very moving story follows him into the later years of his life.

Evaluating Narrative Nonfiction

In order to focus on elements that are particular to narrative nonfiction, let's compare two books on one topic: the 1871 Chicago fire. **The Great Fire,** by Jim Murphy, is a nonfiction book that radiates interest, from the colorful picture of the fire on the cover through the provocative last chapter. Murphy's whole presentation demonstrates his burning desire to know what really prevented the fire from being contained and whether or not blame can be placed. Because he has chosen to tell a large part of the story through the eyes of four people who were present throughout the fire, his narrative is compelling. This book, published in 1995, when technology allowed the easy printing of large-sized books filled with photos, maps, and pictures, is physically very attractive.

In *The Story of the Great Chicago Fire, 1871,* Mary Kay Phelan tells the story in an entirely different way. After shar-

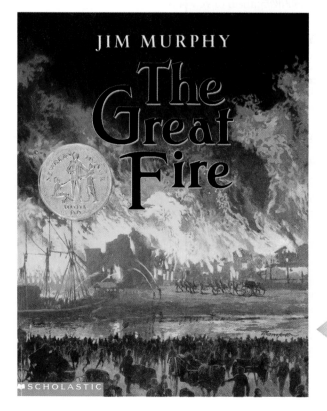

In **The Great Fire,** Jim Murphy not only provides views of the fire from several sections of the city but also examines beliefs about who was to blame.

(From THE GREAT FIRE by Jim Murphy, cover art by John Thompson. Cover art copyright © 1995 by John Thompson. Reprinted by permission of Scholastic Inc.)

ing one very interesting vignette about a speaker who, the night before the fire, predicted a terrible calamity, Phelan turns to explaining the history of the founding and development of Chicago. This book, published in 1971, lacks the visual appeal of Murphy's book. Like many of the older books available in most libraries, this book is likely to seem "old" to younger readers. Phelan's book does not have the same personal appeal as Murphy's book either, because she does not follow any particular eyewitness except the fire chief. Nor does she use the words of the eyewitnesses to describe what happened, although her bibliography cites at least eight eyewitness accounts.

Comparing these two books shows how important an author's choices are with respect to selection of facts and how the story is constructed or organized. Murphy uses only facts that propel the story forward, avoiding any extraneous material that will take our attention away from the fire. Phelan, an expert on the fire and the history of the city, mentions many things—including that Bret Harte's "Outcasts of Poker Flat" appeared in a Chicago newspaper that week. This kind of information appears throughout the book. While fascinating in itself, it prevents the story from moving forward as rapidly as it could. The boxed feature Applying the Criteria: Evaluating Narrative Nonfiction shows how each book stacks up with respect to the main concerns in narrative nonfiction.

Applying the Criteria *Evaluating Narrative Nonfiction*

Comparison of *The Great Fire,* by Jim Murphy, and *The Story of the Great Chicago Fire, 1871,* by Mary Kay Phelan.

1. **Organization or structure.** Organization is one of the first things readers notice in nonfiction.

Although Murphy's *The Great Fire* is divided into chapters, the information is organized around the question of what went wrong and why the fire wasn't extinguished. This focus keeps the reader reading and wondering what else could possibly go wrong. Because the fire is shown mainly through the eyes of four eyewitnesses, readers are taken from one part of the city/fire to another and can easily follow the narrative.

In Phelan's *The Story of the Great Chicago Fire, 1871,* the organization follows a chronological approach, beginning with a vignette, moving into the history of Chicago, and then turning to how the fire moved through buildings and businesses. The emphasis is on the destruction of the physical Chicago and not on how people responded to the fire.

2. **Author's involvement with the subject.** Does the author bring the subject to life and make it matter to the reader? Does the author sound excited about and interested in what she or he is discussing? When an author is not fully engaged with the subject, the book is less interesting and immediate.

Murphy is very involved with his subject and wants the reader to become immersed in the Great Fire and all its complexities. He is especially persis-

tent and passionate in his last chapter, called "Myth and Reality," about who was blamed for the fire. He wants very much to set the record straight so that the "vicious personal attacks" by the newspaper on Mrs. O'Leary and the poor are shown to be false.

Phelan is also very involved in this subject, as shown by the immense amount of research she did and her scrupulous attention to detail. She explained what was happening in the city the week of the fire, from the opening of the Opera House to the appearance of a now-famous Bret Harte story in the newspaper. However, the accumulation of all these precise details overwhelms the reader; it is difficult to see why this information is included.

3. **Setting.** Although setting is certainly not an element in all nonfiction, getting the feeling that we are in the place being described is important. Setting gives the reader another layer through which to experience the text.

Murphy brings us into the setting immediately in the first chapter, as we accompany Peg Leg Sullivan on his search for a little company, which leads to his discovery of the fire. Much of the book consists of accounts of people who were there, and the sights and sounds eyewitnesses describe keep readers right in the burning city.

Phelan's book gives us a sense of what was happening in the city, but we get only bits and pieces of what the setting was like. Because we don't see the ravages of the fire through the eyes of an eyewitness, it is difficult to feel we are actually in the city, experiencing its burning.

(continued)

4. **Qualities of writing.** When looking at informational books, notice whether the author creates a mood conducive to wanting to explore the subject further.

   The Great Fire, a Newbery Honor Book, clearly embodies the qualities of excellent writing, which entice the reader into the subject. Murphy uses details to make readers feel as if they were in Chicago. Quotations from people involved and the friendly authorial voice invite readers into the book.

   Phelan's book contains much good writing, but the use of the present tense—as if the event were happening today—is distracting. Her clear writing and excellent description are marred by a distant authorial voice and an overabundance of detail.

5. **Emotional impact.** Does the information entice us, making us want to know more?

   Murphy's selection of details and use of participants' own words make the fire vivid and real. We recoil when sparks from tall buildings are blown across the river, igniting buildings there. We see people fleeing in horror and stamping out sparks on their own clothing. Murphy's discussion of the fire in terms of people and the effects it had on them heightens the emotional impact.

   In Phelan's book, it is difficult to feel much emotional impact because so much time is spent talking about how building owners attempted to save their goods. No single consistent eyewitness is used, so the reader has no one but the fire chief to identify with. Thus, there is little emotional pull to make the book memorable.

6. **Imaginative impact.** One aspect of imaginative impact is whether the book opens up new possibilities and new ways of thinking. When information is presented with no sense of excitement and no attempt to raise questions, readers may feel deadened by all the information and may not see new openings for their thinking.

   The excitement with which information is presented in Murphy's book makes us question the established accounts of the fire. The reader may wonder whether other aspects of history suffer from such inaccuracy. *The Great Fire* encourages readers to examine other accounts of urban living to see how they have been handled by authors.

   Phelan's book raises few issues or questions. Her factual approach makes it seem as if there were no questions left to be asked.

7. **Vision of the author or attitude toward the topic.** As you assess nonfiction, ask yourself whether the author makes the world seem like an amazing place by bringing up interesting-to-explore mysteries, which show how complex the world is. Or does the author plod from point A to point B without invoking a sense of wonder and mystery? Are interesting speculative questions raised? Since almost every subject is value laden, does the author bring up controversies and uncomfortable facts or just scratch the surface? Does the author make us see the world as a place of interest, filled with fascinating information? How an author feels about his or her subject comes out in many ways in his or her writing.

   Murphy clearly sees the Chicago fire as an incident with many causes, as he works to piece together why it burned so long and spread so far. He is very concerned with the equitable treatment of people, as he provides evidence showing how the placing of the blame on Mrs. O'Leary and the "drunk" firefighters was unfounded. He seems passionate about uncovering attempts to capitalize on the friction between the rich and the poor in placing blame. The tone of the book indicates the author's interest in exploring the deeper equity issues that lie beneath the event itself.

   Phelan's book does not provide any indication of an expansive vision of the world. She characterizes Chicago more in terms of its buildings than its people. Since she brings up none of the social issues surrounding the fire, it is hard to get a sense of her vision of the world.

8. **Authenticity.** Is the book based on solid research? How did the author learn about the subject? Murphy's acknowledgments indicate that he was in Chicago frequently to get a sense of the city he wanted to write about. He did research there, as his bibliography and sources indicate. Much of his research included eyewitness accounts. Phelan also used research extensively, as indicated by her bibliography.

   Be aware that the same fact base can lead to different interpretations, viewpoints, and opinions. For instance, Phelan explains that William Lee rushed to the drugstore where the nearest alarm box had been installed and "Mr. Goll [the druggist] pulls down the lever, but for some unknown reason the signal does not register at the central fire headquarters in the courthouse" (p. 40). However, Murphy says that Druggist Goll would not give William Lee the key to the alarm box because Goll said a fire truck had already passed, and thus this first alarm signal was never sent (p. 26).

9. ▶ **Design and illustrations.** Information is made accessible through placement of illustrations and through the way the book is designed. Design elements include type size, kinds of fonts, and titles and subheads. (More elements are mentioned in the discussion of the evaluation of nonnarrative nonfiction, where they are more frequently used.)

The large size of Murphy's book, the large clear print, and the frequent maps, photos, and drawings quickly bring the reader into the story. This is not a cluttered, busy-looking book, but one whose design makes it look inviting and interesting. Because Phelan's book was published before the advent of recent technology, only a few black-and-white drawings of mediocre quality are included in the book, and they add little to its appeal.

Nonnarrative Nonfiction

Nonnarrative informational books for children are what people often think of as books written to explain. The text is usually expository. According to Christine Pappas (in Mallett, 1992), there are three obligatory elements. The first is the *topic presentation;* it introduces the subject. The second is the *description of attributes;* it sets out the essential features of the subject of the book. These two elements can be interspersed throughout the book or given in one block of text. The third element, called the *characteristic events,* is usually the largest element in non-narrative informational books. The events usually include typical processes, like feeding or giving birth for animals and cycles of growth for plants. The optional features Pappas mentions are *category comparison, final summary,* and *afterword.* For instance, if the topic is squirrels, the category comparison might talk about kinds of squirrels and how they differ. The final summary usually wraps up the topic, and the afterword adds extra information at the end of the book. Margaret Mallett believes that another important optional feature is *retrieval devices,* or aids provided to help readers find information in the book. Retrieval devices include the table of contents, index, and glossary (Mallett, 1992).

Formats of Nonnarrative Nonfiction

When people think of nonnarrative nonfiction, they often oversimplify and don't realize the enormous range of formats within this seemingly narrow category. Let's look closely at three nonnarrative books and see how Pappas's and Mallett's descriptors fit these books.

The Brain: Our Nervous System, by Seymour Simon, uses expository writing but does not have subheads, a glossary, or many of the other elements readers might expect to find in nonfiction. This book depends on the stunning visuals, working in conjunction with the text to provide information. Each double-page spread is a separate unit explaining one aspect of the brain. The text on one page explains the aspect of the brain, and the facing page is filled with a photo or picture. When all these separate units are taken together, they give a complete description of the brain. Simon does present an overview of the topic, describe different aspects of the brain, and show a characteristic event (how the brain gets the message when something hot is touched). The only optional feature Simon includes is a summary.

Sickle Cell Anemia (Diseases and People), by Alvin Silverstein, Virginia Silverstein, and Laura Silverstein Nunn, is an informational book in chapter-book format. The short titled chapters each begin with a vignette or brief story about someone who has the disease. The rest of the chapter is written in an explanatory manner, with subheads and photos throughout. All three of Pappas's obligatory elements are present in this book. Of the optional elements, this book has an index, a glossary, and an afterword, which gives sources for further information. No summary or category comparison is included.

W

For excellent suggestions of nonnarrative nonfiction books, see Literature in the Math and Science Classroom at http://enc.org/topics/across/lit.

Although the coverage of each section is by necessity brief, the intent is to encourage you to explore for yourself and see that every classification holds books that are magical, informative, or interesting.

000: Generalities

The 000 classification of the Dewey decimal system includes bibliographies, library and information science, news media, journalism, and general collections. This section has a lot more to offer than you might expect.

ETs and UFOs: Are They Real?, by Larry Kettelkamp, gives an overview of reported sightings of UFOs and encounters with aliens, as well as the agencies that monitor and investigate such claims. *Bigfoot and Other Legendary Creatures,* by Paul Robert Walker, explores myths and scientific inquiries surrounding repeated sightings of such legendary creatures as the Loch Ness monster, Bigfoot, and the Yeti. A book on just the Yeti, *Yeti: Abominable Snowman of the Himalayas,* by Elaine Landau, recounts sightings throughout history and considers the reliability of the evidence. Students could use books such as these to examine evidence or investigate differences in cultural acceptance of unproven phenomena.

The Cat's Elbow and Other Secret Languages, collected by Alvin Schwartz, presents instructions for speaking 13 secret languages, including Pig Latin. It could be used to immerse students in language issues and to explore the appeal of and reasons for secret languages. Ideas for creating math news or science news are offered in *Extra! Extra! The Who, What, Where, When, and Why of Newspapers,* by Linda Granfield, which explains the history of the newspaper and how news was gathered. *The Furry News: How to Make a Newspaper,* by Loreen Leedy, shows animals working hard at writing, editing, and printing a newspaper, with tips for students on how to make their own.

100: Philosophy and Psychology

In the children's area of the library, the 100 section is not usually a very large one. One part of the classification that is absorbing is the paranormal phenomena. Around Halloween, students might like to read about our historical fascination with ghosts. *Ghosts of the Southwest: The Phantom Gunslinger and Other Real-Life Hauntings,* by Ted Wood, describes homes, hotels, restaurants, and towns in Arizona, New Mexico, Oklahoma, and Texas and the ghosts that haunt them. Woods explains that his first lesson in ghost hunting was that ghosts can be anywhere someone died suddenly or wrongfully. He found out that some ghosts play tricks, such as turning on and off lights, fans, and radios. They also hide objects, spin silverware, and roll toilet paper in front of helpless, shocked bathroom users. This book includes great photos of the places discussed. Similarly, *Ghost in the House,* by Daniel Cohen, tells nine stories about some of the best-known haunted houses in the world, including one called the Octagon in Washington, DC. Kathleen Krull's *They Saw the Future: Oracles, Psychics, Scientists, Great Thinkers, and Pretty Good Guessers* will involve students in the predictions of those who have speculated about or claimed to see the future, from the oracles of ancient Greece to such modern figures as Edgar Cayce and Jeane Dixon. Students might investigate whether current-day psychics have had more success with predictions than their counterparts in the past.

Another part of this section focuses on psychology and contains such books as the delightful *How Are You Peeling? Foods with Moods.* Authors Saxton Freymann and Joost Elffers combed New York for expressive produce. All the photos show vegetables and fruits with twinkling or glaring black-eyed peas for eyes. Children will be amazed at how expressive a green pepper can be! The book has much to say to children of all ages about feelings and how we react to others.

200: Religion

Although teachers might be tempted to skip the 200 classification completely, thinking there would be nothing suitable for sharing in public school classrooms, they would be wrong.

CD-ROM

If you are attracted to *delightful* books, search Favorite Authors for authors who write them.

First of all, some beautiful poetry is part of this classification. In *All God's Children: A Book of Prayers,* edited by Lee Bennett Hopkins, bright, colorful pictures accompany both traditional prayers and prayers by well-known authors. Lois Duncan's "Song for Something Little" thanks God for little things: "Fuzzy mittens, butterflies/Baby colts with solemn eyes."

To help students learn about the multitude of sacred traditions, dip into such books as *This Is the Star,* by Joyce Dunbar and Gary Blythe, a beautiful book about the birth of Christ. This cumulative presentation, which uses rhyme to describe the night Christ was born, is delightful to hear. In *A Great Miracle Happened There: A Chanukah Story,* by Karla Kuskin, a mother tells her family and a young guest the story of the holiday's origin. Because the information is embedded in the story of the family's celebration, it is interesting and engaging. Unfamiliar terms are explained in understandable ways, making this an excellent choice to share with children who are not familiar with Chanukah. Norma Simon's *The Story of Hanukkah* explains the history and traditions that are part of the Jewish holiday. Softly blurred images in muted colors give the mixed-media illustrations an otherworldly quality. Other books in this classification include stories of different denominations, such as *Amish Home,* by Raymond Bial, which depicts the Amish way of life through photos and text.

300: Social Sciences

The 300 section covers such topics as political science and government, civil and political rights, slavery and emancipation, military science, social problems and services, education, commerce, communications, transportation, customs, etiquette, and folklore (discussed in Chapter 8). Just reading these categories doesn't prepare you for the magnitude of topics and the gems in this area. For instance, the gorgeous picture book *I Have a Dream,* by Martin Luther King, Jr., and Coretta Scott King, would give students a new look at King's famous speech because it is illustrated by 15 Coretta Scott King Award and Honor Book artists. The illustrations give added life to the speech and help students visualize King's words.

To begin a social studies unit on poverty or homelessness read a book such as *Lives Turned Upside Down: Homeless Children in Their Own Words and Photographs,* by Jim Hubbard. This book features what four homeless children have photographed of their lives, accompanied by Hubbard's interviews with them. The vibrancy and immediacy of this book make it memorable.

To help students understand in a concrete way the limitations of our planet's resources, read Molly Bang's *Common Ground: The Water, Earth, and Air We Share.* It tells the story of a village commons, which is supposed to be for everyone to use but is misused by a group of villagers who try to graze whole flocks of sheep on it. Eventually they leave when they are told that they can graze only one sheep per family. Bang then shows how the world is like that village, with the commons being our parks, reserves, and natural resources, such as water and air. She ends by pointing out that, unlike the villagers who could just move somewhere else, we don't have anywhere else to go. Although this book is a bit didactic, Bang articulates the interdependence of all living things in such a clear way that even very young children can understand this important concept.

The marvels of transportation can be studied through such books as Gail Gibbons's *The Great St. Lawrence Seaway.* The lovely, inviting watercolors throughout tell the history of the St. Lawrence Seaway, which opened in 1959. We learn that in 1954 Canada and the United States agreed to work together to build this 2,400-mile continuous waterway from the Atlantic Ocean to the Great Lakes.

Students will gain a new appreciation for the complexity of early ship building through David Macauley's *Ship.* The focus on details in this fascinating book brings the subject to life. The last half of the book shows in exquisite detail a boat being constructed in the 15th century. Students will be amazed to see how such complex things were built by hand without the help of machines.

Students can learn about burial practices in *The Best Book of Mummies,* by Philip Steele, a real page-turner. It tells you everything you ever wanted to know about mummies, including the background belief system, how people were mummified, what the coffins

Details in the text and illustrations of Ted Lewin bring to life different types of markets around the world.
(Cover of *Market!* by Ted Lewin. Used by permission of HarperCollins Publishers.)

looked like, and what was in them. Students could focus on what can be learned about a culture through looking at burial practices.

Another eye-opening book, ***Breaking Ground, Breaking Silence: The Story of New York's African Burial Ground,*** by Joyce Hansen and Gary McGowan, tells what archaeologists and anthropologists have learned by "reading" the bones and artifacts of this long-ignored burial site, opened in 1991. Students can see not only that life stories can be pieced together from remains and artifacts but also that historians can choose to ignore contributions of whole groups of people.

Ted Lewin's ***Market!*** is about the market-day practices in five different parts of the world, including Russia, Ireland, and Uganda. The lovely watercolor paintings give as much information as the words.

400: Language

The 400 section, which includes books dealing with many aspects of language, will interest children in issues of language. Ruth Heller has written a unique series on the parts of speech, using inventive imagery that will charm children as they learn the forms and functions of the parts of speech. One book in the series, ***Mine, All Mine: A Book About Pronouns,*** introduces various types of pronouns, explains how and when to use them, and provides whimsical glimpses of what our language would be without them. The text explains that pronouns take the place of nouns so that we don't have to say them over and over again. The author shows how King Cole would sound without the pronouns *his* and *he.* The bright pictures accompanying the text, as well as the clear, often zany examples, make this usually rather staid topic interesting. Heller's books would appeal to older students who need to review these concepts. Rather than bore them with the same old tedious drills, the books use humor to reinforce concepts that have been missed.

What in the World Is a Homophone?, by Leslie Presson, is a dictionary of homophones (words that sound alike but have different spellings and different meanings). It uses colorful, whimsical pictures to demonstrate the difference between words such as *shear* and *sheer.*

Taxi: A Book of City Words, by Betsy Maestro and Giulio Maestro, shows non-city people what's in a city. The reader is introduced to such typical city words as *theater, museum, office building,* and *train station* as a taxi travels in and around the city on a hectic workday. Colorful illustrations give the reader a real feel for what a big city looks like. After reading it, children can be encouraged to create their own dictionary of words for a specific place, such as a farm, a zoo, or a planetarium.

Earth Words: A Dictionary of the Environment, by Seymour Simon, introduces children to words commonly used to discuss the environment. The words are paired with vivid, delightful illustrations.

Cathi Hepworth's ***Bug Off!*** is a collection of words that contain the names of insects, accompanied by droll drawings of the insects. This book provides children with the challenge of finding even more words that contain "bugs."

Also in this category is ***Handtalk School,*** by Mary Beth Miller and George Ancona. Bright, clear photos show children using American Sign Language during a typical school day.

To introduce children to the idea of multiple languages, ***Table—Chair—Bear: A Book in Many Languages,*** by Jane Feder, presents illustrations of objects found in a child's room, labeled in Korean, French, Arabic, Vietnamese, Japanese, Portuguese, Lao, Spanish, Tagalog,

For fun with words, go to ***Richard Lederer's Verbivores*** at *http://pw1.netcom.com/~rlederer/.*

The word play in this delightfully illustrated book focuses on locating names of insects within words.

(From BUG OFF! by Cathi Hepworth, copyright © 1998 by Catherine Hepworth. Used by permission of G. P. Putnam's Sons, an imprint of Penguin Putnam Books for Young Readers, a division of Penguin Putnam Inc.)

Cambodian, and Navajo. *First Words,* by Ivan Chermayeff and Jane Clark Chermayeff, resulted from their efforts to teach their son words in French, Spanish, German, and Italian while they were living in Europe. Each commonly used word, such as *cat,* is written in the four languages and illustrated by a photo from a museum.

To make children aware that some languages have different ways to represent letters, use *At the Beach,* by Huy Voun Lee, in which a mother amuses her son at the beach by drawing Chinese characters in the sand. Children may be surprised to see that Chinese uses pictures instead of symbols for sounds. *Alef-bet: A Hebrew Alphabet Book,* by Michelle Edwards, shows a family doing everyday activities, with labels on the activities in Hebrew. The delightful, often humorous pictures are lively enough to capture children's attention as they learn the Hebrew alphabet.

This section of the library also includes books written in Spanish and English. *A Gift for Abuelita: Celebrating the Day of the Dead,* by Nancy Luenn, shows a child dealing with the loss of her grandmother. *Gathering the Sun: An Alphabet in Spanish and English,* by Alma Flor Ada, is a collection of poems in both Spanish and English, organized around the alphabet scheme.

500: Natural Sciences and Mathematics

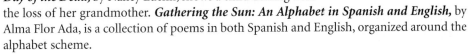

The 500 classification includes books about natural history, mathematics, astrology and allied sciences, physics (heat, light, sound), chemistry, earth sciences, fossils, life sciences, biology, and ecology, as well as plants and animals. To give students an unforgettable experience of what a vernal lake is and the functions it performs, read them *Disappearing Lake: Nature's Magic in Denali National Park,* by Debbie S. Miller. The stunning paintings on glossy paper bring this national park to life, as the text describes the formation of the seasonal lake and the various creatures that make their homes in and around it. In Miller's lyrical language, the book eloquently teaches that this process of going from meadow to lake to meadow contributes to the animals' food supply.

The ecosystem of the giant saguaro cactus is the subject of *Desert Giant: The World of the Saguaro Cactus,* by Barbara Bash, which documents its life cycle and the desert animals it helps support. The ecological importance of the saguaro and its contributions to the ecosystem are shown concretely. Students will learn that this cactus can grow as tall as 50 feet, weigh up to several tons, and live for 200 years! The accordion-like pleats in its skin expand in the rain, storing extra water for the long dry times. After reading this book, students will never forget that the cactus is a source of food for both animals and humans.

Aliki's *Dinosaur Bones* could be used to engage students in the fascinating study of fossils. The book discusses how scientists, studying fossil remains, provide information on how dinosaurs lived millions of years ago. Aliki takes us back about 200 years to the beginnings of modern human awareness of dinosaurs, when a woman in England found a dinosaur tooth in her garden. Aliki's delightful pictures are clear and intriguing, making the book very engaging. *Digging Up Dinosaurs,* also by Aliki, briefly introduces various types of dinosaurs whose skeletons and reconstructions are seen in museums and explains how scientists uncover, preserve, and study fossilized dinosaur bones. Students visiting a museum that houses dinosaur skeletons will look at them with new appreciation after they read about the complexity and delicacy of removing dinosaur bones from one site and reconstructing them in another.

Unusual facts about animals can be used to arouse interest in learning more about the animals. *Chickens Aren't the Only Ones,* by Ruth Heller, is an original and fascinating book on the subject of eggs and all those animals that produce them. The delightful, colorful pictures engage readers immediately, as they learn unusual facts—for example, that the duck-bill platypus is one of two mammals that lay eggs.

The delightful book *Animals Don't Wear Pajamas: A Book About Sleeping,* by Eve B. Feldman, describes human sleeping habits and rituals and then shows comparable animal ones. For instance, in connection with a picture of human children with their blankets, Feldman says, "Perhaps the strangest blanket of all is made by the parrot fish. This bubble-like covering oozes out of the fish's skin" (unpaged). Each morning, the parrot fish has to struggle out of the ooze, only to cover itself with this "blanket" again the next night.

Rattlesnake Dance: True Tales, Mysteries, and Rattlesnake Ceremonies, by Jennifer Owings Dewey, presents facts and folk beliefs about rattlesnakes, accompanied by an auto-biographical account of three personal encounters with rattlesnakes. Dewey begins the book by sharing her experience of being bitten by a rattlesnake as a child and intersperses rattlesnake facts throughout the account.

Look to the North: A Wolf Pup Diary, by Jean Craighead George, is composed of brief diary entries that mark the passage of the seasons and introduce events in the lives of three wolves, as they grow from helpless pups to participants in their small pack's hunt. The for-mat, in which each diary entry is tied to what is happening in school at that time of year, makes it easy to assimilate the information about the wolves.

They Swim the Seas, by Seymour Simon, is an excellent description of the migration of marine animals and plants through rivers, seas, and oceans. Simon always includes intriguing information:

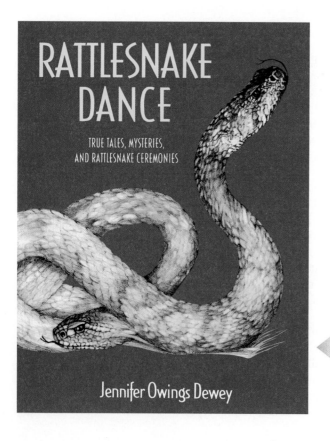

Jennifer Owings Dewey

The oceans cover almost three-quarters of the world, yet only the smallest fraction of the water is visible. Underneath the oceans' windblown surfaces the waters go down to an average depth of sixteen thousand feet. The deepest parts of the seas stretch about seven miles below the surface. Mount Everest, the highest mountain on the land, could easily disappear below the waves in those depths. (unpaged)

Through comparisons such as these, the reader easily experiences the immensity of the ocean. The watercolor illustrations by Elsa Warnick seem magical, showing waves and beach here, a turtle or jellyfish there.

To help young readers understand math concepts, use books such as *How Much Is a Million?,* by David M. Schwartz. Through text and pictures, readers are helped to conceptualize a million, a billion, and a trillion. The examples and Steven Kellogg's zany pictures are compelling. Students will find out that counting from one to one billion would take them 95 years!

This unusual informational book weaves boxed information in with three stories about rattlesnakes (including the author's own experience of being bitten by one).

(Illustration copyright © 1997 by Jennifer Owings Dewey from *Rattlesnake Dance: True Tales, Mysteries, and Rattlesnake Ceremonies* by Jennifer Owings Dewey. Published by Boyds Mills Press, Inc. Reprinted by permission.)

600: Technology (Applied Sciences)

Included within the 600 classification are medical sciences, diseases, engineering, agriculture, hunting, fishing, conservation, home economics, family living, food and drink, child rearing, manufacturing (iron, lumber, textiles, manufacturing for specific uses), hardware, leather, fur, and buildings.

To stimulate students' interest in learning about inventors and the early part of the 20th century, use *Inventors,* by Martin W. Sandler. This beautifully designed, lively book involves the reader through its photographs, drawings, boxed quotations, and short pieces of text. Here we learn that the ferris wheel was invented in 1893, that there were many other African American inventors besides Elijah McCoy, and that high schools gave classes designed to teach young women the proper way to board trolley cars in their long skirts! The whole book is packed with interesting information.

The Wright Brothers: How They Invented the Airplane, by Russell Freedman, describes the lives of the Wright brothers and how they developed the first airplane. The text is interspersed with wonderful old photos. Although written in the narrative style, the book has several features of nonnarrative nonfiction, including an index, "About the Photographs," "Places to Visit," and "For Further Reading."

Bones: Our Skeletal System, by Seymour Simon, will leave students with clear memories of the skeletal system. This visually stunning book describes the skeletal system and outlines the many important roles the bones play in the healthy functioning of the human body. Now that scanners have made it possible to peer inside the body, we see the inside of bones and what the plates look like that make them up. Seymour's clear language adds to the impact of the book: "Your bones are like the framework of a building. Without a framework, the building would collapse." We learn that "bones grow and change just as you do. You begin life with about three hundred bones in your body. As you get older, some of those bones join together, so that by the time you are an adult you will have only about two hundred six bones" (unpaged).

To encourage students to do research on pets and to familiarize them with another format they can use to write, introduce them to *The True-or-False Book of Cats,* by Patricia Lauber, which is set up in a quiz format. A statement such as "Cats don't like to be stared at" is followed on the next page by the answer, which in this case is "true" because cats see staring as a threat. Readers also find out why it is that cats often sit in the laps of guests who don't like cats.

Spots, Feathers, and Curly Tails, by Nancy Tafuri, is another question-and-answer book for young readers. It highlights some outstanding characteristics of farm animals, such as a chicken's feathers and a cow's spots. The text is supported by illustrations.

Students in even the earliest grades will enjoy reading a true story about children creating a business. In *Once upon a company . . . A True Story,* Wendy Anderson Halperin chronologically tells the story of the Christmas wreath business her three children set up and operated to raise money for college. The lovely drawings with soft, inviting colors and the little pictures of the children's activities filling every left-hand page would be enough to make this book satisfying. But on top of that, it really does teach you how to set up a business, as it

Find an abundance of resources on the topic of flying at **NASA's** *website. Go to www.nasa.gov/.*

Wendy Halperin's lovely illustrations and first-person narrative from the point of view of a child enliven the seemingly dry topic of starting a business.

(From a cover of ONCE UPON A COMPANY by Wendy Anderson Halperin. Published by Orchard Books, an imprint of Scholastic Inc. Copyright © 1998 by Wendy Anderson Halperin. Reprinted by permission.)

shows how the business developed over five years. This book certainly proves that *no* topic has to be written about in a less than interesting way.

To broaden students' understanding of differently abled people, use the delightful story *A Button in Her Ear,* by Ada B. Litchfield. This picture storybook tells how a little girl's hearing deficiency is detected and then corrected with the use of a hearing aid. Because the subject of deafness is dealt with in such a straightforward manner, children will find it easy to talk about and understand.

The American Family Farm: A Photo Essay, with text by Joan Anderson and photos by George Ancona, gives students a close-up look at the lives of three farm families. In this pictorial essay on the American family farm, the focus is on daily life at three different kinds of farms. The first-person narratives, along with the photos, will make students feel as if they had real contact with these three families.

700: The Arts (Fine and Decorative)

The 700 classification contains civic and landscape art, architecture, drawing and decorative arts, painting, graphic arts, photography, music, and recreational and performing arts. Sports are included in this section because they are part of the recreational arts.

Books on architecture are a good complement to a unit on any country. *A Greek Temple,* written by Fiona MacDonald and illustrated by Mark Bergin, is part of the *Inside Story* series, which includes books on structures around the world, such as an Egyptian pyramid and a medieval cathedral. This book, a series of illustrated explanations, focuses on such topics as prayer and sacrifices, festival games, temple design, and what it's like inside the Parthenon. Cut-away illustrations let readers see inside the structure of the temple.

One way to share the world of Shakespeare is to read the story of the Globe Theater, in which many of his works were performed. *William Shakespeare & the Globe,* by Aliki, tells the story of Shakespeare and the famous theater. We hear, "Comedy, tragedy, history, fairy tales—Shakespeare wrote about them all in words that dance off the tongue" (p. 11). With Aliki's characteristic mix of delightful pictures and clear text, this book brings us close to the time when Shakespeare lived. Interesting information is put in boxes under the illustrations, and we see pictures of Elizabeth I, James I, and Ben Johnson.

Dance!, by Bill T. Jones and Susan Kuklin, introduces the basic concepts of dance through poetic text and lovely photographs. *Martha Graham: A Dancer's Life,* by Russell Freedman, is a lovely photobiography of the American dancer, teacher, and choreographer, who was born in Pittsburgh in 1895 and became a leading figure in the world of modern dance. Through his research, Freedman always seems to uncover the essence of his subjects. He tells us that Graham was an ambitious young woman who wanted to create a new kind of dance. She spent many hours at New York City's Central Park Zoo, where she would sit on a bench across from a lion in its cage and watch the animal pace back and forth, from one side of the cage to the other. "She was fascinated . . . by the purity of its movements" (p. 11). Readers learn that Graham looked upon dance as an exploration, a celebration of life, a religious calling that required absolute devotion.

CD-ROM

To see what genres Aliki writes in, use the CD-ROM database.

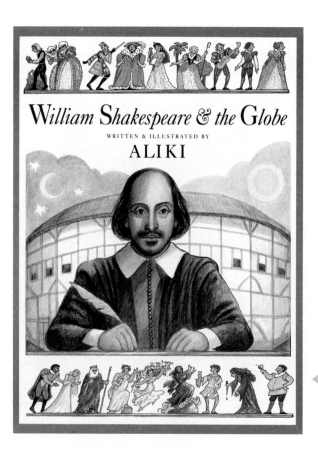

The life of Shakespeare unfolds slowly through text written in short acts and scenes and images drawn in Aliki's characteristic engaging style.

(Cover art from *William Shakespeare & the Globe* by Aliki. Cover art copyright © 1999 by Aliki. Used by permission of HarperCollins Publishers.)

A favorite category of students is books on riddles and word fun. These books are entertaining to read and to figure out and will inspire students to want to explore and think about our language. *Bunny Riddles,* by Katy Hall and Lisa Eisenberg, is an *Easy-to-Read* book with very funny riddles: "What would you get if you crossed a bunny with a giant? A tall tail!" (p. 44). Such books as *Eight Ate: A Feast of Homonym Riddles,* by Marvin Terban, can be used during those few minutes before the bell rings to signal the end of class. Kids love to figure out that a smelly chicken is a "foul fowl."

This section of the library includes a whole range of books on sports. *Leagues Apart: The Men and Times of the Negro Baseball Leagues,* by Lawrence S. Ritter, tells the story of segregation in baseball through short sketches of some of the greats who had to play in the Negro Leagues because of racial discrimination. Smokey Joe Williams played from 1905 to 1932, mainly for the Chicago American Giants, the New York Lincoln Giants, and the Homestead Grays. He had a fastball that was said to zip in at well over 90 miles an hour, about as fast as that of the legendary Walter Johnson. Williams's name is "unknown to most baseball fans because he was never permitted to wear a major league uniform" (unpaged). Students could look at the records set back then in the major leagues and see whose records would not be standing if these men had played in the major leagues.

To help students learn more about different sports and recreation opportunities, encourage them to delve into David Hautzig's *1000 Miles in 12 Days: Pro Cyclists on Tour,* which deals with the complex, competitive world of pro cyclists. The fabulous photos capture the excitement and fast pace of this sport. *Night Dive,* by Ann McGovern, describes the underwater life a twelve-year-old girl sees while scuba diving at night in the Caribbean. The first-person narrator and the photos of glowing fish, by Martin Scheiner and Jim Scheiner, make readers feel as if they were there.

Yahoo! Arts and Humanities has reading lists, reviews, and more at http://d3.dir.dcx.yahoo.com/ arts/humanities/literature/ genres/children_sl.

CD-ROM

To find other artists noted for their use of light, search Favorite Authors for the key word *light.*

800: Literature and Rhetoric

Although most of the 800 classification is made up of fiction and shelved in a different part of the children's section, there are nonfiction books in this category that can be helpful to students. *What's Your Story? A Young Person's Guide to Writing Fiction,* by well-known author Marion Dane Bauer, is a beautifully written, well-explained book on writing. Bauer talks about a story plan, telling her readers that stories "take time to grow in the author's head, time to write down, and time to rework until they are ready to be read" (p. 7). She talks about choosing your best idea, choosing your point of view, and why characters are the key to good stories.

The Divide, by Michael Bedard, relates how the young Willa Cather came to appreciate the beauty of the plains of Nebraska, even though she was unhappy when her family moved there. In the afterword, Bedard tells us that people now remember Cather for her descriptive novels about this area and its people. She wrote "of the harsh beauty of that flat land, and of the women who had taught her what strength and courage meant. Her heart hid somewhere in the long grass always. It sang a new song that had never been sung before" (unpaged).

900: Geography and History

Travel, biography (discussed in Chapter 12), genealogy, the history of the ancient world, and general history of Europe, Asia, Africa, North America, South America, and other areas of the world are all contained in the 900 classification. This is a section teachers can turn to for information and stories that will enrich the teaching of social studies.

Here you can find such books as *Angels of Mercy: The Army Nurses of World War II,* by Betsy Kuhn, which focuses on the nurses who served on the front lines. Through their stories, often told in their own words, we see another side of the war and get a close-up view of some of the 59,000 nurses who served in the army.

Joseph Bruchac's *Lasting Echoes: An Oral History of Native American People* gives the histories of seven generations of American Indian people from an American Indian perspective. Bruchac skillfully weaves the testimony of more than a hundred American Indians into this compelling story. Morgan Monceaux and Ruth Katcher's beautifully illustrated *My Heroes, My People: African Americans and Native Americans in the West* tells the stories of

Visit The U.S. Holocaust Memorial Museum at www.ushmm.org/.

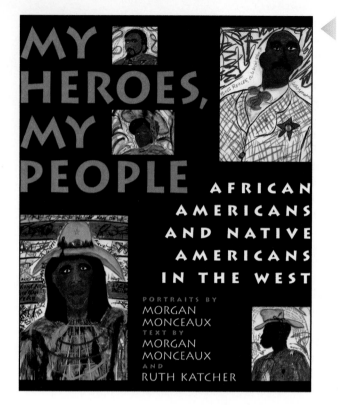

By showing the role that independent-minded African Americans and American Indians played in the development of the West, this book enlarges on what is generally known about the history of the West.

(Jacket design from MY HEROES, MY PEOPLE: AFRICAN AMERICANS AND NATIVE AMERICANS IN THE WEST by Morgan Monceaux and Ruth Katcher. Text copyright © 1999 by Ruth Katcher. Pictures copyright © 1999 by Morgan Monceaux. Reprinted by permission of Farrar, Straus and Giroux, LLC.)

the African Americans and American Indians who were leaders in the West. Cheryl Harness's *The Amazing Impossible Erie Canal* packs fascinating facts and masterfully drawn paintings into this picture book, which gives us a real sense of what it took to make this project a reality. *Pioneers,* by Martin W. Sandler, is filled with photographs and drawings from the Library of Congress that take us into the lives of this country's pioneers. We see mining towns, frontier families, and cowboys, as well as recognition of American Indians' loss of land.

Frozen Girl, by David Getz, discusses the discovery, history, and significance of an Incan mummy found frozen in the mountains of Peru. The fascinating thing about this book is that to tell the story the author used one-on-one interviews with the men who discovered the mummy. His opening line promises a lot—"He had just wanted to get a closer look at an awakened volcano" (p. 3)—and piques readers' curiosity. The archaeologist and mountain climber Johan Reinhard told him he wanted to have a look at the erupting volcano: "The last thing I expected to find was the frozen body of a girl sacrificed five hundred years ago" (p. 5). After reading this introduction, it is almost impossible not to continue reading. The information about the journey to get the frozen mummy out of the ground and to the university was fascinating, as was the way they pieced together the story of the child's life.

As you can see, the nonfiction section holds all kinds of information and stories that you would not have expected to find. Spend time there and see what other treasures you can uncover.

 Nonfiction Series Books

Many of the nonfiction books published today are part of a series. Publishers find what they consider a winning format and then publish several books on like topics, using the same format. The wonderful thing about series books is that when you find a high-quality, appealing book within a series, you can usually count on finding the same quality and appeal in the rest of the books in the series. The same is true for mediocre series books. Once you discover that the book does not have the qualities you look for in nonfiction, you can generally assume that the rest of the series suffers from the same defects. The brief sampling of series books that follows is intended to whet your appetite for more, so you won't overlook these books. Note, however, that series books are not shelved together in the library but within their library classifications.

A series used with younger readers is *In My Neighborhood,* by Kids Can Press. One of these books, *Garbage Collectors,* by Paulette Bourgeois, shows in a step-by-step manner what garbage collectors do. It is packed with fascinating facts—for example, every year each family throws out 200 bags of garbage. This thorough and thoughtful text encourages readers to think about the implications of all these piles of garbage and to discuss how they can help reduce garbage in their families.

The series *I Want to Be,* produced by Stephanie Maze, includes *I Want to Be a Firefighter,* by Catherine O'Neill Grace, which is packed with information and photographs about this occupation. There is a "Where to start" section, a "Kinds of" section, and an "In Practice" section, as well as sections on training, education, specialties, and even firefighting vocabulary. The book ends with famous firefighters, international firefighters, and other sources of information This well-designed series integrates text with frequent photos in an appealing layout. Other titles include *I Want to Be an Engineer* and *I Want to Be a Dancer,* both by Catherine O'Neill Grace.

Lerner's *People's History* is a series that includes such titles as *Buffalo Gals: Women of the Old West,* by Brandon Marie Miller, and *Farewell, John Barleycorn: Prohibition in the United States,* by Martin Hintz. *Dressed for the Occasion: What Americans Wore 1620–1970,* by Brandon Marie Miller, typifies the series because it is full of wonderful photographs and startling information. For example, Miller tells us that in colonial days most clothes were rarely washed. Only clothes made of linen, such as aprons, caps, and underclothes, were washed every six weeks or so! And bathing was considered unhealthy, so people perfumed themselves liberally to mask their smell.

Another excellent series is *The Young Person's Guide to . . . .* One book in the series, *The Young Person's Guide to the Orchestra: Benjamin Britten's Composition on CD,* narrated by Ben Kingsley and written by Anita Ganeri, contains fascinating information in a well-designed book. Each page has a photograph or drawing, boxed information, different text fonts, large colorful dropped letters to begin the text, and headings in white letters within black boxes. On the CD accompanying this book are the sounds made by each instrument. Unusual anecdotes and amazing facts make the information in the book accessible and memorable. Other books in the series include *The Young Person's Guide to Ballet* and *The Young Person's Guide to Shakespeare,* both by Anita Ganeri.

Children's Press has two series by author/illustrator Mike Venezia. One is *Getting to Know the World's Greatest Artists* and the other is *Getting to Know the World's Greatest Composers,* and both are excellent. The books have 32 pages, like most picture books. The books on artists are stuffed with photos of the artists' paintings, cartoons about the paintings, and simply written but insightful descriptions to help children understand both the painter and the paintings. The books on composers are filled with photos and cartoons and text that captures the personality and achievements of the composers.

In an article about series books, Barbara Elleman (1995) says that the *Eyewitness Books,* a series by DK Publishing that includes many science titles as well as art titles, has set a new level of quality in nonfiction by placing sharp, close-up photos on white paper. With their clear labels, eye-catching design, and crisp writing, she says that these books herald a new age in photo nonfiction. Because of the stunning use of photography and the inclusion of so many graphic devices, the series is a standard by which to measure other series of this kind. Now similar books are being produced by Children's Press, Thomson Learning, Chelsea House, Millbrook, Reader's Digest, Time Life, and National Geographic. These series tackle a multitude of subjects, have straightforward material helpful for children's school assignments, and include a generous supply of full-color illustrations and other graphics. They may take a large topic—say, "ancient civilizations"—and relegate a whole book to each civilization.

Reference Books

The main types of references used by five- to eleven-year olds are dictionaries, encyclopedias, thesauruses, and atlases. Although their purposes are the same—to provide information—the quality of these books varies widely, and it's important to pick out excellent ones for the classroom. The better dictionaries are those that stress the concept that words are fascinating and open up ideas.

On the title page of *The Dorling Kindersley Children's Illustrated Dictionary* is a picture of a child jumping for joy. This title page sets the tone for the whole book, which is cheerful and exuberant. The Editor's Introduction explains that the pictures will help draw young readers into the book. The frontmatter has a section "All About Words," which explains all the parts of speech so that children will understand the notations that appear in italics under each word in the dictionary. The color photos are beautiful, and the design makes excellent use of boxes and rectangles of irregular size. The use of different fonts and type sizes to prioritize the headings in this section of the dictionary is especially helpful. For instance, the category heading "verbs" is in a larger type size than the headings "helping verbs" and "verb tenses." The "How to Use This Dictionary" section describes a dictionary game that can be used to involve young readers in using the words. In the body of the dictionary, many entries have a sentence or a picture to contextualize the word and make it more understandable to children.

Scholastic Children's Dictionary uses lots of color throughout and has a clear, appealing introduction to the dictionary section. A dictionary entry is shown close up, with each part of the entry explained in a nearby oval. The graphics and language make this introduction inviting, encouraging children to feel confident about using the dictionary. The body of the book has two columns of text on each page, in large (probably 12-point) type. Sentences are given only when the word might not be known. Two or three pictures are usually on each double page. The layout seems very spacious and thus very appealing. An occasional word history or language note interrupts the columns, helping to keep the pages interesting looking. Some words, such as *architecture*, are highlighted and have a full page devoted to them. In this particular definition, many different buildings are shown.

Webster's New World Children's Dictionary is not as colorful as the other dictionaries. But it does have double columns; pictures every few pages; a large, readable typeface; and sentences for words that may be unfamiliar (such as *authoritative*).

The American Heritage Student Dictionary, aimed at grades 6 to 9, is very dense, with smaller type than the other dictionaries. The whole book is in black and white. Because the dictionary is aimed at an older audience, there are few sentences accompanying the entries. The guide to using the dictionary is long and quite dense; however, the body of the dictionary has two columns of text on the inside of the page and photos and drawings in the outer column. Occasional notes on the history of a word, word building strategies, or regional variation add interest.

In the boxed feature Criteria for Evaluating Dictionaries are guidelines, developed by Margaret Mallett, for choosing a classroom dictionary. The boxed feature Criteria for Evaluating Encyclopedias contains Mallett's excellent advice on choosing classroom or school encyclopedias.

Early atlases and map books for young children should have clear, colorful, and accurate illustrations and an inviting, large format. The better books use features like information

*C*riteria for Evaluating *Dictionaries*

The following criteria were adapted from Mallett (1992, p. 30).

1. The concept that words are fascinating and open up ideas is reinforced.

2. The words are contextualized through sentences or pictures when needed.

3. The definitions are not always free of controversy. On the whole, they are illuminating rather than confusing or drearier than they need to be.

4. The definitions are clear, and the amount of knowledge assumed is appropriate for the age group for which the dictionary is intended.

5. The design and layout—including placement of pictures, type size, type font, and use of white space—add to the appeal and ease of use.

Criteria for Evaluating *Encyclopedias*

The following criteria were adapted from Mallett (1992, pp. 31–33).

1. Be aware of what entries elementary children are likely to use most, and look at these entries. Make sure they provide a good, clear treatment of the topics most important at the elementary level.

2. As in most kinds of nonfiction, look for sound factual information but also ideas and speculation that will awaken curiosity and interest.

3. Make sure the indexing is adequate, directing children to appropriate parts of the volumes.

4. See whether illustrations, photographs, and drawings are included to make the reference book inviting. Color illustrations are generally more numerous in updated encyclopedias. Sometimes the illustrations vary in quality from volume to volume.

5. Check out the language. Encyclopedias specially designed for the primary years usually avoid dry, reference-book language. Stories, bits of biography, and ideas for projects all help to interest and motivate. The long dreary sentences typical of the genre are offputting.

6. Look at the whole format and how the text is integrated with the illustrations.

7. Particularly for younger children, make sure the print is large enough.

8. Look for recently prepared or updated encyclopedias that avoid a narrow ethnocentric view of the world. Mallett mentions one encyclopedia that refers to the implications of colonialism under the term *aborigines.* Rather than assuming that the land was unoccupied, the entry makes it clear that the aborigines resented settlers taking over their land (p. 32).

boxes to help children make links between what they know and the new information. For upper elementary children, the best atlases are also clear, aesthetically pleasing, up to date, and accurate, but they have more detailed information—for example, political and religious background on countries and statistics on health and population.

A Note on Blended Books

Within the genre of nonfiction are books called blended books. Usually these books are fictionalized accounts of something, and so some people call them informational fiction. But because the author creates a story around the information, often these books, although based on true information or a true event, are categorized as fiction. One such case is the wonderful ***Letting Swift River Go,*** Jane Yolen's fictionalized account of building a dam on Swift River in Massachusetts. Carol Avery (1998), who used the book with primary school students, says, "Though the book is told from the perspective of a fictional character, the information about the process of creating a reservoir is so detailed that the book qualifies as nonfiction in our classroom. *Faction* is the word the children and I often use for books such as this" (p. 218).

There is another kind of blended book that does not get high marks from Penny Colman (1999), noted nonfiction writer for children. She says, "Needless to say, I reject the trend in recent years in which some writers add fiction to their nonfiction books in order to move the story along or to make it more dramatic or to introduce facts" (p. 217). The practice of including fiction, which then flows into nonfiction and back again, is known as "edutainment." Colman states that, although this practice is not readily accepted in adult literature, "It has been widely accepted in the world of children's literature, perhaps because

Kettelkamp, Larry (1996). *ETs and UFOs: Are They Real?* New York: Morrow.

King, Martin Luther, Jr., and Coretta Scott King (1997). *I Have a Dream.* New York: Scholastic Trade.

Krementz, Jill (1993). *How It Feels to Be Adopted.* New York: Knopf.

Krull, Kathleen (1999). *They Saw the Future: Oracles, Psychics, Scientists, Great Thinkers, and Pretty Good Guessers.* Illus. Kyrsten Brooker. New York: Atheneum.

Kuhn, Betsy (1999). *Angels of Mercy: The Army Nurses of World War II.* New York: Atheneum.

Kuskin, Karla (1993). *A Great Miracle Happened There: A Chanukah Story.* New York: Perlman.

Landau, Elaine (1993). *Yeti: Abominable Snowman of the Himalayas.* Brookfield, CT: Millbrook.

Lauber, Patricia (1998). *The True-or-False Book of Cats.* Illus. Rosalyn Schanzer. New York: National Geographic Society.

Lee, Huy Voun (1994). *At the Beach.* New York: Holt.

Leedy, Loreen (1990). *The Furry News: How to Make a Newspaper.* New York: Holiday.

Lewin, Ted (1996). *Market!* New York: Lothrop, Lee & Shepard.

Litchfield, Ada B. (1976). *A Button in Her Ear.* Illus. Eleanor Mill. Morton Grove, IL: Whitman.

Livingston, Carole (1978). *"Why Was I Adopted?"* Illus. Arthur Robins. New York: Stuart.

Luenn, Nancy (1998). *A Gift for Abuelita: Celebrating the Day of the Dead.* Illus. Robert Chapman. Flagstaff, AZ: Northland.

Macauley, David (1993). *Ship.* Boston: Houghton Mifflin.

MacDonald, Fiona (1992). *A Greek Temple (Inside Story).* Illus. Mark Bergin. Broomall, PA: Bedrick.

Maestro, Betsy, and Giulio Maestro (1990). *Taxi: A Book of City Words.* New York: Clarion.

McGovern, Ann (1984). *Night Dive.* Illus. Martin Scheiner and James B. Scheiner. New York: Macmillan.

Miller, Brandon Marie (1995). *Buffalo Gals: Women of the Old West.* Minneapolis: Lerner.

—— (1999). *Dressed for the Occasion: What Americans Wore 1620–1970.* Minneapolis: Lerner.

Miller, Debbie S. (1999). *Disappearing Lake: Nature's Magic in Denali National Park.* Illus. Jon Van Zyle. New York: Walker.

Miller, Mary Beth, and George Ancona (1991). *Handtalk School.* New York: Four Winds.

Monceaux, Morgan, and Ruth Katcher (1999). *My Heroes, My People: African Americans and Native Americans in the West.* New York: France Foster.

Murphy, Jim (1995). *The Great Fire.* New York: Scholastic.

Neufeldt, Victoria, ed. (1991). *Webster's New World Children's Dictionary.* New York: Macmillan.

Paulsen, Gary (1991). *Woodsong.* New York: Puffin [1985].

Phelan, Mary Kay (1971). *The Story of the Great Chicago Fire, 1871.* New York: Crowell.

Presson, Leslie (1996). *What in the World Is a Homophone?* Illus. Jo-Ellen Bosson. Hauppauge, New York: Barrons.

Ritter, Lawrence S. (1995). *Leagues Apart: The Men and Times of the Negro Baseball Leagues.* Illus. Richard Merkin. New York: Morrow.

Sandler, Martin W. (1996). *Inventors.* New York: HarperCollins.

—— (1994). *Pioneers.* New York: HarperCollins.

Scholastic (1996). *Scholastic Children's Dictionary.* New York: Author.

Schwartz, Alvin, ed. (1988). *The Cat's Elbow and Other Secret Languages.* Illus. Margot Zemach. New York: Farrar, Straus & Giroux.

Schwartz, David M. (1993). *How Much Is a Million?* Illus. Steven Kellogg. New York: Mulberry.

Silverstein, Alvin, Virginia Silverstein, and Laura Silverstein Nunn (1997). *Sickle Cell Anemia (Diseases and People).* New York: Enslow.

Simon, Norma (1997). *The Story of Hanukkah.* Illus. Leonid Gore. New York: HarperCollins.

Simon, Seymour (1998). *Bones: Our Skeletal System.* New York: Morrow.

—— (1997). *The Brain: Our Nervous System.* New York: Morrow.

—— (1995). *Earth Words: A Dictionary of the Environment.* Illus. Mark Kaplan. New York: HarperCollins.

—— (1998). *They Swim the Seas.* Illus. Elsa Warnick. New York: Browndeer.

Steele, Philip (1998). *The Best Book of Mummies.* New York: Kingfisher.

Tafuri, Nancy (1988). *Spots, Feathers, and Curly Tails*. New York: Greenwillow.

Terban, Marvin (1982). *Eight Ate: A Feast of Homonym Riddles*. Illus. Guilio Maestro. Boston: Houghton Mifflin.

Walker, Paul Robert (1992). *Bigfoot and Other Legendary Creatures*. Illus. William Noonan. San Diego: Harcourt Brace.

Warren, Andrea (1998). *Orphan Train Rider: One Boy's True Story*. Boston: Houghton Mifflin.

Wood, Ted (1997). *Ghosts of the Southwest: The Phantom Gunslinger and Other Real-Life Hauntings*. New York: Walker.

Yolen, Jane (1995). *Letting Swift River Go*. Illus. Barbara Cooney. New York: Little, Brown.

12

Biography and Autobiography

"*I* want to give characters to readers that they won't forget. I want the characters to stand up and walk into the lives of readers and never leave," says Jacqueline Briggs Martin (2000), author of *Snowflake Bentley,* about writing biography. She believes that writing a good biography demands much more than factual knowledge. "It's our passion that gives meaning to our work," she explains. When writing *Snowflake Bentley,* she wanted to create a book with as much emotional power as factual truth.

Biographies written by authors who are passionate about their subjects can make a powerful impact, leaving the reader with unforgettable memories of the subject and her or his life. Biographies can be written as mysteries, as adventures, as romances, as coming-of-age stories, or as sports stories. Because all lives involve elements of drama, biographies can make us sit on the edge of our seats, overwhelm us with emotion, surprise and startle us, and make us laugh out loud.

The charm and the value in biographies and autobiographies—the stories of people's lives—lie in the kinds of people we meet. Christine Duthie (1998) says that these books have the "unique ability to reach into the soil of human experience and till it for the reader; these genres embrace humanness and allow the reader to gaze at the world through the eyes and experiences of another" (p. 220). For children, she says, these genres also offer valuable role models who successfully face challenges and problems. Through biography, readers can deal with human experience, issues of historical significance, and social concerns. Children have strong views on the value of biography, as the boxed feature Children's Voices shows.

Mark Twain's determination is captured in Barry Moser's watercolors.
(Cover illustration from A BRILLIANT STREAK: THE MAKING OF MARK TWAIN by Kathryn Lasky Knight, illustrations copyright © 1998 by Barry Moser, reprinted by permission of Harcourt, Inc.)

In *Mark Twain? What Kind of Name Is That? A Story of Samuel Langhorne Clemens,* Robert Quackenbush uses an entirely different design, framing the story around Twain's affection for cats. We find out that Twain grew up with 19 cats! On every page, cartoons of cats provide asides—such as "Run! Here comes trouble!"—which reinforce what is said in the text. Much of the book explores what Sam was like as a child and how even his writings got him in trouble. His first 31 years are emphasized; only six pages are devoted to the entire rest of his life. On the last page, the author ties cats back into the body of the text, telling us that a cat occupied every room of the last house Twain lived in.

Kathryn Lasky's *A Brilliant Streak: The Making of Mark Twain,* illustrated by Barry Moser, begins and ends with Halley's Comet. In between, she illuminates the experiences, ideas, and actions associated with the "brilliant streak" that was Mark Twain. She shows us what made Twain tick, how he thought, what excited him, and how his imagination contributed to his brilliance. Most of the story is devoted to his boyhood and early adult years, showing how his experiences shaped him into the person he became. "He played hard, fought for every underdog, never stopped dreaming of buried treasure, learned to pilot a steamship from St. Louis to New Orleans, discovered war is stupid and politicians often more so" (p. 37). He always found the forbidden attractive and didn't worry about how others viewed him. This attitude allowed him to write with candor and humor, making fun of institutions that were "sacred cows" and considered inappropriate to mock.

CD-ROM

For a list of Kathryn Lasky's books, use the CD-ROM database.

Types of Biographies

Biographies are written in many different ways. Four common types of biographies are complete biographies, partial biographies, fictional biographies, and collective biographies.

Complete Biographies

Complete biographies look at the subject's whole life, focusing on the impact the person made through her or his life. *Isadora Dances,* by Rachel Isadora, is a complete biography written in the picture-book format. This brief biography of Isadora Duncan tells the story of a woman whose unique style of dance was not readily accepted by audiences at the turn of the 20th century. Duncan believed that true dance came from the soul, untouched and free. Because of Duncan and the dance school she founded, bare feet became as acceptable as shoes in dance. She never conformed to the ideas of the world in which she lived, and eventually the world came to understand her and the world changed.

Partial Biographies

Partial biographies focus on one significant event in the subject's life or one part of the subject's life. The majority of picture-book biographies are partial ones. When William Miller

(2000) writes biography, he tries to find the most important moment in the early life of the character. He thinks in terms of the inner conflicts of the character, not in terms of a beginning, a middle, and an end. "The bottom line is always the character and ending the story on a life-affirming note." In the partial biography **Richard Wright and the Library Card,** Miller focuses on how Wright managed to gain access to a library card even though black people at that time were not allowed to own a library card. He shows the impact this action had on Wright's life.

Fictional Biographies

Fictional biographies focus on a real person, but a story or context is created through which to tell the happenings. Although some fictional biographies are told from the subject's point of view, with a first-person or third-person narrator, divergent approaches may be used, such as viewing the person through the eyes of a neighbor child or a son or daughter; focusing on a significant event from the subject's life and adding characters and events that bring the subject into focus; inventing letters or diary entries by real or fictitious characters; and using art or poetry to tell the story of a creative life.

 Riding Freedom, by Pam Muñoz Ryan, is a fictionalized account of the life of Charlotte Parkhurst, a woman who lived as a man so that she could do what she loved—work with horses. She also voted more than 50 years before any woman could vote in federal elections. To fill in details of early parts of Parkhurst's life about which there was no information, Ryan added characters to the story.

 She's Wearing a Dead Bird on Her Head, by Kathryn Lasky, is a fictionalized account of the two women who founded the Audubon Society. This lively picture-book story of how the two women reacted to the fashion of decorating hats with whole bodies of birds has only one or two created incidents in it. The author explains in the Author's Note that, while there is no record of the two women having gone into a hat store to determine the source of the illegal feather trade, she based this created part of the story on the conventions of the times.

 A very inventive fictional biography is **If a Bus Could Talk: The Story of Rosa Parks,** by Faith Ringgold. In this picture book, a bus tells of the events in Parks's life that caused her to be called the mother of the civil rights movement.

 Occasionally, authors change the name of the subject of their biography when they fictionalize it. Milton Meltzer (1994) is one such author. His intended biography of Calvin Fairbank turned into the fictional **Underground Man** when he decided that his research hadn't unearthed enough evidence to do justice to the story. He simply could not make up characters, events, and dialogue that were in accord with the minimal facts. Changing the hero's name removed the barriers to invention. Although everything about the character is solidly rooted in fact, Meltzer could then "put ideas in his head, words in his mouth, and feelings in his heart that sprang from my own understanding of such a man's character and temperament" (p. 52).

Collective Biographies

Collective biographies give the reader glimpses into the lives of several subjects. Such collections are usually organized around the lives of subjects with a common ethnicity, gender, or occupation.

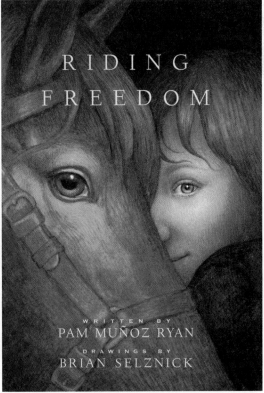

Charlotte's affinity for horses, so clearly shown on this cover, shapes the course of her life.

(From RIDING FREEDOM by Pam Muñoz Ryan. Cover art copyright © 1998 by Brian Selznick. Reprinted by permission of Scholastic Inc.)

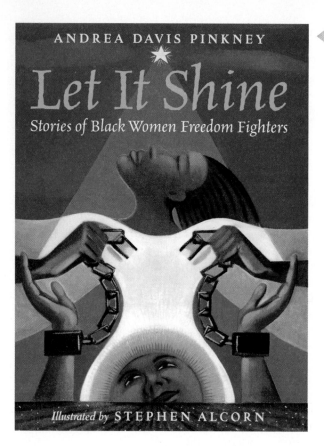

Stephen Alcorn's illustration suggests the strength and joy that characterized the lives of many of these freedom fighters.
(Cover illustration from LET IT SHINE: STORIES OF BLACK WOMEN FREEDOM FIGHTERS by Andrea Davis Pinkney, illustrations copyright © 2000 by Stephen Alcorn, reproduced by permission of Harcourt, Inc.)

Kathleen Krull has written several entertaining and informative collective biographies. Her *Lives of the Artists: Masterpieces, Messes (and What the Neighbors Thought)* contains fascinating tidbits about the lives and work of 16 artists. For instance, Leonardo da Vinci, a vegetarian, had to invent a water-operated alarm clock to get himself out of bed in the morning; Georgia O'Keefe killed rattlesnakes by chopping off their heads with hoes; and Andy Warhol never went out without wearing one of his 400 wigs. The caricatures by Kathryn Hewitt are priceless, and the many hints about the subjects' lives leave readers wanting to know more. In *Lives of the Musicians: Good Times, Bad Times (and What the Neighbors Thought),* we learn that the concerts of Clara Schumann, German composer and pianist, were so popular that police had to be called in to control the crowds. We also find out that Gilbert and Sullivan collaborated on their operettas by correspondence because they didn't like each other. Krull's *Lives of the Athletes: Thrills, Spills (and What the Neighbors Thought)* reveals what these 20 athletes were like as people. We learn mostly admirable but occasional quirky information about them. Babe Ruth was known for his stupendous belch. Babe Didrikson Zaharias's appearance and dress were always discussed before her considerable accomplishments in track and field or golf were. Each of these *Lives of* books is packed to the gills with information and remarkable illustrations by Kathryn Hewitt.

A quieter collection by Cynthia Rylant is called *Margaret, Frank, and Andy: Three Writers' Stories.* In her lean but lyrical language, Rylant takes us to the heart of the lives of the beloved Margaret Wise Brown, L. Frank Baum, and E. B. White. Young children who know the work of these authors will sit still to hear this lovely book read to them.

Gold Rush Women, a collection by Claire Rudolf Murphy and Jane G. Haigh, highlights the achievements of the women who participated in the Alaska gold rush. This lively book, peppered with interesting photographs, paints a much different portrait than we usually get. One interesting fact is that native women made significant contributions. *Girls Think of Everything: Stories of Ingenious Inventions by Woman,* by Catherine Thimmesh, describes what women have done in this scientific field. Collective biographies that focus on the achievements of people of color include *One More River to Cross: The Stories of Twelve Black Americans,* by Jim Haskins; *Let It Shine: Stories of Black Women Freedom Fighters,* by Andrea Davis Pinkney; and *Standing Tall: The Stories of Ten Hispanic Americans,* by Argentina Palacios. All are interesting and very readable, highlighting the events in the lives of subjects who are brought vividly to life.

Autobiographies

An autobiography is the story of a person's life written by that person. Because the whole retelling is from the subject's point of view, no people need be interviewed. But since memory is the main source of information, an autobiography can lead to a skewed view of the subject. Most writers of autobiography mention that the story is their impression of their own life; they know full well that other participants in their life might not see things the same way. Imagine how your own life story would vary, depending on whether it was

This memoir takes us into the heart of Harlem and the childhood of Walter Dean Myers, prolific writer of novels for children.
(From BAD BOY by Walter Dean Myers. Cover illustrated by Robert Andrew Parker. Used by permission of HarperCollins Publishers.)

written by you or by a jealous friend or hostile sibling. Interpretations of incidents and even events selected for inclusion would differ markedly. Thus, in an autobiography, we learn what the writer believes is important about his or her life.

Writers' autobiographies are often of interest to older children, who want to see what influences shaped the writer and ultimately the writing. Jerry Spinelli's *Knots in My Yo-Yo String: The Autobiography of a Kid* takes us into Spinelli's neighborhood, where we meet characters and places he often writes about. Walter Dean Myers's *Bad Boy: A Memoir* helps us see why Myers so clearly understands how kids can get in trouble and why so many of Myers's stories are set in New York. Other engaging autobiographies of writers include *A Girl from Yamhill: A Memoir,* by Beverly Cleary; *Homesick: My Own Story,* by Jean Fritz; *Boy: Tales of Childhood,* by Roald Dahl; *26 Fairmont Avenue,* by Tomie dePaola; *My Life in Dog Years* and *Guts: The True Story Behind the Hatchet and Brian Books,* by Gary Paulsen; *Bowman's Store: A Journey to Myself,* by Joseph Bruchac; and *The Abracadabra Kid: A Writer's Life,* by Sid Fleischman.

Life stories of entertainers are also popular. *Savion: My Life in Tap,* by Savion Glover and Bruce Weber, is the story of the young tap dancer who brought tap back to Broadway. With photographs of Savion and the story of his climb to the top of the tap world, this autobiography will command the attention of older readers.

Autobiography also includes extraordinary stories of ordinary people. *Taking Flight: My Story,* by Vicki Van Meter with Dan Gutman, is the partial autobiography of a twelve-year-old girl who flew across the Atlantic in a single-engine plane. *From Where I Sit: Making My Way with Cerebral Palsy,* by Shelley Nixon, tells of a child living with the condition. *Chinese Cinderella: The True Story of an Unwanted Daughter,* by Adeline Yen Mah, recounts her difficult early life in China. *Zlata's Diary: A Child's Life in Sarajevo,* by Zlata Filipovic, describes living in a city torn by war.

An interesting series of short autobiographies about children's writers is *Meet the Author,* published by Richard G. Owen. Each 32-page book, filled with photos of the author, describes the author's views on writing and how she or he became involved with it. Among the writers covered are Verna Aardema, Eve Bunting, Jean Fritz, Paul Goble, Karla Kuskin, Margaret Mahy, Patricia Polacco, Cynthia Rylant, and Jane Yolen. Young children could be motivated to turn to the author's work after reading one of these short books.

What Kinds of People Can Children Meet Through Biographies and Autobiographies?

Children can be brought into the center of the lives of many memorable people through biographies and autobiographies. Although they have most often been about famous people, they are beginning to be published about people who are not famous but whose lives are deemed worthy of being brought to the attention of a wider audience.

People Famous in Their Field

Just about every field imaginable is represented through biographies. Bessie Coleman, the first African American woman to earn a pilot's license (in 1921), is portrayed in *Fly, Bessie,*

Non-Series versus Series Biographies

Because publishers want to provide biographies of current celebrities and other people in whom there is popular interest, many series have been created. Unlike non-series biographies, these biographies follow a similar format from book to book.

Differences Between Series and Non-Series Biographies

Most writers of non-series biographies are intensely curious about the lives of the people they choose as their subjects. This is often the major characteristic separating a well-written biography from a mediocre biography. Series biographies can be more vulnerable to mediocrity, especially if the same person writes many books in the series without having a passion for the subject. In such books, the facts are usually accurate, but the reader isn't given a real feel for the person and sees only the outer aspects of her or his life. Although chapter-book biographies published in series have strengths of their own, often they lack information about the author and his or her interest in the subject. This is unfortunate, since such information can often help us decide whether we want to read a book.

A wide range of series biographies are published on sports and entertainment figures. Some are hurriedly published to capitalize on the current popularity of a specific celebrity, while others are carefully researched and written in lively prose. Many series sports biographies incorporate interesting information from the subject's life and illustrate why it is important. One quick way to evaluate whether a series book is worth your time is to read the first few pages of the text. If the opening commands your attention, then often the rest of the writing will be good too. If the introduction is simply a dull and plodding recitation of facts, this probably will not be a memorable book. One special strength of some series books is that they have a consultant to the series. If the consultant is a professional historian, then often the research will be scholarly and the sociopolitical context of the subjects' life will be included. However, sometimes a consultant merely writes an introduction for the whole series and her or his name does not ensure research or accuracy. Many series books are strong on graphic interest, created by the generous use of photos. Series books also tend to contain features that make it easy for students to find out more about the subject—lists of works or accomplishments of the subject, sources of further reading, and relevant websites. The wonderful thing about series biographies is that once you find one outstanding book in a series, you know that the other books will probably be of equal worth.

One thing I realized through my own reading is that if I really wanted to know about a subject, especially a celebrity, I read eagerly, without concern for writing style or research. Oftentimes the subject of a biography is enough to draw the reader into the book.

Comparison of Series and Non-Series Biographies of Eleanor Roosevelt

To see the range of quality that exists across series and non-series biographies, let's look at twelve biographies written about Eleanor Roosevelt. These biographies are from the children's section in one public library. This selection is representative of the mix of biographies often found in school libraries and public libraries, which don't contain just the newest books. After looking at the strengths and weaknesses of this group of biographies, you should be able to apply the process to similar mixes of biographies.

At the very high end of the quality spectrum is Russell Freedman's ***Eleanor Roosevelt: A Life of Discovery.*** In this beautifully written book, with glorious photographs, we learn about the interior life of Eleanor and come away feeling as if we knew the woman. Freedman turned not only to Eleanor's diaries but also to the diaries of her family and friends to give the reader a comprehensive look at this remarkable woman. This book is intended for readers who want more than just a bare-bones view of Eleanor for a report, since it encourages reflection on the qualities that contributed to Eleanor's personal achievements.

In addition to providing information about the setting, the cover illustration hints at Eleanor's loneliness as a child.

(From ELEANOR by Barbara Cooney, copyright ©1996 by Barbara Cooney. Used by permission of Viking Penguin, an imprint of Penguin Putnam Books for Young Readers, a division of Penguin Putnam Inc.)

Eleanor

Story and pictures by
BARBARA COONEY

Another non-series biography is the picture book *Eleanor,* by Barbara Cooney. While focusing on only a small part of Eleanor's life, it gives readers a sense of the person. Cooney's three years of research and her lovely writing allow readers to come away from the story knowing what Eleanor was like. This book would work well as an introduction to Eleanor Roosevelt because it gives readers a real empathy for her and a desire to know more about her. Students who have had such an introduction may then be able to read the more "facts only" biographies about her with interest because they care about her and can place the facts in an already established framework.

Several series biographies have been written for the early elementary child. David A. Adler's *A Picture Book of Eleanor Roosevelt,* part of the *Picture Book of . . .* series, contains many of the essential facts about Eleanor's life. Although it occasionally tells us how Eleanor felt, the connection with Eleanor is not strong enough to make readers care about her. *Eleanor Roosevelt: A Photo-Illustrated Biography,* by Lucile Davis, part of the *Photo-Illustrated Biography* series, is intended as a basic introduction for very young readers. Although it gives useful addresses and Internet sites for readers who want more information, what readers mainly get is a view of the roles Eleanor played. They do not come away from the book with a sense of what Eleanor was like as a person. Like the photo-illustrated biography by Davis, *Learning About Integrity from the Life of Eleanor Roosevelt,* by Nancy Ellwood, from the *Character-Building Book* series, takes a rather heavy-handed approach. In none of these books is any information given about the author's connection to or interest in the subject. In the case of all three of these books, it would be interesting to look at other books in the series and see how the format differs from book to book, if at all. Many of the headings seem as if they could fit almost any subject—"Growing Up," "Learning Integrity," "A Turning Point," and so on. This is one weakness of some series books: Instead of the subject's life shaping the framework of the book, the subject's life is made to fit into a specified format.

Eleanor Everywhere, by Monica Kulling, a chapter book that is part of the **Step into Reading** series, does not seem to be limited by the fact that it is intended for beginning readers. In this lively, engaging book of only 48 pages, the author gets to the heart of who Eleanor was. On the copyright page, the author says, "with grateful acknowledgment to Scott Rector, of the Eleanor Roosevelt National Historic Site in Hyde Park, New York, for his time and expertise in reviewing this book." This information lets us know that the author was very concerned with not misrepresenting her subject.

Eleanor Roosevelt: First Lady of the World, by Doris Faber, part of the **Women of Our Time** series, is a well-written and engaging book. In "About This Book" at the end, we learn that the author, as a reporter, actually covered many meetings that Eleanor attended and has been interested in her ever since. This book provides a good example of why a book should not be rejected by readers simply because of an early publication date. Published in 1985, it does a superior job of helping us understand Eleanor's fears and pain at being orphaned, allowing us to see her accomplishments in a new light. Faber is also a master of "showing, not telling," which seems to be lacking in some series biographies. Instead of telling us that Eleanor's mother-in-law was very proper and inflexible, Faber quotes her as saying to one of Eleanor's sons, "Don't say your hands are dirty. The proper word is soiled." That one detail shows us much about Sara Roosevelt. Although this book does not comment as much on the later accomplishments of Eleanor, it makes the reader want to know more about her.

(W)

*One site devoted to achievements of women is **4000 Years of Women in Science**. Find it at www.astr.ua.edu/4000ws/4000ws.html.*

the text, she gets into the drawings. Reading her books is an adventure.

Kathleen Krull focuses on collective biographies. In the few pages she has to write about each character, readers are given memorable information based on meticulous research. Her light touch and engaging writing make her books favorites with students.

Kathryn Lasky's picture-book biographies demonstrate her ability to connect to her subjects and to frame the stories in such a way that readers view the subjects in new ways.

Patricia McKissack's prose sparkles with the energy and passion that characterize her subjects.

Milton Meltzer frequently writes about the lives of reformers and change agents. Clear, clean prose, love of research, and the desire to capture the essence of his subject in honest ways are the marks of his work.

Carolyn Meyer writes relatively long biographies based on research and interest in her subjects. She is mindful of accuracy in re-creating scenes.

Andrea Davis Pinkney writes lively, engrossing picture-book biographies, which demonstrate her love of language and willingness to play with it.

Diane Stanley, both a writer and an illustrator, is a careful researcher who

gives her readers views of subjects never unearthed before. Her biographies are picture books but are intended for older readers.

Mike Venezia writes about the lives of artists. He involves young readers with cartoons and photographs and short snippets of the artists' lives.

Invitations

Choose several of the following activities to complete:

1. After reading several picture-book biographies, respond to them in terms of the characteristics you most admire in the subjects and the characteristics you would most like to have.

2. Write the story of a childhood incident you remember clearly that was also witnessed by someone else—a sibling, parent, coach, or friend. Then ask that person to write up the same incident. What differences do you notice? What implications do these differences have for accuracy in biographies and autobiographies?

3. Bring to class a picture-book biography. Share this biography with the rest of your group, and then as a group talk about what each subject would have to say to the subjects of the other books. What questions would they have? What actions of the others would they admire? What actions would they disagree with? Could they have been friends?

4. Read two or more biographies on one subject. Compare them in terms of the form the author uses to present the subject. Which did you prefer and why? Share your findings with your group.

5. In either the library or the bookstore, find a series book that is not mentioned in the chapter. Summarize the qualities present in the book and evaluate it. Is this a series you could see yourself using in a classroom? Explain your reactions to your small group.

6. After reading a biography, select several poems that the subject would like. Share the poems with your small group, explaining what appeal the poems would have to the subject of your biography. Do the same thing with a picture book or an informational book.

7. Do you remember reading biographies when you were in school? Compare your attitudes to those of the children in Children's Voices.

Classroom Teaching Ideas

1. Have students read a biography of someone they are interested in. Ask them to keep secret the identity of the person they read about. Decide on a day when everyone will come dressed as the person he or she read about. Allow students to ask questions of one another to discover each person's identity.

2. Many famous people have known each other—Thomas Jefferson and Alexander Hamilton, Ralph Waldo Emerson and Henry David Thoreau, as well as contemporary friends Oprah Winfrey and Maya Angelou, to name a few. Have students read biographies in pairs, with an eye for how friendships or rivalries are reported, and compare them. Have them report their findings to the class.

3. Select biographies of several people from the same time period who were not acquainted (for example, a slave and a Civil War general), and have students compare the events in their lives.

4. After reading several picture-book biographies or autobiographies together to see what kinds of events are presented in them, have students write and illustrate their own autobiography.

5. Have each student select someone within the class to write her or his biography. As a class, formulate a list of the kinds of information to be included. Remember to leave room for including something unique to the individual. When the biography is written, allow the student who is the focus of the work to review it for accuracy and inclusion of appropriate material. The subject may wish to illustrate it, or the author may illustrate it.

6. Ask students to think about writing a biography of someone in their family who is no longer living. Talk about how students would have to interview relatives, neighbors, or others who knew this person to get the information they would need.

7. Have students compare several biographies of the same person. How are they different? How are they similar? Do you get a clearer or more personal picture from one than from another? Which one is most interesting?

Internet and Text Resources

1. **Biographies: The Scientists** is a great source for hundreds of biographies of scientists. There is a brief description of their work, along with links to more sites that continue the study. Find it at

   www.blupete.com/Literature/Biographies/Science/Scients.htm

2. **Biographical Dictionary** contains information on more than 28,000 notable men and women. Find it at

   www.s9.com/biography/

3. **Lives, the Biography Resource** provides links and information only on famous people who have died. Go to

   http://amillionlives.com

4. **New Perspectives on the West** is packed with biographies of the men and women who lived in the Old West. Find it at

   www.pbs.org/weta/thewest/people

5. **4000 Years of Women in Science** provides biographies of female scientists. Go to

   www.astr.ua.edu/4000ws/4000ws.html

1987 *The Whipping Boy,* by Sid Fleischman. Illus. Peter Sis. Greenwillow.

Honor: *On My Honor,* by Marion Dane Bauer. Clarion.

Volcano: The Eruption and Healing of Mount St. Helens, by Patricia Lauber. Bradbury.

A Fine White Dust, by Cynthia Rylant. Bradbury.

1986 *Sarah, Plain and Tall,* by Patricia C. MacLachlan. Zolotow/Harper.

Honor: *Commodore Perry in the Land of the Shogun,* by Rhoda Blumberg. Lothrop, Lee & Shepard.

Dogsong, by Gary Paulsen. Bradbury.

1985 *The Hero and the Crown,* by Robin McKinley. Greenwillow.

Honor: *The Moves Make the Man,* by Bruce Brooks. Harper.

One-Eyed Cat, by Paula Fox. Bradbury.

Like Jake and Me, by Mavis Jukes. Illus. Lloyd Bloom. Knopf.

1984 *Dear Mr. Henshaw,* by Beverly Cleary. Illus. Paul O. Zelinsky. Morrow.

Honor: *The Wish Giver: Three Tales of Coven Tree,* by Bill Brittain. Illus. Andrew Glass. Harper.

Sugaring Time, by Kathryn Lasky. Illus. Christopher G. Knight. Macmillan.

The Sign of the Beaver, by Elizabeth George Speare. Houghton Mifflin.

A Solitary Blue, by Cynthia Voigt. Atheneum.

1983 *Dicey's Song,* by Cynthia Voigt. Atheneum.

Honor: *Graven Images,* by Paul Fleischman. Illus. Andrew Glass. Harper.

Homesick: My Own Story, by Jean Fritz. Illus. Margot Tomes. Putnam.

Sweet Whispers, Brother Rush, by Virginia Hamilton. Philomel.

The Blue Sword, by Robin McKinley. Greenwillow.

Doctor De Soto, by William Steig. Farrar, Straus & Giroux.

1982 *A Visit to William Blake's Inn: Poems for Innocent and Experienced Travelers,* by Nancy Willard. Illus. Alice Provensen and Martin Provensen. Harcourt.

Honor: *Ramona Quimby, Age 8,* by Beverly Cleary. Illus. Alan Tiegreen. Morrow.

Upon the Head of the Goat: A Childhood in Hungary 1939–1944, by Aranka Siegal. Farrar, Straus & Giroux.

1981 *Jacob Have I Loved,* by Katherine Paterson. Crowell.

Honor: *The Fledgling,* by Jane Langton. Illus. Erik Blegvad. Harper.

A Ring of Endless Light, by Madeleine L'Engle. Farrar, Straus & Giroux.

1980 *A Gathering of Days: A New England Girl's Journal, 1830–1832,* by Joan W. Blos. Scribner.

Honor: *The Road from Home: The Story of an Armenian Girl,* by David Kheridan. Greenwillow.

(For a complete list, go to www.ala.org/alsc/newbery.html.)

Caldecott Awards

The winner of the award is the illustrator, whose name appears in boldface.

2002 *The Three Pigs,* by **David Wiesner.** Clarion/Houghton Mifflin.

Honor: *The Dinosaurs of Waterhouse Hawkins,* by Barbara Kerley. Illus. **Brian Selznick.** Scholastic.

Martin's Big Words: The Life of Dr. Martin Luther King, Jr., by Doreen Rappaport. Illus. **Bryan Collier.** Jump at the Sun/Hyperion.

The Stray Dog, by **Marc Simont.** HarperCollins.

2001 *So You Want to Be President,* by Judith St. George. Illus. **David Small.** Philomel.

Honor: *Casey at Bat,* by Ernest Lawrence Thayer. Illus. **Christopher Bing.** Handprint.

Click, Clack, Moo: Cows That Type. by Doreen Cronin. Illus. **Betsy Lewin.** Simon & Schuster.

Olivia, by **Ian Falconer.** Atheneum.

2000 *Joseph Had a Little Overcoat,* by **Simms Taback.** Viking.

Honor: *A Child's Calendar,* by John Updike. Illus. **Trina Schart Hyman.** Holiday.

Sector 7, by **David Wiesner.** Clarion.

When Sophie Gets Angry—Really, Really Angry, by **Molly Bang.** Scholastic.

The Ugly Duckling, by Hans Christian Andersen, adapted by **Jerry Pinkney.** Morrow.

1999 *Snowflake Bentley,* by Jacqueline Briggs Martin. Illus. **Mary Azarian.** Houghton Mifflin.

Honor: *Duke Ellington,* by Andrea Davis Pinkney. Illus. **Brian Pinkney.** Hyperion.

No David!, by **David Shannon.** Blue Sky/Scholastic.

Snow, by **Uri Shulevitz.** Farrar, Straus & Giroux.

Tibet: Through the Red Box, by **Peter Sis.** Foster/Farrar, Straus & Giroux.

1998 *Rapunzel,* by **Paul O. Zelinsky.** Dutton.

Honor: *The Gardener,* by Sarah Stewart. Illus. **David Small.** Farrar, Straus & Giroux.

Harlem, by Walter Dean Myers. Illus. **Christopher Myers.** Scholastic.

There Was an Old Lady Who Swallowed a Fly, by **Simms Taback.** Viking.

1997 *Golem,* by **David Wisniewski.** Clarion.

Honor: *Hush! A Thai Lullaby,* by Minfong Ho. Illus. **Holly Meade.** Kroupa/Orchard.

The Graphic Alphabet, by **David Pelletier.** Ed. Neal Porter. Orchard.

The Paperboy, by **Dav Pilkey.** Jackson/Orchard.

Starry Messenger, by **Peter Sis.** Foster/Farrar, Straus & Giroux.

1996 *Officer Buckle and Gloria,* by **Peggy Rathmann.** Putnam.

Honor: *Alphabet City,* by **Stephen T. Johnson.** Viking.

Zin! Zin! Zin! A Violin, by Lloyd Moss. Illus. **Marjorie Priceman.** Simon & Schuster.

The Faithful Friend, by Robert D. San Souci. Illus. **Brian Pinkney.** Simon & Schuster.

Tops & Bottoms, adapted by **Janet Stevens.** Harcourt.

1995 *Smoky Night*, by Eve Bunting. Illus. **David Diaz.** Harcourt.

Honor: *Swamp Angel*, by Anne Isaacs. Illus. **Paul O. Zelinsky.** Dutton.

John Henry, by Julius Lester. Illus. **Jerry Pinkney.** Dial.

Time Flies, by **Eric Rohmann.** Crown.

1994 *Grandfather's Journey*, by **Allen Say.** Houghton Mifflin.

Honor: *Peppe the Lamplighter*, by Elisa Bartone. Illus. **Ted Lewin.** Lothrop, Lee & Shepard.

In the Small, Small Pond, by **Denise Fleming.** Holt.

Owen, by **Kevin Henkes.** Greenwillow.

Raven: A Trickster Tale from the Pacific Northwest, by **Gerald McDermott.** Harcourt.

Yo! Yes?, by **Chris Raschka.** Orchard.

1993 *Mirette on the High Wire*, by **Emily Arnold McCully.** Putnam.

Honor: *The Stinky Cheese Man & Other Fairly Stupid Tales*, by Jon Scieszka. Illus. **Lane Smith.** Viking.

Working Cotton, by Sherley Anne Williams. Illus. **Carole Byard.** Harcourt.

Seven Blind Mice, by **Ed Young.** Philomel.

1992 *Tuesday*, by **David Wiesner.** Clarion.

Honor: *Tar Beach*, by **Faith Ringgold.** Crown.

1991 *Black and White*, by **David Macauley.** Houghton Mifflin.

Honor: *Puss in Boots*, by **Fred Marcellina.** di Capua/Farrar, Straus & Giroux.

More More More Said the Baby, by **Vera B. Williams.** Greenwillow.

1990 *Lon Po Po: A Red-Riding Hood Story from China*, by **Ed Young.** Philomel.

Honor: *Color Zoo*, by **Lois Ehlert.** Lippincott.

Hershel and the Hanukkah Goblins, by Eric Kimmel. Illus. **Trina Schart Hyman.** Holiday.

Bill Peet: An Autobiography, by **Bill Peet.** Houghton Mifflin.

The Talking Eggs, by Robert D. San Souci. Illus. **Jerry Pinkney.** Dial.

1989 *Song and Dance Man*, by Karen Ackerman. Illus. **Stephen Gammell.** Knopf.

Honor: *Mirandy and Brother Wind*, by Patricia C. McKissack. Illus. **Jerry Pinkney.** Knopf.

Goldilocks and the Three Bears, by **James Marshall.** Dial.

The Boy of the Three-Year Nap, by Diane Snyder. Illus. **Allen Say.** Houghton Mifflin.

Free Fall, by **David Wiesner.** Lothrop, Lee & Shepard.

1988 *Owl Moon*, by Jane Yolen. Illus. **John Schoenherr.** Philomel.

Honor: *Mufaro's Beautiful Daughters: An African Tale*, by **John Steptoe.** Lothrop, Lee & Shepard.

1987 *Hey, Al*, by Arthur Yorinks. Illus. **Richard Egielski.** Farrar, Straus & Giroux.

Honor: *The Village of Round and Square Houses*, by **Ann Grifalconi.** Little, Brown.

Alphabatics, by **Suse MacDonald.** Bradbury.

Rumpelstiltskin, by **Paul O. Zelinsky.** Dutton.

1986 *The Polar Express*, by **Chris Van Allsburg.** Houghton Mifflin.

Honor: *The Relatives Came*, by Cynthia Rylant. Illus. **Stephen Gammell.** Bradbury.

King Bidgood's in the Bathtub, by Audrey Wood. Illus. **Don Wood.** Harcourt.

1985 *Saint George and the Dragon*, retold by Margaret Hodges. Illus. **Trina Schart Hyman.** Little, Brown.

Honor: *Hansel and Gretel*, retold by Rika Lesser. Illus. **Paul O. Zelinsky.** Dodd.

The Story of Jumping Mouse: A Native American Legend, retold by **John Steptoe.** Lothrop, Lee & Shepard.

Have You Seen My Duckling?, by **Nancy Tafuri.** Greenwillow.

1984 *The Glorious Flight: Across the Channel with Louis Bleriot*, by **Alice Provensen** and **Martin Provensen.** Viking.

Honor: *Ten, Nine, Eight*, by **Molly Bang.** Greenwillow.

Little Red Riding Hood, retold by **Trina Schart Hyman.** Holiday.

1983 *Shadow*, by Blaise Cendrars. Trans. **Marcia Brown.** Scribner.

Honor: *When I Was Young in the Mountains*, by Cynthia Rylant. Illus. **Diane Goode.** Dutton.

A Chair for My Mother, by **Vera B. Williams.** Greenwillow.

1982 *Jumanji*, by **Chris Van Allsburg.** Houghton Mifflin.

Honor: *Where the Buffaloes Begin*, by Olaf Baker. Illus. **Stephen Gammell.** Warne.

On Market Street, by Arnold Lobel. Illus. **Anita Lobel.** Greenwillow.

Outside Over There, by **Maurice Sendak.** Harper.

A Visit to William Blake's Inn: Poems for Innocent and Experienced Travelers, by Nancy Willard. Illus. **Alice Provensen** and **Martin Provensen.** Harcourt.

1981 *Fables*, by **Arnold Lobel.** Harper.

Honor: *The Grey Lady and the Strawberry Snatcher*, by **Molly Bang.** Four Winds.

Truck, by **Donald Crews.** Greenwillow.

Mice Twice, by **Joseph Low.** McElderry/Atheneum.

The Bremen-Town Musicians, retold by **Ilse Plume.** Doubleday.

1980 *Ox-Cart Man*, by Donald Hall. Illus. **Barbara Cooney.** Viking.

Honor: *Ben's Trumpet*, by **Rachel Isadora.** Greenwillow.

The Treasure, by **Uri Shulevitz.** Farrar, Straus & Giroux.

The Garden of Abdul Gasazi, by **Chris Van Allsburg.** Houghton Mifflin.

(For a complete list, go to www.ala.org/alsc/caldecott.html.)

1986 *The Patchwork Quilt*, by Valerie Flournoy. Illus. **Jerry Pinkney.** Dial.

Honor: *The People Could Fly: American Black Folktales*, by Virginia Hamilton. Illus. **Leo Dillon** and **Diane Dillon.** Knopf.

1985 No award given.

1984 *Ma Mama Needs Me*, by Mildred Pitts Walter. Illus. **Pat Cummings.** Lothrop, Lee & Shepard.

1983 *Black Child*, by **Peter Magubane.** Knopf.

Honor: *I'm Going to Sing: Black American Spirituals*, by **Ashley Bryan.** Atheneum.

Just Us Women, by Jeannette Caines. Illus. **Pat Cummings.** HarperCollins.

All the Colors of the Race, by Arnold Adoff. Illus. **John Steptoe.** Lothrop, Lee & Shepard.

1982 *Mama Crocodile: An Uncle Arnadou Tale from Senegal*, adapted by Rosa Guy. Trans. Birago Diop. Illus. **John Steptoe.** Delacorte.

Honor: *Daydreamers*, by Eloise Greenfield. Illus. **Tom Feelings.** Dial.

1981 *Beat the Story Down, Pum-Pum*, by **Ashley Bryan.** Atheneum.

Honor: *Grandma's Joy*, by Eloise Greenfield. Illus. **Carole Byard.** Philomel.

Count on Your Fingers African Style, by Claudia Zaslavsky. Illus. **Jerry Pinkney.** Crowell.

1980 *Cornrows*, by Camille Yarbrough. Illus. **Carole Byard.** Coward-McCann.

(For a complete list, go to www.ala.org/srrt/csking/winners.html.)

Michael L. Printz Awards

2002 *A Step from Heaven*, by An Na. Front Street.

Honor: *The Ropemaker*, by Peter Dickinson. Delacorte.

Heart to Heart: New Poems Inspired by Twentieth-Century American Arts, by Jan Greenberg. Abrams.

Freewill, by Chris Lynch. HarperCollins.

True Believer, by Virginia Euwer Wolff. Atheneum.

2001 *Kit's Wilderness*, by David Almond. Delacorte.

Honor: *Many Stones*, by Carolyn Coman. Front Street.

The Body of Christopher Creed, by Carol Plum-Ucci. Harcourt.

Angus, Thongs, and Full-Frontal Snogging, by Louise Rennison. HarperCollins.

Stuck in Neutral, by Terry Trueman. HarperCollins.

2000 *Monster*, by Walter Dean Myers. Scholastic.

Honor: *Skellig*, by David Almond. Delacorte.

Speak, by Laurie Halse Anderson. Farrar, Straus & Giroux.

Hard Love, by Ellen Wittinger. Simon & Schuster.

(For a complete list, go to www.ala.org/yalsa/printz/index.html.)

Boston Globe–Horn Book Awards

2002

Fiction and Poetry Book: *Lord of the Deep*, by Graham Salisbury. Delacorte.

Honor: *Saffy's Angel*, by Hilary McKay. McElderry.

Amber Was Brave, Essie Was Smart, by Vera B. Williams. Greenwillow.

Nonfiction Book: *This Land Was Made for You and Me: The Life and Songs of Woody Guthrie*, by Elizabeth Partridge. Viking.

Honor: *Handel, Who Knew What He Liked*, by M. T. Anderson. Illus. Kevin Hawkes. Candlewick.

Woody Guthrie: Poet of the People, by Bonnie Christensen. Knopf.

Picture Book: *"Let's Get a Pup!" Said Kate*, by Bob Graham. Candlewick.

Honor: *I Stink!*, by Kate McMullan. Illus. Jim McMullan. Cotler/Harper.

Little Rat Sets Sail, by Monika Bang-Campbell. Illus. Molly Bang. Harcourt.

2001

Fiction and Poetry Book: *Carver: A Life in Poems*, by Marilyn Nelson. Front Street.

Honor: *Everything on a Waffle*, by Polly Horvath. Farrar, Straus & Giroux.

Troy, by Adèle Geras. Harcourt.

Nonfiction Book: *The Longitude Prize*, by Joan Dash. Illus. Dusan Petricic. Foster/Farrar, Straus & Giroux.

Honor: *Rocks in His Head*, by Carol Otis Hurst. Illus. James Stevenson. Greenwillow.

Uncommon Traveler: Mary Kingsley in Africa, by Don Brown. Houghton Mifflin.

Picture Book: *Cold Feet*, by Cynthia DeFelice. Illus. Robert Andrew Parker. DK Ink.

Honor: *Five Creatures*, by Emily Jenkins. Illus. Tomek Bogacki. Foster/Farrar, Straus & Giroux.

The Stray Dog, retold by Marc Simont. HarperCollins.

2000

Fiction and Poetry Book: *The Folk Keeper*, by Franny Billingsley. Atheneum.

Honor: *King of Shadows*, by Susan Cooper. McElderry.

145th Street: Short Stories, by Walter Dean Myers. Delacorte.

Nonfiction Book: *Sir Walter Ralegh and the Quest for El Dorado*, by Marc Aronson. Clarion.

Honor: *Osceola: Memories of a Sharecropper's Daughter*, edited by Alan Govenar. Illus. Shane W. Evans. Jump at the Sun/Hyperion.

Sitting Bull and His World, by Albert Marrin. Dutton.

Picture Book: *Henry Hikes to Fitchburg*, by D. B. Johnson. Houghton Mifflin.

Honor: *Buttons*, by Brock Cole. Farrar, Straus & Giroux.

a day, a dog, by Gabrielle Vincent. Front Street.

Fiction and Poetry Book: *Holes,* by Louis Sachar. Foster/Farrar, Straus & Giroux.

Honor: *The Trolls,* by Polly Horvath. Farrar, Straus & Giroux.

Monster, by Walter Dean Myers. Illus. Christopher Myers. HarperCollins.

Nonfiction Book: *The Top of the World: Climbing Mount Everest,* by Steve Jenkins. Houghton Mifflin.

Honor: *Shipwreck at the Bottom of the World: The Extraordinary True Story of Shackleton and the Endurance,* by Jennifer Armstrong. Crown.

William Shakespeare & the Globe, by Aliki. HarperCollins.

Picture Book: *Red-Eyed Tree Frog,* by Joy Cowley. Illus. Nic Bishop. Scholastic.

Honor: *Dance!,* written by Bill T. Jones and Susan Kuklin. Hyperion.

The Owl and the Pussycat, by Edward Lear. Illus. James Marshall. diCapua/HarperCollins.

Special Citation: *Tibet: Through the Red Box,* by Peter Sis. Foster/Farrar, Straus & Giroux.

Fiction and Poetry Book: *The Circuit: Stories of the Life of a Migrant Child,* by Francisco Jimenez. University of New Mexico Press.

Honor: *While No One Was Watching,* by Jane Leslie Conly. Holt.

My Louisiana Sky, by Kimberly Willis Holt. Holt.

Nonfiction Book: *Leon's Story,* by Leon Walter Tillage. Illus. Susan L. Roth. Farrar, Straus & Giroux.

Honor: *Martha Graham: A Dancer's Life,* by Russell Freedman. Clarion.

Chuck Close, Up Close, by Jan Greenberg and Sandra Jordan. DK Ink.

Picture Book: *And If the Moon Could Talk,* by Kate Banks. Illus. Georg Hallensleben. Foster/Farrar, Straus & Giroux.

Honor: *Seven Brave Women,* by Betsy Hearne. Illus. Bethanne Andersen. Greenwillow.

Popcorn: Poems by James Stevenson. Greenwillow.

Fiction and Poetry Book: *The Friends,* by Kazumi Yumoto. Trans. Cathy Hirano. Farrar, Straus & Giroux.

Honor: *Lily's Crossing,* by Patricia Reilly Giff. Delacorte.

Harlem, by Walter Dean Myers. Illus. Christopher Myers. Scholastic.

Nonfiction Book: *A Drop of Water: A Book of Science and Wonder,* by Walter Wick. Scholastic.

Honor: *Lou Gehrig: The Luckiest Man,* by David A. Adler. Illus. Terry Widener. Gulliver/Harcourt.

Leonardo da Vinci, by Diane Stanley. Morrow.

Picture Book: *The Adventures of Sparrowboy,* by Brian Pinkney. Simon & Schuster.

Honor: *Home on the Bayou: A Cowboy's Story,* by G. Brian Karas. Simon & Schuster.

Potato: A Tale from the Great Depression, by Kate Lied. Illus. Lisa Campbell Ernst. National Geographic.

Fiction and Poetry Book: *Poppy,* by Avi. Illus. Brian Floca. Jackson/Orchard.

Honor: *The Moorchild,* by Eloise McGraw. McElderry.

Belle Prater's Boy, by Ruth White. Farrar, Straus & Giroux.

Nonfiction Book: *Orphan Train Rider: One Boy's True Story,* by Andrea Warren. Houghton Mifflin.

Honor: *The Boy Who Lived with the Bears: And Other Iroquois Stories,* by Joseph Bruchac. Illus. Murv Jacob. Harper.

Haystack, by Bonnie and Arthur Geisert. Illus. Arthur Geisert. Houghton Mifflin.

Picture Book: *In the Rain with Baby Duck,* by Amy Hest. Illus. Jill Barton. Candlewick.

Honor: *Fanny's Dream,* by Caralyn Buehner. Illus. Mark Buehner. Dial.

Home, Lovely, by Lynne Rae Perkins. Greenwillow.

Fiction and Poetry Book: *Some of the Kinder Planets,* by Tim Wynne-Jones. Kroupa/Orchard.

Honor: *Jericho,* by Janet Hickman. Greenwillow.

Earthshine, by Theresa Nelson. Jackson/Orchard.

Nonfiction Book: *Abigail Adams: Witness to a Revolution,* by Natalie S. Bober. Atheneum.

Honor: *It's Perfectly Normal: Changing Bodies, Growing Up, Sex, and Sexual Health,* by Robie H. Harris. Illus. Michael Emberley. Candlewick.

The Great Fire, by Jim Murphy. Scholastic.

Picture Book: *John Henry,* retold by Julius Lester. Illus. Jerry Pinkney. Dial.

Honor: *Swamp Angel,* by Anne Isaacs. Illus. Paul O. Zelinsky. Dutton.

Fiction and Poetry Book: *Scooter,* by Vera B. Williams. Greenwillow.

Honor: *Flour Babies,* by Anne Fine. Little, Brown.

Western Wind, by Paula Fox. Orchard.

Nonfiction Book: *Eleanor Roosevelt: A Life of Discovery,* by Russell Freedman. Clarion.

Honor: *Unconditional Surrender: U. S. Grant and the Civil War,* by Albert Marrin. Atheneum.

A Tree Place and Other Poems, by Constance Levy. Illus. Robert Sabuda. McElderry.

Picture Book: *Grandfather's Journey,* by Allen Say. Houghton Mifflin.

Honor: *Owen,* by Kevin Henkes. Greenwillow.

A Small Tall Tale from the Far Far North, by Peter Sis. Knopf.

Fiction and Poetry Book: *Ajeemah and His Son,* by James Berry. Harper.

Honor: *The Giver,* by Lois Lowry. Houghton Mifflin.

Nonfiction Book: *Sojourner Truth: Ain't I a Woman?,* by Patricia C. McKissack and Fredrick L. McKissack. Scholastic.

On Market Street, by Arnold Lobel. Illus. Anita Lobel. Greenwillow.

Jumanji, by Chris Van Allsburg. Houghton Mifflin.

1980

Fiction and Poetry Book: *Conrad's War,* by Andrew Davies. Crown.

Honor: *The Night Swimmers,* by Betsy Byars. Delacorte.

Me and My Million, by Clive King. Crowell.

The Alfred Summer, by Jan Slepian. Macmillan.

Nonfiction Book: *Building: The Fight Against Gravity,* by Mario Salvadori. Illus. Saralinda Hooker and Christopher Ragus. Atheneum/McElderry.

Honor: *Childtimes: A Three-Generation Memoir,* by Eloise Greenfield. Illus. Jerry Pinkney. Crowell.

Stonewall, by Jean Fritz. Illus. Stephen Gammell. Putnam.

How the Forest Grew, by William Jaspersohn. Illus. Chuck Eckart. Greenwillow.

Picture Book: *The Garden of Abdul Gasazi,* by Chris Van Allsburg. Houghton Mifflin.

Honor: *The Gray Lady and the Strawberry Snatcher,* by Molly Bang. Greenwillow.

Why the Tides Ebb and Flow, by John Chase Bowden. Illus. Marc Brown. Houghton Mifflin.

Special Citation: *Graham Oakley's Magical Changes,* by Graham Oakley. Atheneum.

(For a complete list, go to www.hbook.com/bghb.shtml.)

Mildred L. Batchelder Awards

2002 Cricket Books/Carus Publishing for *How I Became an American,* by Karin Gündish. Trans. James Skofield.

Honor: Viking Press for *A Book of Coupons,* by Susie Morgenstern. Illus. Serge Bloch. Trans. Gill Rosner.

2001 Scholastic/Arthur A. Levine for *Samir and Yonatan,* by Daniella Carmi. Trans. Yael Lotan.

Honor: Godine for *Ultimate Game,* by Christian Lehmann. Trans. William Rodarmor.

2000 Walker and Company for *The Baboon King,* by Anton Quintans. Translated from Dutch by John Nieuwenhuizen.

Honor: R & S Books for *Vendela in Venice,* by Christina Björk. Illus. Inga-Karin Eriksson. Translated from Swedish by Patricia Crampton.

Farrar, Straus & Giroux for *Collector of Moments,* by Quint Buchholz. Translated from German by Peter F. Neumeyer.

Front Street for *Asphalt Angels,* by Ineke Holtwijk. Translated from Dutch by Wanda Boeke.

1999 Dial for *Thanks to My Mother,* by Schoschana Rabinovici. Translated from German by James Skofield.

Honor: Viking for *Secret Letters from 0 to 10,* by Susie Morgenstern. Translated from French by Gill Rosner.

1998 Henry Holt for *The Robber and Me,* by Josef Holub. Ed. Mark Aronson. Translated from German by Elizabeth D. Crawford.

Honor: Scholastic Press for *Hostage to War: A True Story,* by Tatjana Wassiljewa. Translated from German by Anna Trenter.

Viking Publishing for *Nero Corleone: A Cat's Story,* by Elke Heidenrich. Translated from German by Doris Orgel.

1997 Farrar, Straus & Giroux for *The Friends,* by Kazumi Yumoto. Translated from Japanese by Cathy Hirano.

1996 Houghton Mifflin for *The Lady with the Hat,* by Uri Orlev. Translated from Hebrew by Hillel Halkin.

Honor: Henry Holt for *Damned Strong Love: The True Story of Willi G. and Stephan K.,* by Lutz Van Sijk. Translated from German by Elizabeth D. Crawford.

Walker and Co. for *Star of Fear, Star of Hope,* by Jo Hoestlandt. Translated from French by Mark Ploizzotti.

1995 Dutton for *The Boys from St. Petri,* by Bjarne Reuter. Translated from Danish by Anthea Bell.

Honor: Lothrop, Lee & Shepard, for *Sister Shako and Kolo the Goat: Memories of My Childhood in Turkey,* by Vedat Dalokay. Translated from Turkish by Guner Ener.

1994 Farrar, Straus & Giroux for *The Apprentice,* by Pilar Molina Llorente. Translated from Spanish by Robin Longshaw.

Honor: Farrar, Straus & Giroux for *The Princess in the Kitchen Garden,* by Annemie Heymans and Margriet Heymans. Translated from Dutch by Johanna H. Prins and Johanna W. Prins.

Viking for *Anne Frank Beyond the Diary: A Photographic Remembrance,* by Ruud van der Rol and Rian Verhoeven, in association with the Anne Frank House. Translated from Dutch by Tony Langham and Plym Peters.

1993 No award given.

1992 Houghton Mifflin for *The Man from the Other Side,* by Uri Orlev. Translated from Hebrew by Hillel Halkin.

1991 E. P. Dutton for *A Hand Full of Stars,* by Rafik Schami. Translated from German by Rika Lesser.

1990 E. P. Dutton for *Buster's World,* by Bjarne Reuter. Translated from Danish by Anthea Bell.

1989 Lothrop, Lee & Shepard for *Crutches,* by Peter Hartling. Translated from German by Elizabeth D. Crawford.

1988 McElderry Books for *If You Didn't Have Me,* by Ulf Nilsson. Translated from Swedish by Lone Thygesen Clecher and George Blecher.

1987 Lothrop, Lee & Shepard for *No Hero for the Kaiser,* by Rudolph Frank. Translated from German by Patricia Crampton.

1986 Creative Education for *Rose Blanche,* by Christophe Gallaz and Robert Innocenti. Translated from Italian by Martha Coventry and Richard Craglia.

1985 Houghton Mifflin for *The Island on Bird Street,* by Uri Orlev. Translated from Hebrew by Hillel Halkin.

1984 Viking Press for *Ronia, the Robber's Daughter,* by Astrid Lindgren. Translated from Swedish by Patricia Crampton.

1983	Lothrop, Lee & Shepard for *Hiroshima No Pika*, by Toshi Maruki. Translated from Japanese through Kurita-Bando Literacy Agency.
1982	Bradbury Press for *The Battle Horse*, by Harry Kullman. Translated from Swedish by George Blecher and Lone Thygesen Blecher.
1981	William Morrow & Co. for *The Winter When Time Was Frozen*, by Els Pelgrom. Translated from Dutch by Maryka Rudnik and Raphael Rudnik.
1980	E. P. Dutton for *The Sound of the Dragon's Feet*, by Aliki Zei. Translated from Greek by Edward Fenton.

(For a complete list, go to www.ala.org/alsc/batch.html.)

NCTE Poetry Award for Excellence

2000	X. J. Kennedy
1997	Eloise Greenfield
1994	Barbara Juster Esbensen
1991	Valerie Worth
1988	Arnold Adoff
1985	Lilian Moore
1982	John Ciardi
1981	Eve Merriam
1980	Myra Cohn Livingston
1979	Karla Kuskin
1978	Aileen Fisher
1977	David McCord

(For more information, go to www.ncte.org/elem.poetry/.)

Pura Belpré Award

Where the winner of the award is the illustrator, the illustrator's name appears in boldface.

2002

Narrative: *Esperanza Rising*, by Pam Muñoz Ryan. Scholastic.

Honor: *Breaking Through*, by Francisco Jiménez, Houghton Mifflin.

Illustration: *Chato and the Party Animals*, by Gary Soto. Illus. **Susan Guevara.** Putnam.

Honor: *Juan Bobo Goes to Work*, by Marisa Montes. Illus. **Joe Cepeda.** HarperCollins.

2000

Narrative: *Under the Royal Palms: A Childhood in Cuba*, by Alma Flor Ada. Atheneum.

Honor: *From the Bellybutton of the Moon and Other Summer Poems/Del ombligo de la luna y otros poemas de verano*, by Francisco X. Alarcon. Illus. Maya Christina Gonzalez. Children's Book Press.

Laughing Out Loud, I Fly: Poems in English and Spanish by Juan Felipe Herrera Illus. Karen Barbour. HarperCollins.

Illustration: *Magic Windows*, by **Carmen Lomas Garza.** Children's Book Press.

Honor: *Barrio: Jose's Neighborhood*, by **George Ancona.** Harcourt Brace.

The Secret Stars, by Joseph Slate. Illus. **Felipe Davalos.** Marshall Cavendish.

Mama and Papa Have a Store, by **Amelia Lau Carling.** Dial.

1998

Narrative: *Parrot in the Oven: Mi vida*, by Victor Martinez. Cotler/HarperCollins.

Honor: *Laughing Tomatoes and Other Spring Poems/Jitomates Risuenos y otros poemas de primavera*, by Francisco X. Alarcon. Illus. Maya Christina Gonzalez. Children's Book Press.

Spirits of the High Mesa, by Floyd Martinez. Arte Publico.

Illustration: *Snapshots from the Wedding*, by Gary Soto. Illus. **Stephanie Garcia.** Putnam.

Honor: *In My Family/En mi familia*, by **Carmen Lomas Garza.** Children's Book Press.

The Golden Flower: A Taino Myth from Puerto Rico, by Nina Jaffe. Illus. **Enrique O. Sanchez.** Simon & Schuster.

Gathering the Sun: An Alphabet in Spanish and English, by Alma Flor Ada. English translation by Rosa Zubizarreta. Illus. **Simon Silva.** Lothrop, Lee & Shepard.

1996

Narrative: *An Island Like You: Stories of the Barrio*, by Judith Ortiz Cofer. Kroupa/Orchard.

Honor: *The Bossy Gallito/El gallo de bodas: A Traditional Cuban Folktale*, by Lucia Gonzalez. Illus. Lulu Delacre. Scholastic.

Baseball in April, and Other Stories, by Gary Soto. Harcourt.

Illustration: *Chato's Kitchen*, by Gary Soto. Illus. **Susan Guevara.** Putnam.

Honor: *Pablo Remembers: The Fiesta of the Day of the Dead*, by **George Ancona.** Lothrop, Lee & Shepard.

The Bossy Gallito/El gallo de bodas: A Traditional Cuban Folktale, by Lucia Gonzalez. Illus. **Lulu Delacre.** Scholastic.

Family Pictures/Cuadros de familia, Spanish text by Rosa Zubizarreta. Illus. **Carmen Lomas Garza.** Children's Book Press.

(For a complete list, go to www.ala.org/alsc/belpre.html.)

Edgar Allen Poe Awards for Best Juvenile Mystery

2002	*Dangling*, by Lillian Eige. Simon & Schuster/Atheneum.
Nominated:	*Ghost Soldier*, by Elaine Marie Alphin. Holt.
	Ghost Sitter, by Peni R. Griffin. Penguin-Putnam/Dutton.
	Following Fake Man, by Barbara Ware Holmes. Random/Knopf.
	Bug Muldoon, by Paul Shipton. Penguin-Putnam/Viking.
2001	*Dovey Coe*, by Frances O'Roark Dowell. Atheneum.
Nominated:	*Trouble at Fort La Pointe*, by Kathleen Ernst. American Girl.

1986   *Sarah, Plain and Tall*, by Patricia C. MacLachlan. Harper & Row.

1985   *The Fighting Ground*, by Avi. HarperCollins.

1984   *The Sign of the Beaver*, by Elizabeth George Speare. Houghton Mifflin.

(For updates, go to www.scottodell.com/sosoaward.html.)

Orbis Pictus Award for Outstanding Nonfiction for Children

2002   *Black Potatoes: The Story of the Great Irish Famine, 1845–1850*, by Susan Campbell Bartoletti. Houghton Mifflin.

Honor: *The Cod's Tale*, by Mark Kurlansky. Illus. S. D. Schindler. Penguin Putnam.

The Dinosaurs of Waterhouse Hawkins: An Illuminating History of Mr. Waterhouse Hawkins, Artist and Lecturer, by Barbara Kerley. Illus. Brian Selznick. Scholastic.

Martin's Big Words: The Life of Dr. Martin Luther King, Jr., by Doreen Rappaport. Illus. Bryan Collier. Hyperion.

2001   *Hurry Freedom: African Americans in Gold Rush California*, by Jerry Stanley. Crown.

Honor: *The Amazing Life of Benjamin Franklin*, by James Cross Giblin. Illus. Michael Dooling. Scholastic.

America's Champion Swimmer: Gertrude Ederle, by David A. Adler. Illus. Terry Widener. Gulliver.

Michelangelo, by Diane Stanley. HarperCollins.

Osceola: Memories of a Sharecropper's Daughter, by Alan B. Govenar. Illus. Shane W. Evans. Jump at the Sun.

Wild and Swampy, by Jim Arnosky. HarperCollins.

2000   *Through My Eyes*, by Ruby Bridges and Margo Lundell. Scholastic.

Honor: *At Her Majesty's Request: An African Princess in Victorian England*, by Walter Dean Myers. Scholastic.

Piano Virtuoso, by Susanna Reich. Clarion.

Mapping the World, by Sylvia A. Johnson. Atheneum.

Snake Scientist, by Sy Montgomery. Illus. Nic Bishop. Houghton Mifflin.

The Top of the World: Climbing Mount Everest, by Steve Jenkins. Houghton Mifflin.

1999   *Story of Shackleton and the Endurance*, by Jennifer Armstrong. Crown.

Honor: *Black Whiteness: Admiral Byrd Alone in the Antarctic*, by Robert Burleigh. Illus. Walter Lyon Krudop. Atheneum.

Fossil Feud: The Rivalry of the First American Dinosaur Hunters, by Thom Holmes. Messner.

Hottest, Coldest, Highest, Deepest, by Steve Jenkins. Houghton Mifflin.

No Pretty Pictures: A Child of War, by Anita Lobel. Greenwillow.

1998   *An Extraordinary Life: The Story of a Monarch Butterfly*, by Laurence Pringle. Illus. Bob Marstall. Orchard.

Honor: *A Drop of Water: A Book of Science and Wonder*, by Walter Wick. Scholastic.

A Tree is Growing, by Arthur Dorros. Illustrated by S. D. Schindler. Scholastic.

Charles A. Lindbergh: A Human Hero, by James Cross Giblin. Clarion.

Kennedy Assassinated! The World Mourns: A Reporter's Story, by Wilborn Hampton. Candlewick.

Digger: The Tragic Fate of the California Indians from the Missions to the Gold Rush, by Jerry Stanley. Crown.

1997   *Leonardo da Vinci*, by Diane Stanley. Morrow.

Honor: *Full Steam Ahead: The Race to Build a Transcontinental Railroad*, by Rhonda Blumberg. National Geographic.

The Life and Death of Crazy Horse, by Russell Freedman. Holiday.

One World, Many Religions: The Ways We Worship, by Mary Pope Osborne. Knopf.

1996   *The Great Fire*, by Jim Murphy. Scholastic.

Honor: *Dolphin Man: Exploring the World of Dolphins*, by Laurence Pringle. Illus. Randall S. Wells. Atheneum.

Rosie the Riveter: Women Working on the Home Front in World War II, by Penny Colman. Crown.

1995   *Safari Beneath the Sea: The Wonder World of the North Pacific Coast*, by Diane Seanson. Sierra.

Honor: *Wildlife Rescue: The Work of Dr. Kathleen Ramsay*, by Jennifer Owings Dewey. Boyds Mills.

Kids at Work: Lewis Hine and the Crusade against Child Labor, by Russell Freedman. Clarion.

Christmas in the Big House, Christmas in the Quarters, by Patricia C. McKissack and Fredrick L. McKissack. Scholastic.

1994   *Across America on an Emigrant Train*, by Jim Murphy. Clarion.

Honor: *To the Top of the World: Adventures with Arctic Wolves*, by Jim Brandenburg. Walker.

Making Sense: Animal Perception and Communication, by Bruce Brooks. Farrar, Straus & Giroux.

1993   *Children of the Dust Bowl: The True Story of the School at Weedpatch Camp*, by Jerry Stanley. Crown.

Honor: *Talking to Artists*, by Pat Cummings. Bradbury.

Come Back, Salmon, by Molly Cone. Sierra.

1992   *Flight: The Journey of Charles Lindbergh*, by Robert Burleigh. Philomel.

Honor: *Now Is Your Time! The African-American Struggle for Freedom*, by Walter Dean Myers. HarperCollins.

Prairie Vision: The Life and Times of Solomon Butcher, by Pam Conrad. HarperCollins.

1991   *Franklin Delano Roosevelt*, by Russell Freedman. Clarion.

Honor: *Seeing Earth from Space*, by Patricia Lauber. Orchard.

Arctic Memories, by Normee Ekoomiak. Holt.

1990   *The Great Little Madison*, by Jean Fritz. Putnam.

Honor: *The Great American Gold Rush*, by Rhoda Blumberg. Bradbury.

The News about Dinosaurs, by Patricia Lauber. Bradbury.

(For a complete list go to www.ncte.org/elem/orbispictus/.)

Kate Greenaway Medals

2000 Lauren Child, *I Will Not Ever Never Eat a Tomato*. Orchard.

1999 Helen Oxenbury, *Alice's Adventures in Wonderland*. (text by Lewis Carroll). Walker.

1998 Helen Cooper, *Pumpkin Soup*. Doubleday.

1997 P. J. Lynch, *When Jessie Came Across the Sea* (text by Amy Hest). Walker.

1996 Helen Cooper, *The Baby Who Wouldn't Go to Bed*. Doubleday.

1995 P. J. Lynch, *The Christmas Miracle of Jonathan Toomey*. Walker.

1994 Gregory Rogers, *Way Home* (text by Libby Hathorn). Andersen Press.

1993 Alan Lee, *Black Ships before Troy*. Frances Lincoln.

1992 Anthony Browne, *Zoo*. Julia MacRae.

1991 Janet Ahlberg, *The Jolly Christmas Postman* (text by Allan Ahlberg). Heinemann.

1990 Gary Blythe, *The Whales' Song* (text by Dyan Sheldon). Hutchinson.

1989 Michael Foreman, *War Boy: A Country Childhood*. Pavilion.

1988 Barbara Firth, *Can't You Sleep, Little Bear?* (text by Martin Waddell). Walker.

1987 Adrienne Kennaway, *Crafty Chameleon* (text by Mwenye Hadithi). Hudder & Stoughton.

1986 Fiona French, *Snow White in New York*. Oxford University Press.

1985 Juan Wijngaard, *Sir Gawain and the Loathly Lady* (text by Selina Hastings). Walker.

1984 Errol LeCain, *Hiawatha's Childhood*. Faber.

1983 Anthony Browne, *Gorilla*. Julia MacRae.

1982 Michael Foreman. *Long Neck and Thunder Foot* (text by Helen Piers); and *Sleeping Beauty and other Favorite Fairy Tales* (selected by Angela Carter). Kestral and Gollancz.

1981 Charles Keeping, *The Highwayman*. Oxford University Press.

1980 Quentin Blake, *Mr. Magnolia*. Cape.

(For a complete list, go to www.carnegiegreenaway.org.uk/green.html.)

Carnegie Medals

2000 Beverly Naidoo, *The Other Side of Truth*. Puffin.

1999 Aidan Chambers, *Postcards from No Man's Land*. Bodley Head.

1998 David Almond, *Skellig*. Hodder.

1997 Tim Bowler, *Riverboy*. Oxford University Press.

1996 Melvin Burgess, *Junk*. Andersen.

1995 Phillip Pullman, *His Dark Materials: Northern Lights* (published in the United States as *The Golden Compass*). Scholastic.

1994 Theresa Breslin, *Whispers in the Graveyard*. Methuen.

1993 Robert Swindells, *Stone Cold*. Hamish Hamilton.

1992 Anne Fine, *Flour Babies*. Hamish Hamilton.

1991 Berlie Doherty, *Dear Nobody*. Hamish Hamilton.

1990 Gillian Cross, *Wolf*. Oxford University Press.

1989 Anne Fine, *Goggle-eyes*. Hamish Hamilton.

1988 Geraldine McCaughrean, *A Pack of Lies*. Oxford University Press.

1987 Susan Price, *The Ghost Drum*. Faber & Faber.

1986 Berlie Doherty, *Granny was a Buffer Girl*. Methuen.

1985 Kevin Crossley-Holland, *Storm*. Hinemann.

1984 Margaret Mahy, *The Changeover*. Dent.

1983 Jan Mark, *Handles*. Kestral.

1982 Margaret Mahy, *The Haunting*. Dent.

1981 Robert Westall, *The Scarecrows*. Chatto and Windus.

1980 Peter Dickinson, *City of Gold*. Gollancz.

(For a complete list, go to www.carnegiegreenaway.org.uk/carnegie/list.html.)

Text Credits

p. 31, From THE POLAR EXPRESS by Chris Van Allsburg. Copyright © 1985 by Chris Van Allsburg. Reprinted by permission of Houghton Mifflin Company. All rights reserved; From THE WHALES' SONG by Dyan Sheldon, copyright © 1992 by Dyan Sheldon. Used by permission of Dial Books for Young Readers, an imprint of Penguin Putnam Books for Young Readers, a division of Penguin Putnam Inc.; p. 52, From *The Lotus Seed* by Sherry Garland. Reprinted by permission of Harcourt, Inc.; p. 59, From "How to Choose Great Books for the Classroom," by Katherine Paterson, *NEA Today,* May, 2001. Reprinted by permission of the National Education Association; p. 62, From "Supporting Critical Conversations in Classrooms," speech by Jerome Harste to Michigan Council of Teachers of English, October 9, 1998. Used by permission of Jerome Harste; p. 73, From *Alison's Zinnia* by Anita Lobel. Reprinted by permission of HarperCollins Publishers Inc.; From *Aster Aardvark's Alphabet Adventure,* by Steven Kellogg. Reprinted by permission of HarperCollins Publishers Inc.; From QUENTIN BLAKE'S ABC by Quentin Blake. Reprinted by permission of Random House Children's Books, a division of Random House, Inc.; p. 74, From *The Ocean Alphabet* by Jerry Pallotta. Copyright © 1986 by Jerry Pallotta. All rights reserved. Used with permission by Charlesbridge Publishing, Inc.; From A IS FOR AFRICA by Ifeoma Onyefulu, copyright © 1993 by Ifeoma Onyefulu. Used by permission of Cobblehill Books, an affiliate of Dutton Children's Books, an imprint of Penguin Putnam Books for Young Readers, a division of Penguin Putnam Inc.; From THE ABC BUNNY by Wanda Gag, copyright 1933 by Wanda Gag, renewed © 1961 by Robert Janssen. Used by permission of Coward-McCann, an imprint of Penguin Putnam Books for Young Readers, a division of Penguin Putnam Inc.; From *The ABC Mystery,* by Doug Cushman. Reprinted by permission of HarperCollins Publishers Inc.; p. 78, From *Hello! Good-bye!* by Aliki. Reprinted by permission of HarperCollins Publishers Inc.; p. 84, From *Silly Tilly's Valentine* by Lillian Hoban. Reprinted by permission of HarperCollins Publishers Inc.; From *The Fat Cat Sat on the Mat* by Nurit Karlin. Reprinted by permission of HarperCollins Publishers Inc.; From *Wizard and Wart at Sea* by Janice Lee Smith. Reprinted by permission of HarperCollins Publishers Inc.; From *Sid and Sam* by Nola Buck. Reprinted by permission of HarperCollins Publishers Inc.; From *The Great Snake Escape* by Molly Coxe. Reprinted by permission of HarperCollins Publishers Inc.; p. 189, From *Wizard and Wart at Sea* by Janice Lee Smith. Reprinted by permission of HarperCollins Publishers Inc.; From *Toby, Where Are You?* by William Steig. Reprinted by permission of HarperCollins Publishers Inc.; From *Noel the First,* by Kate McMullan. Reprinted by permission of HarperCollins Publishers Inc.; p. 204, From TAR BEACH by Faith Ringgold. Reprinted by permission of Crown Children's Books, a division of Random House, Inc.; p. 205, *Heroes* text copyright © 1995 by Ken Mochizuki. Permission arranged with LEE & LOW BOOKS Inc., New York, NY 10016; p. 233, From UNDER THE CHERRY BLOSSOM TREE by Allen Say. Copyright © 1997 by Allen Say. Reprinted by permission of Houghton Mifflin Company. All rights reserved; p. 236, From JOSEPH HAD A LITTLE OVERCOAT by Simms Taback, copyright © 1999 by Simms Taback. Used by permission of Viking Penguin, an imprint of Penguin Putnam Books for Young Readers, a division of Penguin Putnam Inc. All rights reserved; From BIT BY BIT by Steve Sanfield, copyright © 1995 by Steve Sanfield, text. Used by permission of Philomel Books, an imprint of Penguin Putnam Books for Young Readers, a division of Penguin Putnam Inc. All rights reserved; p. 244, From *Mike Fink* by Steven Kellogg. Reprinted by permission of HarperCollins Publishers Inc.; p. 245, From SWAMP ANGEL by Anne Isaacs, copyright © 1994 by Anne Isaacs. Used by permission of Dutton, a division of Penguin Putnam Inc.; From *The Bunyans* by Audrey Wood. Reprinted by permission of Scholastic Inc.; From *Sally Ann Thunder Ann Whirlwind Crockett* by Steven Kellogg. Reprinted by permission of HarperCollins Publishers Inc.; From *Keelboat Annie* by Janet P. Johnson. Copyright © 1998 by Troll Communications L.L.C. Published by and reprinted with permission of Troll Communications, L.L.C.; From JOHN HENRY by Julius Lester, copyright © 1994 by Julius Lester. Used by permission of Dial Books for Young Readers, an imprint of Penguin Putnam Books for Young Readers, a division of Penguin Putnam Inc.; From *Paul Bunyan: A Tall Tale* by Steven Kellogg. Reprinted by permission of HarperCollins Publishers Inc.; p. 246, From SEVEN BLIND MICE by Ed Young, copyright © 1992 by Ed Young. Used by permission of Philomel Books, an imprint of Penguin Putnam Books for Young Readers, a division of Penguin Putnam Inc.; p. 337, From "Song for Something Little" by Lois Duncan, in *All God's Children,* compiled by Lee Bennett Hopkins. Reprinted by permission of Harcourt, Inc.; p. 341, From *Bones— Our Skeletal System* by Seymour Simon. Reprinted by permission of HarperCollins Publishers Inc.; p. 342, From *William Shakespeare & the Globe* by Aliki. Reprinted by permission of HarperCollins Publishers Inc.; p. 360, From *A Brilliant Streak: The Making of Mark Twain* by Kathryn Lasky. Reprinted by permission of Harcourt, Inc.; p. 364, From JOAN OF ARC by Josephine Poole. Reprinted by permission of Alfred A. Knopf Children's Books, a division of Random House, Inc.; p. 365, Excerpt from STARRY MESSENGER by Peter Sis. Copyright © 1996 by Peter Sis. Reprinted by permission of Farrar, Straus and Giroux, LLC.; p. 372, From ELEANOR by Barbara Cooney, copyright © 1996 by Barbara Cooney. Used by permission of Viking Penguin, an imprint of Penguin Putnam Books for Young Readers, a division of Penguin Putnam Inc.

Name and Title Index
for Children's Books

A

A Is for Africa (Onyefulu), 74
A Is for Asia (Chin-Lee), 74
Aardema, Verna, 201, 363
Abbott, Tony, 261
ABC Bunny, The (Gag), 74
ABC Mystery, The (Cushman), 74
Abeel, Samantha, 156
Abelove, Joan, 63
Abracadabra Kid, The: A Writer's Life
  (Fleischman), 363
Ada, Alma Flor, 207, 210, 253, 339
Adedjouma, Davida, 156
Adler, David A., 371
Adoff, Arnold, 151, 156, 157, 158, 161, 162,
  164
Adoption Is for Always (Girard), 326
*Adventures of Brother Sparrow, Sis Wren
  and Their Friends, The* (Hamilton), 207
Aesop's Fables (Aesop), 245
After the Dancing Days (Rostkowski), 280
Ahlberg, Allen, 78
Ahlberg, Janet, 78
Alan Mendelsohn: The Boy from Mars
  (Pinkwater), 312
Alarcon, Francisco X., 22, 151, 204, 210
Alcott, Louisa May, 190
Alef-bet: A Hebrew Alphabet Book
  (Edwards), 339
Alexander, Lloyd, 302, 318
*Alexander and the Terrible, Horrible, No
  Good, Very Bad Day* (Viorst), 100
Alice in Wonderland (Carroll), 301, 319
Alicia: My Story (Appleman-Jurman), 367
Aliki, 78, 96, 100, 206, 250, 269, 339, 341,
  349
Alison's Zinnia (Lobel), 73, 100
All About Scabs (Yagyu), 219
All by Herself (Paul), 151, 157
All God's Children: A Book of Prayers
  (Hopkins), 337
All I See (Rylant), 127
All in a Day (Anno), 217

All the Colors of the Race (Adoff), 162
All the Places to Love (MacLachlan), 49
Allard, Harry, 265
Allen, Pamela, 137
Allison (Say), 268
Almond, David, 307, 318
Alphabet City (Johnson), 75
Alvarez, Julia, 204
Always My Dad (Wyeth), 49, 50, 125, 206,
  269
Am I Blue? Coming Out from the Silence
  (Bauer), 21, 193
Am I Naturally This Crazy? (Holbrook),
  161
Amazing Grace (Hoffman), 21
Amazing Impossible Erie Canal, The
  (Harness), 344
Amber Brown Sees Red (Danzinger), 267
American Family Farm, The: A Photo Essay
  (Anderson), 342
Amish Home (Bial), 337
Amistad: A Long Road to Freedom (Myers),
  22, 207
Among the Hidden (Haddix), 313
Anastasia Krupnik (Lowry), 263
Anaya, Rodolfo, 210
Ancona, George, 63, 206, 337, 349
Anderson, Joan, 342
Angel and the Soldier Boy, The
  (Collington), 81
Angell, Judie, 265
Angelou, Maya, 146
*Angels of Mercy: The Army Nurses of World
  War II* (Kuhn), 343
Anholt, Laurence, 366
Animal Numbers (Kitchen), 75
Animal Shapes (Wildsmith), 77
Animalia (Base), 73
*Animals Don't Wear Pajamas: A Book About
  Sleeping* (Feldman), 340
Anna Banana: 101 Jump-Rope Rhymes
  (Cole), 232
Anna Is Still Here (Vos), 367
Anna of Byzantium (Barrett), 279

Anne of Green Gables (Montgomery), 190
Annie on My Mind (Garden), 264
Anno, Mitsumasa, 79, 217
Anno's Journey (Anno), 217
Anno's USA (Anno), 79
Another Day (Sachs), 268
Antelope Woman: An Apache Folktale
  (Lapaca), 234
ANTICS (Hepworth), 73
Anzaldúa, Gloria, 206
Appleman-Jurman, Alicia, 367
April and the Dragon Lady (Namioka), 268
Arcellana, Francisco, 217
Archambault, John, 100, 145, 146, 158
Arctic Stories (Kusagak), 206
Are You There God? It's Me, Margaret
  (Blume), 264
Armageddon Summer (Yolen and Coville),
  21, 189
Armstrong, Robb, 86
Armstrong, William H., 263
Arnold, Carolyn, 349
Arrow Over the Door, The (Bruchac), 207
Arrow to the Sun: A Pueblo Indian Tale
  (McDermott), 246
Art Dog (Hurd), 91
Art Lesson, The (dePaola), 127
Arthur's Back to School Day (Hoban), 266
Asch, Frank, 162
Ashabranner, Brent, 349
Ashanti to Zulu: African Traditions
  (Musgrove), 201
Asim, Jabari, 288, 289
Aster Aardvark's Alphabet Adventure
  (Kellogg), 73
*At Her Majesty's Request: An African
  Princess in Victorian England* (Myers),
  207
At the Beach (Lee), 339
Auerbacher, Inge, 367
Aunt Flossie's Hats (and Crab Cakes Later)
  (Howard), 95
*Aunt Harriet's Underground Railroad in the
  Sky* (Ringgold), 94, 101

Exactly the Opposite (Hoban), 77, 78
Extra! Extra! The Who, What, Where, When and Why of Newspapers (Greenfield), 336
Extra Innings: Baseball Poems (Hopkins), 162

F

F Is for Fabuloso (Lee), 207
Faber, Doris, 371
Fables (Lobel), 246
Facing the Music (Willey), 267
Families: Poems Celebrating the African American Experience (Strickland), 159
Fang, Linda, 207
Far North (Hobbs), 261
Farewell, John Barleycorn: Prohibition in the United States (Hintz), 345
Faria, Rosana, 217
Farm Team (Weaver), 266
Farmer, Nancy, 314
Farmer Duck (Waddell), 85
Farmer's Garden: Rhymes for Two Voices (Harrison), 156
Farrell, Kate, 160, 163
Fast Sam, Cool Clyde, and Stuff (Myers), 207
Fat Cat Sat on the Mat, The (Karlin), 84
Father and Son (Lauture), 161
Father Sky and Mother Earth (Oodgeroo), 176
Fathers, Mothers, Sisters, Brothers: A Collection of Family Poems (Hoberman), 161
Favorite Greek Myths (Osbourne), 247
Feder, Jane, 337
Feelings, Muriel, 76
Feelings, Tom, 76, 146, 206, 209
Feldman, Eve B., 340
Fenner, Carol, 201, 269
Fernandez, Laura, 282
Festivals (Livingston), 161
Fiesta Fireworks (Ancona), 206
Filipovic, Zlata, 363
Finding Providence: The Story of Roger Williams (Avi), 368
Fine, Howard, 41, 42
First Dog, The (Brett), 85, 95
First Words (Chermayeff), 339
Fisher, Aileen, 164
Fisher, Leonard Everett, 162, 349, 365
Fishes (Wildsmith), 36, 37
Fitzhugh, Louise, 265
Flat Stanley (Brown), 86
Fleischman, Paul, 63, 156, 161, 165, 269, 281, 287, 308
Fleischman, Sid, 363
Fleischner, Jennifer, 367
Fleming, Denise, 75, 77
Fletcher, Ralph, 63, 159
Flicker Flash (Graham), 150

Flight (Burleigh), 364
Flight: Fliers and Flying Machines (Jefferis), 332, 333, 334
Flora McDonnell's ABC (McDonnell), 72, 73
Florian, Douglas, 143, 147, 150, 151, 162, 164
Flournoy, Valerie, 203, 269
Flower Garden (Bunting), 85
Fly, Bessie, Fly (Colman), 363, 364
Fly Away Home (Bunting), 264
Flying Solo (Fletcher), 63
Folk Tales and Fables of the Middle East and Africa (Hayes), 238
Follow the Drinking Gourd (Winter), 137
Follow the Leader (Winslow), 63
Follow the Moon (Weeks), 21, 53, 88
Foot Book, The (Seuss), 84
For the Love of the Game: Michael Jordan and Me (Greenfield), 162
Forbes, Esther, 292
Foreman, Michael, 283
Forever Family, A (Banish), 328
Forged by Fire (Draper), 268
Forrester, Sandra, 63
45th Street: Short Stories (Myers), 207
Four Perfect Pebbles: A Holocaust Story (Perl), 367
Fox, Mem, 87, 97, 137, 217
Fox, Paula, 63, 290
Fradin, Dennis Brindel, 367
Francie (English), 21, 214, 215, 216
Frankenstein Moved In on the Fourth Floor (Levy), 308
Frasier, Debra, 39, 46, 47, 89
Freak the Mighty (Philbrick), 131, 264, 268
Freaky Friday (Rodgers), 307
Freedman, Russell, 341, 342, 349, 365, 369, 370, 377
Freedom Like Sunlight: Praisesongs for Black Americans (Lewis), 157
Freedom River (Rappaport), 366
Freedom's Fruit (Hooks), 282
Freymann, Saxton, 336
Friedman, Judith, 326
Friedrich (Richter), 280
Friends, The (Guy), 205
Friends, The (Yumoto), 218
Friends from the Other Side (Anzaldúa), 206
Frindle (Clements), 266
Fritz, Jean, 349, 363, 377
Frog and Toad Are Friends (Lobel), 83, 128, 131
Frog Jumps: A Counting Book (Kellogg), 75
Frog Prince Continued, The (Scieszka), 95
From the Bellybutton of the Moon and Other Summer Poems (Alarcon), 157
From the Notebooks of Melanin Sun (Woodson), 21, 264
From Where I Sit: Making My Way with Cerebral Palsy (Nixon), 363

Frost, Robert, 158
Frozen Girl (Getz), 344
Furlong, Monica, 240, 310
Furry News, The: How to Make a Newspaper (Leedy), 336
Further Tales of Uncle Remus: The Misadventures of Brer Rabbit, Brer Fox, Brer Wolf, the Doodang, and Other Creatures (Lester), 238

G

Gag, Howard, 74
Gag, Wanda, 5, 74, 96
Gallaz, Christophe, 219
Gallow's Hill (Duncan), 308
Galvez, Daniel, 203
Gammell, Stephen, 82, 96
Gandhi (Fisher), 365
Ganeri, Anita, 345
Gantos, Jack, 263
Garbage Collectors (In My Neighborhood) (Bourgeois), 344
Garden, Nancy, 21, 264, 290
Garden of Abdul Gasazi, The (Van Allsburg), 41, 95
Gardener, The (Stewart), 52, 54, 129, 269
Gardener's Alphabet, A (Azarian), 46, 74
Gardiner, John Reynolds, 263
Garland, Sherry, 49, 52, 53, 94, 100, 133, 202, 203, 206, 269, 279
Garner, Alan, 309, 318
Garza, Carmen Lomas, 211
Gathering, The (Hamilton), 207
Gathering of Days, A: A New England Girl's Journal, 1830–1832 (Blos), 278
Gathering the Sun: An Alphabet in Spanish and English (Ada), 339
George, Jean Craighead, 263, 268, 340, 349
George, Kristine O'Connell, 159, 162
George, Twig C., 263
Gerstein, Mordicai, 308
Geter, Tyrone, 63
Getting Near to Baby (Couloumbis), 271, 272
Getz, David, 344
Ghost Canoe (Hobbs), 261
Ghost in the House (Cohen), 336
Ghosts of the Southwest: The Phantom Gunslinger and Other Real-Life Hauntings (Wood), 336
Giacobbe, Beppe, 156
Giants! Stories from Around the World (Walker), 237
Gibbons, Gail, 337, 349
Giblin, James Cross, 349
Gideon's People (Meyer), 280
Giff, Patricia Reilly, 22, 86, 128, 268, 276, 290
Gift for Abuelita, A: Celebrating the Day of the Dead (Luenn), 339
Gilden, Mel, 313

Z

Zachary's Ball (Tavares), 41
Zeely (Hamilton), 207
Zel (Napoli), 240
Zelinsky, Paul O., 98, 228, 250
Zemach, Margot, 336
Zlata's Diary: A Child's Life in Sarajevo
    (Filipovic), 363
Zughaib, Helen, 22

General Index

Minorities
    characterization of, 21
    as heroes, 181
    as publishers, 175
Miscues in reading, 17
Mixed media, effects created by, 47
Moore, Lilian, 142
Mora, Pat, 203
Morals in fables, 246
Mother Goose rhymes, 229–230
Movement, as response to literature, 132–134
Multicultural literature, 22, 199–208
    availability of, 22
    awards for, 58
    benefits of, 200–204
    evaluating, 213–214
    across genres, 204, 206–207
    importance of discussion about, 212
    issues in using, 212–213
    issues in writing, 208, 211, 212
    literary merit and, 199, 201, 213
    the read-aloud and, 124
    themes in, 203
    types of, 204
Murray, Donald, 129
Muse, Daphne, 213
Music, as response to literature, 134–135
Mysteries, 265
Myths, 246–250
    analyzing, 247–248
    heroes in, 246
    purposes of, 246
    universal messages in, 248

N
Naive art in illustrations, 50–51
Narrative, first-person. See First-person narrative
Narrative nonfiction, 326–331
    evaluating, 328–331
    formats of, 326, 328
Narrative poems, 147
Narrator
    in biographies, 361, 373
    in realistic fiction, 267, 269
Natural sciences, 339–340
NCTE Poetry Award for Excellence, 58, 397
Newbery, John, 229
Newbery Award, 4, 5, 21, 55, 57, 201, 214, 240, 272, 330, 385–386
Nixon, Jean Lowery, 265
Non-series biographies, 370–372
Nonfiction, 326
    authenticity and, 22, 330, 334
    author's notes in, 334
    award for, 58
    children's reactions to, 325
    classroom uses of, 336–344
    elements of, 335

evaluating, 328–331, 332, 333–334
formats of, 326, 328
history of, 190
literary qualities of, 332, 335
multicultural, 204, 206–207
purpose of, 326
selection of, 348
series, 344–345
technology and, 190, 328
types of, 326
Nonnarrative nonfiction, 326, 331–335
    elements of, 331
    evaluating, 332
    expository writing and, 326, 331
    formats of, 331–332
    optional features of, 331
Nordstrom, Ursula, 189, 190
Nursery rhymes, 150, 229–230

O
O'Connor, Sheilah, 313
Oil paint, effects created by, 46
Older readers
    biographies for, 364, 365
    books for, 4, 92
Oliver, Mary, 146
Onomatopoeia in poetry, 145
Opie, Iona, 229
Opie, Peter, 229
Opie Collection of Children's Literature, The, 229
Opitz, Michael, 231
Oral tradition, and folk literature, 228
Orbis Pictus Award for Outstanding Nonfiction for Children, 58, 400
Organization, in evaluating nonfiction, 329, 333
Oversimplification in biographies, 375
Oxford University, 229

P
Paintings as illustrations, 42
Pappas, Christine, 331
Parallel cultures, 177, 187
    multicultural literature and, 200, 201
Parents' rights in selecting books, 271
Partial biographies, 360
Passion of author, 4, 357
Pastels, effects created by, 41
Paterson, Katherine, 287
Pen and ink, effects created by, 40
Pencil, effects created by, 41
People of color
    in collective biographies, 361–362
    stereotypes of, 172, 174, 177, 180, 191
Perfect, Kathy, 150
Perrault, Charles, 229
Philosophical speculations in reading, 20
Philosophy, 336
Phonemic awareness, 231

Phonics, 231
Photo story format in narrative nonfiction, 328
Photography in fiction, 47
Piaget, Jean, 11–12
Picture books, 6, 71, 326. See also Picture storybooks
    authors and illustrators of, 96–98
    awards for, 57, 58
    biographies as, 363–366, 367
    historical fiction as, 281–283
    imagination and, 90
    multicultural, 204, 206
Picture storybooks
    characteristics of, 92–96
    plot structures of, 100
    purposes of, 87–92
Plot(s), 33, 213
    comparing in two folk tales, 236
    in evaluating biographies, 373, 374
    in evaluating fantasy, 315
    in evaluating historical fiction, 288, 289
    in evaluating realistic fiction, 272
    of picture storybooks, 100
    racism/sexism and, 181
    in traditional literature, 228, 251, 252
Poetic ability of children, 153
Poetry, 6, 22, 141–163
    alliteration in, 143, 145
    approaching, 142, 143
    art in books of, 157
    award for, 58
    bilingual, 155
    biographical, 151, 156–157
    characteristics of, 144–147
    children's joy in, 141
    children's language and, 153
    choral reading of, 154
    collections of, 158–160
    concrete, 149
    consonance in, 145
    criteria for evaluating, 163
    experiencing, 141, 144
    free-verse, 149
    imagery in, 144–145
    lyric, 148
    as model for writing, 151
    multicultural, 204, 206
    narrative, 147
    need for variety in, 163
    power of, 150
    rationale for using, 150–151
    read-aloud and, 124, 143
    social issues in, 156
    sound devices in, 145
    sounds of, 143–144
    themes in, 161–162
    trends in, 155
    types of, 147–150
    unmotivated readers and, 150
    writing, 152

Point(s) of view, 204
    author's, 172, 175, 181, 191, 228, 287
    multiple, 202, 203
    as objective, 202
    reader's, 112
Poster paint, effects created by, 43
Pourquoi stories, 228
Power
    racism/sexism and, 177, 181
    in relationships, 186
    sources of, in folk literature, 232, 233, 234
Pre-Columbian days, in historical fiction, 279
Predictability, and accessibility, 15, 18
Prejudice, in realistic fiction, 269
Printmaking, effects created by, 46
Privileged reading, 174, 175
Psychology, 336
Publishing
    effects of houses of, 4, 23, 190
    by minorities and women, 175
    parameters in, 172
    tax laws and, 23
Puns, 230
Pura Belpré Award, 58, 397
Purposes
    in book selection, 60
    historical, of children's literature, 188–189
Purves, Alan, 124

Q

Quests, in fantasy, 309

R

Race, 7, 117, 118
Racism, 173, 174, 175, 176, 177, 179, 187, 204
    author's world view and, 181
    copyright date and, 181
    criteria for evaluating books for, 180–183
    historical, 191
    in illustrations, 180
    plot and, 181
    power and, 177
Read-aloud, the, 76
    implementing, 124
    poetry and, 124, 143
    value of, 124, 131
Readers
    community of, 8, 9
    point of view of, 112
    response of, 7, 110–111
Readers theater, 130
Reading, 6, 7, 67, 113–115
    child development and, 11–12
    constructing meaning in, 6, 115
    cueing systems and, 15, 17
    drama and, 131

literature-based programs of, 17
    poetry and, 150
    privileged, 174–175
    reasons for, 19–21
    to share genres, 317
    skills involved in, 113–114
    strategies for, 76, 115
Reading comprehension, 114–115
Reading workshop, 9
Realism
    in fiction, 260
    in illustrations, 49
Realistic fiction, 259–271
    adventure stories in, 261
    appeals of, 260–261
    awards for, 58, 59
    controversy in, 260
    cultural awareness in, 268
    evaluating, 272, 273, 274
    formats in, 267, 269
    growing-up stories in, 263
    homosexual characters in, 266
    humor in, 264
    multicultural, 204, 207
    series, 270
    themes in, 267–269
    types of, 261, 263–267
Reese, Debbie, 214
Reference books, 345–346
Religion, 7, 247–248, 336. *See also* Spiritual elements
Repertoires, 7, 118
Repetition
    in early reader books, 84
    in poetry, 146
Representations in literature, 201
Research
    in biographies, 22, 359
    on creating classroom communities, 9
    on *Dick and Jane* and *Henry and Mudge*, 15
    in historical fiction, 22, 259, 277, 278, 284, 285
    for illustrations, 251, 283
    on inclusion and exclusion, 93
    on learning phonemic awareness, 231
    on listening to voices of those you wish to include, 214
    on literature-based reading programs, 17
    in nonfiction, 22
    on the read-aloud, 76
    on Vygotsky and literature for children, 61
Resources, teacher, 24, 65, 102, 138, 166, 195–196, 220–221, 255–256, 293, 320, 352, 379
Responding, 10, 30–33, 110–111, 119–120. *See also specific responses*
    through art, 123–128
    through drama, 129–131

to first readings, 116, 117, 119
    to historical fiction, 119
    making meaning and, 110
    through movement, 132–134
    through music, 134–135
    to a picture book, 116, 117
    through talk, 120–123
    through writing, 128–129
Response log, 116
Rhetoric, 343
Rhyme
    in early reader books, 84
    as link between oracy and literacy, 150
    nursery, 150, 229–230
    in poetry, 143, 145
    power of, 152
    street, 230–231
Rhythm
    in early reader books, 84
    learning language use through, 150
    in poetry, 145
Robots, in science fiction, 313–314
Rogers, Theresa, 124
Rogovin, Paula, 186, 187, 204
Role-playing
    as classroom community builder, 131
    as response to literature, 130
Rollins, Charlemae, 200
Romances, 265–266
Rosenblatt, Louise, 110–111, 173
Rountree, Helen, 376
Routman, Regie, 9, 17, 76, 152, 231

S

Same-gendered parents, in children's literature, 193
Saul, Wendy, 274
School stories, in realistic fiction, 266
Science fiction, 110
    adventure stories in, 312
    appeal of, 311–312
    authors of, 318
    bias toward, 317
    evaluating, 315
    versus fantasy, 311
    getting started with, 317
    questions about life's meaning and, 311
    social concerns and, 312
    themes in, 314–315
    thinking deeply through, 310
    variety in, 312–314
Scott O'Dell Historical Fiction Award, 58, 399–400
Scratchboard, effects created by, 41
Scripting, as response to literature, 130
Seale, Doris, 180, 182, 184, 185
Seeing oneself in reading, 20
Selection of books, 11–12, 57, 163, 348
    censorship and, 271
    considerations in, 59–65, 213–214
Self-image, and children, 181, 183, 185

Trends in children's literature
    as influenced by marketing and technology, 23
    as influenced by sociopolitical factors, 21–23
Trickster tales, 228, 237
Truth
    in fantasy, 305
    in myths, 247
    in traditional literature, 228

U

Unconscious delight in reading, 20
Universal issues, 227
Universal messages in myths, 248

V

Valsner, Jaan, 61
Values, 5, 59, 175, 190
    in award-winning books, 56
    in biographies, 376
    in fantasy, 309
    in folk literature, 232, 234, 235, 236, 240, 241
    in science fiction, 315
    in tall tales, 244
van der Veer, Rene, 61
Vicarious experience in reading, 20
    through fantasy, 305, 308
Victorian England, in historical fiction, 279
Vision of author
    in evaluating fantasy, 317
    in evaluating nonfiction, 330, 333

in evaluating realistic fiction, 272, 274
in evaluating traditional literature, 252
Visual, the
    accuracy of, in traditional literature, 251, 252
    learning and, 74–75
    in nonnarrative nonfiction, 332
    responding to, in picture books, 36–38
Visual expression, 125
Vocabulary, controlling, 15
Vygotsky, Lev, 61, 123, 154

W

Walsh, Jill Paton, 286
Walter, Mildred Pitts, 285
Watercolor, effects created by, 43–45
Websites for children's literature, 24, 65, 102, 138, 166, 195–196, 220–221, 255–256, 293, 320, 352, 379
Webster, Renee, 122
Werlin, Nancy, 265
White space, use of
    in nonnarrative nonfiction, 332
    in poetry, 146
Whitin, Phyllis, 123
Whole language experience, 231
Wilhelm, Jeff, 131
Williams, Carol Ann, 234
Wolf, Dennie Palmer, 119, 120, 123
Women
    as characters. *See* Female characters
    as publishers, 175
    stereotypes of, 172

Wonder, in fantasy, 301
Wordless books, 79–82
    characteristics of, 82
    purposes of, 79–82
World view, 172
    of authors of historical fiction, 287
    of authors of traditional literature, 228
    expanding, 202
    factors affecting, 173
    in folk tales, 233
    reading and, 174
    recognizing our own, 173, 176
World War II, in historical fiction, 280
Writing
    of biography, 358–359
    expository, 326, 331
    of historical fiction, 284–287
    of nonfiction, 335
    outside one's culture, 229
    as response to literature, 128–129
    styles of, 34, 213, 236, 252, 272, 273, 316, 330, 333, 373, 374
Writing workshop, 9

Y

Yolen, Jane, 208

Z

Ziegler, Alan, 152
Zimmerman, Susan, 115, 116, 117, 118
Zone of proximal development, 15, 61, 154